CHALLENGES OF URBAN EDUCATION AND EFFICACY OF SCHOOL REFORM

ADVANCES IN EDUCATIONAL ADMINISTRATION

Series Editor: Richard C. Hunter

Volumes 1–5: Series Editor Paul W. Thurston

ADVANCES IN EDUCATIONAL ADMINISTRATION
VOLUME 6

CHALLENGES OF URBAN EDUCATION AND EFFICACY OF SCHOOL REFORM

EDITED BY

RICHARD C. HUNTER
College of Education, University of Illinois at Urbana-Champaign, USA

FRANK BROWN
School of Education, University of North Carolina at Chapel Hill, USA

2003

JAI
An Imprint of Elsevier Science

Amsterdam – Boston – London – New York – Oxford – Paris
San Diego – San Francisco – Singapore – Sydney – Tokyo

ELSEVIER SCIENCE Ltd
The Boulevard, Langford Lane
Kidlington, Oxford OX5 1GB, UK

First edition 2003

Library of Congress Cataloging in Publication Data
A catalog record from the Library of Congress has been applied for.

British Library Cataloguing in Publication Data
A catalogue record from the British Library has been applied for.

ISBN: 0-7623-0426-X

∞The paper used in this publication meets the requirements of ANSI/NISO Z39.48-1992 (Permanence of Paper).
Printed in The Netherlands.

DEDICATION

To our loving and dedicated wives, Margo and Joan,
who have supported our careers.

CONTENTS

ABOUT THE AUTHORS *xi*

PREFACE
Kern Alexander *xvii*

INTRODUCTION: CHALLENGES OF URBAN EDUCATION EFFICACY OF URBAN EDUCATION
Richard C. Hunter and Frank Brown *1*

PART I: URBAN SCHOOLS AND THEIR STUDENTS

1. DIVERSITY AND REFORM
A. Reynaldo Contreras *15*

2. HISTORICAL STRUGGLES FOR EQUITY: POLITICS OF EDUCATION AND LANGUAGE POLICIES AND ITS IMPLICATIONS FOR ASIAN AMERICANS
Ji-Yeon O. Jo and Xue Lan Rong *25*

3. UPDATE ON SCHOOL DESEGREGATION
Charles J. Russo *49*

4. BACK TO THE FUTURE WITH THE END OF *BROWN*: COMMUNITY CONTROL OF NEIGHBORHOOD SCHOOLS
Frank Brown *65*

5. DISCRIMINATION IN TRACKING AND SPECIALIZED EDUCATION PROGRAMS
Richard C. Hunter and Saran Donahoo *87*

6. URBAN ECONOMICS AND FINANCIAL FACTORS AFFECTING EDUCATION
Steven B. Lawton *101*

PART II: ACCOUNTABILITY AND EQUITY

7. THE STRUCTURE OF INEQUALITY: TRACKING AND EDUCATIONAL OPPORTUNITY IN AMERICA'S PUBLIC SCHOOLS
Paul Green 123

8. THE DIGITAL DIVIDE IN AMERICA'S PUBLIC SCHOOLS
Philip T. K. Daniel 145

9. SUPERVISION'S PRIMARY TASK: SYNTHESIZING PROFESSIONAL DEVELOPMENT TO MEET INDIVIDUAL TEACHER NEEDS AND ATTAIN SCHOOL ORGANIZATIONAL GOALS
Stephen Earl Lucas 165

10. SCHOOL LEADERSHIP FOR 21st-CENTURY URBAN COMMUNITIES
Leonard A. Valverde 187

11. ADEQUACY ISSUES IN FINANCING URBAN SCHOOLS
James G. Ward 199

12. STANDARDIZED TESTING AND ASSESSMENT POLICY: IMPACT ON RACIAL MINORITIES AND IMPLICATIONS FOR EDUCATIONAL LEADERSHIP
Dawn G. Williams and Laurence Parker 207

13. INSTRUCTIONAL EFFICIENCY VERSUS SOCIAL REFORM: FUNDAMENTALS OF THE TRACKING DEBATE
Arthur E. Lehr 221

PART III: SCHOOL REFORM STRATEGIES

14. INITIATING WORK TEAMS TO REFORM THE AMERICAN HIGH SCHOOL
Terri H. Mozingo 239

15. CHOICE, VOUCHERS AND PRIVATIZATION AS EDUCATION REFORM OR THE FULFILLMENT OF RICHARD NIXON'S SOUTHERN STRATEGY?
Frank Brown 255

16. FILING FOR ACADEMIC BANKRUPTCY: THE IMPACT AND ECONOMICS OF STATE TAKEOVERS
Richard C. Hunter and Saran Donahoo 283

17. AFRICAN AMERICAN PARENTAL INVOLVEMENT IN URBAN SCHOOL REFORM: IMPLICATIONS FOR LEADERSHIP
Linda C. Tillman 295

18. RECONSTITUTION, SMALL SCHOOLS, SCHOOL-BASED MANAGEMENT, ETC.
James E. Lyons 313

ABOUT THE AUTHORS

Kern Alexander joined the Department of Educational Organization and Leadership at the University of Illinois at Urbana-Champaign in the spring of 2002. He is the most recent past president of Murray State University. He also served as the seventh president of Western Kentucky University and a faculty member at the University of Florida at Gainesville and Virginia Polytechnic Institute. Dr. Alexander has conducted educational research in various areas including education finance and law. He earned his Ph.D. from Indiana University.

Frank Brown is the Cary C. Boshamer Professor of Education and former dean of the School of Education at the University of North Carolina at Chapel Hill. He has published numerous articles and books in the areas of school law, policy studies, minority education, and educational administration. He is also an active participant in the American Educational Research Association and National Organization for Legal problems on Education, and he serves on the editorial boards of several academic journals.

A. Reynaldo Contreras is Professor of Administrative and Interdisciplinary Studies (DAIS) in the College of Education at San Francisco State University. Formerly he was department chair at San Francisco State University and Professor of Educational Leadership and Policy Studies at Indiana University, Bloomington. Professor Contreras received his Doctor of Philosophy degree from Stanford University where he studied administration and policy analysis. His research interests include policy research in education, minority educational leadership, and education in emerging metropolitan contexts. Currently he is conducting research on home-school partnerships and in the transformation of urban education. He has contributed to journals and books on urban education and educational leadership and continues to serve on editorial boards of professional publications in education.

Philip T. K. Daniel is a professor of education and law at The Ohio State University who has been teaching in postsecondary education for over 28 years. In 1993, he received The Ohio State University Alumni Award for Distinguished

Teaching and was inducted into The Ohio State University Academy of Distinguished Teaching. He received his B.S. from Cheyney University of Pennsylvania, M.S. and Ed.D. from the University of Illinois, and J.D. from Northern Illinois University. His primary research area is education law with special attention to discrimination and equal protection, students with disabilities, health and safety, gifted education, Internet regulation, and church-state issues.

Saran Donahoo is a doctoral student in Higher Education Administration at the University of Illinois at Urbana-Champaign. She earned her B.A. in secondary education at the University of Arizona and her M.A. in history at the University of Illinois. She has also served as a teacher in a charter school. In addition, she has also authored and co-authored articles on various public education issues including charter schools, homeschooling, privatization and vouchers. Her current research interests include the history of higher education, women and minorities in higher education, curriculum and assessment, and transitions between higher education and secondary schools.

Paul Green is an Assistant Professor of Educational Politics, Policy and Law at the University of California's Washington Center in Washington, D.C. His area's of expertise include the politics, policies and practices of decision making at the federal, state and local levels, which either impede of advance access and opportunity for poor students and students of color in elementary, secondary and post-secondary institutions.

Richard C. Hunter joined the Educational Organization and Leadership Department at the University of Illinois at Urbana-Champaign as both faculty and department head in 2000. Formerly chair and faculty member in Educational Leadership at the University of North Carolina at Chapel Hill, he has also served in the public schools of America as a teacher, assistant principal, assistant coordinator, compensatory education consultant, principal, assistant superintendent, associate superintendent, and superintendent.

Ji-Yeon O. Jo is a doctoral student in the School of Education at the University of North Carolina at Chapel Hill. She taught Korean language to college students and adults. She is currently serving as an assistant principal at the Chapel Hill-Durham Korean language school. Her academic interests are on the issues of heritage language retention and attrition, identity of language minority students, and language policies and politics in education.

Stephen B. Lawton, Ph.D. Full Professor and Chair, Department of Education Administration and Community Leadership, Central Michigan University, and Professor Emeritus, Department of Theory and Policy Studies, Ontario Institute for Studies in Education, University of Toronto. School finance, economics, and policy with a current emphasis on school choice, comparative education finance, and school system structures at the national, state/province, and local levels (including schools) and their link to educational effectiveness. Current and recent articles focus on Arizona school finance, school choice in Canada and the U.S., information systems in education, and administrative roles of state education agencies.

Arthur E. Lehr is currently a visiting assistant professor the Department of Educational Organization and Leadership and AT&T Technology Fellow at the University of Illinois at Urbana-Champaign. A former secondary and gifted education teacher, his research interests include student placement, school administration, curriculum, and collaborative instruction.

Stephen Earl Lucas is an assistant professor of educational administration at the University of Illinois at Urbana-Champaign, where he teaches instructional supervision, the political-social context of schools, and research methods. A former California middle school teacher and administrator, he conducts research on middle school principals, collaborative administrator-teacher leadership, and the relationship between transformational leadership and school culture.

James E. Lyons is Professor of Educational Administration in the Department of Educational Administration, Research, and Technology at the University of North Carolina at Charlotte. Previously, he served as a high school teacher, principal, a school management consultant with the Ohio Department of Education, and university department chairperson for fifteen years. His research interests include the principalship, the superintendency, human resources development and administration, and organizational development. Articles presenting his research have been published in The Journal of School Leadership, Education and Urban Society, The Journal of Cases in Educational Administration, School Business Affairs, and the NASSP Bulletin. Professor Lyons earned the Ph.D. at The Ohio State University.

Terri H. Mozingo has more than 20 years in public education. Her previous positions include teacher, assistant principal, project coordinator, and curriculum director. She is currently assistant superintendent for curriculum and instruction with the Charlotte-Mecklenburg (NC) School System. Her research interests include organizational change, work teams, and restructuring secondary schools.

Laurence Parker is an associate professor in the Department of Educational Policy Studies at the University of Illinois at Urbana-Champaign. His research and teaching interests include educational leadership and diversity, education law and teacher testing, and diversity and evaluation.

Xue Lan Rong is Associate Professor in School of Education at the University of North Carolina at Chapel Hill. Her research focuses on cultures, race/ethnicity and education, and the effects of immigrant generation on immigrant children's schooling. Her previous publications include *Educating Immigrant Students: What we need to know to meet the challenge* (with J. Preissle, 1998), and *The effects of immigrant generation and ethnicity on educational attainment among young African and Caribbean Blacks in the United States* (with F. Brown) in Harvard Education Review (2001).

Charles J. Russo is the Panzer Chair in Education and professor in Educational Leadership at the University of Dayton. He is also editor of *Education and Urban Society*. He earned both his J.D. and Ed.D. in Educational Administration and Supervision from St. John's University in New York City. His teaching and research interests include education law and policy, equity and school desegregation.

Linda C. Tillman is an associate professor in the Department of Educational Leadership and Policy Studies at Wayne State University. Her research interests focus on mentoring African American faculty, teachers and administrators, the education of African Americans in K-16 education, principalship preparation, and culturally responsive research approaches using qualitative research methods.

Leonard A. Valverde is professor of Education Leadership and Policy Studies at Arizona State University. Also, he is the Executive Director of the Hispanic Border Leadership Institute, a eight member consortium of higher education institutions. Over his 30 year career, he has researched and published extensively on matters relating to the education of students of color, primarily in urban settings. His focus the past ten years has been on leadership and how persons of color can make a positive difference in the learning of students. His scholarship perspective has been complimented by serving in the role of a program director and teacher supervisor at the K-12 school level as well as college dean and academic vice president at the university level.

James G. Ward is Professor of Educational Administration at the University of Illinois at Urbana-Champaign where he specializes in education finance, educational politics, and organization and democratic theory. He is a past president of the American Education Finance Association. He has been a classroom teacher, an educational policy analyst, and served from 1977 to 1985 as Director of Research, American Federation of Teachers. He has been an elected school board member in a small urban school district.

Dawn G. Williams is a Doctoral Candidate in Educational Policy Studies with a concentration in Policy Analysis at the University of Illinois at Urbana-Champaign. She is a former Virginia and North Carolina elementary school teacher and now also serves as a Teaching Assistant in the departments of Educational Policy Studies and Curriculum and Instruction. Her research interests include the achievement gap between African American and white students, standardized-based reform and federal involvement in local education.

PREFACE

The idea of the public common school as it was conceptualized in the era of the Enlightenment has found its greatest trial in the cities of America. That virtuous governments could exist only if structured on a system of universal mass education delivered by the means of public schools was a cornerstone and basic tenent of American democracy. The weight of a churning population of races, cultures, nationalities, ethnic groups, with a never ending polyglot of tongues that issued forth a foundation of educational complexities is American cities constitutes the ultimate crucible for public schools. Before this great educational experiment came into existence aristocratic and religious organizations ruled the people by arbitrary power and caprice in nearly all the lands with these two powerful institutions opposed and sought to stamp out state secular schools in spite of the fact that under the old regime illiteracy rates were enormous. Fully aware that the labors of ignorant are easily exploited and controlled with simplistic myth and superstitions, the seats of monarchial and church power, doggedly held to the status quo. This state of affairs existed as late as the 19th and 20th centuries from the Atlantic to the Bosporus and beyond. Women were uniformly denied organized education of any real substance, as were social, ethnic, religious and other minorities. Churches jealously guarded their prerogatives to control the education of the youth in both Christian and Islam cultures, with the unhappy result that shortly before 1800 only one out of 52 young men in France had any secondary education and women much less and the new United States was not much better off. Denominational schools sought to educate a few, in accordance with religious doctrines, to a level of minimal literacy sufficient only to understand moral principles for salvation. The Enlightenment idea of universal education upset this system of controlled illiteracy and with the advent of the industrial revolution the value of widespread knowledge and scientific advancement began to require that the common person become exposed to more widespread knowledge. Driven by the decline in the apprenticeship system as an alternative to schooling and the limited social interests of the denominational schools, the need for education to become more widely diffused was recognized and accepted in America even though in mother England there existed great and serious debate as to the efficacy and wisdom of educating the poor.

In America as the cities populations increased with the immigration of penniless and jobless aliens, poverty tended to define the city and as squalor and slums increased. In that benighted setting of the cities there arose a belief that a system of efficient public schools was not merely desirable, but an absolute social necessity. The task of education was magnified as the industrial revolution exacerbated problems of the poor; rather than helping to resolve the dilemma of urban poverty, the industrial revolution drove the poor deeper into destitution as aggressive capitalists used cheap labor to increase their profits. During the 19th century the growth of the cities had proceeded at an extraordinarily rapid pace, and the overcrowding in American cities such as Chicago, Baltimore, Boston, Cleveland, were America's examples of the Emile Zola's Paris. The statistics bear out the stress that was placed on the American cities. Chicago, for example, had a mere 30,000 people in 1850, but forty years later it was the sixth largest urban center in the world with over one million population. As Hobsawn said in *The Age of Capital* "The city was indeed the most striking outward symbol of the industrial world . . ." (pp. 2, 6) The rate of urbanization and volume of growth in the United States, from 1850 to 1900, far exceeded the rates in nearly all western countries. In the late 19th century the urban growth had produced unusual phenomenon such as New York's Lower East side, one of the most overcrowded slums in the western world, were congregated over 520 undernourished persons per acre. During the decade from 1845 to 1854 flight from Europe, especially from Ireland and Germany, over 80% of the immigrants crowded into the cities along the eastern seaboard of the U.S.

Universal education by means of public common schools stood almost alone as a solution to urban poverty, hopefully serving as a safely valve to prevent social instability that had upset European countries during the revolutions of 1848. Substantial hinderances were posed by industrialists who sought to increase their profits by paying low wages to working children and by parents who allowed and even encouraged the exploitation of their children. The public schools were, thus, largely ineffective until the states enacted in tandem child labor laws and compulsory attendance laws that prevented child exploitation by businessmen and parents. Therefore, after much struggle and reactive opposition pitting progressive school advocates against businessmen, backward parents, and church schools, there emerged a strong belief and acceptance that urban life would be greatly improved by universal public schooling that would raise the productivity of all the people, diminish rampant crime, and prevent poverty.

The public schools, thereby, became the essential vehicle in which faith and security was placed to mitigate the deprivations of the urban masses. These new uniquely American institutions began to churn out an unprecedented explosion of economic development and a constantly rising standard of living, quickly becoming the envy of the world. The urban public schools created the means for social mobility, amply demonstrated as generation after generation were educated, intellectually elevated, and economically uplifted moved to suburbia, exurbia, and beyond.

Then throughout the late 19th and first one-half of the 20th century city schools received new challenges as an interstate migration of African-Americans from the poor Southern conservative states with discriminating laws established as a matter of systematic state segregation policies, began to move north seeking jobs in the urban industrial states, and pursuing new freedoms. The numbers of deprived African-Americans were greatly supplemented by the underprivileged whites of Appalachia, the Ozarks, and other poor rural areas where the public schools had been throttled by conservative political leaders who had convinced ignorant whites to vote against their own self interests. Walter Hines Page, the great journalist, described the situation in his famous "Forgotten Man" speech at the turn of the century in North Carolina. He pointed out that the percent of the white persons in that state could not read nor write and that they along with southern African Americans existed in a stationary social condition where illiteracy reigned and became intergenerational. These benighted people knew no better and were devoid of knowledge aspiration, and became the forgotten ones of society. As Hines observed, "The Forgotten Man was content to be forgotten. He became a dead weight, but a definable opponent of social progress. He faithfully heard the politicians on the stump praise him for the virtues that he did not have." The Forgotten Man was told that the "other politicians had some hairbrained plan to increase his taxes . . . told him to distrust anybody who wished to change anything. What was good enough for his forefathers was good enough for him. Thus, the Forgotten Man became a dupe, became thankful for being neglected."

Yet, it was many of these forgotten ones of the South that broke the bonds of discrimination and ignorance who exited the South descending on the northern industrial cities seeking educational, social and economic opportunities that were withheld in a reluctant South. The public schools of the cities of the north were thereby inundated by this relentless movement of underdeveloped human capital. The ravages of backwardness and anti-intellectualism of the South was fully visited upon public schools of the cities of the North placing a concentrated educational burden on the resources of the public schools that was a new social phenomenon and nearly impossible to remediate.

In spite of these burdens, however, the public schools of the cities continued to assimilate and provide opportunities to the multitudes who would ultimately be woven into the fabric of a productive national economic and social system. Building on the foundation of the public schools, the nation gained strength through two world wars and continued to generate economic strength that enabled it to finally stand alone as the greatest world power since the Roman Empire. Any attempt to determine the productivity of public schools must recognize that they found the intellectual base for the masses on which this great world hegemon found its prestige and economic power.

Yet, the machinery of the public schools of our cities, however, have never been able to function free of political interests that have weighted the schools with conditions and constraints. Preeminent among these is, of course, the reluctance of taxpayers, legislatures, and city politicians to adequately finance the schools. Implicit in the idea of public schools is the assumption that a sufficiency of public resources would be provided to permit an operation of an efficient system of schools, especially where those schools were largely inhabited by African-Americans whose educations were so detrimentally affected by the racial discrimination visited upon their forebears.

One need only peruse the plethora of litigation, since 1954, wherein the courts of America have been called upon to remediate the effects of political and social impositions of the majority that have deprived the public school children in the cities of proper and appropriate educational opportunity. Nearly every big city school system in the U.S. has a long record of litigation in which, as a last resort, judicial authority has been sought to correct the inadequacies of financial provision for the city schools.

The dilemma has become more pronounced as the core cities have been politically underweighted as the more affluent residents of suburbia have demonstrated little interest in the plight of the schools of the central cities. Yet, in spite of unrealistic resources and the great educational overburdens of deprived minority children, including today the vast Hispanic migration, the public schools of the cities continue as the most important and effective societal vehicle for maintaining social stability, a productive economy, and a reasonably effective democracy.

With an air of optimism this book discusses the problems and issues of the city schools of today arguing that with appropriate innovation and change, that these same public schools of the cities will continue to serve as the most essential institution in the dissemination of education and assimilation of peoples in forming a nation of vitality, energy, and virtue.

Kern Alexander

INTRODUCTION: CHALLENGES OF URBAN EDUCATION EFFICACY OF URBAN EDUCATION

Richard C. Hunter and Frank Brown

ABSTRACT

As the primary target of the school reform movement, urban education remains the most difficult to assess and repair. Indeed, the crisis evident in urban school systems mirrors many of the problems found in big cities themselves – poor economic conditions for schools and families, personnel shortages and high turnover rates, improper facilities and materials, and political struggles over issues of structure and control. This book analyzes the problems effecting urban schools and their students and some of the efforts that have been developed to make these schools more accountable and effective.

Considerable attention is focused on reforming public education in America. This is due, in part, to knowledge that our children have not successfully competed with their counterparts in other industrialized nations (National Commission of Excellence, 1982). Some maintain that our children have failed to demonstrate basic educational skills. This conclusion is supported by comparisons of our elementary and middle school students to students in other industrialized nations. Bracey (2000) reported slippage on math and science scores for our grade four and grade eight students on the Third International

Challenges of Urban Education and Efficacy of School Reform, Volume 6, pages 1–11.

ISBN: 0-7623-0426-X

Mathematics and Science Study (TIMMS). The data from this examination revealed that American fourth grade students scored 12th out of 26 nations in math and were third out of 26 countries in science, while eighth grade American students' scores in both math and science were considered average when compared to the same nations. In spite of this data, others express outrage that public schools have become "whipping posts" for the failure of society to address complex social problems that have a significant impact on educational performance (Berliner & Biddle, 1997a).

It should be noted that failures in the educational system are worse in large urban centers, which have high percentages of poor African, Hispanic, and Asian American students. Consider that one in every four students in public education in the United States attend schools in an urban environment, which also enroll a disproportionate number of the nation's poor children and contain 43% of all minority students (Kozol, 1992; Orfield, 1993; Olson & Jerald, 1998). Interesting data from the *African American Education Data Book: Preschool Through High School Education-Volume II Executive Summary* (1997) further illustrates the impoverished conditions urban education offers to African-American students. Selected conclusions from this report indicate that:

- Poverty appears to limit participation of African American parents in their children's education and their opportunity to gain access to private school education.
- African American children participate in preschool programs at higher rates than White students and their participation increases with income.
- African American preschool students demonstrate comparable abilities compared to White students in verbal memory skills and produce lower scores on tests measuring vocabulary. The achievement gap for African American students persists and widens as students take examinations in reading, writing, geography, mathematics, and history in grades 4, 8, and 12.
- Most of the African American public school population is located in the southern region of the country, 56.2% of all students. This region also includes 63.7% of African American teachers, and 51.0% of all African American principals.
- Almost one-third (30.2%) of African American students attend public schools in large central cities. Also, 56.2% of all African American teachers and 57.7% of school principals are employed in public urban schools.
- African American students are over-represented in special education (28.7%), vocational education (29.8%), and alternative education or other public school programs (23.0%) as opposed to (16.1%) in regular public schools.

- African American students make up 50.0% of enrollments in only 9.7% of the public schools in the U.S.
- The share of African American students who remain in America's public schools has declined from 16.4% of students in grades K–5 to 15.3% of students in grades 9–12. This may suggest that African American students leave school at higher rates than their counterparts in other racial or ethnic groups.

Clearly, the data on African American students suggests that there are unique and challenging problems for large numbers of children in the urban environments. Further, similar problems exist in urban schools for Asian and Hispanic American students.

Because urban school districts have numerous social problems that derive from the high concentrations of families in whose social mobility is limited by poverty and minority status, repeated efforts have been taken to reform their education. Some of the special efforts to reform urban education and especially the education of African American students include the following:

- Implementation of the landmark decision of the United States Supreme Court in *Brown v. Board of Education* in 1954, that struck down the longstanding practice of "separate but unequal" education for African American students. Public school desegregation resulted from legal challenges that were brought on behalf of African Americans students. Efforts to eliminate racially segregated public education have not been successful after several decades and large expenditures of public money (Orfield, 2001). The lack of success of public school desegregation can, in part, be attributed to the strong and determined will of majority citizens to resist and recent efforts of the U.S. Supreme Court and the Justice Department to stop reviewing and/or enforcing cases (Brown, 1997).
- President Johnson's 1960 "Great Society" programs, including the Headstart Program and the Elementary and Secondary Education Act of 1965 are examples of compensatory education programs. Compensatory education programs were designed to give students from economically poor family backgrounds greater educational opportunities. (Wirt & Kirst, 1982).
- An additional program that has effected urban education is special education. Supported by federal legislation, special education can be viewed as compensatory education. Special education is not limited to minority students and enrolls students from all races regardless of socio-economic background. Even today, a disproportionate number of special education students in the U.S. are African American.

- Another legally based program that influences urban education is the school finance litigation movement that began in the 1970s. School finance litigation is an attempt to provide equal funding for poor, minority, and other students, who often receive less economic support from state governments for their public education than other student groups. The historic practice of providing some school districts with greater state financial support has violated a number of education clauses in state constitutions.
- Yet, another legally based initiate that has had profound impacts on urban education is affirmative action. Affirmative action programs were the result of federal legislation and has permitted organizations to use quotas or favorable status for certain groups in employment, university admission decisions, special scholarships, and the awarding of government contracts. Affirmative action programs have been used to compensate minorities and women for the sins of past discrimination. Recent challenges in the federal courts by majority citizens have severely limited the use of affirmative action.
- A practice in the public education system that has ameliorated some of the positive effects of efforts to improve urban education is the system of ability grouping and tracking students into certain academic groups and courses. This practice has restricted the access of many minority students to higher-level subject matter and diminished their overall educational opportunities and economic benefits (Nolan, 1985).

In spite of set backs and limited assistance, the high school and university completion rates for poor and minority students has increased (Berliner & Biddle, 1997b). Some recognize that the demographic conditions that characterize urban education for many minorities in the U.S. are part of a history of discrimination that has severely limited the opportunities for an equal education for many students. With each passing generation, there appears to be less support for the government to address the effects of this past and ever lingering discrimination. Still, others believe that urban schools have used these demographic problems and the historic discrimination against minority students as excuses to rationalize the failure of these schools (Carter, 2001; Bush, 2001). As such, public policy in the U.S. is preoccupied with making the education system more accountable. According to Pipho (1997), this paradigm shift in public policy "can be traced to the more than 20 years that the triumvirate of standards, assessment, and accountability has occupied the minds of state education policy makers." Further, he recounts that in 1976, California, Colorado, and Florida passed legislation dealing with minimum competency testing for high school graduation. Mather (2001a) suggested that the Russians' launching of the satellite Sputnik in 1957 and the U.S. government's issuance of the 1983 report *A Nation at Risk* were events that created the change in public education accountability policy. Mintrom and Vergari (1997) concluded that the interest in the standards movement was generated by comparisons of the educational curricula of the U.S. with those of other industrialized nations.

The emphasis on accountability can also be traced to ideological changes that began to emerge in this country during President Ronald Reagan's administration, which sought to eliminate several of the compensatory programs of the "Great Society," including public school desegregation and affirmative action. This ideological change also supported the development of a market driven educational system and greater interests in private education. Structures such as school vouchers for public education and the privatization of selected school services are examples of the market driven educational system. These initiatives were later followed by plans to takeover low-performing schools and school districts. The evolution of efforts to improve urban public education and education for minority students is also characterized by a change in the definition of what a quality education means. Quality public education was largely determined by comparing "input variables;" schools with smaller class sizes or more computers were considered superior to those with larger class sizes or fewer computers (Mathers, 2001b). Urban schools often fail to meet such standards simply because they lack both funds and the facilities needed to provide these services to their students.

In summary, the primary target of the school reform movement is urban public schools and they remain the most difficult to assess and repair. Indeed, the crisis evident in urban school systems mirrors many of the problems found in big cities themselves – poor economic conditions for schools and families, personnel shortages and high turnover rates, improper facilities and materials, and political struggles over issues of structure and control (Hunter, 1997). This book analyzes the problems effecting urban schools, their students, and efforts to make these schools more accountable and effective.

The book is organized into three parts. Part I provides an overview of the issues facing urban school districts, their students and their communities including meeting the needs of racially, ethnically, linguistically and culturally diverse populations, financing schools located in economically disadvantaged areas, and the shortage of qualified teachers. Part II examines the impact that demands for increased accountability and equity have on urban education reform. The issues discussed in this section include academic standards and high stakes testing, technology and the digital divide, the role of leadership, teacher quality and minority teacher and administrator shortages, and school finance and public policy. Part III focuses on strategies developed to reform and improve urban school systems. These chapters examine federal education policy, the impact of school choice and related issues such as privatization and vouchers, the influence of community involvement, and state sponsored reform and reorganization efforts.

PART I: URBAN SCHOOLS AND THEIR STUDENTS

In his paper titled, "Diversity and Reform," Reynaldo Contreras maintains that any vision of school reform must lead to high-quality education for every child. Contreras quotes David Perkins' (1992) book, *Smart Schools*, to describe the difficulty educators face today in meeting the challenges of diversity in light of current social changes. Perkins (1992) notes that, "we want schools to deliver a great deal of knowledge and understanding to a great many people of greatly differing talents and with a great range of interests and a great variety of cultural and family backgrounds" (p. 2). According to Contreras, the American educational system faces two major problems as it considers school reform and addresses the needs of an increasingly diverse population: (1) the system's growth includes a large number of native-born minorities who arrive as immigrants with limited or no proficiency in English. In spite of this these individuals must be prepared for the American society of the 21st century, and (2) the educational system's historic failure to provide academic success for all students. There is growing recognition today that a variety of factors, including the current demographic changes in schools challenge every segment of society, including educators, parents, and the greater community to work together in partnerships to forge needed educational improvements.

Ji-Yeon Jo and Xue Lan Rong's paper titled, "Historical Struggles for Equity: Politics of Education and Language Policies and Implications for Asian Americans," discusses immigrant education and bilingual and multi-cultural education by using recent incidents and various political movements to foster greater understanding of the subjects. The authors analyze three bodies of research literature: educating immigrant children; the social, economic and political interactions between immigrant and non-immigrant residents; and the education policies that affect the life and advancement of immigrants, their families and communities. Rong and Jo use several important questions to guide their research, such as "what positions have the general public taken toward immigration and immigrants at "good" and "bad" times?"

Charlie Russo's chapter, "Update on School Desegregation," contains a thorough discussion of important decisions of the United States Supreme Court on school desegregation. The author reviews efforts of school districts to achieve unitary status, key court rulings on student admissions and transfers, school district consolidation, and deconsolidation, inter district remedies, and attorney fees. Russo maintains that the U.S. Supreme Court has discontinued its activist role in school desegregation and has done so by refusing to hear cases on the subject.

Frank Brown also discusses school desegregation in his chapter, "Back to the Future with the End of *Brown*: Community Control of Neighborhood Schools." The author suggests that public school desegregation is no longer an American goal or a viable alternative for minorities in this country. Brown posits that the re-segregation of public schools has been a bi-product of the lack of the judicial intervention mentioned above.

Richard C. Hunter and Saran Donahoo's paper, "Discrimination in Tracking and Specialized Education Programs," discusses how these educational approaches have limited educational opportunities for poor and minority students. Data that identifies a disproportionate rate of participation in these specialized programs for poor and minority students is presented. The authors suggest that even though these programs do not produce positive results for minority students that big-city school districts continue to use them to provide needed funding. It must be noted, that many urban school districts are under funded (Kozol, 1992).

Stephen B. Lawton presents urban economics and financial factors that affect education in his chapter titled, "Urban Economics and Financial Factors Affecting Education." The author maintains that trends in urban economies affect the way urban school systems perform. He discusses the love-hate relationship that exists regarding the central cities in the U.S. and the use of urban school systems as laboratories for educational experimentation. Finally, Lawton recommends a return to school finance reform and a focus on the equitable allocation of funds to school districts as a means to improve the quality of urban education, instead of tinkering with administrative processes, such as charter schools.

PART II: ACCOUNTABILITY AND EQUITY

Paul Green's paper, titled "The Structure of Inequality: Tracking and Educational Opportunities in America's Public Schools," identifies schooling as the primary avenue of upward mobility for minorities. Green concludes that the structure of tracking in public education has limited minority students' upward mobility and widened the gap in academic achievement over time between students in upper and lower tracks. However, the author also maintains that tracking limits the opportunities of both upper track and lower ability student groups, but with vastly different consequences.

Philip T. K. Daniel's article titled, "The Digital Divide in America's Public Schools," discusses technology in response to national and state reform movements. The author points out that some believe that educators can do little to reduce the digital divide existing today between the "haves" and "have nots." Daniels maintains that the digital divide is not simply about the budgets of school districts, but is largely about the availability of teacher training in a field that is experiencing staggering growth.

Stephen E. Lucas' chapter titled, "Supervision's Primary Task: Synthesizing Professional Development to Meet Individual Teacher Needs and Attain School Organizational Goals," presents the leadership function of instructional supervision through the lenses of organizational improvement, teacher development, and student growth and achievement. The author maintains the view that quality supervision by principals must link individual teacher professional development needs with the attainment of organization goals. According to Lucas, principals must maintain a trifocal view of schooling that includes: (a) improving schools as organizations, (b) developing teacher capacity, and (c) addressing the growth and achievement needs of students.

Leonard A. Valverde's article titled, "School Leadership for 21st Century Urban Communities," maintains that dynamic leadership is necessary in urban schools. He adopts this view because these schools have historically failed to satisfactorily educate students of color. Valverde maintains that urban school leaders must focus on several important issues, including improving pedagogy, developing a thorough knowledge of the student body of the school, and by expanding beyond learning to serve community needs, and building capacity for schools to network and form partnerships with various segments of community.

James Ward's chapter, "Adequacy Issues in Financing Urban Schools, " traces events in financing urban school districts from the major urban stress period of the late 1970s to the present. Ward discusses the political, economic, and social environment surrounding urban schools and concludes that future prospects for increased funding are not good. Instead, the political system seems to favor new public management systems (NPM) approaches to improve accountability in public education. Ward describes the new public management in education (NPME) approach as including:

- A decline of funding
- Greater use of privatization, vouchers, and charter schools
- Increased power over public education by mayors

- An emphasis on technology in management and instruction
- A high concern for international student performance comparisons

Finally, Ward suggests that the insufficient supply of high quality teachers in urban schools will worsen in the years to come, thus making it more difficult to improve educational quality.

Chapter 12 by Dawn G. Williams and Laurence Parker titled, "Standardized Testing and Assessment Policy: Impact on Racial Minorities and Implications for Educational Leadership," provides a thorough discussion of the student academic achievement gap that exist today in public schools between majority and minority students. The authors present the impact racism has had on this important phenomenon in public education. Data on the National Assessment of Educational Progress (NAEP) are presented, which document the magnitude of the problem. The authors also discuss the *No Child Left Behind Act* (2001) and present several strategies to close the achievement gap, including increasing the number of minority teachers and using multiple assessments to gauge student performance.

Art Lehr's chapter, titled "Instructional Efficiency Versus Social Reform: Fundamentals of the Tracking Debate," offers a thorough discussion of the ability grouping controversy in secondary education. This practice has been advocated to provide efficient instruction, while some maintain that ability grouping has resulted in depriving minority students with equal access to a meaningful education. Both perspectives on tracking are presented in this chapter, as well as a discussion of the uphill battle that educators face who support the de-tracking of secondary education.

PART III: SCHOOL REFORM STRATEGIES

Terri H. Mozingo's chapter, "Initiating Work Teams to Reform the American High School," discusses the lingering problem of bureaucracy and offers key lessons from business and industry that could be used to reform America's high schools. Mozingo suggests that organizing teaching and learning in work teams will yield greater results than are produced by the current educational system. Second, school systems must be committed to involving employees in work teams. Finally, the third lesson is that work teams provide an alternative to the isolation that teachers experience in their normal work settings.

The first chapter written by Frank Brown is titled, "Choice, Vouchers and Privatization as Education Reform or the Fulfillment of Richard Nixon's Southern Strategy?" and presents an exhaustive discussion of school choice, privatization, and vouchers and traces formal public education for African Americans from the Civil War. The Brown article addresses numerous issues in public education and focuses on the future of education for African Americans in neighborhood schools. Professor Brown offers a five-fold rationale for his position on the return to neighborhood schools. First, white Americans fled the inner cities to escape poorly funded schools for the suburbs. Second, whites are returning to inner cities due to changing demographics. White families are now smaller and many no longer desire to live in the suburbs. Third, the federal courts are no longer willing to force schools to desegregate because it is claimed that current racial segregation is due to private action and not state action. Fourth, due to a confluence of events, wide spread desegregation of K-12 public education is not likely to become a reality in America soon. Finally, the political options that are open to African Americans to improve public education for their children is discussed.

Richard C. Hunter and Saran Donahoo's article, "Filing for Academic Bankruptcy: The Impact and Economics of State Takeovers," discusses the pressure to reform low performing schools and to improve test scores for all students. They point out that many states have turned to school takeovers as a way of bringing about radical reform. Although it has been more than a decade since the first state sponsored school takeover occurred, this reform strategy has yet to be proven effective. The article begins with a brief description of school takeovers, which is followed by a critical analysis of how school takeovers were constructed and carried out in school districts in Logan County, West Virginia; Newark, New Jersey; and Compton, California. Several questions provide an instructive framework for the discussion of school takeovers.

Chapter seventeen written by Linda C. Tillman is titled, "African American Parental Involvement In Urban School Reform: Implications for Leadership," and is about parents and their role in school reform. The author maintains that much has been written about urban school reform and the contributions of teachers, principals, and central office administrators. While these individuals play a critical role in school reform, the literature is less instructive on the role of parents. Tillman discusses the importance of parental involvement in school reform, especially in urban school settings, where large numbers of poor and minority children have been under-served and under-educated. Tillman in addition to discussing the community environment, cultural norms, and collective vs. individual decision making, also talks about the role of *race* in the level of parental involvement in school reform.

Chapter eighteen by James E. Lyons is titled, "Reconstitution, Small Schools, School Based Management, Etc." The chapter addresses these reform strategies as a means to improve teaching and learning and to better student academic performance on standardized tests. This chapter provides a rationale for these initiatives, discusses the level of adoption and implementation of each, and assesses the perceived efficacy of them as vehicles for school improvement.

REFERENCES

Berliner, D. C., & Biddle, B. J. (1997). *The manufactured crisis: Myths, fraud, and the attack on America's public schools*. White Plains, NY: Longman Publishing USA.

Bracey, G. W. (2000). *Bail me out*. Thousand Oak, CA: Corwin Press, Inc.

Brown v. Board of Education, 347 U.S. 483 (1954).

Brown, F. (1997, Spring). Major changes in school integration litigation, 1954–1979. *Educational Administration Quarterly, 15*(2), 76–97.

Bush, G. W. (2001, January). *No child left behind* [On-line]. Retrieved March 4, 2001, from http://www.ed.gov/inits/nclb/index.html

Carter, S. C. (2001). *No excuses: Lessons from 21 high-poverty schools*. Washington, D.C.: The Heritage Foundation.

Hunter, R. C. (1997, February). The mayor vs. the school superintendent: Political incursions into metropolitan politics. *Education and Urban Society, 29*(2), 217–222. Thousand Oaks, CA.

Kozol, J. (1992). *Savage Inequalities: Children in America's Schools*. New York: Harper Perennial.

Mathers, J. K. (2001, April). State performance-based accountability systems: A national perspective. *Phi Delta Kappan, 67*(9), 6–12.

Mintrom, M., & Vergari, S. (1997, Spring). Education reform and accountability in an intergovernmental context. *Publius, 27*, 143–166.

National Commission on Excellence in Education (1983). *A nation at risk: The imperatives for educational reform*. Washington, D.C.: U.S. Government Publishing Office.

Nettles, M. T. & Perna, L. W. (1997). *The African American education data book: Volume II – Pre-school through high school education*. New York: Frederick D. Patterson Research Institute of the College Fund/UNCF.

No Child Left Behind Act (2002). Washington, D.C.: United States Department of Publications.

Nolan, T. (1985). The effects of ability grouping. Dissertation, University of Colorado, Boulder.

Olson, L., & Jerald, C. D. (1998). The challenges: Quality counts 98 barriers to success. *Education Week, 17*(17), 9.

Orfield, G. (1993). *The growth of segregation in Americas schools: Changing patterns of separation and poverty since 1968*. Alexander, VA: National School Board Association.

Orfield, G. (2001, July). *Schools more separate: Consequences of a decade of resegregation*. Cambridge, MA: The Civil Rights Project, Harvard University.

Perkins, D. (1992). *Smart Schools: From Training Memories of Educating Minds*. New York: The Free Press.

Pipho, C. (1997, May). Standards, assessment, accountability: The tangled triumvirate. *Phi Delta Kappan, 67*(9), 6–12.

Wirt, F., & Kirst, M. (1982). *The politics of education: Schools in conflict*. New York: McCutchan Publishing Corporation.

PART I: URBAN SCHOOLS AND THEIR STUDENTS

1. DIVERSITY AND REFORM

A. Reynaldo Contreras

ABSTRACT

A vision of school reform is to achieve a high-quality education for every child. However, there is a growing recognition today that a variety of factors including the current demographic changes in schools play a role and influence the notion that the process of education involves every segment of society and requires educators, parents and the greater community to come together in new roles and partnerships. This chapter discusses some of the ways diversity issues influence modern school reform efforts.

INTRODUCTION

We are probably more aware today of the changing student population than at any time in the history of our nation's education system. Communities that historically have been composed of one or two racial or ethnic groups find their public schools enrolling children from heterogeneity of social and cultural backgrounds. The shifting demography represents new kinds of challenges for education, many of which are being addressed within the educational reform movement.

Educational leaders and concerned citizens are coming together for genuine and sustained discussion about their expectations of educational organizations and the strategies that they are willing to support for creating and sustaining change. Community discourses offers reform movements an opportunity to bring communities and their schools together. In doing so, schools must include the

Challenges of Urban Education and Efficacy of School Reform, Volume 6, pages 15–23.

ISBN: 0-7623-0426-X

perspectives of diverse students and their families. Without common understanding among all segments of society regarding educational missions, goals and ways of measuring progress, most reforms are likely to be short-lived and ineffective, at least with regard to the needs of under-served students.

Community conversations, as a mode for connecting reform and diversity, has evolved as a way to examine conditions and factors that support and hinder the public deliberation process. This process is crucial as distinct groups come together for authentic and sustained debate about education. Community conversations thus can be used to bring together educators and the communities they serve to focus on educational reform.

This chapter addresses what schools and communities may need to consider in employing community conversations as an approach to ascertaining educational reform strategies for addressing contemporary issues of diversity.

A Perspective of Diversity

There is diversity in an education system. In every system, no one organization is the same as another, if for no other reason than that each organization has its own particular history, its own particular faculty and students, and its own particular geographical location. If looked at nationally, there is obvious variety also in the way in which different state educational systems have formally organized and reorganized themselves. However, what is of concern to both education policy and research is not diversity per se as some absolute state of affairs, but desirable degrees of difference and similarity coupled with an understanding of the forces which push educational organizations and systems in one direction or another. In terms of education policy it is what is intended to be achieved by diversity that is of value, rather than its mere existence. Moreover, an increase or decrease in degrees of diversity is a consequence of how educational organizations respond to external social, political, economic and other environmental pressures, pressures they themselves help to elicit and shape.

The environment is, in part, a political arena where educational organizations and interest groups within educational organizations vie with one another to maximize status, prestige and financial rewards. Diversity becomes part of the political process, inasmuch as one or the other state of affairs may advantage one set of educational organizations or interest groups over others, setting in motion efforts by the 'disadvantaged' to modify the circumstances. Much has been written about diversity in education (e.g. Berman et al., 1995; Okun, 1996; Quintero, 1999; Suarez-Orozco & Suarez-Orozco, 1995).

This literature falls into those who view education in terms of an inevitable trend towards ever-increasing differentiation and those who see a natural tendency for educational organizations to converge in terms of structure, activities, status and prestige. Clark (1983, p. 195), for example, argues that 'Explicit sectors thus seem to be the chief answer to the macro organization of an evermore extended division of academic labor', while Neave (1983) maintains that: 'all systems of ... education display a dynamic towards integration ... there is ... an indisputable move towards integration, even though from the policy-makers perspective, it constitutes a regression toward the priorities, values and practices found in the 'noble' sector'.

Whatever the perspective, what seems to be crucial is how it is applied to the understanding of the interaction between educational organizations and their environment. The environment should not be regarded as something 'out there,' totally independent of the educational organization. The environment structures institutional behavior, but the action of educational organizations in turn helps structure the environment. In line with Giddens (1977), the environment can be viewed as both the medium and outcome of social interaction. Viewed from this perspective, change in education, by definition, cannot be regarded as linear. One of the reasons why questions of diversity in education are so complex is because educational organizations not only adapt to their environment, but the environment in turn adapts to the educational organization. Furthermore, the environment is not unitary. Educational organizations interact with the environment on many different levels: a policy environment as defined by government (which educational organizations also help structure), commerce and industry, interest groups, and so on. Particular histories and cultural norms and values should also be regarded as important aspects of the environment.

Clearly, in many locales new patterns of government-education relationships are emerging. Many of those are based on a governance model that emphasizes organizational autonomy, and one that has resulted in an increasingly market-oriented framework for educational organizations. Thus, rather serious questions can be formulated with respect to its inevitability as a result of deregulation and market mechanisms. Approaches to the manner of dealing with diversity must be influenced by experiential evidence. It is hoped that the reasoning presented in this chapter will form the basis for an improved understanding of how diversity in education can be better approached.

Our Increasing Diversity

The shifting demographic patterns are already evident in the country's urban school districts. Most non-traditional students attend school districts with enrollments of 10,000 students or more. In the 2000–2001 school year, there were 47.2 million students enrolled in public elementary and secondary schools in the 50 states and the District of Columbia. Of these students, 55.5% were in pre-kindergarten through grade 6, an additional 43.4% were in grades 7 through 12, and the remaining 1.2% was ungraded students.

California had the most public elementary and secondary school students with 6.1 million, followed by Texas with 4.1 million and New York with 2.9 million. Thirteen states had enrollments of over 1 million public elementary and secondary students in the 2000–2001 school year. The District of Columbia (68,925), Wyoming (89,940), and Vermont (102,049) had the fewest students (NCES, 2001).

The 47.2 million students enrolled in the 2000–2001 school year represents a 14.6% increase in the number of students being served in the public elementary and secondary school system since the 1990–1991 school year. Between the 1990–1991 and 2000–2001 school years, Nevada had the largest percentage increase (69.2%) in the number of students. Seven states and the District of Columbia had a decrease in the number of students between these years (the District of Columbia, Louisiana, Maine, Mississippi, North Dakota, South Dakota, West Virginia, and Wyoming). The District of Columbia had the largest percentage decrease in students with a 14.6% drop.

In the 2000–2001 school year, white, non-Hispanic students made up the majority of students (61.2% 4) followed by Black, non-Hispanic and Hispanic students (17.2 and 16.3%, respectively). Asian/Pacific Islander students made up 4.1% of the public school population and American Indian/Alaska Native students made up 1.2%. In six states (California, Hawaii, Louisiana, Mississippi, New Mexico, and Texas) and the District of Columbia, 50% or more of students were non-white. Black non-Hispanic students made up more than 50% of all students in the District of Columbia and Mississippi. New Mexico reported 50.2% of its students as Hispanic, and Hawaii reported 72.3% of its student body as Asian/Pacific Islander. On the other hand, five states (Iowa, Maine, New Hampshire, Vermont, and West Virginia reported that over 90% of their students were White, non Hispanic. Changes in the racial/ethnic composition of student enrollments have altered the diversity in the Nation's schools. Although variety in student backgrounds can enhance the learning environment, it can also create challenges for schools. Awareness of the shifting racial/ethnic distribution of public school students can be helpful to schools in planning for this change.

Immigrant students bring with them much diversity. Ten years ago Hispanic immigrants came from Mexico, Puerto Rico and Cuba. Mexico still dominates this group, but significant numbers also come from Columbia, Peru, Ecuador, Venezuela, and the Dominican and Central American countries (Valdivieso & Nicolau, 1992). Asian immigrants also come from many different locations, such as Vietnam, Korea, Laos, Cambodia, Hong Kong, Taiwan, Malaysia, and the Philippines. Many of these immigrant students enter the educational system, from preschool to high school, speaking no English. Some immigrants are illiterate in their native language, while others have had excellent schooling (McLeod, 1995).

Numerous non-traditional students in schools underachieve academically. They enroll in fewer academic courses and fall behind in literacy skills. Many explanations for the educational failure of non-traditional students are shaped by the assumptions that the student's sociocultural background is deficient and impedes academic success. Most non-traditional students are economically disadvantaged. Some students are fourth, fifth and sixth generation native-born who may or may not be limited English proficient. Others are limited English proficient whose families rarely speak English at home. Because the lack of English language skills is often equated with the lack of academic potential, recently arrived immigrant students are typically placed in the lower track classes with the least demanding curriculum, almost guaranteeing low academic success. Because of tests that do not consider language and cultural differences, Hispanics have been mistakenly placed in special education, where they are over-represented. Fortunately, many educational programs today are abandoning instructional practices based on these assumptions. There is growing recognition today that a variety of factors play a role and influence the outcomes of non-traditional students (Ovando & Collier, 1998).

Educators are trying to retain the hundreds of thousands of diverse young adults that leave the educational system each year without successfully completing high school. According to Dropout Rates in the U.S., (NCES, 2001), some 3.8 million young adults were not enrolled in a high school program and had not completed high school. These youths accounted for 10.9% of the 34.6 million 16- through 24-year-olds in the U.S. in 2000. The dropout rate for Whites in 2000 remained lower than the rate for Blacks, but over the past three decades, the difference between the rates for Whites and Blacks has narrowed. However, this narrowing of the gap occurred during the 1970s and 1980s. Since 1990, the gap has remained fairly constant. In addition, Hispanic young adults in the United States continued to have a relatively high dropout rate when compared to Asian/Pacific Islanders, Whites, or Blacks.

The dropout rate for Asian/Pacific Islander young adults was lower than for young adults from all other ethnic groups. The rate for Asian/Pacific Islanders was 3.8% compared with 27.8% for Hispanics, 13.1% for Blacks, and 6.9% for Whites. Approximately 44.2% of Hispanic young adults born outside of the United States were high school dropouts. Hispanic young adults born within the United States were much less likely to be dropouts. However, when looking at just those young adults born within the United States, Hispanic youths were still more likely to be dropouts than other young adults.

Educators need to address both the strengths and needs of these students. The challenge of educating children from these different backgrounds is complex. Motivation, social organization, and ways of thinking and speaking that vary with education, income, and class status impact educational experiences and participation. Educators are striving to better understand the cultural characteristics and the socioeconomic variables that affect these students' learning. They are developing new ways of teaching diverse students and connecting with the home. In fact, the success of the reform movement will be measured by how accurately educators determine and respond to the needs of all students. The magnitude of the current demographic changes in educational programs coupled with the assumption that the process of educating involves every segment of society requires educators, parents, and the extended community to come together in new roles and partnerships.

The Challenge of Diversity

Gerzon (1996, p. xxii) describes the challenge of debate: "As citizens on the eve of the next millennium, in a nation exploding with diversity, our challenge is to listen to fellow citizens who anger us, disturb our thoughts, expose our preconceptions, and even impugn our integrity." Community conversations offer communities the opportunity to change the way they approach problems. It encourages disengaged people and families to be involved and to make acting together a community practice and responsibility.

The education of all children is a community responsibility. Educators, along with community members and organizations, must work together to create schools that will perform more effectively in our diverse society. Educational reform is essentially about widening the circle of a conventional, formal education system to include the concerns, expectations, desires, and wisdom of the extended community. Policy-makers, parents, business people, religious and civic groups, retired persons, recently arrived immigrants, and average taxpayers must join educators to help prepare our children and youth.

Today, change affects students, parents, teachers, school administrators, and the general community especially if it is transforming the community. Consequently, educators and policymakers are looking beyond the schools for support in helping all students to achieve high academic standards. To this end, current reform efforts must call for establishing positive relationships with parents and communities by making them partners in the educational process.

The Pursuit of Reform

The vision of educational reform is to achieve high-quality learning opportunities for every child. The literature aptly describes how difficult it is to meet this challenge in light of current school demographic changes. As one scholar notes "We want schools to deliver a great deal of knowledge and understanding to a great many people of greatly differing talents and with a great range of interests and a great variety of cultural and family backgrounds" (Perkins, 1992, p. 2). As a result, the contemporary educational system faces two major problems as it considers reform amidst the needs of diverse students: (1) the system's growth that includes large numbers of minorities and recent immigrants whose first language is not English, and (2) the system's historical failure to provide for academic success by many minority students.

As noted by the Education Commission of the States (1997*),* reforms are better supported, better understood, and more effective when communities play an integral role in their creation. Educators need to build community involvement and understanding into the reform process early and not as an afterthought. When educational leaders communicate with the community throughout the reform process, they need to become aware of the larger community's concerns and needs. This awareness enables educators to examine and modify ideas, practices and policies in light of the community's leadership. The consequences will include greater community trust of and advocacy for defined reforms.

Community conversations serve to bring diverse groups of community members together to achieve understanding of and consensus on a range of community issues ranging from violence in the community to the role of education. These are conversations promoting local discourse that is personal, civil, deliberative, inclusive, and relevant. Insights into the potential role of community conversations about educational reforms hold promise for helping educators and policymakers make progress toward gaining community approval, support, and legitimacy necessary to realize the promise of high-quality education for all students (SEDL, 1995).

However, if community conversations are to be a mechanism for providing effective education for all children, an effort must be made to ensure that all members of the greater community are engaged in the conversations. All too frequently, linguistically, culturally, and racially different members of the community are excluded from participation in collective discourse. Their exclusion may result from a perceived lack of skills needed to participate or because the topic and activity appear irrelevant (SEDL, 1995). Forethought requires not only setting aside time for people to meet and interact, but also the nurturing of a sense of safety and connection for all involved (Olsen et al., 1994).

Voices from the greater community are essential to the conversations about educational reform. They provide a window into the experiences of students that teachers and other educators do not have. For students from diverse families of a school community, the window helps to link the school and the home by fostering better understanding of their socio-cultural backgrounds. Without this input, educators are at a disadvantage in identifying and implementing appropriate reforms, and students are at risk of being misunderstood, mis-educated, or excluded (Olsen et al., 1994).

Common ground between the greater community and its educational system emerges when community members share purposes, courtesy, language, issues, processes and a pledge to work together. In many communities, parents, educators, and community members have reached an understanding that the community's role must go beyond merely electing school boards, paying taxes, or participating in special events. Educators alone cannot decide how programs will be provided for a diverse community of learners. The greater community must take responsibility for fulfilling its role in helping create the educational program that will serve its vision.

CONCLUSION

In conclusion, community conversations can be an effective mechanism to help a community "generate greater clarity and broad agreement" (Wagner, 1997). The unique characteristics of community conversations including: adaptability, inclusiveness, accessibility, and emphasis on shared problem solving make it an important medium as educators seek to change the way they teach and prepare students for an emerging complex society. Once integrated into a community culture, forethought looks like a revolving-door process (Ledell, 1996). "If we think of education as part of our work as citizens, it changes our relationship to schools, making it more likely that we will see them as our agents, as educational organizations that help carry out public responsibilities" (Mathews, 1996, p. 54).

Today's students are expected to become critical thinkers, to possess a high level of competency in the emerging learning technologies, to apply their knowledge to daily problem solving, to be able to work cooperatively, and to become lifelong learners. Helping them meet these expectations when so many diverse students do not gain a solid grounding in literacy skills is a major challenge for educational leaders in the pursuit of reform. Clearly little progress will be made unless educators and the communities they serve face the challenge of a broadened conversation about the kinds of strategies needed to produce desired outcomes. Meeting these expectations requires a better understanding of how such factors as culture, race, language, and national background affect the lives and needs of diverse students. Educators and the community must work as partners and begin an exchange that creates plans and practices that are inclusive and truly provide all students with an equal educational opportunity.

REFERENCES

Berman, P., McLaughlin, B., McLeod, B., Minicucci, C., Nelson, B., & Woodworth, K. (1995). *School reform and student diversity*. Santa Cruz, CA: National Center for Research on Cultural Diversity and Second Language Learning.

Clark, B. R. (1983). *The higher education system: A cross-national perspective*. Berkeley, CA: University of California Press.

Education Commission of the States. (1997). *So you have standards . . . now what?* Denver, CO: Author.

Gerzon, M. (1996). *A house divided.* New York, NY: G. P. Putnam's Sons.

Giddens, A. (1977). *Central problems in social theory: Action, structure and contradiction in social analysis*. London, England: Macmillan.

Ledell, M. A. (1996). Common ground: A way of life, not a checkoff item. *The School Administrator*, *53*(10), 8–11.

Mathews, D. (1996). *Is there a public for public schools?* Dayton, OH: Kettering Foundation Press.

McLeod, B. (1995). *School reform and student diversity: Exemplary schooling for language minority students.* Santa Cruz, CA: National Center for Research on Cultural Diversity.

Okun, B. F. (1996). *Understanding diverse families: What practitioners need to know*. New York, NY: Guilford Press.

Olsen, L., Chang, H., De La Rosa Salazar, D., Leong, C., Perez, Z., McClain, G., & Raffel, L. (1994). *The unfinished journey: Restructuring schools in a diverse society*. San Francisco, CA: California Tomorrow.

Ovando, C., & Collier, V. (1998). *Bilingual and ESL classrooms: Teaching in multicultural contexts.* Boston, MA: McGraw Hill.

Perkins, D. (1992). *Smart schools: From training memories to educating minds*. New York, NY: The Free Press.

Quintero, E. (1999). The new faces of Head Start: Learning from culturally diverse families. *Early Education And Development*, *10*(4), 475–497 EJ 593 721.

Southwest Educational Development Laboratory (1995). Diversity in dialogue: A proposal for a Task 5, LNP project in language and cultural diversity. Unpublished manuscript.

Suarez-Orozco, C., & Suarez-Orozco, M. (1995). *Transformations: Immigration, family life and achievement motivation among Latino adolescents.* Stanford, CA: Stanford University Press.

U.S. Department of Education, National Center for Education Statistics (2001). *The condition of education 2001* (NCES 2001-072). Washington, D.C.: U.S. Government Printing Office.

Valdivieso, R., & Nicolau, S. (1992). *Look me in the eye: A Hispanic cultural perspective on school reform* (Report No. RC 019 293). Palo Alto, CA: American Institute for Research in the Behavioral Sciences.

Wagner, T. (1997). The new village commons: Improving schools together. *Educational Leadership*, *54*(5), 25–28.

2. HISTORICAL STRUGGLES FOR EQUITY: POLITICS OF EDUCATION AND LANGUAGE POLICIES AND ITS IMPLICATIONS FOR ASIAN AMERICANS

Ji-Yeon O. Jo and Xue Lan Rong

ABSTRACT

Many see the United States as a country of immigrants, but an examination of the past 150 years of education and language policies regarding immigrant children shows a tendency toward the disservice and underservice of many immigrant children. In this study, the authors conduct a historical analysis of how immigration, education, and language-related legal issues have affected the schooling of Asian Americans. The authors hope that this case study will improve educational policies and practices making them equitable educational opportunities for all immigrant children.

INTRODUCTION

Educating immigrant students has always been a pressing and challenging issue for American public, social, and educational institutions. Census data of 2000 reported an estimated 29 million immigrants reside in the United States and

Challenges of Urban Education and Efficacy of School Reform, Volume 6, pages 25–47.

ISBN: 0-7623-0426-X

nine million students in U.S. elementary and secondary schools are from immigrant families (Camarota, 2001). Immigration was and still is an issue particularly for urban schools because urban school districts have absorbed the largest number of immigrants and low-income students, many of whom need special attention. According to the Current Population Report (Lollock, 2001), almost half the immigrants who live in urban areas tend to be poorer, less educated, and have a lower proficiency in spoken English compared to immigrants who live in suburban areas (see Rong & Preissle, 1998).

The current wave of immigration has broadened the diversity of U.S. society. The Hispanic population has been the fastest growing population – from less than one million at the turn of the last century to 34 million in 2000 – and has become the largest minority population in the United States. More than one million school-age children, accounting for 36% of all immigrant students in the United States, were born in Mexico. This figure is up from 15% in 1970 (Zehr, 2002). The Asian population in the United States has shown a similar pattern of rapid growth – from less than 250,000 in 1900 to 11 million in 2000. Currently, about 85% of foreign-born children are not European whites, including 25% Asian, 51% Hispanic, and 7% Black (Lollock, 2001).

Large-scale immigration with vast and growing diversity demands schools to be reflective of and responsive to on-going demographic, social, political, and economic changes. Morse (1994) reminds people who have worked with immigrant children and families that their jobs are becoming more difficult and that solutions must therefore become more inventive. Although more immigrants have arrived in the last decade, the federal government has reduced or restricted a few of the existing programs that have assisted new immigrants in integrating into the economic, social, and civic life of the United States Federal funding for refugees, legalized aliens, and immigrant education programs has been delayed or cut substantially. For the most part, the responsibility for integrating immigrants into society has been left to state and local governments, private organizations, and (mostly) immigrants themselves.

How schools cope with these declining federal and local supports but still effectively integrate immigrant children into U.S. society will greatly affect the future of our nation. Questions related to immigrant children's education have often triggered heated debate: What have been the dilemmas and paradoxes surrounding laws and policies regarding the education of immigrant children? What are the promises and problems, challenges and opportunities when society and its schools deal with policy issues regarding the education of large numbers of immigrant students with enormous diversity? What are the differences between the temporary and long-term solutions, the simplified and the more comprehensive solutions? We hope this study, examining equality and equity issues in educational and language policies for Asian American children, will shed light on these questions.

In our study, we will examine Asian American immigration, education, and language experiences in the United States. It is our hope that our study will serve as an example to capture ways in which immigrants have been incorporated into American schools and other social institutions. Asian Americans have historically suffered from exclusion, alienation, and marginalization, but many people may not acknowledge the racial nature of the actions against this group of people or may interpret the anti-Asian actions differently because of the deeply rooted "Model Minority" stereotype. By formulating our study as a historical case study, we invite readers to compare the experiences we recount here to the experiences of other immigrant minority groups and to consider how it relates to possible and necessary changes in school policies and practices. Moreover, comparing current trends with past trends may suggest future changes to how we deal with these issues and may result in useful recommendations on how the U.S. public and U.S. schools can accommodate such changes.

In our historical analysis we focus on educational language policies; however, we believe these policies must be examined in a larger context to understand where they came from, how they were implemented, how they are interrelated, and whose interests they have served. Due to these considerations, we first examine U.S. immigration policies, then the policies and legal issues related to Asian Americans' educational and language status. We focus our examination on Asian Americans' encounters with major U.S. institutions (local, state, and federal legislatures, as well as schools) and mainstream communities. We provide a historical perspective on these encounters by analyzing societal responses to immigration movements and reviews of politicians', as well as the general public's and educators' ideas and philosophies regarding how immigrant children should be educated. We will discuss a wide range of stereotypes that have been imposed upon Asian Americans from Coolie (contract hard labor), to urban gangster, to permanent alien/exotic oriental, to the more contemporary stereotype of "the model minority" (Lee, 2001). However, as pointed out by many scholars (Lee, 1996; Rong & Preissle, 1998), this new "model minority" stereotype may mask other more negative stereotypes such as "marginal minority" and "double minority," while at the same time enhancing the more resentful but hidden stereotype – the "cross-overs." We will also discuss our understanding of what kind of language policies embody equal and equitable educational opportunities for immigrant children. Finally, we will outline the special needs of Asian immigrant children and make recommendations for educators and policymakers. We hope the examination of Asian American education history might also suggest lessons educators and policy makers can draw on when working with other immigrant children and their communities.

ASIANS IN THE UNITED STATES: A HISTORY OF ASIAN IMMIGRATION

Asians are one of the fastest growing minority groups in the United States. The recent surge in immigration from Asian countries could be interpreted as a result of changes in immigration policies in the United States (*Hart-Cellar Act of 1965*)[1] as well as an increase in international migration due to globalization (Suarez-Orozoco, 2001). Asian immigration to the United States has expanded dramatically in the last two decades. Although Asians have been immigrating to the country for more than 150 years, over 90% of Asian Americans are recent immigrants who have arrived after the 1965 Immigration Act. The number of immigrants from Asian countries has risen rapidly since then, and the Asian American population has approximately doubled in each of the last three decades – 1.7 million in 1970, 3 million in 1980, 6.8 million in 1990, 11 million in 2002, and a projected 17 million in 2010 (Rong & Brown, 2002a).

The term "Asian American" leads to the common misconception that this is a homogeneous group. Asian Americans actually comprise many very diverse groups of peoples; "Asian" does not work as conveniently or neatly as some would like. "Asian" can be a marker of the geographic origin of people, or of certain physical characteristics – such as color of skin, shape of eyes and nose, height, etc. – or of certain cultural practices. There are different physical features among Asians, for example between Japanese and Asian Indians, or between geographic regions like Russia and Malaysia. Diverse languages such as Tagalog, Vietnamese, Tamil, Gujarati, Japanese, Mandarin Chinese, Cantonese, and Korean are spoken in Asia. More than 50 languages are spoken by Asian immigrants, and many dialects are also spoken within a single nationality such as Chinese, which alone encompasses eight different dialects (Rong & Preissle, 1998). The misconception is all the more problematic because some of the people whom we call "Asians" may not identify with each other. For example, many Koreans identify themselves as Koreans but do not identify themselves with Filipinos or Japanese (Lee, 1996).

However, the term "Asian" is still used to signify a greatly diverse group of people and use of the term is often politically motivated to homogenize and control a certain group of people. The social and political boundaries for Asians have been often contested and negotiated within the history of racial politics in the United States. Below, we will explore the contested and negotiated arena of Asian racial politics by examining Asian immigration history to the United States and immigration policies in the United States.

The United States Asian immigrant population consists of a large percentage of recent immigrants, as well as a number of Asian immigrant descendents who have lived in the United States for many generations. Asian immigration history goes back more than 150 years. Though some Chinese laborers were present in Hawaii before 1835 (Takaki, 1998), a considerable number of immigrants started to immigrate from Asia beginning in the 1850s. The majority of these immigrants were from China (Weinberg, 1997). The booming sugar industry in Hawaii and a lack of native labor led plantation owners to consider importing labor from other countries. As a result, Chinese contract laborers started to arrive in Hawaii in the early 1850s (Takaki, 1998). The labor demand from the California mining industry and the cross-continental railroad construction industry also influenced Chinese migration to California and to the other parts of the U.S. mainland. Most of them came to this country as sojourners to temporarily escape the economic turmoil in their home country, and to earn good money and return home with "pride and prosperity." The contract laborers (also called Coolies) were predominantly single men who left their families in their home country. Since neither the immigration of Chinese women nor miscegenation with whites was allowed by the U.S. government, most of the laborers could not easily establish their own families in the United States. As the possibility of returning home with "pride and prosperity" became scarce for the contract laborers, they started to settle and work in labor-intense industries like farming, laundry, etc. (Takaki, 1998).

Although Asian immigrants made the United States their home, their rights were not guaranteed by the U.S. Constitution; nor could they become citizens of the United States. In 1790, Congress passed a law stating that "a foreigner could become a naturalized citizen only if he or she is *white*" (Weinberg, 1997, p. 18). This rhetoric persisted for more than 100 years. We would argue that it had led to entrenched racism that continued to prohibit Chinese and other Asians from procuring citizenship and equal rights, including the right to be educated. Asians' struggles to become citizens of the United States and their fight for equal opportunities decorate the history of Asians in the United States, but their stories are conspicuously absent from U.S. history books. (Lee, 1996; Takaki, 1998). In this sense, they have been consistently marginalized.

The *Naturalization Law of 1790* that specified citizenship eligibility only to whites was in effect until 1952 (Takaki, 1998). During this period, many Asians suffered from inconsistent and illogical interpretation and implementation of this law. Thus, the rights and benefits that come with citizenship were also not granted to most Asians, no matter how many years they had lived in this country, no matter how Americanized their way of life, and no matter how white their skin colours. Under this law, Asians' right to own property, their right to marry (especially with whites), and their right to public education were consistently denied. The laws limiting both the number of Asian immigrants and their opportunities, rights, and entitlements made Asian Americans an invisible and marginal minority in U.S society for a very long time.

While the *Naturalization Law of 1790* was in place and Asians attempted to gain citizenship through court hearings, the notion of "white" was changed to exclude non-European whites from obtaining citizenship. Court cases like the *Ozawa* case (1922), *U.S. v. Balsara* (1910), the *Aikoy Kumar Mazumdar* decisions (1913), *U.S. v. Bhagat Singh Thind* (1923), etc., indicate that the term 'White' changed to exclude any colored person or non-European descendents from gaining citizenship. The notion of "white" initially referred simply to the color of the skin; however, it was used as equivalent to the term "Caucasian" when Ozawa, a Japanese immigrant, asserted that his skin complexion was as white as most of the whites in the United States. However, when Bhagat Singh Thind, an Asian Indian, asserted his Caucasian heritage and claimed his right to citizenship, the definition of "Caucasian" (white) changed again to "immigrant from northern or western Europe" (Spring, 2001, p. 59; Takaki, 1998, pp. 298–299). Since Asians could not obtain citizenship, their human rights were not guaranteed by the U.S. Constitution. This was arguably a strategic exclusion of Americans to legitimize the long-term exploitation of Asian laborers in this country and the racialization of Asian as an inferior species.

Though the immigrant generation could not obtain citizenship by naturalization, their descendents could acquire citizenship by birth (e.g. the case of Nisei, second generation Japanese). However, these second-generation citizens were not immune from racial discrimination and social injustice. This institutional racism manifested in reduced employment opportunity had a covert influence on student performances and career aspirations. A study of the Nisei conducted by researchers from Stanford University from 1928 to 1933 (Chan, 1991, p. 114) revealed that Nisei students' academic achievement was comparable to or somewhat higher than their European-American counterparts until the 7th grade; their academic achievement started to decline after 8th grade seemingly without reason. The researchers also found that high school Nisei's number one career aspiration was in agriculture, which reflected most of Issei's[2] profession at that time. Thus, there could be institutional pressures for the Nisei to succeed their parents' occupation and it may have lowered their academic achievement as they got older (Spring 2001, p. 66). However, the Stanford researchers provided various reasons that Nisei should not aspire to become professionals or white-collar workers and urged them to accept existing occupational barriers. This recommendation provides a glimpse of society's prevailing low expectations and systematic injustice practiced upon second-generation Japanese Americans.

There are other examples of discriminatory immigration laws in the early years of Asian immigration history. The *Chinese Exclusion Act of 1882* and the *1917 Immigration Law* were enacted to prohibit Chinese and Asian Indian immigration, respectively. *The 1924 Immigration Act*,[3] however, set quotas for immigration. This quota system was in effect until the *Hart-Cellar Act of 1965* (Johnson et al., 1997, p. 1057).

The immigration and naturalization process for Asians in the United States is a constant reminder for Asians that they are foreigners and aliens. The very term "permanent resident alien" is still in use today to classify immigrants who received a green card from the U.S. government. We would argue that immigrants are constantly reminded of their foreignness, and their civil rights are rejected, especially in the event of a national crisis. The USA Patriot Act passed by Congress in the aftermath of the September 11th terrorist attack is a recent example of immigrant discrimination. Under this immigration provision, the U.S. government has authority to hold an illegal alien suspected to threaten national security for seven days without filing any charges (*Time*, December 6, 2001).[4] Furthermore, this provision also allows the government to monitor foreign students who are legally in the United States, and allows the FBI to monitor telephone and Internet activities (ACLU Legislative Analysis on USA Patriot Act). Some say civil rights are not really for immigrants and that these rights are only for American citizens. However, enacting immigrant laws in reaction to a terrorist attack shows the irrational application of a patriotism that paints all immigrants, even legal immigrants, as the ultimate "other" – in some sense, as the "enemies within". Thus, Asian immigrants are still "situated in a differential relationship to the political and cultural institutions of the nation-state" (Lowe, 1996).

STRUGGLE FOR INCLUSIVE AND EQUITABLE EDUCATIONAL OPPORTUNITIES

Injustice and inequity regarding Asian-American children's educational opportunities have been exemplified in over 100 years of federal and state education policies and have been embodied in the struggles of Asian-Americans striving for inclusion.

During the mid-19th century, the United States established tax-based public schools, but these schools were open only to white children. Both African-American slaves and Chinese immigrants were forbidden to learn how to read and write. The Chinese community's fight for equal and equitable educational opportunities lasted for more than a century. In 1857, Chinese community leaders requested that the San Francisco School Board admit Chinese children into public schools, but their request was denied. Instead, they were told to send their children to segregated African-American schools. After two years of persistent requests by the Chinese community, the San Francisco School Board opened California's first Chinese public school in 1859, but it soon faced opposition from the public. Though it was reorganized as a night school in the following year, opposition from the public and some policy makers persisted for a decade (Wollenberg, 1995). In 1869, Superintendent James Denman campaigned against the Chinese school and finally closed the school on Feb. 14, 1871. Although the *Burlingame treaty*[5] (1868), signed by the Chinese and U.S. governments, ensured equal rights among citizens of both countries, this provision was not enforced by the United States, and Chinese children's access to regular public education was consistently denied (Wollenberg, 1995; Weinberg, 1997, p. 18).

Much of the discrimination against the Chinese was based on the interpretation of the School Law of 1872, which stated (Low, 1982, p. 48), ". . . every school, unless otherwise provided by special statute, must be opened for the admission of *all white children* [emphasis added] between five and twenty-one years residing in a district . . . ." According to this law, public schools were only for white students and thus relegated non-white children to separate schools. The district repeatedly denied its obligation to provide equal educational opportunities for non-white children.

The *Tape v. Hurley* case in California in October 1884 was a fight to obtain access to non-segregated public education (Takaki, 1998; Spring 2001; Wollenberg, 1995, p. 3). Mamie Tape was an American-born Chinese girl whose enrollment in the Spring Valley School in California was prohibited by the principal, Jennie Hurley. Hurley refused to admit Mamie because the San Francisco school board did not allow Chinese students to attend public schools. The Tape family took court action. The presiding judge, Judge Maguire, ordered the district to provide public educational access to Mamie Tape and other Asian students. However, only two weeks after the decision, the California legislature found a loophole in Judge Maguire's decision and revised the California school code so that Chinese children would have to be educated in "segregated" schools (Spring, 2001; Weinberg, 1997). Thus, as a result of the *Tape v. Hurley* ruling, a segregated Chinese school, the "Oriental School," was created in 1885 (Wollenberg, 1995 p. 9).

Because the Chinese were paying taxes, the district could not refuse to provide public education; instead, it sought to exclude Chinese students from being in the same class with white students. This "separate but equal" educational policy persisted until the early 1950s, when African-Americans pressured for school desegregation. Whites started to open their schools to Chinese-Americans as the desegregation efforts of African-Americans became more intense (Weinberg, 1997, p. 34).

While Chinese children were educated in the segregated Oriental School, Japanese children could attend integrated schools in the late 19th century. The Japanese student population was much smaller in number and did not live in a clustered region like the Chinese in San Francisco. Between 1871–1880, only 149 Japanese lived in the United States compared to 123,201 Chinese during the same period (Weinberg, 1997, p. 3). Also, Americans' anti-Japanese feeling had not yet developed in the late 19th century.

As anti-Japanese sentiment increased in the early 20th century, so, too, did public demand to segregate Japanese students from integrated schools. Tensions heightened in 1905 with an influx of Japanese labor immigrants and the attendance of older Japanese students in primary grades in regular public schools. Primarily for economic reasons, Japanese students were traditionally kept in regular public schools. However, after the 1906 San Francisco earthquake, many Chinese immigrants moved out of San Francisco's Chinatown, and more spaces became available for the ninety-three Japanese children to attend the Oriental School. Thus, the San Francisco School Board turned the segregated Oriental School for Chinese immigrants into a segregated school for Japanese, Chinese and Korean students in 1906 (Spring, 2001; Takaki, 1998).

Reaction from the various ethnic communities was mixed. Many Japanese parents resisted this segregated school and most of them kept their children at home. They also boycotted the school and tried to win public opinion in Japan to force the U.S. government to take favorable action toward Japanese Americans (Spring 2001). However, most of the Korean parents sent their children to school; for them, the segregated educational opportunities were better than nothing (Takaki, 1998).

The tension between federal and state governments continued in *Aoki v. Deane* in 1907. Keikichi Aoki was denied public education in a desegregated institution because "children of Mongolian or Chinese descent should not be admitted to any other school when segregated Oriental schools were established" (Wollenberg, 1997). The Aoki family hired U.S. attorney Devlin, who argued that the "Japanese are not Mongolians" and claimed that the Japanese were a different race than the Chinese. He also argued that the San Francisco school district could not segregate Japanese children, thereby depriving them of their treaty (the treaty of 1894) rights as citizens of "the most favored nation." The *Aoki v. Deane* case was dismissed eventually, but it became the most serious school segregation conflict prior to the 1950s, resulting in the political rearrangement of the Japanese immigrant labor agreement and migration policy (e.g. Gentlemen's Agreement, 1908) (Takaki, 1998; Wollenberg, 1995).

Interestingly enough, while all of the Asian students were educated in segregated schools, San Francisco's German, Italian, and French immigrants were taught in their native languages in regular public schools[6] (Rothstein, 1998). Thus, the injustice and inequality in education that the Asians experienced in California was not solely based on their immigrant status. Instead, the educational injustice and inequality leveled against Asian students was a result of their skin color and overt racism by the white community and its institutions.

EDUCATIONAL LANGUAGE POLICIES AND POLITICS OF LANGUAGE EDUCATION

We believe that immigrant children's language learning process includes acquiring English and also the loss or maintenance of heritage language.[7] We do not view English learning as an isolated process. Instead, we see language learning and transitions of children as a holistic process that is continuously formed and reformed by interplay among three activities: acquisition of English, retention of heritage language, and attrition of heritage language. We observed that language-learning efforts with different focuses and scopes might result in different outcomes from monolingual (either in English or in the heritage language) proficiency, to bi/multilingual proficiency, to incompetence in any language. We believe that the three linked activities of the language learning and transition processes contribute to a child's linguistic adaptation. Thus, the interplay of all these activities deserves to be studied simultaneously. Without understanding the whole process of language learning, we cannot fully comprehend why some immigrant children learn English more effectively than others.

We also believe that the processes of learning English and learning and maintaining home languages are affected by many factors that may not always be controllable by either the child or the family. Scholars (e.g. Jiobu, 1988; Heath, 1986) have argued that many factors are involved in English acquisition: place of birth, age at arrival, length of U.S. residency, social class, parental education, family language, neighborhood language diversity, English environment, availability of schooling, quality of ESL or bilingual education programs, etc. They believe that the outcome of a child's language transition will be the result of the interplay of all these elements.

In addition to the aforementioned factors, many other factors are recognized as relevant to children's language retention and attrition (i.e. a child's cultural heritage, ethnic identity, language preference, religion, ethos, political beliefs, values, etc.) (Portes & Rumbaut, 1996). These may be compounded by other factors such as SES and a child's language status. Poor and/or uneducated immigrants may find themselves in an undesirable situation where they can neither help their children develop English proficiency fast enough to cope with the school requirements nor locate the resources and authority to help their children retain their heritage language for effective communication with parents and community members.

Acquiring English fluency has been viewed as crucial for immigrant children's academic success. Likewise maintaining the ability to communicate in home language with family and community members is recognized as necessary for immigrant children's socialization and psychological well-being. However, historical examination reveals that the language policymaking process in the United States has been highly politically charged and as a result these policies have not been successful in properly educating immigrant children for either purpose.

1850–1950s: LANGUAGE POLICIES FOR SCHOOLING

Educational language policies from the 1850s to the 1950s are closely related to the immigrant policies and educational policies described above. Furthermore, the educational language policies also reflect intra/international political and economic circumstances (i.e. annexation, colonization, diplomatic relationships between the United States and other countries, war, international trade, etc.). Before the 1850s, German bilingual schools flourished in the United States, and in the Southwest region of the U.S., Spanish-English bilingual schools and French-English bilingual schools were also present. However, school-related English-only laws aimed at German Catholics were passed in 1889, shortly after German immigration peaked in the United States (Wiley, 2002, pp. 43–44).

German language instruction gradually declined in the early 1900s and was subsequently banned or dropped in most states during WWI. At this time, many states passed laws that prohibited languages other than English as an instructional language in schools. The ban on German language instruction was overturned by the U.S. Supreme Court in 1923 (*Meyer v. Nebraska, 262 U.S. 390*), but German language instruction never recovered its pre-war levels (Wiley, 2002, p. 54).

In another Supreme Court case, *Farrington v. Tokushige 273 U.S. 284,298* (1927), the justices also ruled that restrictions on private or community-based

Japanese, Korean, and Chinese instruction imposed by the territorial governor of Hawaii were unconstitutional. However, during WWII, the right to Japanese instruction was prohibited in the federal Japanese internment camps (Wiley, 2002, p. 54). As the historical struggle for language education illustrates, the movement toward English as the only language and restrictions on the instruction of immigrants' native languages in schools are "closely corresponded to the general level of hostility of the dominant group toward various language minority groups" (Tse, 2001; Wiley, 2002, p. 46).

1950s–PRESENT: BILINGUAL EDUCATION vs. THE ENGLISH-ONLY MOVEMENT

Asian Americans have continuously experienced unequal educational opportunities in U.S. schools, and even after schools were desegregated, proper education for immigrant children was still in question. Especially after the *Hart-Cellar Act of 1965*, when many more emigrated from Asian countries, the education of these immigrant children, including language instruction, became an issue. The immigrant community realized that gaining equal access to public schools was not enough for the proper education of these children. Many Asian students were failing or dropping out from school because of their difficulty in learning English and the racism they experienced from their peers and from school officials. Children who spoke English as a second language did not receive proper assistance from school programs intended to provide the amount of effective English instruction necessary for immigrant children's success in school. These programs were often ineffective because these children's psychological, cultural, and linguistic needs were often neglected by teachers, schools, and education boards.

In 1970, the families of Kinney Kinmon Lau and twelve other Chinese American students sued the San Francisco Unified School District and asked them to provide special English classes taught by bilingual teachers (Spring, 2001; Wang, 1995; Weinberg, p. 28). The school district argued that since all Chinese children were receiving the same educational opportunities as other students in the district, learning English was not a legal right of ESL students. The lower courts ruled in favor of the school district, but the U.S. Supreme Court later overturned those decisions.

The *Lau v. Nichols* case has important significance. Although the earlier cases (i.e. *Farrington v. Tokushige*, *Tape v. Hurley*, *Aoki v. Deane*, etc.) influenced school choice and instructional language policy, those cases were influential to only Asian communities. The *Lau v. Nichols* case influenced many other immigrant communities (including the Latino(a) community) and greatly influenced bilingual education in the United States. In contrast to the English-only instruction in most of the schools that was implemented before the *Lau* decision, three types of bilingual programs were proposed: (1) transitional bilingual education; (2) bilingual/bicultural education; and (3) multilingual/multicultural education. The bilingual educational policy known as the Lau Plans was aggressively enforced from 1975 to 1981 in nearly five hundred school districts, mostly in the Southwestern region of the U.S. (Crawford, 2000).

However, the prescriptive implementation of bilingual education provoked a backlash by English only advocates. Proposition 227 in California, the so-called "English for the children movement"(1998) is one of the examples of this backlash, and the current politically-inclined English-only movement led by California millionaire Ron Unz is a forceful continuation of the backlash against bilingual education.

CRITICAL ISSUES IN THE CURRENT POLITICS OF LANGUAGE IN EDUCATION

The English-only initiative is currently spreading rapidly in the United States. Recently, 20 states have passed official English laws and over a dozen other states have comparable versions of similar legislation pending (Tse, 2001,p. 1). There were state-level propositions in California (Proposition 227[1998]) and Arizona (Proposition 203[2001]), and similar bills have been introduced in Massachusetts, Oregon and Rhode Island (Zehr, 2001). A popular rhetorical device for the English-only movement is the proclamation that the English-only movement is "helping immigrants adjust in the new country." A front-line English-only supporters' network, "U.S. English," claims that official English legislation is pro-immigrant (Tse, 2001, p. 76; U.S. English website). In addition, proponents of the English-only movement have accused bilingual education of being a "linguistic welfare" system that is prohibiting immigrant children's acquisition of English and is responsible for the high dropout rates and school failures among immigrant students, restricting them, ultimately, to low-skill, low-paying jobs (Tse, 2001, p. 77).

More interestingly, some of the forerunners of this movement are immigrant descendents themselves (i.e. software millionaire Ron Unz and Senator S. I. Hayakawa); their version of "success" in the United States necessitates the acquisition of English and a quick assimilation into mainstream culture. This position is quite different from the earlier English-only movement of the early 20th century, which was often supported by white, Anglo-Saxon, English-speaking people who wanted to ban other languages because of their xenophobia. Bilingual proponents attribute the current spread of the debate to lawmakers taking advantage of "political opportunism." They believe it demonstrates a continued societal misconception about bilingual education programs (Zher, 2001).

It is our belief that the English-Only proponents misinform the general public. We will detail the biases and inaccuracies of their claims in the next section.

CRISIS OF ENGLISH: TRUE OR FALSE?

The English-only movement is largely manufactured, we argue, by rhetoric suggesting there is a "crisis of/in English," which is similar to the rhetoric of Anglo-decline (Hage, 2000). Similar to Hage's argument that Anglo-decline is an unfounded claim, we contend that the crisis-of-English or English-decline rhetoric is a largely falsified claim as well. We think three English crises have been invented to misinform the public. First, English usage is declining and the dominant language in the United States will soon be Spanish. Contrary to this claim of declining English usage, there is plenty of evidence to suggest that English is actually gaining more dominance, both domestically and internationally. For instance, widespread use of the Internet has contributed to the dominance of English as a global language. Consequently, English and English acquisition has become more important than ever. Furthermore, some scholars (Sach, 1990; Skutnabb-Kangas, 2000) have argued that, due to globalization, over 90% of world languages are going to disappear in the next century.

The second evidence of the crisis-of-English rhetoric can be found in the rationales given by politicians for the English-only movement, arguing that "English unites the country and multilingualism is divisive."[8] (Tse, 2001, p. 3). The ideology of "cultural and linguistic unification is accompanied by the imposition of the dominant language and culture as legitimate and by the rejection of all other languages into indignity" (Bourdieu, 1998, p. 46). This and the tendency of "language restrictionism" are actually the reflection of adverse feelings toward the people who speak languages other than English and have little to do with language itself[9] (Tse, 2001, p. 75).

These policies of language restrictionism result mainly from the social, political, and economic climate, both locally and internationally, that promote linguistic, cultural, and economic unity (sometimes homogeneity) across the globe (Sachs, 1992). This globalization effort increasingly homogenizes global culture and reduces linguistic diversity. In this context, pluralism is often seen as the foe of civil unity in the contemporary nation-state (Ricento, 2000). Lucy Tse (p. 76) claims that "Language is often a tool or symbol of covert social, political, or economic battles and a proxy for other agendas." According to Portes and Rumbaut (1990), language in the United States has a meaning broader than the instrumental value of communication and language homogeneity has been seen as the cornerstone of collective identity. Nativists have insisted that non-accented English and the dropping of native languages are symbols of an immigrant's commitment to Americanization and his/her patriotism. It is not hard to explain why immigrants have been compelled not only to speak English well, but also to speak English only, as a prerequisite for social acceptance and mobility.

The third claim used to support the crisis-of-English rhetoric is that "immigrants do not learn English" (Tse, 2001). There is overwhelming evidence that immigrants are acquiring English at the expense of losing their heritage languages (Woodrum, 1981 cited in Goodis, 1986: Rong & Preissle,1998). Instead of blaming newcomers' arrogance, inassimilability, or unwillingness to learn English, McDonnell and Hill (1993) argue that although we are at the peak of the fourth wave of immigration to the United States, government at all levels has not provided adequate services to help newcomers learn English. No federally financed program exists to teach adult immigrants English, though states have the option of using federal adult-education money for that purpose. Community-based organizations and volunteer literacy organizations around the country undertake the task of teaching immigrant literacy. However, these organizations reported unmet needs for more classes, especially at times and in places convenient for working people (see Rong & Preissle, 1998). Scholars have argued that the common rhetoric of immigrants who resist learning English (Tse, 2001, p. 1) has proven to be an unfounded claim (Kouritzen, 1999; Tse, 2001, p. 29; Tuan, 1998).

In the process of learning English, immigrants and their children are losing their native languages rapidly. A language shift from the heritage language to English often occurs within the lifetime of young immigrants (Tse, 2001, p. 31); within two generations their heritage languages have been almost completely forgotten (Tuan, 1998). Rong & Preissle (1998) report that among second-generation Asians, more than 95% reported speaking English very well, and the proportion of children reported speaking a language other than English dropped to less than 20%. Among those in the third generation, all reported speaking English very well, and the percentage of children who reported speaking a language other than English at home decreased to less than 5%. In Woodrum's (1981) study of the language shift of Japanese immigrants, first-generation Japanese reported 100% Japanese/17% English fluency; there was, however, a dramatic language shift in the second and third generations (second generation – 19% Japanese/93% English fluency, third generation – 2% Japanese/100% English fluency) (Goodis,1986). Well-known linguistic human rights scholar Skutnabb-Kangas (2000) has argued that language losses are often the result of formal education: every time indigenous or minority children were educated in a dominant language, there were complete language shifts. Skutnabb-Kangas termed this phenomenon of language loss not as "language shift," but as "language genocide."[10]

POWER OF LANGUAGE OR LANGUAGE OF POWER?

Despite the advent of the English-only movement in K-12 levels of educational and governmental services, foreign language instruction is flourishing in the post-secondary level. In some colleges, foreign language has become a part of the undergraduate curriculum requirement. More and more students are taking foreign language courses. The English-only movement does not seem threatened by the foreign language courses offered at the college level. Thus, we argue that the source of English-only proponents' "discontent" is not related to the foreign language issue itself, but rather who uses that language and who allows that usage. If an immigrant uses a language other than English, it is seen as a threat to the unity of the United States and possibly even a threat to national security[11] (Tse, 2001). But if a nonimmigrant white person uses a foreign language, it is seen as the accumulation of cultural and social capital (Hage, 2000, p. 56). For English-speaking dominant Americans, English is not questioned as hampering the retention or aggravating the attrition of other languages, but immigrants' home languages are constantly portrayed as hampering the immigrants' English language acquisition. This common myth that immigrants' native language inhibits their English acquisition has proved to be unfounded in the area of second language acquisition (SLA) research (Ovando & Collier, 1998).

Despite evidence of a rise in English acquisition, it is unclear why some still think English is declining and bilingual education is so divisive that it threatens national unity. Why does language policy remain an emotional political issue? Sonia Nieto (1996) has argued it is because bilingual education has the potential to empower traditionally powerless and subordinate groups and give them the power to control, to some extent, their and their family members' Americanization process

The "absolute dominance of the English language in both public and private life actively discourages bilingualism" (Alba & Nee, 1996) and leads to a limited or minimal retention of heritage languages among immigrant children (Tuan, 1998, p. 107). When immigrants lose their heritage language, they also lose many aspects of their heritage culture. Research has also shown that Asian immigrants who have given up their heritage languages and cultures to completely assimilate into American society report that they experience identity loss or confusion and feelings of ambivalence – living in the United States as an American while still being treated as "exotic Orientals" and "permanent aliens" (Kouritzin, 1999; Tuan, 1998).

DISCUSSION

The history we have reviewed here strongly suggests that the processes of educational policy making usually involve political, social, racial, and economic battles. How schools accommodate their immigrant students is inextricably linked to broader societal attitudes about immigration, and schools throughout the century have found themselves in a recurring pendulum swing between assimilation and pluralism (Schnaiberg, 1999). Immigrants, especially immigrant linguistic minorities, are likely to be convenient scapegoats in times of political crisis and economic downturns when nativist feelings are high (Ravitch, 1974; Tyack, 1974). While poorer immigrants were often demeaned as a "societal burden and welfare addicted," middle class immigrants were resented as "cross-overs."

Immigrant Asians who are unfamiliar with the American legislative and legal process and who lack social and political connections may find themselves powerless to influence the policy making process (Lujan, 1989; Portes & Rumbaut, 1996). Although the Asian population has rapidly increased in the United States in the last three decades, in many states and counties, Asian-Americans are still a first-generation immigrant population, a small percentage of the population and likely vulnerable to discrimination of all kinds. Current monolingual/monocultural movements and immigrant bashing are severely challenging the commitment to providing equitable and effective education to all students; however, these movements may cause the most damage to Asian-American children who are working class, low SES, and learning disabilities.

Gibson (1995) articulated two different models in terms of working with immigrant children, the subtractive assimilation model and the additive acculturation model, and their philosophical differences represented by the English-only movement in the United States and bilingual-bicultural education policies respectively. Gibson's study concluded that an educational policy reinforcing additive acculturation will in the long run prove more effective than one that presses for subtractive or coercive assimilation because additive acculturation better utilizes the social and cultural capitals of immigrant students.

In regard to social and cultural capital, a key point is to understand and value the immigrants' parenting ideas and strategies (Waters, 1999). Educators need to understand and pay special attention to home language factors. Home languages and other home elements are givens, not choices, but immigrant children's English learning is affected by these givens (Steven, 1994). Educators must understand the home language situation and the language options that may open to adults and children. In many cases, linguistic cognition and language development for adult immigrants are far beyond their control. Although their English-spoken ability can always be improved, late language learners may never achieve the fluency of a native speaker. Therefore, immigrant adults often prefer to use their native tongues at home, especially if they have spouses who prefer and are able to speak the same language (Rong & Preissle, 1998).

Rong and Preissle (1998) have also pointed out that many experienced teachers, social workers, and sociologists agree that open and effective communication between children and parents helps the child profoundly in many ways that directly or indirectly relate to their schooling and later career. Children need parental guidance and direction during their growth. Immigrant children who acculturate into a society unfamiliar and alienating at best, hostile and rejecting at worst, may need more communication with and comfort from their parents than do native-born children (Portes & Rumbaut, 2001). Conversations on intimate topics, such as religious belief, friendship, dating, and marriage, are difficult enough without attempting them across language barriers. It is difficult to imagine effective communication on these topics between home-tongue-speaking parents and English-only-speaking children.

Gibson (1995) also observed that at the local level, assimilationist policies tend to be more implicit than explicit. According to Gibson's research, many teachers claimed to believe in the additive acculturation model at an abstract level, but their practices implicitly carried a subtractive form of assimilationist beliefs. Based on these concerns, Rong and Preissle (1998) made several recommendations in their book on how teachers can assess and handle the whole family's linguistic situation, including the family's language backgrounds, the parents' English proficiency, and parental education.

First, schools should not see a child's speaking a language other than English as a hindrance to the child's improvement of his or her English learning. Instead, they should develop partnerships with parents and immigrant communities in an effort to assist in the children's language development. Historically, efforts advocated in U.S. schools for English acquisition have ignored invisible endeavors for heritage language retention and the sorrow for heritage language attrition of immigrant children and their families. U.S. schools cannot effectively teach every immigrant child English unless all links of linguistic adaptation are addressed. Furthermore, if acquisition of the new language in schools is seen as the first step in losing the native tongue (it may even be seen as the first step in rejecting the homeland cultures), the schools' practices may consequently be resisted by children themselves or their parents (Rodriguez, 1982).

Second, schools should make efforts to encourage children to retain their mother tongues – both in formal class instruction and in informal activities, such as cultural and social occasions. Teachers should be aware of the difficulty English-only-speaking students can have in communicating with their non-English-speaking parents. Teachers should encourage their immigrant students to participate in weekend language schools and make other extra efforts to retain their native tongues, as well as connecting to the parents' home cultures. Involving children and parents in international festivals and foreign language speech competitions can encourage immigrant students to be multilingual and multicultural, but more importantly the immigrant children's heritage culture, language, and knowledge should be incorporated into their everyday learning.

Finally, in regard to language policies, policy makers should consider the process of language learning in the institutional context of the public schools as a mutual adaptation between school and immigrant children and an accommodation among multiple ethnolinguistic groups in particular structural contexts. Making policies and setting up programs designed to help Asian immigrant children's schooling and language learning must involve Asian parents and their communities. Policy makers and school administrators should take a lesson from history. When integration became incorporation and acculturation became Anglicization, schools were likely to find themselves in battles with immigrant parents and communities. Establishing a true partnership that addresses issues from multiple sides may not be easy or trouble-free, but it can produce workable policies that strengthen the ties between school, family, and community. School districts also need to know the number of languages spoken in their districts and the size of the incoming and outgoing student populations who speak various languages to make long- and short-term plans for language instruction and other services. School districts hiring bilingual and ESL teachers and school workshops that train teachers to speak a foreign language need to map out local language needs. Recruitment plans must target teachers who are able to speak various dialects of a language or several languages.

Studies of the language and schooling experience of Asian-Americans (the so called "double minority") in the United States reveal an interesting yet common American juxtaposition – social and economic opportunities with motivation, effort, and self-empowerment on the one hand, the restriction of opportunities with racial exclusion, xenophobia and ethnic stereotypes that slow the progress of racial minorities (during certain periods) on the other. For a more equal and equitable educational opportunity for Asian-American children and all immigrant children, Rong and Brown (2002b) suggested that educators should advocate a constructivist approach, focusing on mutual accommodation from both schools and newcomers. Schools should not treat immigrant students and their communities as passive learners and service receivers; rather, they should encourage immigrant children to become active and critical participants in their own learning and to become their own agents for changes (Borman & Baber, 1998; Nieto, 1995). Rong and Brown believed that the subtractive model with rapid assimilation would bring more discrimination and fewer resources for offsetting discrimination against immigrant groups. Additive acculturation that will enhance social and cultural capitals of immigrant minority children may be the way to lead them to a relatively lasting success in schools.

NOTES

1. Hart-Cellar Act of 1965 eliminated an annual quota for immigration created by the racist and ethnocentric 1924 Immigration Act (Spring 2001, p. 114; Weinberg 1997, p. 24).

2. Issei means a first generation Japanese and Nisei means a second generation Japanese.

3. The 1924 immigration act set immigration quotas for individual countries based on the percentage that each nationality group comprised of the total population of the United States in 1920 (Spring, 2001, p. 114). Since the early immigration population was consisted of European immigrants, the implementation of immigration quotas resulted in favoring European immigrants and consequently protecting and maintaining the existing racial composition of the time.

4. The initial proposal by Attorney General Ashcroft was an indefinite detention.

5. This treaty, signed by the U.S. and Chinese governments, ensured equal rights, including the right to education, of both countries' citizens when they resided in each other's country.

6. During the 1700s, school instructions throughout Pennsylvania, Maryland, Virginia and the Carolinas were given in German, often to the exclusion of English. The bilingual education or non-English education of German continued in many other states until 1913 (Rothstein, 1998). Many of the children in California and New Mexico schools were taught in Spanish, initially state-supported (Gonzalez, 1979). In the late 19th century, there were seven Czech-language schools supported by the Texas state school fund (Rothstein, 1998).

7. We trade largely on Valdés's and Fishman's definition of heritage language and heritage language learner in this study. Heritage language refers to a language with which individuals have a personal connection (Fishman, 2001). It is the historical and personal connection to the language that is salient and not the actual proficiency of individual speakers (Valdés, 2001, p. 38). As currently used in the United States, the term heritage language refers to all non-English languages, including those spoken by Native-American peoples. A heritage language speaker is someone who has been "raised in a home where a non-English language is spoken" and "who speaks or merely understands the heritage language, and who is to some degree bilingual in English and the heritage language" (Peyton et al., 2001, p. 1).

8. Table 1.1. Frequency of reasons given in congressional speeches for supporting English-Language Amendments, 1981–1998 (Tse, 2001).

9. Another example can be found in Japanese Language schools in Hawaii (Wollenberg, 1995).

10. Definition of linguistic genocide: "Prohibiting the use of the language of the group in daily intercourse or in schools, or the printing and circulation of publications in the language of the group." This definition was included in the final draft of The Convention on the Prevention and Punishment of the Crime of Genocide (Article III), but in the final vote in General Assembly, Article III was voted down and is Not (emphasis added by Skutanabb-Kangas) part of the final Conventions (Skutnabb-Kangas, 2000, p. 26).

11. Evidence can also be found in the 1919 annual governmental report in Hawaii (Tse, 2001).

REFERENCES

Alba, R., & Nee, V. (1998). Rethinking assimilation theory for a new era of immigration. *International Migration Review*, *31*, 826–874.

Borman, K. M., & Baber, M. Y. (1998). *Ethnic diversity in communities and schools: Recognizing and building on strengths*. Stamford, CT: Ablex Pub. Corp.

Bourdieu, P. (2001). *Language and symbolic power*. Cambridge, MA: Harvard University Press.

Camarota, S. (2001). *Immigrants in the United States – 2000*. Excerpted from Center for Immigration Studies. Retrieved April 2, 2002, from http://www.cis.org/articles/2001/back101.html

Chan, S. (1991). *Asian Americans: An interpretive history*. Boston, MA: Twayne Publishers.

Crawford, J. (2000). *At war with diversity: U.S. language policy in an age of anxiety*. Tonawanda, NY: Multilingual Matters Ltd.

English for the children [web-site]. Available: URL (http://www.onenation.org).

Gibson, M. A. (1995). Additive acculturation as a strategy for school. In: R. G. Rumbaut & W. A. Cornelius (Eds), *California's Immigrant Children* (pp. 77–106). San Diego, CA: Center for U.S.-Mexican Studies.

Goodis, T. A. (1986). *Adaptation processes of recent immigrants to the United States: A review of demographic and social aspects*. Washington, D.C.: The Urban Institute.

Gonzalez, J. M. (1979). Coming of age in bilingual/bicultural education. In: H. T. Trueba & C. Barnett-Mizrahi (Eds), *Bilingual Multicultural Education*. (pp. 1–19). Rowley, MA: Newbury House Publishers, Inc.

Hage, G. (2000). *White nation: Fantasies of White supremacy in a multicultural society*. New York: Routledge.

Hall, S. (1997). Old and new identities, old and new ethnicities. In A. D. King (Ed.), *Culture, Globalization and the World-system: Contemporary Conditions for the Representation of Identity* (pp. 41–68). Minneapolis, MN: University of Minnesota Press.

Heath, S. B. (1986). Sociocultural contexts of language development. In: *Beyond Language: Social and Cultural Factors in Schooling Language Minority Students* (pp. 143–186). Sacramento, CA: State Department of Education, Bilingual Education Office.

Jiobu, R. M. (1988). *Ethnicity and assimilation*. Albany, NY: State University Press of New York.

Johnson, Jr., J. H., Farrell, Jr., W. C., & Guinn, C. (1997). Immigration reform and the browning of America: Tensions, conflicts and community instability in metropolitan Los Angeles. International Migration Review, *31*(4), 1055–1095.

Kouritzin, S. G. (1999). *Face[t]s of first language loss*. Mahwah, NJ: Lawrence Erlbaum Associations, Inc.

Lee, J. S. (2001). More than "model minorities" or "delinquents": a look at Hmong American high school students. *Harvard Education Review*, *71*(3), 505–528.

Lee, J. S. (1996). *Understanding the "model minority" stereotype: Listening to Asian American youth*. New York: Teacher's College Press.

Lollock, L. (2001). *The foreign-born population in the United States*. U.S. Census Bureau, Current Population Reports, Series P20-534, Washington, D.C.: Government Printing Office.

Low, V. (1982). *The unimpressible race: A century of educational struggle by the Chinese in San Francisco*. San Francisco, C.A.: East/West Publishing Company, Inc.

Lowe, L. (1996). *Immigrant Acts*. Durham, NC: Duke University Press.

Lujan, H. D.(1989). Asian Americans and the quality of education: A policy view. In: G. M. Nomura, R. E. S. H. Sumida & R. C. Long (Eds), *Frontiers of Asian American studies*. Pullman, WA: Washington State University Press.

McDonnell, L. M., & Hill, P. R. (1993). *Newcomers in American schools – meeting the educational needs of immigrant youth*. Santa Monica, CA: RAND.

Morse, A. (1994). *America's newcomers*. Washington, D.C.: National Conference of State Legislatures.

Nieto, S. (1995). From brown heroes and holidays to assimilationist agendas: reconsidering the critiques of multicultural education. In: C. E. Sleeter & P. L. Mclaren (Eds), *Multicultural Education, Critical Pedagogy, and Politics of Difference* (pp. 191–220). Albany, NY: SUNY Press.

Nieto, S. (1995). *Affirming diversity: The sociopolitical context of multicultural education*. White Plains, NY: Longman Publishers.

Ovando, C. J., & Collier, V. P. (1998). *Bilingual and ESL classrooms: Teaching in multicultural context* (2nd ed.). Boston, MA: McGraw-Hill.

Peyton, J. K., McGinnis, S., & Ranard, D. A. (Eds) (2001). *Heritage languages in America: Preserving a national resource*. McHenry, IL: CAL & Delta Systems Co., Inc.

Portes, A. (1995). Segmented assimilation among new immigrant youth: a conceptual framework. In: R. G. Rumbaut & W. A. Cornelius (Eds), *California's Immigrant Children* (pp. 71–76). San Diego, CA: Center for U.S.-Mexican Studies.

Portes, A., & Rumbaut, R. G. (1996). *Immigrant America: A portrait* (2nd ed.). Berkeley, CA: University of California Press.

Portes, A., & Rumbaut, R. G. (2001). *Legacies: The story of the immigrant second generation*. Berkeley, CA: University of California Press.

Ravitch, D. (1974). *The great school wars: A history of the New York City public schools*. New York: Basic Books.

Ricento, T (Ed.) (2000). *Ideology, politics and language policies: Focus on English*. Philadelphia, PA: John Benjamins Publishing Company.

Rodriguez, R. (1982). *Hunger of memory: The education of Richard Rodriguez*. New York: Bantam.

Rong, X. L., & Brown, F. (2002a). Immigration and urban education in the New millennium: the diversity and the challenges. *Education and Urban Society*, *34*(2), 112–133.

Rong, X. L., & Brown, F. (2002b). Socialization, culture and identities – educating Black immigrant children: What Educators need to know and do. *Education and Urban Society*, *34*(2), 247–273.

Rong, X. L., & Jo, J. Y. (2002, April). Hitting in opposite directions? A comparison of the adaptive strategies of Chinese and Jamaican immigrant teens and their families. Paper presented at the annual meeting of the American Educational Research Association, New Orleans, LA.

Rong, X. L., & Preissle, J. (1998). *Educating immigrant students: What we need to know to meet the challenge*. Thousand Oaks, CA: Sage-Corwin Press, Inc.

Rothstein, R. (1998). Bilingual education. *Phi Delta Kappan, 79*(9), 672–678.

Sachs, W. (1992). One world. In: W. Sachs (Ed.). *The development dictionary*. Atlantic Highlands, NJ: Zed Books.

Schnaiberg, L. (1999) Immigrants: Providing a lesson in how to adapt. *Education Week, 18*(20), 34–35.

"Should we keep them out?" (2001, December 6), *Time* [On-line]. Retrieved April 12, 2002, from http://www.time.com/time/nation/article/0,8599,179255,00.html

Skutnabb-Kangas, T. (2000). Linguistic human rights and teachers of English. In: J. K. Hall & W. G. Eggington (Eds), *The Sociopolitics of English Language Teaching* (pp. 22–44). Tonawanda, NY: Multilingual Matters, Ltd.

Spring, J. (2001). *Deculturalization and the struggle for equality* (3rd ed.). New York: McGraw-Hill Companies.

Suarez-Orozoco, M. (2001). Globalization, immigration, and education: The research agenda. *Harvard Education Review, 71*(3), 345–365.

Stevens, G. (1994). The English language proficiency of immigrants in the U.S. In: B. Edmunston & J. S. Passel (Eds), *Immigration and Ethnicity: The Adjustment of America's Newest Immigrants* (pp. 163–185). Washington, D.C.: Urban Institute.

Takaki, R. (1998). *Strangers from a different shore* (2nd ed.). Boston, MA: Back Bay Books.

Tollefson, J. (Ed.) (2002). *Language policies in education: Critical issues*. Mahwah, NJ: Lawrence Erlbaum Associates, Publishers.

Tse, L. (2001). *"Why don't they learn English?" Separating fact from fallacy in the U.S. language debate*. New York: Teachers College Press.

Tuan, M.(1998). *Forever foreigners or honorary Whites?: The Asian ethnic experience today*. Princeton, NJ: Rutgers University Press.

Tyack, D. B. (1974). *The one best system*. Cambridge, MA: Harvard University Press.

USA Patriot Act boosts government powers while cutting back on traditional checks and balances. *ACLU Legislative Analysis on USA Patriot Act* [On-line]. Retrieved April 14, 2002, from http://www.aclu.org/congress/1110101a.html

Waters, M. C. (1999). *Black identities*. Cambridge, MA: Harvard University Press.

Wang, Ling-Chi. L. (1995). Lau v. Nichols: History of struggle for equal and quality education. In: D. T. Nakanish & T. Y. Nishida (Eds), *The Asian American Educational Experience: A Source Book for Teachers and Students* (pp. 58–91). New York: Routledge.

Weinberg, M. (1997). *Asian-American Education: Historical background and current realities*. Mahwah, NJ: Lawrence Erlbaum Associate, Publishers.

Wiley, T. G. (2002). Accessing language rights in education: A brief history of the U.S. context. In: J. W. Tollefson (Ed.), *Language Policies in Education: Critical Issues* (pp. 39–64). Mahwah, N.J.: Lawrence Erlbaum Associates, Publishers.

Woodrum, E. (1981). An assessment of Japanese American assimilation, pluralism, and subordination. *American Journal of Sociology, 87*(1), 157–169.

Wollenberg, C. M. (1995). "Yellow Peril" in the schools (I and II). In: D. T. Nakanish & T. Y. Nishida (Eds). *The Asian American Educational Experience: A Source Book for Teachers and Students* (pp. 58–91). New York: Routledge.

Zehr, M. A. (2002). Educating Mexico. *Education Week, 21*(27), 22–28.

Zehr, M. A. (2001). Immigration Spawns Bills Similar to Proposition 227. *Education Week, 20*(31), 24–27.

3. UPDATE ON SCHOOL DESEGREGATION

Charles J. Russo

ABSTRACT

Since the late 1970s, the Supreme Court has shown little interest in hearing and resolving school desegregation issues. In recent years, this pattern has also trickled down to the lower courts limiting judicial action in educational equity and opportunity issues. This chapter provides an update on litigation pertaining to school desegregation. It pays particular attention to cases since 1990.

INTRODUCTION

The Supreme Court's monumental decision in *Brown v. Board of Education* in 1954, wherein it held "that in the field of public education the doctrine of "separate but equal" has no place. Separate educational facilities are inherently unequal" (p. 495) set the stage for the overdue onslaught of cases challenging segregated schooling. In fact, between 1954 and 1979 a busy Supreme Court resolved more than thirty cases involving K-12 school desegregation (Russo, Harris, & Sandidge, 1994). The 1980s signaled what may be viewed as the beginning of the end of the Court's active role in fighting segregation in public schools since during that decade it took on only two relatively minor cases, both on the same day in 1982, when it examined the legality of state-approved voter initiatives that limited the impact of desegregation plans. In the first, the

Challenges of Urban Education and Efficacy of School Reform, Volume 6, pages 49–64.

ISBN: 0-7623-0426-X

Court rejected Washington state's proposed action (*Washington v. Seattle Sch. Dist.*, 1982) but in the second upheld California's amendment of its state constitution (*Crawford v. Board of Educ. of the City of Los Angeles*, 1982).

The 1990s opened on a promising note for proponents of school desegregation when, after the longest time during which it had not heard such a case, the Court agreed to intervene in the long-running dispute from Kansas City, Missouri. In *Missouri v. Jenkins I*, (1990), a closely divided Court surprised many in upholding the authority of federal judges to increase taxes to pay for the cost of desegregating the public schools in Kansas City. The ray of hope was short lived since supporters of desegregation in K-12 settings lost in the three remaining cases that the Court would address in the interim: *Board of Education of the Oklahoma City Public Schools v. Dowell* (1991), *Freeman v. Pitts* (1992), and *Missouri v. Jenkins II* (1995).

Since 1979, the Supreme Court's apparent lack of interest in school desegregation cases has impacted on the lower federal courts as they have followed its lead and have begun to disengage in the process of providing equitable educational opportunities for all children. In light of legal developments in this area, this chapter is divided into two major parts. The first part reviews the four most Supreme Court cases on desegregation stretching back to 1990. The second section reviews selected lower federal court cases to give a flavor of where the judiciary has gone, or more properly, not gone, in the important, but neglected, area of school desegregation. The chapter ends with a briefly reflection on the status, and importance, of school desegregation.

SUPREME COURT CASES

The Supreme Court opened the 1990s by examining a case that was more concerned with the authority of the federal judiciary to impose a tax increase to fund a remedy in a formerly dual system than it was with the substantive aspects of school desegregation. After having refused to hear an earlier appeal in the controversy, *Missouri v. Jenkins* (1987), in *Missouri v. Jenkins I* (1990) a typically closely divided Court, in a five-to-four decision, reasoned that the state of Missouri and the Kansas City Public School District maintained a segregated system. However, since the state constitution placed a cap on property tax increases, a federal trial court imposed a tax increase to pay for implementing a desegregation order. In *Jenkins I* the Court surprisingly affirmed the authority of federal judges to increase taxes to pay for the cost of desegregating the public schools in Kansas City. The extension of judicial power in *Jenkins I* set the stage for the case's return to the High Court later in the decade in a dispute over whether there should be limits on funding a desegregation remedy.

The next two cases dealt with substantive issues in school desegregation. *Board of Education of the Oklahoma City Public Schools v. Dowell* (1991) concerned the appropriate standards for determining whether a formerly segregated school system had achieved unitary status. In other words, the Court questioned whether the school board had eliminated segregation and its vestiges such that the system operated in a unitary, rather than a segregated dual, fashion in providing equal educational opportunities for all students. In reversing the Tenth Circuit, the Court dissolved the desegregation order that had been in place since 1972. The Court ruled that since desegregation orders were not meant to operate in perpetuity, it was necessary to consider whether a district has complied in good faith with the decree and whether the vestiges of past discrimination had been eliminated to the extent practicable. Further, the Court ascertained that in reaching its judgment, a lower court should not view a board's adoption of a given plan as a breach of good faith even if it had been technically flawed where the plan was accepted in reliance on the express language of a court order which found that the system had achieved unitary status. Finally, in considering whether the vestiges of segregation were eradicated and whether a system achieved unitary status, the Court continued to rely on the six principles enunciated in *Green v. County Sch. Bd. of New Kent County* (1968). These so-called *Green* factors that must be taken into a account in determining whether a district has achieved unitary status are the composition of the student body, faculty, staff, transportation, extracurricular activities, and facilities.

In *Freeman v. Pitts* (1992) the Court considered whether judicial supervision of a desegregation order can be terminated incrementally before full compliance has been achieved. After a federal trial court in Georgia, relying on the *Green* factors, relinquished its control incrementally, the Eleventh Circuit reversed and reinstated the entire plan. The Supreme Court, in turn, reversed. The Court was of the opinion that a federal judge has the authority to relinquish supervision and control over a school district in stages while retaining jurisdiction as long as the court is satisfied that a board has made a good faith commitment to comply with the dictates of its order.

The Court revisited the on-going litigation in Kansas City In *Missouri v. Jenkins II* (1995). This time, a typically divided Court, led by the dissent in *Jenkins I*, reversed an earlier judgment in favor of the plaintiffs and signaled a further retrenchment in the struggle to end racial segregation in the schools. In this, the second action between the parties to reach the Court on its merits, the majority declared that a federal trial court in Missouri, in a judgment that was subsequently affirmed by the Eighth Circuit, exceeded the bounds of its broad discretion in mandating a costly desegregation remedy. The trial court had ordered the State to pay for both across-the-board salary increases for virtually all personnel and the quality education programs in KCMSD, at a total cost of more than $1.3 billion dollars, because student achievement levels were still at or below national norms at many grade levels. Even though the Court stopped short of dismantling the desegregation program in Kansas City, *Jenkins II* is noteworthy as its most recent pronouncement on desegregation.

LOWER COURT CASES

The lower federal courts reviewed a variety of issues arising in conjunction with desegregation plans and other racial classifications in America's primary and secondary schools. This activity continues largely because, based the most recently updated report from the Civil Rights Division of the Office of the Assistant Attorney General of the U.S., there are still "more than 400 school districts currently covered by desegregation orders in over 200 desegregation cases in which the United States is a party" (2001, p. 12). This section reviews cases under the headings of whether a school board has complied with its desegregation plan and achieved unitary status, student admissions and transfers, district consolidation and deconsolidation of a school system, teacher rights, inter district remedies, and attorney fees.

Achieving Unitary Status

As reflected by the cases discussed in this section, disputes over whether a school system has achieved unitary status often continue on for decades in attempts to eradicate the pernicious effects of segregated schooling. In recent years, the majority of lower federal courts, following the lead of the Supreme Court, have unfortunately continued to disengage as they have been satisfied that school systems are acting in conformity with their orders in seeking to ensure unitary status.

Perhaps the best know case among the recent disputes over unitary status involved the continuation of the original *Swann v.Charlotte-Mecklenburg Board of Education* (1971) wherein the Court introduced the concept of busing to the national lexicon of school desegregation. After vacating and remanding a desegregation suit which a White student sought relief on the basis of reverse discrimination (*Belk v. Charlotte-Mecklenburg Board of Education,* 2000), the Fourth Circuit granted a rehearing (2001). In affirming that the district achieved unitary status by complying with its desegregation plan, the court returned control to the integrated school board which demonstrated its commitment to a desegregated school system. At the same time, the court reversed the injunction which required the board to refrain from the use of race-based lotteries, preferences, and set-asides in student assignments as unwarranted since nothing in the record suggested that it would use race in an unconstitutional manner. The Supreme Court's refusal to hear an appeal means that this long-running litigation has probably come to an end (2002).

In the first of two cases from the Eleventh Circuit, the court affirmed that a school district in Mississippi achieved unitary status where the board of education proved that any remaining racial imbalances in its schools were the result of demographic changes (*Lockett v. Board of Educ. of Muscogee County Sch. Dist.*, 1997). The court asserted that the district achieved unitary status because it eliminated the vestiges of de jure, based on law or some official state classification, segregation to the extent practicable through a good faith commitment to and compliance with the desegregation plan.

A school board in Florida challenged a federal trial court's rejection of its motion for unitary status in a forty-year old desegregation case. The court refused to issue such an order since the district still had racial imbalances in student assignments and failed to achieve an effective majority-to-minority transfer program. On further review, the Eleventh Circuit reversed and remanded in favor of the board in holding that the imbalances were the result of demographic factors over which the board did not have control (*Manning v. School Bd. of Hillsborough County*, 2001a, b). The court noted that the lack of an effective transfer plan was not a sufficient ground on which to conclude that the board had not complied in good faith with the desegregation order. Previously, a federal trial court in Florida ended its twenty-seven years of jurisdiction over a district because it pointing out that school officials had done all that they could to eliminate a dual system of education (*United States v. Board of Pub. Instruction of St. Lucie County*, 1997).

The Third Circuit found that a cross-district remedial plan had achieved unitary status despite performance disparities where school official provided evidence that the disparities were caused by socioeconomic factors, not de jure segregation (*Coalition To Save Our Children v. Board of Educ.*, 1996). This ruling ended almost four decades of judicial supervision in Northern New Castle County, Delaware.

On further review of a trial court's denial of a school board's motion to terminate oversight in a twelve year-old desegregation suit from Illinois, the Seventh Circuit reversed and remanded in contending that the board eliminated the consequences of segregation (*People Who Care v. Rockford Bd. of Educ.*, 2001). The court observed that while there were no white-only or minority-only schools in the district and the education of minority children was behind that of whites, there was no evidence that this lag was greater than in other school systems. According to the court, it had no choice but to end its oversight because the plaintiffs could not produce a single instance showing that the school board violated any provision of the desegregation decree.

In Texas, a federal trial court conclude that a school district achieved unitary status with regard to student assignments, despite an increase in the number of single race schools and primarily minority schools since its initial desegregation decree in 1971 (*Tasby v. Woolery*, 1994). The court decided that there were no further reasonable measures that could have been taken to achieve racial balance where the district implemented several remedial measures such as redrawing attendance zones, implementing majority to minority transfer policies, creating magnet schools, allowing curriculum transfers and developing an honors program. Even though the court believed that the school system had achieved unitary status and ended more than two decades over oversight, it retained jurisdiction over the case for a three-year monitoring period.

On remand after the Supreme Court refused to hear an appeal, the federal trial court in Colorado wrote that Denver, home to the first school desegregation suit not involving primarily African Americans (*Keyes v. School Dist.* No. 1, 1973), achieved unitary status (*Keyes v. Congress of Hispanic Educators*, 1995, 1997). The court based its judgment on the fact that the board eliminated the vestiges of past discrimination to the extent practicable despite existing racial and ethnic differences in program participation, test scores, and discipline

A federal trial court in Kansas ruled that a public school system in the Kansas City area, in a dispute that began in 1973, achieved unitary status because it complied with all areas of the desegregation plan (*United States v. Unified Sch. Dist.* No. 500 (1997). The court was content that the district improved student attendance, raised the level of quality in its extracurricular activities, improved the racial balance among its faculty and the staff, and enhanced the racial equity in its facilities and transportation.

In a three decade old school desegregation case from Michigan, a federal trial court dissolved a permanent injunction and relinquished its jurisdiction (*Davis v. School Dist. of City of Pontiac*, 2000). The court maintained that the school board was not required to continue making adjustments in the racial compositions of student bodies once the duty to desegregate was completed through official action. The court was of the view that the board made a good faith compliance with its decree and eliminated past discrimination.

In Kentucky, parents challenged a school board's student assignment plan and racial composition guidelines on the ground that they violated equal protection. A federal trial court decreed that the desegregation order remained in effect which permitted the board to use racial classifications to prevent the re-emergence of racially identifiable schools (*Hampton v. Jefferson County Bd. of Educ.*, 1999). The court added that the board's efforts to comply with its order were immune from a constitutional challenge until it was dissolved. In a continuation of the same case, parents again sought to dissolve the desegregation decree. A federal trial court granted the parents' request since the board met the requirements of an initial 1975 decree (*Hampton v. Jefferson County Bd. of Educ.*, 2000). The court also reviewed the district's voluntary maintenance plan of assigning African-Americans students to magnet schools and struck it down as a violation of equal protection. As such, the court directed the board to admit any African-American students who were denied enrollment to a high school be admitted prior to the 2000–2001 school year. Further, the court called for a new hearing on the plan but would not order an immediate change in the reassignment of students until the 2002–2003 school year.

When a school board in Pennsylvania sought a declaration of unitary status and an end to judicial oversight that traced its origins to 1971, the plaintiff class opposed the motion. A federal trial court partially granted the motion in explaining that the board acted in sufficiently good faith in complying with the *Green* factor since remaining disparities in test scores and occurrences of discipline did not preclude granting its request (*Hoots v. Commonwealth*, 2000). However, the court refused to grant the entire motion in positing that the board failed to comply fully with an order to eliminate tracking.

As reflected by the following cases, not all courts have released districts from oversight. In the most recent remand in more than twenty years of litigation in the ongoing desegregation suit from Yonkers, a federal trial court in New York indicated that vestiges of segregation remained in the district with respect to academic tracking, disciplinary practices, administration of special education programs, pupil personnel services, and services for limited English proficiency students (*United States v. Yonkers Branch-NAACP*, 2000). The court referred the matter to a monitor to recommend a suitable remedy.

In a related action from Yonkers, New York State challenged a court order allocating the expenses of compliance with its desegregation decree between it and a city's public schools. The Second Circuit held that the trial court did not abuse its discretion in failing to continue to give the State credit for magnet school aid that the city received from it pursuant to a statewide magnet aid program, in failing to credit the State for categorical grants under four statewide aid programs, or in shifting universal pre-kindergarten costs from an educational improvement plan (*Yonkers Branch – NAACP v. City of Yonkers*, 2000).

The federal trial court in South Carolina was not satisfied with a district's progress under a desegregation plan that traces its origins to 1962. As such, it ordered the implementation of a magnet program in a historically black high school to further desegregate the schools there (*Stanley v. Darlington County Sch. Dist.*, 1995, 1996).

In Michigan, a federal trial court rejected a motion filed by a school board and the state seeking unitary status and the termination of judicial oversight in a case that started in 1967. The court acknowledged that the board and state, rather than the claimants, had the burden of establishing that differences in student achievement levels between races were vestiges of past segregative conduct (*Berry v. School Dist. of City of Benton Harbor*, 2001).

Student Admissions and Transfers

The use of racial classifications in admission or transfer decisions in K-12 education continues to receive judicial attention. Litigation in this area typically occurs after a school board, either on its own, or compliance with a state statute, implements a policy that relies on race to limit the number of students who can be admitted or who can transfer into or between schools. As reflected in the ensuing discussion, school officials have mixed results in defending their policies.

In Boston, after a finding of de jure segregation and the subsequent 1987 relinquishment of court-enforced remedies (*Morgan v. Nucci*, 1987), some city schools were accused on violating equal protection again in 1996 by making admission decisions pursuant to a policy that reserved seats for Black and Latino students (*McLaughlin v. Boston Sch. Comm.*, 1996). This set aside policy was subsequently revised in 1996 and replaced by flexible racial/ethnic guidelines to be used in admissions actions. Under the new policy, a white female student was denied admission to the Boston Latin School but admitted to the Boston Latin Academy even though she would have been admitted had all applicants been selected solely on grade point averages and test scores. The admission policy provided that students applying to the examination schools, which include the Boston Latin School, the Boston Latin Academy, and the John D. O'Bryant School of Mathematics and Sciences, were included in the Applicant Pool for each school that the applicants designated. Each student was ranked within the applicant pool based on his or her composite score, a combination of grade point average, and score on the Independent School Entrance Examination. All students ranked in the top half of the applicant pool were designated as the Qualified Applicant Pool. Fifty percent of the available seats in each school were filled on a straight-from-the-top basis according to composite score. The remaining seats for each school were filled based on a combination of composite score ranking and flexible racial/ethnic guidelines. Under these guidelines, the remaining seats were allocated based on composite score rank in proportion to the racial/ethnic composition of the school's remaining qualified applicant pool.

The student unsuccessfully challenged the admissions policy on the basis that it violated the Fifth and Fourteenth Amendments. School officials argued that they had a compelling interest in the policy not only because a diverse student body increases the quality of education but also because it was designed as a remedy for past discrimination. After the federal trial court in Massachusetts rejected the student's request for an injunction that would have permitted her to enter the Boston Latin school (*Wessmann v. Boston Sch. Comm.*, 1998), she sought further review.

The First Circuit reversed in reasoning that the admissions program was not sufficiently narrowly tailored to further a compelling governmental interest (*Wessmann v. Gittens*, 1998). The court determined that school officials failed to demonstrate a compelling interest in a policy to promote student diversity because it was not in any way tied to the vigorous exchange of ideas. Moreover, the court declared that statistical evidence of an achievement gap between students of different races was insufficient to prove that vestiges of the school system's past discrimination remained. The court was of the opinion that school officials produced evidence sufficient to prove a compelling interest in diversity or in remedying past discrimination. Thus, the court maintained that the policy was not designed to redress past discrimination insofar as it was simply a method for achieving the constitutionally impermissible goal of racial and ethnic balance.

The first of related developments from Boston involved a parental challenge to the elementary school assignment process on the ground that their children were denied preferred assignments based on race. The First Circuit ruled that several plaintiffs lacked standing since they had not applied to change schools (In re Boston's Children First, 2001). Insofar as the court asserted that the remaining plaintiffs may have had a damages claim, it refused to dismiss these allegations and set the course for future litigation by allowing discovery on the issue of standing.

Parents of white children in Boston unsuccessfully filed suit claiming that their children were denied their preferred school assignments because of their race. The First Circuit decided that even thought the earlier order had the practical effect of denying an injunction, it was not immediately appealable since the parents failed to demonstrate the existence of serious harm (*Anderson v. City of Boston*, 2001).

In Massachusetts, parents questioned the validity of their school board's plan to improve schools by preserving racial diversity while ending racial isolation and imbalance by limiting student transfers. In response to board's motion to dismiss, the federal trial court agreed that Eleventh Amendment immunity protections prevented the parents from suing unconsenting officials in a federal venue because the Commonwealth was not a "program or activity" for purposes of title VI liability (*Comfort ex rel. Neumyer v. Lynn Sch.*, 2001). In a related development parents unsuccessfully challenged a school board's transfer policy that was created in order to gain additional funding from the Massachusetts Racial Imbalance Act as based on unequal treatment due to race. The federal trial court noted that while the parents lacked standing to seek an injunction since they had already been granted transfers for their children, they could seek nominal damages under their claim of unequal treatment based on race (*Comfort v. Lynn Sch. Comm.*, 2001).

Parents in Washington sought further review of a judgment which upheld an open choice assignment plan which used a racial integration tie-breaker on the ground that it served a compelling government interest and was narrowly tailored to do so, it did not violate equal protection. The Ninth Circuit reversed in concluding that the tie breaker was inappropriate since it violated a state law which prohibits granting preferential treatment to students in public schools on the basis of race. (*Parents Involved in Community Schools v. Seattle School Dist.*, No. 1, 2002a). The court subsequently granted the parents request to enjoin the use of the racial tiebreaker pending any further appeals in the case (*Parents Involved in Community Schools v. Seattle School District*, No. 1, 2002b).

In New York, parents of an elementary student sued a school board and officials for denying their daughter a transfer from a city to a suburban school after several districts had set up an urban-suburban inter-district transfer program to reduce racial isolation to ameliorate de facto segregation. The child met all of the criteria for admission except that she was white and only minority students were eligible for the program. After a federal trial court granted the preliminary injunction requiring the transfer, the Second Circuit vacated the injunction and remanded, pointing out that the parents failed to demonstrate a likelihood of success on the merits of their claim (*Brewer v. West Irondequoit Cent. Sch. Dist.*, 2000). Even so, the court did allow the child to finish the current academic year at the suburban school.

A case from Maryland also dealt with racial classifications. The Fourth Circuit found that schools that choose to implement policies using race as a classification face the presumption that they cannot be sustained (*Eisenberg v. Montgomery County Pub. Sch.*, 1999). Here the parents of a seven-year-old sued after school officials denied their request to transfer him to a mathematics and science magnet school because doing so would have reduce the racial balance in the school that he wanted to leave. Even though the school system had never been the target of a court ordered desegregation policy, officials voluntarily desegregated their schools by creating magnet programs to establish a diverse student body. The Fourth Circuit struck the policy down as an impermissible use of racial balancing on the ground that it was not sufficiently narrowly tailored insofar as there was no determination of whether diversity is a compelling interest. In addition to vitiating the policy, the court entered a preliminary injunction requiring school officials to admit the student and a final injunction requiring them to reconsider his application without considering his race. The Supreme Court refused to hear an appeal in the dispute (2000).

In a case that was also discussed under the heading of unitary status, a federal trial court in North Carolina, in part of the extensive litigation involving *Charlotte Mecklenburg, Belk v. Charlotte-Mecklenburg Sch.* (2001), in part, addressed a magnet school admissions policy. Although recognizing that the district achieved unitary status, the Fourth Circuit affirmed that the board's admissions policy as exceeding constitutionally permissible bounds insofar as it was not sufficiently narrowly tailored to achieve its stated goal of racial equity in student placements. The Supreme Court refused to hear an appeal in this case (2002).

District Consolidation and Deconsolidation

In the course of implementing a desegregation plan, some schools have attempted to carry out both consolidation and deconsolidation plans. For example, in Louisiana, a federal trial court denied a school board's request to divide into independent districts because the school was under a desegregation plan and failed to achieve unitary status. The deconsolidation would have left one school district's population with slightly more black than white students and the new district becoming overwhelmingly white. A trial court observed that the school division would have hindered efforts to desegregate the existing school system. Subsequently, the Fifth Circuit vacated the trial court's judgment because the matter was not ripe for review, commenting that there was no imminent threat of harm to the district or the desegregation decrees, only potential harm (*Valley v. Rapides Parish Sch. Bd.*, 1998). Nearly a year later Fifth Circuit revisited the dispute (*Valley v. Rapides Parish Sch. Bd.*, 1999) and remanded the case to the trial court with the instructions that the new district select a board of trustees and conduct more hearings to allow the state and new board the opportunity to demonstrate that the new district would not adversely impact the desegregation plan that was in place in school district.

A county board of education in Alabama successfully petitioned for judicial approval to consolidate a school district that was under a desegregation order and to relocate students within the system after a fire destroyed one school and it was not economically feasible to construct another building (*Lee v. Geneva County Bd. of Educ.*, 1995). A federal trial court indicated that the proposed consolidation plan was acceptable because it neither perpetuated nor reestablished a racially segregated dual school system.

Teacher Rights

The rights of teachers can be at issue incident to a desegregation plan. For example, teachers in Arkansas appealed an order that required them to end a strike against a school district that was subject to a consent decree in a desegregation case. The Eighth Circuit reversed in favor of the teachers, maintaining that the trial court lacked the authority to enjoin the strike because nothing in the desegregation settlement agreement could be read as denying the teachers their right to strike (*Knight v. Pulaski County Special Sch. Dist.*, 1997). The court also mentioned that a strike could not be characterized as a modification of the consent decree since such a change can only be accomplished by a judicial order, not an order by the parties.

Retirement and health insurance plans for teachers have come under judicial scrutiny with respect to desegregation agreements. The Eighth Circuit affirmed that the state school funding system in Arkansas violated desegregation agreements (*Little Rock Sch. Dist. v. North Little Rock Sch. Dist.*, 1998). The court believed that the funding system provided money to school districts to be distributed to teachers based on the number of students in a district and the wealth of the district. The court added that the system provided proportionally less money to teachers at three districts that were under desegregation plans because of mandated staffing increases.

Inter District Remedies

A disagreement over the tuition owed by one board to another relating to students sent to a vocational school led to litigation in Mississippi. The dispute was initially filed in state court but was removed to federal court because the defendant district claimed that the agreement was part of an earlier desegregation order. A federal trial court, affirmed by the Fifth Circuit, which did not issue a formal opinion, disagreed in explaining that it lacked original jurisdiction in this dispute since the defendant district did not demonstrate any causal relationship between the agreement on tuition and the desegregation decree (*Quitman Consol. Sch. Dist. v. Enterprise Sch. Dist.*, 1999, 2000).

Attorney Fees

Based on the discussions of many of the cases in this chapter, it should be evident that desegregation suits last for years, even decades. As such, it is not surprising that the legal costs associated with fighting for equal educational opportunities can become costly. Consequently, since plaintiffs would ordinarily be able to bring suit to ensure equal educational if they had to pay for such costs up front, federal law permits the prevailing party to recover such fees. As many of the school desegregation cases address a variety of issues, one of the topics that the courts must resolve is the important question of who should pay attorney fees.

When the Fourth Circuit affirmed that the Charlotte-Mecklenburg Board of Education achieved unitary status (*Belk v. Charlotte-Mecklenburg Bd. of Educ.*, 2001), one of the issues that it examined was attorney fees. In an unusual aspect of its rationale, the court held that the White student, whose suit challenged the board's use of an allegedly discriminatory magnet school program and led to the district's being declared unitary, was not entitled to attorney fees as the prevailing party. The court took this unusual step because it was of the opinion that the racial quotas that were struck down were enacted pursuant to a judicially imposed desegregation order rather than a voluntary action on the part of school officials. As such, the board was not liable for complying with a judicial mandate.

The plaintiff class in the long-running in Kansas City opposed the Desegregation Monitoring Committee's use of an interactive electronic communication system called ShareNet because it was not part of the original voluntary inter-district transfer plan (*Jenkins by Agyei v. State of Mo.*, 1996). The Eighth Circuit affirmed an award of attorney fees on the basis that the state had to pay attorney fees for defending the desegregation remedy even though it, too, disagreed with the use of ShareNet.

In a second case from Kansas City, the Eighth Circuit affirmed an award of attorney fees for the plaintiff's work in defending the State's appeal that the school system achieved unitary status. The court also granted an award of attorney fees in settlement agreement issues and for the time counsel spent in seeking a stay pending an appeal. However, the court rejected a claim for the time that the attorney spent talking with the media (*Jenkins by Jenkins v. State of Mo.*, 1997). The court asserted that the terms of the settlement did not shift liability to the school board for an award of statutory attorney fees incurred by the plaintiffs in opposing the approval of the agreement.

CONCLUSION

Without a doubt, progress has been made the almost fifty years since the Supreme Court struck down segregation in public schools in *Brown v. Board of Education*. Yet, insofar as more than 200 school systems continue to operate under court-ordered desegregation plans, much more needs to be done. Further, the work of Gary Orfield (1993, 2001) graphically reveals that American public schools, especially with regard to Spanish-speaking students who are infrequently involved in school desegregation litigation, remain segregated and are becoming more so.

As noted, for more than twenty years now, the Supreme Court has discontinued an activist role in ensuring educational equity. In fact, following the eight year period between 1982 and 1990, the Court is on its second longest period of time during which it has not heard a desegregation case since it started doing so in *Brown*. This judicial inactivity has been caused, at least in part, by a combination of the Court's having followed national trends that have unfortunately resisted urban desegregation. Even so, one can only wonder why state (and local) educational agencies have not adopted proactive stances in implementing *Brown*. Thus, it may be that many locations act as if *Brown* had never been decided because the Court's inactivity has signaled that desegregation is no longer a priority among national goals and objectives. As the Supreme Court's final word on the legacy of *Brown*, *Jenkins II* signals the continuation of its retreat from active involvement in school desegregation that has been reflected throughout the remainder of the federal judiciary.

Consistent with the recommendations that in Orfield's most recent report (2001, p. 12), such as the need to promote expertise on desegregation in state departments of education, local school boards documenting the value of integrated schooling, creating bilingual programs in light of the fact that Spanish-speaking students need to be integrated into the mainstream, and having inner city and suburban school systems explore possibilities of teacher exchanges, it is imperative that educational leaders find ways to combat growing resegregation, especially in urban schools. The need to overcome resegregation, and provide equal educational opportunities for all students is crucial not only for our children but also for our collective future.

REFERENCES

Anderson v. City of Boston, 244 F.3d 236 (1st Cir. 2001).

Belk v. Charlotte-Mecklenburg Bd. of Educ., 233 F.3d 232 (4th Cir. 2000), en banc reh'g 269 F.3d 305 (4th Cir. 2001), *cert. denied*, 122 S. Ct. 1537 (2002).

Berry v. School Dist. of City of Benton Harbor, 141 F. Supp.2d 802 (W. D.Mich. 2001).

Board of Educ. of the Oklahoma City Pub. Schs. v. Dowell 498 U.S. 237 (1991).

Brewer v. West Irondequoit Cent. Sch. Dist., 212 F.3d 738 (2nd Cir. 2000).

Brown v. Board of Educ., 347 U.S. 483 (1954).

Civil Rights Division of the Office of the Assistant Attorney General of the United States, Department of Justice (Nov. 2001). http://www.usdoj.gov/crt/activity.html *Educational Opportunities*, 12.

Coalition To Save Our Children v. Board of Educ., 90 F.3d 752 (3rd Cir. 1996).

Comfort ex rel. Neumyer v. Lynn Sch., 131 F. Supp.2d 253 (D. Mass. 2001).

Comfort v. Lynn Sch. Comm., 150 F. Supp.2d 285 (D. Mass. 2001).

Crawford v. Board of Educ. of the City of Los Angeles, 458 U.S. 527 (1982).

Davis v. School Dist. of City of Pontiac, 95 F. Supp.2d 688 (E. D.Mich. 2000).

Eisenberg v. Montgomery County Pub. Sch., 197 F.3d 123 (4th Cir. 1999), *cert. denied*, 529 U.S. 1019 (2000).

Freeman v. Pitts, 503 U.S. 467 (1992).

Green v. County Sch. Bd. of New Kent County 391 U.S. 430 (1968).

Hampton v. Jefferson County Bd. of Educ., 72 F. Supp.2d 753 (W. D.Ky. 1999), 102 F. Supp.2d 358 [145 Educ. L. Rep. 985] (W.D.Ky 2000).

Hoots v. Commonwealth, 118 F. Supp.2d 577 (W. D.Pa. 2000).

In re Boston's Children First, 244 F.3d 164 (1st Cir. 2001).

Jenkins by Agyei v. State of Mo., 73 F.3d 201 (8th Cir. 1996).

Jenkins by Jenkins v. State of Mo., 131 F.3d 716 (8th Cir. 1997).

Keyes v. Congress of Hispanic Educators, 902 F. Supp 1274 (D. Colo. 1995), appeal dismissed by *Keyes v. School Dist.* No. 1, Denver, Colo., 119 F.3d 1437 (10th Cir. 1997).

Keyes v. School Dist. No. 1, 413 U.S. 189 (1973).

Knight v. Pulaski County Special Sch. Dist., 112 F.3d 953 (8th Cir. 1997).

Lee v. Geneva County Bd. of Educ., 892 F. Supp. 1387 (M. D.Ala. 1995).

Little Rock Sch. Dist. v. North Little Rock Sch. Dist., 148 F.3d 956 (8th Cir. 1998).

Lockett v. Bd. of Educ. of Muscogee County Sch. Dist., 111 F.3d 839 (11th Cir. 1997), *reh'g, en banc, denied*, 121 F.3d 724 (11th Cir. 1997).

Manning v. School Bd. of Hillsborough County, 244 F.3d 927 (11th Cir. 2001), *cert. denied*, 122 S. Ct. 61 (2001).

Missouri v. Jenkins, 484 U.S. 816 (1987), 495 U.S. 33 (1990), 515 U.S. 70 (1995).

McLaughlin v. Boston Sch. Comm., 938 F. Supp. 1001 (D. Mass. 1996).

Morgan v. Nucci, 831 F.2d 313 (1st Cir. 1987).

Orfield, G. (1993). *The growth of segregation in American schools: Changing patterns of separation and poverty since 1968.* Alexandria, VA: National School Boards Association.

Orfield, G. (2001, July). *Schools more separate: Consequences of a decade of resegregation.* Cambridge, MA: The Civil Rights Project, Harvard University. Retrieved March 8, 2002, from http://www.law.harvard.edu/groups/civilrights/publications/resegregation01/schoolsseparate.pdf

Parents Involved in Community Schools v. Seattle School Dist., No. 1, 285 F.3d 1236 (9th Cir. 2002a), – F.3d –, 2002 WL 841345 (9th Cir. 2002b).

People Who Care v. Rockford Bd. of Educ., 246 F.3d 1073 (7th Cir. 2001).
Quitman Consol. Sch. Dist. v. Enterprise Sch. Dist., 105 F. Supp.2d 545 (S. D.Miss. 1999), aff'd 226 F.3d 642 (5th Cir. 2000).
Russo, C. J., Harris, J. J., & Sandidge, R. F. (1994). *Brown v. Board of Education* at 40: A legal history of equal educational opportunities in public education. *Journal of Negro Education, 63*(3), 297–309.
Stanley v. Darlington County Sch. Dist., 879 F. Supp. 1341 (D. S. C. 1995), *rev'd in part on other grounds*, 84 F.3d 707 (4th Cir. 1996).
Swann v. Charlotte-Mecklenburg Bd. of Educ., 402 U.S. 1 (1971).
Tasby v. Woolery, 869 F. Supp. 454 (N. D.Tex. 1994).
United States v. Board of Pub. Instruction of St. Lucie County, 977 F. Supp. 1202 (S. D.Fla. 1997).
United States v. Unified Sch. Dist. No. 500, Kansas City, 974 F. Supp. 1367 (D. Kan. 1997).
United States v. Yonkers Branch-NAACP, 123 F. Supp.2d 694 (S.D. N. Y. 2000).
Valley v. Rapides Parish Sch. Bd., 145 F. 3d 329 (5th Cir. 1998); 173 F. 3d 944 (5th Cir. 1999).
Washington v. Seattle Sch. Dist., 458 U.S. 457 (1982).
Wessmann v. Boston Sch. Comm., 996 F. Supp. 120 (D. Mass. 1998).
Wessmann v. Gittens, 160 F.3d 790 (1st Cir. 1998).
Yonkers Branch – NAACP v. City of Yonkers, 251 F.3d 31 (2nd Cir. 2000).

4. BACK TO THE FUTURE WITH THE END OF *BROWN*: COMMUNITY CONTROL OF NEIGHBORHOOD SCHOOLS

Frank Brown

ABSTRACT

In spite of the intent and promise of Brown v. Board of Education, *most poor and minority children continue to receive an unequal education from the nation's public schools. Furthermore, the political pressure to reform schools has helped to erode Brown by turning judicial attention away from desegregation issues giving new and greater support to the idea of community schools. This chapter discusses changes in school desegregation policy that brought about by recent rulings made by the U.S. Supreme Court that are fostering a return to neighborhood schools.*

INTRODUCTION

This chapter addresses the continuing efforts to seeking racially desegregated schools nearly 50 years after the U.S. Supreme Court in their 1954 *Brown v. Board of Education* decision that de jure or state imposed segregation was unconstitutional; and a recent decision of the Supreme in *Capacchione* (2001) to effectively end the federal court's efforts or involvement promote school

---

Challenges of Urban Education and Efficacy of School Reform, Volume 6, pages 65–86.

ISBN: 0-7623-0426-X

integration as outlined in the High Court's 1971 ruling in *Swann v. Charlotte-Mecklenburg*. Yet, today, most racial and ethnic minority children continue to receive a poor education in public elementary and secondary schools. A closely related education issue tied to *Brown* is the use of "school choice" options to voluntarily racially integrate public schools. However, the school choice issue will be more fully developed in another chapter. I then raise the question, will the end of *Brown* lead minorities communities back to a strategy first pursued in the 1960s, "community control" of neighborhood schools and the realities of operating schools regardless of one's goals and objectives. I also argue that multiple cultures and voices are essential in providing effective leadership in a culturally pluralistic society, but can we bring this reality into our public schools?

A nearly 50 year battle to use race as a factor in implementing the 1954 *Brown v. Board of Education* by the U.S. Supreme Court to desegregate public schools ended April 15, 2002 when the Court rejected the continued use of race in assigning pupils to schools designed to increase the racial desegregation of the Charlotte-Mecklenburg, North Carolina School System (*Belk v. Capacchione*, 2001). The U.S. Supreme Court refused to hear on appeal a case where the Fourth Circuit Court of Appeals ruled that race could no longer be used to integrate Charlotte-Mecklenburg public schools as approved earlier by the Supreme Court (*Swann*, 1971). A federal district court ruled earlier in 2000 that the 109,000-student school system use of race in making pupils' assignment was unconstitutional. A white parent sued to end race as a criterion in the selection of students for enrollment in the Charlotte-Mecklenburg School District's magnet schools for students' assignments for the 1997 school year when his daughter was refused admission to the academically elite magnet school program. The white parents filed their grievance in federal district court and won. On appeal, a three-judge panel of the Fourth U.S. Circuit Court of Appeals reversed and held that the district had not achieved unitary status as endorsed by the High Court in *Swann* (1971) and the use of a student's race in making pupils' assignments to integrate the school system was constitutional. But, the entire 11 member Fourth Circuit Court of Appeals agreed to review the case and September 21, 2001 voted 7–4 against continued race based pupil assignments to achieve school desegregation via the use of magnet schools. Upon appeal to the U.S. Supreme Court the Court in April 15, 2002 refused to hear the case, leaving the decision of the Fourth Circuit in place. The federal courts had also ruled earlier against the use of race in placing students in magnet schools to achieve school desegregation in a Maryland school district and the Boston Public Schools. The U.S. Supreme Court message was clear by endorsing the Fourth Circuit Court's strong opinion against further use of race to achieve racial school desegregation ended the *Brown* era as stated in the Circuit

Court's opinion. Nationwide, urban school districts are asking federal courts to be relieved of federal court's supervision of court ordered school desegregation plans given the small possibility that their plans to achieve racial school integration will be upheld by the U.S. Supreme Court. The former mechanism of having the school districts pay attorney fees for the prevailing party in a school desegregation case appears to be something of the past with the Supreme Court recent holdings against the use of race to promote further school desegregation. Therefore, minority parents as plaintiffs will find it almost impossible to obtain legal counsel necessary to pursue a school desegregation complaint all the way to the U.S. Supreme Court, if no legal support is likely to be awarded which operationally, if not legally, kills further school desegregation suits in federal courts.

The chapter explores the impact of a return to neighborhood schools after a failure of the federal courts to continue to implement the 1954 *Brown* decision that called for the racial integration of public schools. The chapter outlines current solutions to the ineffective education for most minority children and takes us back to the 1960s for possible solutions: community control of schools or making use of other mechanisms to improve education through school choice, privatization of public school administration, and new accountability schemes that calls for the reconstitution of failing public schools.

Racial and ethnic minorities in the U.S. have fought for decades to improve the quality of education for themselves and their children. This battle has centered on such issues as equal funding for segregated schools, school desegregation, community control of neighborhood schools, and the need for multicultural education. In general, the problem is how best to educate poor children in our urban centers and many small towns across the country. A disproportionate percentage of these children come from minority backgrounds. The characteristics of schools in urban communities are by now so well known that I feel little need for an elaborate discussion of urban schools for this chapter. In general, however, urban schools attempt to educate large numbers of at-risk students without adequate financial, human and political resources. The country's minority population is increasing and the majority (European-Americans) percentage is deceasing which changes the politics of education and living patterns in America.

MINORITY POPULATION CHANGES

The minority student population in America increased from 10.4 million in 1985–1986 to 13.7 million in 1994–1995 which constitutes 34% of K-12 schools enrollment in 1994–1995 from 29% in 1985–1986 (Garcia, 2001, p. 25). A majority of the high school graduates in California, Hawaii, Mississippi, New Mexico, and the District of Columbia will be from minority households. By 2006, about 50%% of all K-12 students in America will be minority students (Garcia, 2001, p. 25). Changes in the size and composition of the K-12 student population should have enormous consequences for schools, including the languages and experiences they bring to school will influence the curriculum and how schools functions. In 2000, 64% of the children were white, non-Hispanic, compared to 79% in 1972: 15% are Black, 4% are Asian, 1% Native American, and 16% are Hispanic (Imig, 2002, p. 17). The percentage of school age students speak a language other than English or have difficulty speaking English has doubled over the past two decades, increasing from 2.8% to 5.0% in 1999 (Imig, 2002, p. 17). Two factors serve to increase minority enrollments in our schools: immigration and fertility (Hodgkinson, 1999, p. 13). Nearly 85% of immigrants come to this country from non-European countries; and the average Black female gives birth to 2.6 children compared to 1.7 children for the white population which is not enough to replace the white population (Hodgkinson, 1999, p. 13). By 2020, half of the students will be non-white; and by 2050 or sooner half of all Americans will be non-European Americans. The European Americans (whites) school age population will continue to decline and the minority school age population will continue to increase (Hodgkinson, 1999, p. 13). Today, more than 180 different language groups are represented in LEP programs funded under Title VII (Garcia, 2001, p. 65). Many of these students also qualify for support under Title I programs for at-risk students. Also, many minority students are immigrants and need special services.

Today, most large urban cities are racially segregated and also many suburban communities are becoming racially segregated, from Milwaukee to New York City; and that shift includes a move from primarily white to non-white residential communities. For example, this pattern occurred in a community that planned a racially homogenous community and school in Celebration City, Florida by the Walt Disney Company in Florida (Blair, 2001, p. A21). The schools in this new planned community is 88% white in a county that is only 59% white. The trend is toward racial balkanization. One African American from this Florida County expressed a point of view that goes unstated but is felt by many African Americans when he stated that "I would not want to live there (Celebration City). They (whites) are not comfortable with us and I am not comfortable with them" (Blair, 2001, p. A21). Today, many African Americans and other minority groups are less motivated to fight to live in white communities where they are not welcome. Most demographers feel that housing discrimination is so subtle and forceful that even with the best intentions the decade-old national trend toward suburban segregation would be difficult to reverse. Robert Tennebaum who developed the integrated community in Columbia, Maryland in the 1960 feels that it would be difficult to duplicate such a community today (Blair, 2001, p. A21).

In all major U.S. cities during the last decade, from 1990 to 2000, segregation levels of Black and White children grew sharply as a result of white flight (Schmitt, 2001). In Milwaukee where the voucher experiment began, Black children now made up 61% of the public school population in 2000, up from 46% in 1990 (Schmitt, 2001). Many U.S. cities are gentrifying, increasing their white middle class residents, wealthy whites are returning to the cities in large numbers (Lerman, 2000; Scott, 2001); many big city majors are promoting this movement back to the inner cities (Lerman, 2000; Scott, 2001; Wilgoren, 2001); and many Black Americans are giving up on racially integrated neighborhoods and moving into all Black communities (Nasser, 2001). Oakland (California), Chicago and Harlem New York are excellent examples of gentrification (Lerman, 2000; Scott, 2001; Wilgoren, 2001).

For example, the 2000 U.S. Census revealed that on Long Island, NY that the segregation of Blacks and Whites is the rule, not the exception, across the Island (Lambert, 2002, p. A21). African Americans face more racial isolation than any other minority group. The only cities with a higher index with a higher segregation index than Long Island are Detroit, Milwaukee and Chicago. For example, Blacks live in the almost Black city of Hempstead where the medium income is $46,675 and the mayor and all elected officials are Black and next door is Garden City with an median income of $120,305 is all White with a white mayor and all white elected city officials. Hempstead is "almost like a township in South Africa." (Lambert, 2002, p. A21). How did this segregation practice began? The original suburban tract homes in Levittown, announced in bold letters that the homes could be sold only to members of the Caucasian race, the practice continues and Blacks make up on 1% of this World War II neighborhood (Lambert, 2002, p. A21). The white residents are likely to give up their protected status and there is almost no will on the part of politicians to disturb this segregated social order.

This pattern of racial/ethnic segregation is likely to continue and make community control a de facto matter if not a direct fight by these communities to exercise control over neighborhood schools. This segregation cuts across all income levels, from low-income neighborhoods to wealth minority neighborhoods, where the average price of home is $400,000 in communities surrounding Chicago, Washington, D.C., Atlanta, Birmingham, Houston, Los Angeles and several other large urban areas. This trend is motivated by more than finding suitable housing, but from a realization that the current courts are no longer interested in protecting minority rights as was the original intent of the Bill of

Rights to the U.S. Constitution as applied to the states after the Civil War as defined in the Fourteenth Amendment to the U.S. Constitution in 1868. Prior to the enactment of the Fourteenth Amendment to the U.S. Constitution in 1868 the Bill of Rights only applied to actions by the federal government, not the individual states. Minority rights have fallen victim to wishes of the hegemonic European majority with the power to exercise veto power over the proper implementation of Bill of Rights through political power and the appointment of federal judges. Therefore, the behavior of the federal courts are forcing minority citizens to use different means of achieving a good life in America and must be understood in light of these changes in American's new demographics and political movements.

Consider for a moment the political nature of educational reform. In the 1950s and 1960s, minorities sought improved schooling for their children through school desegregation, community control, and increased funding for urban schools. In the 1970s and 1980s, our national and state leaders, reacting to widespread hostile by European Americans responses to court-ordered desegregation with symbolic language with the goal of reversing the desegregation process (Edelman, 1977; Brown, 1979; Brown, 1990). This symbolic language suggested that parents should have a "choice" in the school their children attend, and proposed other school reform measures for those not interested in choice plans or where school choice simply was not feasible. The school choice movement began with conservative Presidents Ronald Reagan and George Bush, and the strategy so successfully appeased the foes of federal court ordered school integration that even moderate political leaders adopted this strategy for political gains. Because the more moderate voices in public education in America declined to accept all the newly proffered forms of choice, business and industry leaders began to advocate several trendy types of shared decision making or School Based Management (SBM), and among them, site based management-attracted support. This support led to a mandate in most states for some form of SBM, and many moderate state leaders were, in a political sense, forced to join the school reform movement owing to shrinking state resources and a continuing outcry about school failure.

In today's America, both public and non-public schools are racially segregated. We have long sought to integrate the public schools but private schools have been outside of the concept of "state action" within the rights under the Fourteenth Amendment to the U.S. Constitution but non-public schools are also segregated and seek public funds (Schemo, 2001). The Civil Rights Project at Harvard University, in their study of private religious schools, found that Roman Catholic schools are more racially segregated than public schools: 34% of Blacks attend heavily segregated schools where less than 10% of the students are white; and 48% of black children in Catholic schools and 44% in other religious schools are racially segregated (Schemo, 2002, p. A18).

There is a concentration of minority children in one race urban schools where resources are limited and "crime control" is a major safety and political issue. This concentration makes it easier to target minority children for criminal behavior. The recent decision by the U.S. Supreme Court ending their 1954 decision in *Brown v. Board of Education* to racially integrate the public schools will likely increase the ability of local governments to target minority students for greater social control with crime and safety issues. Beginning in 1960 whites left the inner cities for suburbia in large numbers to escape school integration and for whites that remained in the cities, intra-district segregation became the norm with ability grouping or tracking and the placement of minority students in special education classes. The concentration of minority children in single race schools makes it easier to target this population for further regulation through crime control mechanisms.

SCHOOL CHOICE

The school choice strategy was used to reduce the amount of court ordered school desegregation by busing of students according the race of students to achieve racial desegregation. For example, in October 1977, the New York State Department of Education convened a four day meeting involving officials from the U.S. Office of Education to set guidelines for Congressional approval of $7.5 million allocation to use magnet schools within public schools as part of a plan to achieve quality integrated public education. Representatives from school districts across the county with experience with magnet schools participated in the conference and Morton J. Sobel, a New York State Education Department official concluded that (Ambach, 1979, pp. 129–140). The conference participants felt that if there are to be magnet schools with Federal Government support, the government should provide funds to make these schools the best schools possible. Magnet schools have been around for many years but they typically have not been racially desegregated. There is a strong feeling that magnet schools are designed to pacify whites by using a de facto method of voluntarism and not "forced busing" to get white children to attend school with African American children. A major element of concerning about methods of achieving school desegregation is and this is true of magnet schools, is the victim of segregation must take the initiative. It is the victim who is being analyzed, researched, and it is up to the victim to fit the problem: make a selection to get a better education and force the power structure to make our democratic ideals work. There is little evidence that magnet schools will desegregate schools, but they can produce excellent schools that are more likely to develop a desegregated school situation (Ambach, 1979, p. 140). It was this same issue, the use of magnet schools to voluntarily integrate public schools by conservatives that these same forces are now seeking to end the use of magnet schools as a tool to racially desegregate public schools as evident by the U.S. Supreme Court decision to uphold the 2002 holding by the Fourth Circuit Court of Appeals to hold unconstitutional the use of race to desegregate the magnet schools in Charlotte, North Carolina.

Today in America, all appearances aside, social and economic mobility is severely limited. A society stratified by unequal positions of power, income, and social status can hardly alter these conditions through its schools; it can merely reproduce the existing inequalities. Racism is a system of advantage based upon race. Whiteness, in America, has a cash value that includes advantages that come to individuals through profits made from discriminatory markets and networks; unequal education allocated to children of different races; and these advantages are passed on to succeeding generations (Lipsitz, 2000, p. 669).

The restructuring of schools is a political process controlled by ruling majority elites who favor the status quo when it comes to providing access to knowledge for minorities. Thus, when the political restructuring of schooling introduces other issues involving race and ethnicity the winners and losers are easy to predict. The development of a hegemonic majority in American is best revealed in Dahl's (2001, p. 133) paraphrasing of Tocqueville over two hundred years ago:

> Since the very essence of democratic governments is the absolute sovereignty of the majority, which nothing in democratic states is capable of resisting, a majority necessarily has the power to oppress a minority. Just as a man with absolute power to misuse it, so may majority. Given an equality of condition among citizens, we may expect that in democratic countries a wholly new species of oppression will arise. Among citizens all equal and alike, the supreme power, the democratic government, acting in response to the will of the majority, will create a society with a network of small complicated rules, minute and uniform, that none can escape. Ultimately, then, the citizens of a democratic country will, be reduced to nothing better than a flock of timid and industrious animals, of which the government is the shepherd.

In better economic times, school reform would involve equally the three concepts of equity, efficiency and liberty. But equity and liberty as bases of reform are too financially and politically expensive in today's climate; thus, any change in a school's decision making structure will likely be designed to improve organizational efficiency, exclusive of equity and liberty. The strategy calls for no new money, no busing of students to promote desegregation, and no change of school boundaries to improve the balance among students from different economic and social classes. In light of these problems, how can SBM improve schooling for minority students?

Some, of course, doubt the effectiveness of a structural reform accepted only grudgingly by principals and teachers; others believe that this reform initiative can work, regardless of its top-down. Major social changes are difficult to implement when individual or group economic and social advances are constrained. Today in America, all appearances aside, social and economic mobility is severely limited. A society stratified by unequal positions of power, income, and social status can hardly alter these conditions through its schools; it can merely reproduce the existing inequalities. The restructuring of schools is a political process controlled by ruling elates who favor the status quo when it comes to providing access to knowledge for minorities. Thus, when the political restructuring of schooling introduces other issues involving race and ethnicity the winners and losers are easy to predict.

In better economic times, school reform would involve equally the three concepts of equity, efficiency and liberty. But equity and liberty as bases of reform are too financially and politically expensive in today's climate; thus, any change in a school's decision-making structure will likely be designed to improve organizational efficiency, exclusive of equity and liberty. The strategy calls for no new money, no busing of students to promote desegregation, and no change of school boundaries to improve the balance among students from different economic and social classes. In light of these problems, it is doubtful can SBM improve schooling for minority students?

Education is tied to economic success and it has been speculated that the economic situation among certain minority groups are improving. The most talked about took place among African American males (Wilson, 1978). Wilson (1978) reviewed data on African American males in the job market between 1962 to 1973 and concluded that economic success depended more upon the social class status of the father than on the race of the African American male entering the work force. Wilson's logic is fine, but the data used to make this argument are lacking (Hout, 1994, p. 532). The weakest link in the Wilson study was that as a sociologist he should have recognized that the period, 1962 to 1973 was a unique period in the history of African Americans in this country. It was also the beginning of the country's willingness to implement Civil Rights laws evident by the passage of the landmark 1964 Civil Rights statute by Congress and other measures by the states and Congress; and positive rulings by the federal courts striking down Jim Crow laws and forceful support of anti-discrimination laws. Therefore, qualified African American males during this period had greater opportunities to achieve quality job opportunities than before 1962 or after 1973. The failure of an African American sociologist to recognize this fact, even his own appointment to the faculty at the University of Chicago is difficult to understand or comprehend. One should be able to conclude that economic advancement of non hegemonic groups are not likely to improve greatly in the near future and add more positive advancement for public education.

SCHOOLS AS ORGANIZATIONS

If minority communities are to be successful in managing community controlled schools, it is necessary to understand that the organizational norms of school administration will not disappear just because they are under neighborhood control. Given these characteristics, reform leadership is clearly the most difficult kind of organizational leadership (Burns, 1978, p. 169). Reform leadership requires exceptional political skills, commitment, persistence and courage. A school reformer needs to understand street-level politics because symbolic politics cannot save a principal's career (Abbott & Caracheo, 1988; Willower, 1991). Any change that makes a difference will be political and will require the use of social power to resolve the inherent conflict and build consensus (Benveniste, 1989, p. 9).

The body politic establishes public schools to educate discipline and socialize children for successful adult roles; and through its board of education, superintendent, and principals, each community wishes to accomplish these functions without trouble. Thus, communities tend to work hard following the rules and ensuring accountability for expenditure of school funds.

Administratively, we can call schools "loosely coupled organizations." That is, superintendents rarely supervise individual schools closely, and principals rarely supervise individual teachers closely. Once the principal and the teachers reach a consensus, little can encourage teachers to embrace change if that consensus must be re-negotiated. Also, under conditions of a major change, the needs of the teachers may well supersede those of their students unless additional resources are forthcoming. Informing teachers that a new administrative arrangement will improve education is unlikely to motivate a change in their behavior. Since each teacher evaluates change by the meaning it holds for her or him, teachers will resist a change that requires them to re-negotiate their social contract with their principal. Thus, the major participants in school "restructuring" are teachers, and their needs must be met if the reform is to succeed (Fullan & Stiegelbauer, 1991, p. 117).

The teaching profession requires administrative supervision and evaluation; both are strategies for effecting control. Teachers and principals must involve themselves in face-to-face politics involving the interplay of power. But at the same time, educational politics requires that school-site conflict be kept within the school (Marshall & Scribner, 1991).

In schools, principals influence teachers through the political allocation of resources, and teachers counter with coalition politics. As a result of this political interplay, teachers conform to agreed-upon rules and grant a principal their loyalty in exchange for increased autonomy, limited supervision and good evaluations (Blase, 1991).

In five case studies of principals, Dahl and Peterson (1990) found that principals influenced the culture of their schools by the way, in which they resolved conflict. However, its doubtful that one would find a strong relationship between school structure and school function. He believed tradition, norms of practice and competing demands to be more important.

Meanwhile, disadvantaged students must be protected from unproven reforms. The impact of educational reform on the poor appears to be neutral. Nevertheless, the treatment of minority and poor students in our schools remains an intractable problem for the school reform movement (Brown & Contreras, 1991). Schools in affluent neighborhoods tend to perform well on standardized academic tests and the residents are pleased with their schools. Therefore, any talk about school improvement quickly shifts to the "real" education problem: how best to improve schooling for racial and ethnic minorities.

A shift in educational philosophy from an emphasis on equity to an emphasis on excellence hardly changes the problem, but the strategies for solving the problem have changed. The country will not move away from school desegregation, fiscal equity, "market" or "choice" plans to community control and accountability. Other studies on the impact of reform on low achieving students found that principals in restructured schools serving the poor co-opted parents through socialization and coalitions (Kershner & Connolly, 1991; Smey-Richman, 1991). Minorities invariably crowd the lower-level academic tracks and an administrator in a community-controlled school must be committed to improving this situation.

CAREERS AND CHANGE

The career goals of educators provide strong motivating factors both for and against change, including community schools (Miklos, 1988). Teachers and administrators who wish to advance must be careful to avoid violating the norms of the profession. Career advancement opportunities for teachers generally require securing an important sponsor, the principal, and teachers gain this sponsorship by conforming to the norms of the organization. Likewise, school principals who themselves desire sponsorship must also conform to the norms of the organization. In this context, we might well ask, who would be interested in structural change?

The school planning process in education is political (Benveniste, 1989). School planner and administrators are forced to be political in order to survive; and often avoid the participatory process whenever possible because the process is invariably slow and cumbersome; because the group may approve a project they do not fully support; because open democratic forums discourage complex conflict resolution; and because complete openness and disclosure may actually increase conflict or mobilize opposition. Moreover, demonstrable mistakes in any organization endanger professional survival (pp. 46, 99).

An understanding of how schools operate politically is essential to a full understanding of the ways in which schools can be successfully reformed into community schools. School reforms that require political alterations are more difficult to accomplish mainly because they require changes in the organization's production activities and resource allocation (Levin, 1977).

TRADITIONAL BARRIERS TO CHANGE

A school reformer requires exceptional leadership skills and you are a reformer if you wish to change a traditional managed school into a community-controlled school (Burns, 1978). Machiavelli advised the Prince over 400 years ago, it is simply unwise to be a reformer. The Prince learned that nothing is riskier than a new order, for those who stand to gain from the new order will withhold their help until they see results, while those who stand to lose by the change will oppose it vigorously. Like the Prince, any American school board or administrator who wish to restructure a K-12 education using current or new faculty will encounter barriers:

(1) Tradition. Politically powerful Americans, in general, like the schools they have and resist efforts to substitute alternative models for "real schools"; also, they value liberty over equity. The first impact of reforms on schools will result in fighting among stakeholders to re-negotiate their power relations; this may delay the implementation of reforms.
(2) Organization. Schools as organizations generally do not seek to be outstanding; rather, they seek to be good. Because teachers and principals aspire to promotion, they see supporting radical structural reforms as too risky, even if those reforms yield superior student outcomes.
(3) Vested Interests. Micro-school politics follow structural changes among parents, teachers, and principals. All reforms require planning and the planning process itself is political.
(4) Time, money and motivation. Educators have minimum tolerance for reform if they cannot find money for basic programs – renovating buildings, raising low salaries, and other problems. Reforms require extra time and funding for planning and program development.

(5) Trust. Educational reform may ultimately be more symbolic than real. People who jump on the reform bandwagon will not stay the course if serious resistance appears. Teachers are also concerned that "reforms" will dilute their professional power and autonomy in the classroom.
(6) Planning and evaluation. First, evaluation and planning are political processes. Second, evidence from reform experiments reveal that from goal setting to implementation, the process takes a decade or more under the best of conditions.

The minority community seeks equity from schools in the education of their children, but two forms of equity exist, horizontal and vertical. Horizontal equity involves the opportunity to attend school. In general, minority and majority children enjoy an equal opportunity to attend public elementary and secondary schools. Vertical equity, on the other hand, requires that all schools be equal. Here, the evidence is conclusive that minority children do not enjoy the vertical equity majority children enjoy (Oakes, 1985; Noguera, 2001).

Parent participation in education is value-laden and political (Young, 1995). As politicians and educators continue to urge more "parental involvement," they also seem willing to blame minority parents who cannot meet their definition of adequate involvement as measured against parent participation by middle-class white parents (pp. 21, 27). Concomitantly, politicians and educators may lay the blame for poor education outcomes for minority children on minority parents' disengagement with their children's schools. Reviewing educational reforms in Redwood City, California, researchers found that white neighborhoods exercised a powerful influence over the nature and extent of minority participation in these reforms; and this racial conflict may be less in a community school (Kirp & Driver, 1995).

The allocation of educational opportunity in America is socially constructed, political (English, 2002, pp. 298–311; Noguera, 2001) and the politics of education change as individuals who are in a position to wield power and influence over other players in the arenas of education change (Scribner, Reyes & Fusarelli, 1995, pp. 201–212). School reform may produce change, or it may maintain the status quo; either situation is liable to disadvantage minority children without effective participation by alert parents.

The future of the school desegregation movement is questioned given the recent position of the National Association for the Advancement of Colored People (NAACP). The NAACP at its 1997 convention did not take an official position on whether to drop its almost 75 year effort to racial integrate public education but placed the item of continued school desegregation efforts by the organization on their agenda for debate for the first time in its history. This debate may be moot now with the recent holding of the federal courts against further court ordered or supervision of school desegregation but the attitudes of group members may say much about future directions in this area. The organization invited long time opponents to the school desegregation to debate the merits of their school integration efforts as compared to other alternatives for getting a better quality of education for African Americans. There are strong feelings among many African Americans that they have lost the battle against segregated schooling and the community is out of political or judicial resources to effectively battle the new consensus among white Americans to oppose school desegregation. Further, many minority political leaders are found in urban communities when the public schools are almost 100% minority and to continue this fight drains valuable political resources to fight what they perceives as a futile fight away from more tangible goals. And, in communities where there still reside a sizeable number of white children in the public schools minority children are typically separated from their white peers by a variety of means such as tracking and the placement of minority children in special education classes. The public schools are more segregated today than they were in 1970 and we have more racial and ethnic minority children enrolled in our school than in the recent past.

Regarding the quality of education factor, the Court held in *Freeman* and *Jenkins III* that this factor must be tied to a constitutional violation by the school system. Most large urban school districts are composed primarily of minority students and there are few white students enrolled to achieve unitary status by a significant improvement in the racial balance of students; and in districts where improved racial balance of students is possible, the Court (*Freeman*) recognizes new and subtle forms of discrimination and racism in the schooling process. Detroit, Kansas City and other urban schools are focusing more upon improving educational programs to mediate injuries to minority students caused by school systems' unconstitutional violation of their rights. For example, the federal district court in Rockford, Illinois case found that "ability grouping or tracking was the most egregious and blatant form of intentional discrimination against minority school children" (*Rockford II*, 1996, 14). The district court also approved supplemental funding for staff development, human relations programs, multi-cultural programs, weekend programs, summer school programs, tutorial programs and high order thinking programs. The court, however, rejected a preschool program because the school board could not be held accountable for educational progress or a lack of progress for students before they enroll in school. Again, the U.S. Supreme has decided for the moment not to render an opinion on *Brown*, but in a de facto way say no to *Brown* via a lower court opinion by reviewing that opinion in the Charlotte case.

The Supreme Court's use of the five *Green* factors and the one *Freeman* factor to define court-ordered school desegregation remedies for achieving unitary status is a changing standard; and is affected by the Court's preference for ending district court's supervision of offending school systems after decades of court oversight. This preference by the Court encourages district courts to fashion remedies that are "practical" and can be "realistically" implemented. Achieving unitary status should provide minority students with a superior education; greater fairness and equity for the minority community as it relates to minority teachers, administrators and staff; and greater fairness and equity for minority students as it relates to transportation, and participation in extra-curricular activities. The recent holding by the Federal Court of Appeals and the U.S. Supreme Court in the Charlotte, North Carolina case ending race as a factor in desegregating public schools because the idea is no longer practical or realistically; and if desegregation could be achieved with such means, segregation is cause by "state" action (school board) which means there is no violation of the Constitution. Coons and Sugarman (1978, p. 40), two European American law professors who have supported conservative education causes for decades feel strongly that "while our national law forbids and sometimes prevents official segregation, it does not appear likely that affirmative integration will soon become a constitutional norm or a social habit." They do not believe white Americans, as a group will accept racial and social class integration. The segregation of schools, white flight, and decreasing support for urban schools appear to support their conclusion, which makes focusing more upon quality education in achieving unitary status, more important.

The decline of court ordered remedies for producing unitary schools began with the white backlash of the 1970s and continues to this day. On the national sense, former Presidents Richard Nixon, Ronald Reagan, and George Bush promised to appoint federal judges who would move slow in the area of school desegregation; and the appointment of attorney generals who would seek to remove federal court supervision of school districts under court supervision to desegregate their schools. The presidents and their supporters in Congress also made it unlawful by federal statute for any federal agency to spend any federal money for the purpose of eliminating racial segregated schools and also, it is unlawful for any of these federal employees to knowingly encourage local to schools or private agencies to support the elimination of racial segregated schools. This statute was included in the Education Act Amendment of 1972 and is still operative. However, the statute excludes court ordered desegregation. At the same time, these former presidents used a variety of strategies to subvert school desegregation: they funded "magnet" schools, supported voucher plans for students who wished to attend private schools and tuition tax credits for students attending private schools. Similar tactics played out on the national scene were also being played out on the state and local levels. Today, in 2002, court ordered school desegregation is something of the past and publicly funded education vouchers are now constitutional permissive. In short, our government is composed of three components, the legislative, executive, and judicial branches; and, it is clear, that the legislative and executive branch are acting as a check and balance on the judicial branch as witnessed after the 1950s in the direction of European American majority politics.

In summary, the minority communities are back to "square one", how to achieve quality education for their children? The answer may lie in where we want to go as society of diverse populations, where all citizens' equality is the rule, even if the outcomes are not the same. Currently, the rules and the outcomes are different for members of different racial and ethnic groups. Put, another way, public school desegregation is not an American ideal or goal? Today, most minority American communities as indicative by the action taken by majors in cities where the minority student population is in the majority are seeking quality education but are not longer willing to invest political capital in the desegregation fight. White middle class Americans will continue seek various ways to enroll their children in racially segregated magnet schools, move to a racially isolated community (white flight), or enroll their children in private schools. White children from poor families will pay to commute and enroll their children in suburban schools, attend low cost Catholic schools, or drop out of school.

To understand public education in the U.S., political, the states must be viewed as 50 separate countries when assessing the status of public education, which is unlike most countries of the world, except for Canada. The U.S. constitution leaves the role of public education to the individual states and so you have 50 state educational systems with varying degrees of educational services for their citizens.

It is important to note that race plays a critical role in determining who gets to choose the type and kind of education they will receive from the public schools. Generally, middle class European Americans desire that their children attend school with other middle class white students but will accept a minimum level of minority involvement. The major choice and privatization movement began with the 1954 *Brown* decision, which declare racially segregated schools unconstitutional. First, the southern states that enrolled their children in racially segregated schools used "freedom" of choice plans to get around enrolling their children in integrated public schools; and sought public vouchers to fund segregated academies to escape school integration. Politicians seeking the votes of this constituency promised public vouchers, a protection of neighborhood schools, "magnet" schools, the elimination of public funds to support transportation for the purpose of racially desegregating public schools; and later "charter" schools, the use of "market" forces to through private management of public schools to improve their quality with the same resources.

The third major factor is economics. In the U.S. market forces are used to support major allocation of resources among the population. The system assumes that everyone has an equal chance given his/her natural talents or the lack thereof to achieve a good life in America; and if you fail to achieve that good life its your fault, not the poor educational system of your poor state or community. To those who believe that we should live like a big family and share resources, feel that if you live in a poor state the federal government should help and if you live in a poor community, your state government should assist. Naturally, citizens who would have the resources to share to make either of these schemes work generally oppose a redistribution of opportunities for children of the poor.

Privatization should inject market incentives into the system but in America, there are several markets operating and listed in order of priority you will find political (and ideological), economical, and educational markets. Politics "trumps" all other markets. Politics define economic, educational, and other markets or areas of interests. In reality, educational reform is a metaphor for several agendas: political, economical, and educational. At first glance, these agendas should be obvious to the casual observer but due to the complexity and confluence of issues involved the goals of privatization in education become muddled. Other common metaphors for privatization of education are family choice, deregulation, and democratic values. However, the one thing we all know about low academic productivity in America's public education is that poorly educated children are located in poor communities. Further, most low performing schools are located in urban communities where most students come from racial and ethnic minority households. These residents possess less economical and political power than those who live outside of these communities do. Yet, many educational reformers proposing radical solutions to the problems of urban schools are traditionally their opponents, if not the enemies, of residents in these communities. There are no for-profit schools in America; this is true for private and public operated schools. Therefore, for-profit schools are not likely to surface in America.

Education as "political market" is at the top of all "markets" influencing public education. In the educational political fields some players have the power to wield influence over other players. Educational politics fields will determine whether schools have site-based management programs, vouchers, charter schools, home schools, private schools, and states takeovers of failed schools (Brown, 1991;

Mathews, 1997, p. 741). The key players in public school politics are school board members, business leaders, clergy, district employees, parents, students, and the legislature.

"White flight", the exit from or avoidance of racially mixed urban public schools was as strong in the 1990s as it was in the 1960s (Clotfelter, 2001). In a study of 238 metropolitan areas from 1987 to 1996 white losses in urban public school enrollment resulted from white families moving from one district to another, enrolling their children in private schools and avoidance of moving into districts with high minority concentrations (Clotfelter, 2001). This pattern existed across small and large urban communities; and is consistent in both southern and northern urban communities.

In 1999 the Fourth U.S. Circuit Court of Appeals ruled that the Montgomery County Maryland School System policy of using race as a factor in assigning students to public magnet schools was unconstitutional; and in 2001 that same court make a similar ruling in the Charlotte-Mechlenburg, North Carolina Public School and it was upheld by the U.S. Supreme Court (*Belk,* 2001). Several school districts that once used race to assign students to magnet schools to promote racial desegregation voluntarily quickly switched to economic diversity to achieve the same end, greater racial school desegregation. In the Wake County School District (Raleigh, North Carolina) shifted from the use of race to economic measures to achieve racial school diversity? The economic measure used is the percentage of students in each school participating in their Free and Reduced Federal Lunch Program. The goal is to keep the percentage of students enrolled in the Free and Reduced Federal Lunch Program rate below 40% of a school's enrollment. This new economic policy achieves the same results as the use of race in assigning students to such schools by moving some middle-income students from their neighborhood schools and reassigning these students to schools in low-income neighborhoods or just the reverse. The results are the same on two accounts. First, the use of economic measures to make school assignments achieve a similar degree of racial school integration as the race based school assignment plan. Second, the same middle-income parents who objected to the race based student assignment plan objects to the economically based school assignment plan. The strongest argument against any plan to improve racial diversity in our public schools is opposition from middle class parents.

With the end of *Brown* and a strong push to implement the "Southern Strategy" first proposed by former President Richard M. Nixon and supported by every Republican President since Richard M. Nixon (Peterson & Miner, 2000, pp. 819–822); and the resurfacing of racially isolated neighborhoods what is the future of public education for people of color? One practical and tested model is the "community control" of neighborhoods that surfaced in the 1960s

(Byndloss, 2001). The community control concept of public school governance included the hiring and firing of school personnel, selection of the curriculum and general control over school matters. The most recent model of community control is practiced in Chicago, where each school has its own school board composed of parents from the community. In addition to educating children, schools can also provide employment opportunities for community residents. In many states, communities cannot restrict public employment to residents which suggests that isolated minority community can never expect to exercise total control over public education as long as the hegemonic majority is in control of state governments and the federal government. States may enact statutes forbidding such practices and most states do; and the federal government may require the elimination of all federal funds due a school or school district if residential restrictions are enacted for employment and most districts cannot afford to fore go such financial assistance.

America is more diverse now than a decade ago, yet neighborhoods are more segregated by race and ethnicity than it was a decade ago and schools are becoming more neighborhood focused. An increase in single racially identifiable communities are more likely to result in community control of neighborhood schools similar to the ones that surfaced in New York City in the 1960s in large urban cities; in smaller cities and towns where the entire population is composed of a single racial/ethnic group the entire school district may take on a community control philosophy similar to those that are a part of a larger community. Therefore, the new school leadership core for community control schools must respond to this new neighborhood design because its likely to be with us for many decades into the future; and its logically to expect that these communities will want educational leaders who will serve their specific needs regardless of the leadership paradigms espoused: situational, transformational, caring, traditional, or issue focused. Further, if neighborhood schools become more racial and ethnic specific, then the major issue for future leaders in these schools will have show the greatest respect for the parents and nurture the abilities of children in these schools and utilize the leadership most desired by their respective communities. There are other positive implications for community control of public schools: minority residents may feel empowered with a stronger measure of control over the education of their children; students may feel more secure and empowered with more minorities in positions of role model as teachers and community leaders; students and parents may be able to focused more on education and less on daily conflict due to racial differences at school; more minority students will be placed in leadership positions than before; more jobs may flow from the model; and a wider social and economic networks may resulted from this model.

Minorities and particularly, the African American community have waged a 50 year struggle to promote quality desegregated schooling without much success and it appears that with their limited economic and political power its time to seek other alternatives to pursuing quality education for their children where quality school integration opportunities are too high. However, changes in organizational forms and behaviors are never easy and minority control of community schools will also have to deal effectively with organizational rules and regulations; and the career aspirations of employees in delivering quality education to their children.

REFERENCES

Abbott, M. G., & Caracheo, F. (1988). Power, authority, and bureaucracy. In: N. J. Boyan (Ed.), *Handbook of Research on Educational Administration* (pp. 239–258). New York: Longman.

Ambach, G. M. (1979). *Magnet schools for desegregation*. Albany, NY: The University of the State of New York, The State Education Department, and Division of Intercultural Relations.

Belk v. Capacchione, U.S. Court of Appeals for the Fourth Circuit, 269 F.3d 305 (September 21, 2001).

Benveniste, G. (1989). *Mastering the politics of planning*. San Francisco: Jossey-Bass.

Burns, J. M. (1978). *Leadership*. New York: Harper & Row.

Blair, J. (2001, September 23). Failed Disney vision: Integrated city: Community is part of U.S. trend toward suburban segregation. *The New York Times*, p. A21.

Blase, J. (1991). *The politics of life in schools: Power, conflict, and cooperation*. Newbury Park, CA: Sage.

Brown v. Board of Education, 347 U.S. 483 (1954).

Brown, F. (1979, Spring). Major changes in school integration litigation, 1954–1979. *Educational Administration Quarterly*, *15*(2), 76–97.

Brown, F. (1990). The language of politics, education, and the disadvantaged. In: S. L. Jacobson & J. A. Conway, *Educational Leadership in an Age of Reform* (pp. 83–100). New York: Longman.

Brown, F. (1991). School choice and the politics of decline. *Education and Urban Society*, *23*(2), 115–118.

Brown, F., & Contreras, A. R. (1991). Deregulation and privatization of education: A flawed concept. *Education and Urban Society*, *23*(2), 144–158. Washington, D.C.: Brookings Institution Press.

Byndloss, D. C. (November 2001). Revisiting paradigms in Black education community control and African-centered schools. *Education & Urban Society*, *34*(1), 84–100.

Capacchione v. Belk, U.S. Court of Appeals for the Fourth Circuit, 269 F.3d 305 (September 21, 2001).

Clotfelter, C. T. (2001, Spring). Are Whites still fleeing? Racial patterns and enrollment shifts in urban public schools, 1987–1996. *Journal of Policy Analysis and Management*, *20*(2), 199–221.

Coons, J. E., & Sugarman, S. D. (1978). *Education by choice: The case for family control*. Berkeley, CA: University of California Press.

Dahl, R. A. (2001). *How democratic is the American constitution?* (p. 133). New Haven, CT: Yale University Press.

Dahl, T. E., & Peterson, K. D. (1990, September). *The principal's role in shaping school culture.* Office of Educational Research and Improvement, Washington, D.C.: U.S. Department of Education, unnumbered.

Edelman, M. (1977). *The symbolic uses of politics.* Urbana, IL: The University of Illinois Press.

English, F. W. (2002, May). On the intractability of the achievement gap in urban schools and the discursive practice of continuing racial discrimination. *Education and Urban Society, 34*(3), 298–311.

Freeman v. Pitts, 503 U.S. 467 (1992).

Fullan, M. G., & Stiegelbauer, S. (1991). *The new meaning of educational change* (2nd ed.). New York: Teachers College Press.

Garcia, E. E. (2001). *Hispanic education in the United States.* Lanham, MD: Rowman & Littlefield Publishers, Inc.

Green v. New Kent County School Board, 391 U.S. 430 (1968).

Hodgkinson, H. L. (1999, December). The uneven spread and blurring of student diversity. *The School Administrator, 56*(11), 13–14.

Hout, M. (1994). Occupational mobility of Black men: 1962 to 1973. In: D. B. Grusky, *Social Stratification: Class, Race, and Gender in Sociological Perspective* (pp. 531–542). Boulder, CO: Westview Press.

Imig, D. G. (2002, January). American Association of Colleges for Teacher Education President's contextual scan. In: Y. T. Moses, *Scanning the Environment, AAHE Bulletin, 53*(53), 7–9, June 2001.

Jenkins III v. Missouri, 807 F.2d 657, 661, 662 (8th Cir. 1986); 855 F. 2d 1295, p. 1302 (8th Cir. 1988); 11 F.3d 755 (8th Cir. 1993a); 13 F.3d 1170 (8th Cir. 1993b); 19 F.3d 393 (8th Cir. 1994); cert. granted 115 S. Ct. 41 (1994); 115 S. Ct. 2038 (1995).

Kemerer, F. R. (1999). Race and school choice. In: S. D. Sugarman & F. R. Kemerer, *School Choice and Social Controversy: Politics, Policy, and Law* (pp. 174–211). Washington, D.C.: Brookings Institution Press.

Kirp, D. L., & Driver, C. E. (1995). The aspirations of systemic reform meet the realities of localism. *Educational Administration Quarterly, 31*(1), 589–612.

Lambert, B. (2002, June 5). Study says Long Island is the most racially segregated suburb in the U.S. *The New York Times*, p. A21.

Lerman, S. (2000, May 17). Ads spark Oakland gentrification fear. *Oakland (CA) Tribune*, p. 5.

Lewin, T. (1997, April 20). Schools get tough on illegal students from other places. *The New York Times*, p. 1.

Lipsitz, G. (2000). The possessive investment in Whiteness. In: J. Birnbaum & C. Taylor, *Civil Rights Since 1787: A Reader on the Black Struggle* (pp. 669–678). NY: New York University Press.

Marshall, C., & Scribner, J. D. (1991). It's all political: Inquiry into the micropolitics of education. *Education and Urban Society, 23*, 347–355.

Menand, L. (2001, February 12). Civil actions: Brown v. Board of Education and the limits of law. *The New Yorker*, pp. 91–96.

Miklos, E. (1988). Administrator selection, career patterns, succession, and socialization. In: N. J. Boyan, *Handbook of Research on Educational Administration* (pp. 53–76). New York: Longman.

Nasser, H. E. (2001, July 9). Minorities make choice to live with their own, *USA Today*, p. 8A.

Noguera, P. A. (2001, November). Racial politics and the elusive quest for excellence and equity in education. *Education and Urban Society*, *34*(1), 18–41.

Peterson, B. and Miner, B. (2000). Vouchers, the right and the race card. In: J. J. Birnbaum & C. Taylor, *Civil Rights Since 1787: A Reader on the Black Struggle* (pp. 819–822). New York: New York University Press,.

Rockford II Board of Education School District No. 205 v. People Who Care, U.S. District Court Northern District of Illinois Western Division, Case No. 89 C 20168 (1996).

Schemo, D. J. (2001, July 20). U. S. schools turn more segregated, a study finds, *The New York Times*, p. A12.

Schemo, D. J. (2002, June 27). Study finds parochial schools segregated along racial lines, *The New York Times*, p. A18.

Schmitt, E. (2001, May 6). Segregation growing among U.S. children, *The New York Times*, pp. A6, A20.

Scribner, J. D., Reyes, P., & Fusarelli, L. (1995). Educational politics and policy: And the games go on. In: J. D. Scribner & D. H. Layton, *The Study of Educational Politics* (pp. 201–212). Washington, D.C.: Falmer Press.

Smey-Richman, B. (1991). *School climate and restructuring for low-achieving students*. Philadelphia: Research for Better Schools.

Swann v. Charlotte-Mecklenburg Board of Education, 402 U.S. 1 (1971).

Wilgoren, J. (2001, June 15). Chicago uses preschool to lure middle class, *New York Times*, p. A1, A20.

Willower, D. J. (1991). Micrcopolitics and the sociology of school organizations. *Education and Urban Society*, *23*, 442–454.

Wilson, W. J. (1978). *The declining significance of race*. Chicago: University of Chicago Press.

Young, M. D. (1995, October). A parental involvement paradox: Rhetoric and reality. Paper presented at the annual meeting of the University Council for Educational Administration, Salt Lake City, UT.

5. DISCRIMINATION IN TRACKING AND SPECIALIZED EDUCATION PROGRAMS

Richard C. Hunter and Saran Donahoo

ABSTRACT

This chapter will examine how tracking, gifted education, special education, and compensatory education programs have limited the educational opportunities of many poor and minority students. Despite the stated intentions of these educational programs, the situation in the nation's urban schools indicates that these structures are having a detrimental impact on the lives of some students. Statistical information regarding the disproportionate participation of poor and minority students in these programs is included.

INTRODUCTION

Like other school reforms, many of the problems urban students suffer while participating in tracking, gifted programs, special education and compensatory education result from the clash between intentions and reality. In different ways, each of these programs is responsible for providing students with the type and level of academic support most needed. Such intervention programs do benefit some participants; however, many urban and minority students are hurt more than they are helped by these programs.

Challenges of Urban Education and Efficacy of School Reform, Volume 6, pages 87–100.

ISBN: 0-7623-0426-X

The foundation for all of these intervention programs is that children learn better when receiving an individualized education tailored to their needs and ability levels. In reality, these often inflict more damage upon the students they are meant to assist. This chapter examines how tracking and specialized programs such as gifted, special and compensatory education limit educational opportunities for low-income and minority students. It also includes a discussion of the impact teachers' perceptions and attitudes have on the placement, participation and success of disadvantaged students.

TRACKING AND ABILITY GROUPING[1]

Tracking and ability grouping are both long-standing educational practices that allow schools to sort, academically categorize, and place their students. Dating back to the latter years of the Progressive Era, these practices were initially created to help educators place students into different tracks that would prepare them for careers they seemed best suited for later in life (Brown, Carter & Harris, 1978; Donelan, Neal & Jones, 1994; Mallery & Mallery, 1999; Marsh & Raywid, 1994; Oakes, 1995). Since the 1950s and 1960s, these practices have also helped to limit the application of the *Brown* decision by restricting desegregation efforts and the progress of minority students (Darling-Hammond, 1995a; Donelan, Neal & Jones, 1994; Ford, 1995; Kershaw, 1992; Oakes, 1995).

Although tracking and ability grouping continue to be widely used, they are not effective for most students. The only students who truly benefit from these systems are those in the gifted or high-performing track (Donelan, Neal & Jones, 1994; Ford, 1995; Hallinan, 1994; Harris & Ford, 1991; Mallery & Mallery, 1999; Slavin, 1995). These students generally have access to the best teachers, greater resources, and most challenging curricula. On the other hand, students placed in middle and lower performing groups fall further behind rather than improving. The lower standards and poorer quality instruction offered to these students makes it extremely difficult for them to catch or keep up. Students in these tracks tend to start out behind their peers and remain there even as adults (Brown, Carter & Harris, 1978; Donelan, Neal & Jones, 1994; Hallinan, 1994; Kershaw, 1992; Mallery & Mallery, 1999; Oakes, 1985).

The fact that tracking systems impede the educational progress of students who are not placed in high-performing groups is particularly devastating for many low-income and minority students. Both the *Brown* decision and the Elementary and Secondary Education Act (ESEA) of 1965 mandate that all children have an equal educational opportunity regardless of race. However, tracking obstructs the effectiveness of these mandates. Tracking discriminates on the basis of race by using subjective, culturally biased assessments and evaluation criteria to determine which students are high performing, low performing, or average (Braddock, 1990; Brown, Carter & Harris, 1978; Daniels, 1998; Donelan, Neal & Jones, 1994; Ford, 1995; Harris & Ford, 1991; Harry & Anderson, 1994; Hilliard, 1992; Kershaw, 1992; Oakes, 1985).

Schools generally rely on standardized test scores, teacher referrals, counselor recommendations, grades and other academic information to make placement decisions (Brown, Carter & Harris, 1978; Donelan, Neal & Jones, 1994; Hallinan, 1994; Oakes, 1995). Objectivity and fairness rarely accompany the application of these measures. Many schools simply lack clear guidelines for making placement determinations. Even when the implementation process is clearly defined, students often fall victim to inconsistencies in the way various teachers and other school personnel follow outlined procedures (Ferguson, 1998; Hallinan, 1994; Lockwood & Cleveland, 1998; Murphy, 1986; Oakes, 1994a, 1995). Rather than recognize multiple forms of intelligence, tracking establishes white culture and behavior as the norm (Donelan, Neal & Jones, 1994; Ford, 1995; Harris & Ford, 1991; Kershaw, 1992; Oakes, 1985, 1994a, b, 1995). As such, intelligent and successful low-income and minority students are those who best emulate their white classmates in ability, behavior and attitude.

The cultural bias inherent in tracking systems leads to a variety of negative consequences for low-income and minority students. One consequence is the overrepresentation of these students in the least productive academic tracks (Brown, Carter & Harris, 1978; Donelan, Neal & Jones, 1994; Hallinan, 1994; Kershaw, 1992; MacMillan & Reschly, 1998; Mallery & Mallery, 1999; Oakes, 1985, 1994a, 1995). For the most part, tracking works to the advantage of Asian students who are overrepresented in high performing groups.[2] However, Latino and African American students are often hurt since they are more likely to participate in low performing groups regardless of demonstrated academic ability (Braddock, 1990; Ford, 1998; Mallery & Mallery, 1999; Oakes, 1995). Indeed, Oakes (1995) found that only 56% of Latino students scoring in the top 10 percentile enrolled in accelerated classes. Similarly, African Americans students who scored in the top 25 percentile were less likely to participate in college preparation courses than white students who scored in the bottom 25 percentile on the same assessment (Oakes, 1995). According to Crosby and Owens (1993), minority students from low-income families have only a 19% chance of participating in the top academic track compared to a 30% chance of assignment to the vocational or lower track. As such, tracking limits social mobility for these students by preparing them for service and manual labor careers that increasingly do not provide enough compensation to keep a family above the poverty line (Brown, Carter & Harris, 1978; Kershaw, 1992). In this way, tracking not only limits the academic achievement of these students, but also perpetuates a cycle of poverty by denying them access to courses they need to prepare for college and success after high school.

THE LONG ARM OF TRACKING

In addition to general problems, tracking also influences the participation of low-income and minority students in specialized educational programs. Repercussions from tracking include low participation in gifted education, overrepresentation in special education, and the development of compensatory programs specifically targeted at these students.

Gifted Education

As previously mentioned, low-income and minority students are not frequently placed in high performing tracks and ability groups. This underrepresentation includes gifted education programs. Similar to other tracking decisions, cultural bias often keeps low-income and minority students out of these programs (Donelan, Neal & Jones, 1994; Ford, 1995, 1998; Ford & Webb, 1994; Harris & Ford, 1991; Hilliard, 1992).

There are no universal standards for gifted education (Harris & Ford, 1991). The U.S. Office of Education first attempted to establish such a definition in 1972. At that time, the Office of Education defined gifted students as those who possessed or had the potential for general intellectual, specific academic, creative or productive thinking, leadership, and psychomotor abilities (U.S. Commissioner of Education, 1972). The definition provided in the Gifted and Talented Act of the 1978 Reauthorization of the Elementary and Secondary Education Act (ESEA) of 1965 revised the 1972 definition by eliminating consideration for giftedness in psychomotor abilities and by adding performing and virtual arts abilities (Ford, 1995; Ford & Webb, 1994).

Each of the definitions cited above increases the possibility for identifying gifted students by considering a wide range of abilities. However, states and schools limit the effectiveness of these definitions by relying on assessment measures that do not test for multiple forms of intelligence. The standardized tests often used to make such determinations focus on testing reading and math skills. As a result, other forms of intelligence often go untested and unrecognized (Ford, 1995; Gardner, 1983). The fact that some gifted students are underachievers also makes identification difficult since grades and test scores alone do not accurately reflect their abilities and intellect (Ford, 1995).

The inconsistent application of federal definitions for giftedness helps to keep many students out of these programs. Moreover, it actually promotes underrepresentation and limited participation by low-income and minority students. The removal of psychomotor abilities as an area of consideration in the 1978 definition eliminates the possibility that students who excel in athletics may gain access to gifted education (Harris & Ford, 1991). In addition, the cultural bias inherent in standardized tests and other measures decreases the possibility for identification of giftedness or placement of students of color in these programs (Darling-Hammond, 1995a; Ford, 1995, 1998; Ford & Webb, 1994; Harris & Ford, 1991; Samuda et al., 1991).

As part of the 1988 Reauthorization of the Elementary and Secondary Education Act of 1965, the Jacob K. Javits Gifted and Talented Students Education Act provides financial assistance for programs and research on gifted students. In addition, this act also attempts to address representation issues by asking that states, schools, programs and researchers give special attention to identifying and assisting gifted students from traditionally underrepresented student populations. These include low-income, racial and ethnic minority, disabled, and limited English proficient students (Ford, 1998; Ford & Webb, 1994). In spite of this act and the funding that accompanies it, disadvantaged students remain underrepresented in gifted education programs. Indeed, many low-income and minority students may not have access to gifted education programs since schools with large populations of minority students are less likely to offer high-level curricula including accelerated programs, advanced placement and honors courses (Ford, 1998; Oakes & Guiton, 1995). As such, even the most academically successful students attending these schools graduate from high school while ill prepared for college.

Special Education

For the most part, special education is an antithesis to gifted programs and high ability tracks. Whereas low-income and minority students often find it difficult to gain access to gifted programs, they tend to be overrepresented in special education. The same cultural bias that keeps these students out of the best programs actually makes them prime targets for special education services (Coutinho, Oswald & Best, 2002; Daniels, 1998; Harry & Anderson, 1994).

Congress first attempted to formally define and regulate special education in 1975 under the Education for all Handicapped Children Act (EHA). This act was later renamed the Individuals with Disabilities Education Act (IDEA). Similar to the Javits Act, IDEA provides regulations and financial support for the education of students with a wide range and variety of disabilities.

IDEA attempts to resolve some of the issues surrounding special education by providing more clear information regarding which students are eligible for assistance, ways to provide appropriate assistance, parent involvement in the process, and guidelines for outcomes and standards. This act mandates that each child enrolled in special education have access to a free and appropriate public education that abides by both state standards and the guidelines set forth in each individualized educational program (IEP). Amended in 1997, this version of the act describes 13 categories of disabilities. Disabilities covered under IDEA include deafness, mental retardation, hearing impairment, emotional disturbance, specific learning disability, speech or language impairment, and visual impairment such as blindness (Henderson, 2001).

In spite of regulations stipulated by IDEA, the definitions for some disabilities are very flexible, thus allowing bias and abuse to occur. As with gifted education, whether a child receives an evaluation for special education services often depends on how teachers interpret his or her behavior. Children whose behavior or academic performance does not match expectations or emulate cultural norms may receive an improper referral for special needs assistance. The descriptions and evaluation procedures for categories such as Educable Mental Retardation (EMR), Trainable Mental Retardation (TMR), Serious Emotional Disturbance (SED), Speech Impairment (SI) and Specific Learning Disability (SLD) make it easy to misdiagnose and incorrectly place students.

When analyzing data gathered by the Office of Civil Rights (OCR) in a 1992 survey of elementary and secondary schools, Harry and Anderson (1994) found that African American males are primarily overrepresented in EMR, TMR and SED classifications. These students occupied 19.4%, 17.5% and 18.9% of the population of these programs, respectively, yet only made up 8.2% of total school enrollment across the country (Harry & Anderson, 1994). Using OCR data from the 1994–1995 school year, Coutinho, Oswald, and Best (2002) determined that American Indian males are overrepresented in the learning disabilities category at a rate of 9.2% compared to a rate of 5.5% for students of all races in this classification. Likewise, students who are limited English proficient (LEP) or do not speak standard English at home may be incorrectly labeled as SI when such intervention is not really needed (Harry & Anderson, 1994; Ortiz, 1997). Such labeling and intervention can be beneficial or damaging. Some special education categories demonstrate underrepresentation among Hispanic students (Coutinho, Oswald & Best, 2002). This suggests that limited English proficiency, use of non-standard English in the home environment and other linguistic concerns can make it difficult to accurately place students.

Once placed in special education programs, low-income and minority students continue to be targets for discriminatory practices. For the most part, special education students receive needed services and extra help while being mainstreamed into courses with other students. Only 4.2% of all special education students have disabilities severe enough to place them in segregated schools or classrooms. Conversely, African American males referred to special education programs are much less likely to end up in mainstream classes. Of those classified as SED, 13.3% are in segregated schools or classrooms along with a 9.8% segregation rate for African American males diagnosed as EMR (Harry & Anderson, 1994).

Special education programs afford schools an opportunity to meet the individual needs of many students. Appropriate academic and program placement allows students to use their time in school more productively than might otherwise be possible. However, students who are inappropriately labeled may experience even worse academic gains than if placed in regular, lower ability tracks because those students may also adapt to more relaxed performance standards imposed by such programs. Although IDEA dictates that special education provide students with an individualized education, many low-income and minority participants do not acquire the skills needed to succeed outside of school (Harry & Anderson, 1994).

Compensatory Education

Compared to gifted and special education, compensatory education programs appear to have few problems with either the underrepresentation or overrepresentation of low-income and minority students. For the most part, the number of disadvantaged students who participate in these programs is not an issue simply because they are the only students enrolled. Like tracking and other related programs, some disparity exists between what compensatory programs are supposed to do and how they actually affect and influence students.

Dating back to the 1960s, compensatory education programs include Chapter 1 (also called Title I), Head Start, Project Follow Through, Even Start and special services for neglected, delinquent and homeless children. The goal of these programs is to improve the education of students who live in economically and educationally disadvantaged areas (Murphy, 1986; Vinovskis, 1999; Watras, 2000). Like other tracking systems, these programs are based on the idea that low-income and minority students are inherently deviant and ill equipped to perform on the same level as affluent, white students. Under the guise that they are helping to improve academic skills, compensatory education programs generally offer them a limited and overly simplified curriculum that actually maintains the achievement gap (Anderson & Pellicer, 1990; Vinovskis, 1999).

Compensatory education programs produce mixed results. One of the most well-known success stories is that of the Perry Preschool in Ypsilanti, Michigan.

A longitudinal study conducted by High/Scope found that African American students who participated in this program were more likely to graduate from high school, less likely to get involved with youth crime and violence, and earned higher incomes as adults than those who did not participate. Indeed, students who attended the Perry Preschool Program in Ypsilanti, Michigan for just one year received a net income benefit of almost $29,000 after an up front cost of only $5,000 (Cooley, 1981; Murphy, 1986; Sweinhart, Barnes & Weikart, 1993; Sweinhart & Weikart, 1980; Vinovskis, 1999).

In addition, Aughinbaugh (2001) also found that participating in Head Start increased high school completion and college attendance rates among white students and decreased the rate of criminal arrests and convictions for African American students. However, these results appear to be more anomalous than normal. The problem does not seem to be whether or not students receive help, but the quality of the instruction and assistance that is provided by compensatory programs.

Similar to mid-range and lower track students in regular schools and programs, children enrolled in compensatory education programs rarely receive the type of instruction they need to make gains these programs portend to provide. If the goal is to help students so they can return to and succeed in regular classes, many compensatory programs are failing since students have a hard time getting out of these programs once assigned to them. Few students improve enough during their first year of enrollment to move up to other levels since 40% to 75% of these students return the next year. Among those who transition out of a compensatory program, as many as 50% earn test scores making them eligible for re-entry within their first year away from these programs (Anderson & Pellicer, 1990). Even when compensatory programs have a positive influence on academic achievement, their students continue to perform below students in regular classes (Vinovskis, 1999). The watered-down curriculum most compensatory programs provide helps students achieve low-level goals quickly without having a lasting (positive) impact on academic performance. Like other forms of tracking, many compensatory education programs trap students by not giving them the skills they need to succeed for the long term.

TEACHING AND THE TRACKING PROCESS

By far the most significant element of the cultural bias dominating the tracking process is that it frequently denies low-income and minority students access to quality teaching. As a factor used to make tracking decisions, teachers' perceptions not only determine the placement of students but also whether they will succeed in their assigned tracks. Therefore, it is critically important to recognize the influence teachers have in tracking and placement of disadvantaged students.

As with standardized testing, the cultural bias exhibited by teachers against low-income and minority students stems from a assumption and use of white cultural norms as the standard. Minority students dominate urban schools and make up over 50% of the population (Agron, 1998). However, 86% of teachers are white (Darling-Hammond, 1995b; Ford, 1998). Although racial differences between teachers and students do not guarantee that bias is present, it does increase a likelihood that bias may occur. In addition, the fact that suburban, white cultural norms often serve as the basis for structuring of teacher education and certification programs suggests that teachers of all racial and ethnic backgrounds are likely to support and perpetuate similar standards.

The cultural bias exhibited by teachers helps influence placement decisions and the quality of urban schools. Poverty, crime, low support, rundown facilities and a general lack of resources at home, at school and in the community inundate many children in urban areas (Agron, 1998; Darling-Hammond, 1995a, 1995b; Ford, 1998; Kozol, 1992). At the same time, these schools also experience extremely high teacher turnover rates and frequent personnel shortages for certified positions (Darling-Hammond, 1995a, 1995b; Ford, 1998; Kozol, 1992; Miller, 2000). Moreover, some urban school districts offer teachers' salaries equivalent to just over half as much as those offered in wealthy, suburban areas (Miller, 2000). Combined with a reputation for poor working conditions and insufficient resources, these low salaries make it difficult for urban schools districts to either attract or keep qualified staff.

Teachers' abilities, attitudes and interests have a much stronger impact on low-income and minority students than they do on other children. Unlike other students, 81% of black females and 62% of black males are most concerned that their academics and classroom behavior please their teachers but not their parents or themselves (Ferguson, 1998). As such, the underachievement of these students is at least partially the result of low performance expectations communicated by their teachers (Ferguson, 1998; Ford, 1998; Murphy, 1986). Even when the giftedness of minority students is recognized, teachers often continue to maintain lower expectations (Ford, 1998). As a result, many of these students cannot perform to the best of their academic abilities because their efforts go unrecognized by their teachers, leading them to simply give up and become the failures that several of their teachers believe them to be (Ferguson, 1998).

Teachers' perceptions affect the tracking and placement of low-income and minority students as well as their academic performance. By establishing low expectations, teachers make it difficult to appropriately place students. This also makes it difficult for students to do well on the standardized tests so heavily weighted in tracking and placement decisions. Regardless of ability, the test performance gap between black and white students increases after they enter school (Phillips, Crouse & Ralph, 1998). Even when black and white children earn equal test scores, black children experience lower academic gains in the future (Ferguson, 1998). Although not solely responsible, this research conclusion suggests that teachers' perceptions of minority students are major causes for the test performance gap between black and white students. When disadvantaged students encounter teachers who have little interest in helping them to succeed, it is difficult for them to do so.

FINANCING FAILURE IN URBAN SCHOOLS

Although tracking and related programs often further disadvantage low-income and minority students, these programs are very valuable to urban school districts. Compared to districts located in suburban areas, urban school districts have much larger student populations that must be educated on much smaller budgets. The impoverished communities that surround these schools do not provide the same level of tax support available in more affluent areas. At the same time, crime, poverty and other elements of city life actually create new expenditures for big-city school districts as they attempt to provide students with a safe and healthy educational environment. Thus, the combination of insufficient funds allotted to these districts and the availability of federal funds for specialized programs may actually serve as an impetus for misplacement of students to help bring more money into poor districts.

The federal structure for special and compensatory education programs makes misplacement especially tempting. Indeed, the 2002 Reauthorization of ESEA actually mandates that urban school districts receive more support and consideration in the distribution of federal funds. In addition, this reauthorization also provides significant increases in monetary support. Under the 2002 Reauthorization of ESEA, federal support for special education programs, as outlined by IDEA, went from to $6.33 billion to $7.53 billion. At the same time, Title I funds rose to $10.35 billion from $8.75 billion in federal allocations. The Title I allocations alone represent significant budget increases for many urban school districts. As a result of changes to Title I programs, urban school districts in Boston, Los Angeles and New York will receive an additional $11 million, $87 million and $143 million, respectively, this year alone (Robelen, 2002).

Conversely, federal support for gifted education programs is not as large as it is for special and compensatory education. Under the Javits Act, the federal government allocated $11.75 million to gifted education programs and research in 2002

(National Association for Gifted Children [NAGC], 2002). Although this amount is the highest federal allocation ever made to these programs, it represents only.16% of the total federal funds devoted to special education and.11% of the funds for Title I. The additional funds allotted to urban districts in Los Angeles and New York far outpace the total amount available for gifted education programs for distribution among the fifty states. Even if urban schools do receive special consideration in grant and allocation decisions, the comparatively small amount of gifted education funds available does not encourage them to make the effort.

CONCLUSION

Tracking and specialized educational programs have proven to be false friends for most low-income and minority students. Although these programs help bring desperately needed funds into impoverished urban school districts, the money is not doing most students any good. These sorting systems actually serve as impediments to student achievement rather than catalysts. Even so, the poor financial conditions affecting urban schools make it impossible for big-city school districts to turn away federal funds that are somewhat easy to acquire. As such, the financial needs of the districts end up competing with the students' needs, and the children are clearly losing.

Bringing well-trained, interested and culturally aware teachers into urban schools would definitely help to alleviate some of the problems caused by tracking and placement procedures. Although urban schools cannot afford to lose the financing associated with these programs, experienced and knowledgeable teachers can help ensure that these programs actually lead to outcomes they have claimed they will be produced. Regardless of their skills and ability levels, teachers must establish and communicate high expectations for all students.

Tracking, limited access to gifted education, low achievement and skill building in special education and compensatory programs, and disinterest on behalf of teachers are just some of the reasons why urban schools are failing to adequately prepare their students. Although students, teachers and administrators in urban schools bear most of the blame for their problems, they are not solely responsible. The funding formula for public schools in most states forces big-city schools to misplace students in order to receive federal funds for specialized programs, while also making it extremely difficult for these schools to utilize either the funds or the programs to effectively remediate students. In this way, urban school districts actually use cultural bias to their financial advantage. However, once these funds reach urban schools, they generally help to perpetuate cultural bias rather than eliminating it. In spite of dramatic increases in federal funds for gifted, special and compensatory education dictated in the 2002 Reauthorization of ESEA, there is little reason to believe that most disadvantaged students will fare better in these programs.

NOTES

1. Green's "The Structure of Inequality: Tracking and Educational Opportunity," Chapter 7 of this volume, provides additional information on the issue of tracking with special attention to equal opportunity, its theoretical context and the overall impact tracking has equity and achievement in America's schools.
2. This may be misleading since the diversity among Asian students is often overlooked.

REFERENCES

Agron, J. (1998, July). The urban challenge. *American School & University*, *70*(11), 18–20.

Anderson, L. W., & Pellicer, L. O. (1990, September). Synthesis of research on compensatory and remedial education. *Educational Leadership*, *48*(1), 10–16.

Aughinbaugh, A. (2001, Fall). Does Head Start yield long-term benefits? *The Journal of Human Resources*, *36*(4), 641–665.

Brown, F., Carter, D. G., & Harris, J. J., III. (1978, June). Minority students, ability grouping and career development. *Journal of Black Studies*, *8*(4), 477–488.

Braddock, J. H., II. (1990). *Tracking: Implications for student race-ethnic subgroups* (Report No. 1). Baltimore, MD: Center for Research on Effective Schooling for Disadvantaged Students. (ERIC Document Reproduction Service No. ED325600).

Cooley, W. W. (1981, January). Effectiveness of compensatory education. *Educational Leadership*, *38*(4), 298–301.

Coutinho, M. J., Oswald, D. P., & Best, A. M. (2002). The influence of sociodemographics and gender on the disproportionate identification of minority students as having learning disabilities. *Remedial and Special Education*, *23*(1), 49–59.

Crosby, M. S., & Owens, E. M. (1993, March). The disadvantages of tracking and ability grouping: A look at cooperative learning as an alternative. *Solutions and Strategies*, *5*, 1–9.

Daniels, V. I. (1998, Spring). Minority students in gifted and special education programs: The case for educational equity. *The Journal of Special Education*, *32*(1), 41–43.

Darling-Hammond, L. (1995a, Summer). Cracks in the bell curve: How education matters. *Journal of Negro Education, 64*(3), 340–353.

Darling-Hammond, L. (1995b). Inequality and access to knowledge. In: J. A. Banks & C. A. M. Banks (Eds), *Handbook of Research on Multicultural Education* (pp. 465–483). New York, NY: Simon & Schuster.

Donelan, R. W., Neal, G. A., & Jones, D. L. (1994, Summer). The promise of Brown and the reality of academic grouping: The tracks of my tears. *Journal of Negro Education*, *63*(3), 376–387.

Ferguson, R. F. (1998). Teachers' perceptions and expectations and the black-white achievement gap. In: C. Jencks & M. Phillips (Eds), *The Black-White Test Score Gap* (pp. 273–317). Washington, D.C.: Brookings Institution Press.

Ford, D. Y. (1995, Winter). Desegregating gifted education: A need unmet. *Journal of Negro Education*, *64*(1), 52–62.

Ford, D. Y. (1998, Spring). The underrepresentation of minority students in gifted education: Problems and promises in recruitment and retention. *The Journal of Special Education*, *32*(1), 4–14.

Ford, D. Y., & Webb, K. S. (1994, Summer). Desegregation of gifted educational programs: The impact of Brown on underachieving children of color. *Journal of Negro Education*, *63*(3), 358–375.

Gardner, H. (1983). *Frames of mind.* New York, NY: Basic Books.

Hallinan, M. T. (1994, April). Tracking: From theory to practice. *Sociology of Education*, *67*(2), 79–84.

Harris, J. J., III, & Ford, D. Y. (1991, Winter). Identifying and nurturing the promise of gifted black American children. *Journal of Negro Education*, *60*(1), 3–18.

Harry, B., & Anderson, M. G. (1994, Autumn). The disproportionate placement of African American males in special education programs: A critique of the process. *Journal of Negro Education*, *63*(4), 602–619.

Henderson, K. (2001, March). *An overview of ADA, IDEA, and section 504: Update 2001* [ERIC digest]. Arlington, VA: ERIC Clearinghouse on Disabilities and Gifted Education. (ERIC Document Reproduction Service No. ED452627).

Hilliard, A. G., III. (1992, Summer). Behavioral style, culture, and teaching and learning. *Journal of Negro Education*, *61*(3), 370–377.

Kershaw, T. (1992, September). The effects of educational tracking on the social mobility of African Americans. *Journal of Black Studies*, *23*(1), 152–169.

Kozol, J. (1992). *Savage inequalities: Children in America's schools.* New York, NY: HarperPerennial.

Lockwood, J. H., & Cleveland, E. F. (1998). *The challenge of detracking: Finding the balance between excellence and equity.* New York, NY: ERIC Clearinghouse on Urban Education.

MacMillan, D. L., & Reschly, D. J. (1998, Spring). Overrepresentation of minority students: The case for greater specificity or reconsideration of the variables examined. *The Journal of Special Education*, *32*(1), 15–24.

Mallery, J. L., & Mallery, J. G. (1999, Fall). The American legacy of ability grouping: Tracking reconsidered. *Multicultural Education*, *7*(1), 13–15.

Marsh, R. S., & Raywid, M. A. (1994, December). How to make detracking work. *Phi Delta Kappan*, *76*(4), 314–317.

Miller, M. (2000, February 28). Short fall. *The New Republic*, *222*(9), 18, 20–21.

Murphy, D. M. (1986, Autumn). Educational disadvantagement: Associated factors, current interventions, and implications. *Journal of Negro Education*, *55*(4), 495–507.

National Association for Gifted Children. (2002, May 30). *NAGC legislative update: We need support for Javits Act funding*. Retrieved June 24, 2002, from http://www.nagc.org/Policy/update.htm

Oakes, J. (1985). *Keeping track: How schools structure inequality.* New Haven, CT: Yale University Press.

Oakes, J. (1994a, April). More than misapplied technology: A normative and political response to Hallinan on tracking. *Sociology of Education*, *67*(2), 84–89.

Oakes, J. (1994b, April). One more thought. *Sociology of Education*, *67*(2), 91.

Oakes, J. (1995, Summer). Two cities' tracking and within-school segregation. *Teachers College Record*, *96*(4), 681–690.

Oakes, J., & Guiton, G. (1995). Matchmaking: The dynamics of high school tracking decisions. *American Educational Research Journal*, *32*(1), 3–33.

Ortiz, A. A. (1997, May/June). Learning disabilities occurring concomitantly with linguistic differences. *Journal of Learning Disabilities*, *30*, 321–332.

Phillips, M., Crouse, J., & Ralph, J. (1998). Does the black-white test score gap widen after children enter school? In: C. Jencks & M. Phillips (Eds), *The Black-White Test Score Gap* (pp. 229–272). Washington, D.C.: Brookings Institution Press.

Robelen, E. R. (2002, January 9). ESEA to boost federal role in education. *Education Week*, *21*(16), 1, 28–29, 31.

Samuda, R. J., Kong, S. L., Cummins, J., Lewis, J., & Pascual-Leone, J. (1991). *Assessment and placement of minority students*. Lewiston, NY: Hogrefe and ISSP. Intercultural Social Sciences Publications.

Slavin, R. E. (1995, November). Detracking and its detractors: Flawed evidence, flawed values. *Phi Delta Kappan*, *77*(3), 220–221.

Sweinhart, L. J., Barnes, H. V., & Weikart, D. P. (1993). *Significant benefits: The High/Scope Perry Preschool study through age 27*. Ypsilanti, MI: High/Scope.

Sweinhart, L. J., & Weikart, D. P. (1980). *Young children grow up: The effects of the Perry Preschool Program on youths through age 15*. Ypsilanti, MI: High/Scope.

U.S. Commissioner of Education (1972). *Education of the gifted and talented: Report to the Congress of the United States by the U.S. Commissioner of Education*. Washington, D.C.: U.S. Government Printing Office.

Vinovskis, M. A. (1999, May). Do federal compensatory education programs really work? A brief historical analysis of Title I and Head Start. *American Journal of Education*, *107*, 187–209.

Watras, J. (2000). The use and abuse of labels: The concept of a culture of poverty and compensatory education. *Educational Foundations*, *14*(3), 63–81.

6. URBAN ECONOMICS AND FINANCIAL FACTORS AFFECTING EDUCATION

Stephen B. Lawton

ABSTRACT

This chapter focuses on urban economies and demographics and how changes in these areas have influenced the roles of local, state, and federal governments in funding schools. Emphasis is placed on the evolution of urban America in the Post World War II era, the role of immigration, and the accumulation of human, social, and cultural capital. Demonstrated shortfalls in both the quality of educational inputs and results have led to court challenges to education funding systems and responses by state legislatures, resulting in systemic reforms affecting both educational institutions and their regulatory environment. A future of greater funding equity but more diverse educational arrangements is anticipated.

INTRODUCTION

The future of urban education is inextricably linked to the future of urban economies: both will succeed or fail together as the evolution of one feeds or starves the other. Urban economies, like urban schools, vary greatly from one state or region to another. Since 1990, some experienced double-digit growth in

Challenges of Urban Education and Efficacy of School Reform, Volume 6, pages 101–120.

ISBN: 0-7623-0426-X

income and population while others stagnated then slipped backwards, each step forward being matched by two steps back. In many, but not all, population growth equates to increased diversity. Too often, stagnate communities are homogeneous minority communities where a hopeful vision, if it comes, is likely to be that of a government subsidized developer ready to raze their homes for a new stadium, convention center or gated town house development. All the while, the local public schools may be viewed as progenitors of failure, abandoned by the few resident middle class parents whose children attend private schools.

In many ways, the story of contemporary American cities begins with the end of World War II and the abandonment of high-density urban development and close-in suburbs served by interurban transit lines that had arrived in cities with electricity. Like the end of the "Red Car" line of the Pacific Electric Company, told humorously in the Hollywood film, *Who Framed Roger Rabbit?*, the end of these transit systems meant the end of an era, as intercity freeways with inner and outer loops encircled and divided cities while connecting them with other conurbations spread across the country. Even defining what "urban" means today is a challenge; often, we have little choice but to refer to what the U.S. Census defines as Consolidated Metropolitan Statistical Areas (CMSA), Metropolitan Statistical Areas (MSA), or Primary Metropolitan Statistical Areas (PMSA).

Living amidst these interconnected transportation systems of the pre- and post-war periods have been three very different populations and cultures. In the pre-war period, the densely populated cities were both the generators and home to economic wealth. Those of means let their presence by known by mansions on grand boulevards; their ideals, during the first third of the century, were expressed in the "Garden City Movement" which sought to make every town and city an American version of Paris. In education, the great central high schools of the era were planted centrally as symbols of civic pride. The post-war vision, in contrast, was one based on escape from crowded urban areas to idyllic suburbs whose reality sometimes fell short of their pastoral portrayal in developers' brochures. High schools, along with post offices, ceased to be civic buildings of stature since these new developments usually lacked a civic component – the town squares of New England or plazas of the Southwest had been cast aside as city centers were replaced by open and closed malls that, ironically, are now built with "town centers." Businesses too relocated to these so-called "ring cities" (in reference to the circular looped freeways encircling the populated – and sometimes unpopulated – areas). These interconnected entities are the CMSAs, MSAs, and PMSAs of the U.S. Census and "cities" or "urban areas" of concern in this chapter, which uses Chicago, New York, Phoenix as contrasting exemplars of current trends.

In the sections that follow, an overview of the economic trends in U.S. urban areas begins with a sketch of demographic and social trends. A key element of the latter is the rate of development of human, social and cultural capital of different kinds. Provided next is description of the trends in fiscal resources available to schools in urban areas from local, state, federal and private resources. These allocations are the outcome of policy decisions by various bodies, executive, legislative and judicial. Many large urban school districts, such as those in New York and Chicago, are fiscally dependent upon their municipal counterparts for local funds unlike most suburban and rural districts that are fiscally independent; i.e. that retain the power to set local tax rates. Often, it will be seen, courts of law rather than governors, legislatures, city councils or mayors are most accommodating of pleas from urban districts. Finally, new structures and methods for translating fiscal resources into educational services are briefly discussed, including administrative strategies imposed by state and municipal governments. Several of these alternatives, including vouchers and privatization, are the topic of other chapters but are introduced here to close the loop with the local economy since increased efficiency and educational effectiveness are invariably the goal of these initiatives.

URBAN ECONOMICS

The 1990s were a time of rapid economic growth in virtually all parts of the United States, urban as well as rural. Overall, between 1998 and 1999, the total personal income of Americans increased an astounding 5.4%. Even the laggards, areas like Philadelphia and Cleveland, experience income growth over 3%; that is, a growth rate slightly greater than inflation. Urban centers such as New York, Los Angeles, Chicago and Phoenix experienced slightly higher growth that was in the 5% to 7% range. Leading the pack, driven by their silicon supported stock options, were places like San Francisco, Seattle and San Jose, all of which experienced double-digit income growth (Table 1). Subsequent events, including the bursting of the technology bubble and the start of a recession, reduced these exceptional rates of increase; nevertheless they reflect not just the boom of the 1990s but also the success of public and private educational institutions that were critical agents in the development of the human capital that put technological development into overdrive, if only for a brief moment.

Rates of income growth tell of both the past and future. High rates speak of vitality, innovations, change, creativity and, admittedly, recklessness. Low rates – or negative rates – imply the opposite: a slumbering embrace of routine as entropy slowly dissipates the social, economic and physical resources accumulated during

Table 1. Personal Income and Income Growth for Urban Areas, 1998-1999.

Metropolitan area ranked by total 1999 regional income	1999 per capita personal income	Percent of national average	Percent income growth, 1998–1999
United States	28,546	100.0	5.4
New York-No. New Jersey-Long Island	38,539	135.0	5.6
Los Angeles-Riverside-Orange County	28,050	98.3	5.6
Chicago-Gary-Kensoha	33,857	118.6	4.8
San Franciso-Oakland-San Jose	40,858	143.1	10.3
Washington-Baltimore	35,797	125.4	6.8
Boston-Worcester-Lowell-Brockton	36,285	127.1	7.3
Philadelphia-Wilmington-Atlantic City	32,397	113.5	4.5
Detroit-Ann Arbor-Flint	31,140	109.1	5.4
Dallas-Forth Worth	32,482	113.8	7.0
Houston-Galveston-Brazoria	31,543	110.5	4.9
Atlanta	32,486	113.8	7.9
Seattle-Tacoma-Bremerton	35,052	122.8	8.9
Minneapolis-St. Paul	35,250	123.5	6.0
Miami-Fort Lauderdale	26,682	93.5	4.5
Cleveland-Akron	29,905	104.8	3.7
Denver-Boulder-Greeley	35,318	123.7	8.6
Phoenix-Mesa	27,617	96.7	7.2
San Diego	29,489	103.3	8.3
St. Louis	30,382	106.4	3.9
New Haven-Bridgport-Stamford-Danbury-Waterbury	45,267	158.6	5.0
Riverside-San Bernadino	22,060	77.3	6.8
Pittsburgh	29,587	103.6	5.0
Portland-Salem	29,645	103.7	5.5
Tampa-St. Petersburg-Clearwater	28,145	98.6	5.3
Cincinnati-Hamilton	29,485	103.3	5.0
Kansas City	30,225	105.9	6.3
Milwaukee-Racine	31,457	110.2	4.8
Sacramento-Yolo	28,568	100.1	7.1
Indianapolis	30,523	106.9	5.4

Source: *Statistical Abstract of the United States*, 2001, p. 428.

past periods of growth. Yesterday was more lively than today; today is more vital than tomorrow.

Also critical of course is the level of income, as opposed to the rate of growth in income. Although by no means a perfect correlation, some of the metropolitan areas that experienced high rates of income growth in the late 1990s also enjoyed the highest per capita incomes – San Francisco at $49,695, 174% of the national average; San Jose at $46,649, 163% of the average; and Seattle at $39,880 or 140% of the average. In contrast, slow-growth cities like Philadelphia and Cleveland had per capita incomes of $32,397 and $29,905, and 34743 – 114% and 105% of the national average – well below those of the middle-growth cities of New York and Chicago ($38,814 or 136% and $33,857 or 119% of the national average). Los Angeles and Phoenix, although experiencing above-average income growth, have per capita incomes below the national average at $28,050 (98%) and $27,627 (97%) respectively, indicating resource levels more akin to those of slow-growth eastern cities than their northerly West Coast brethren.

URBAN DEMOGRAPHICS

The redesign of American cities in the post-war period was accompanied by a resettlement of populations that, combined with secular trends related to family formation and family structures, increasingly differentiated central cities from suburbs – the vast tracks of developments arrayed along interstate freeways. The wave of rural migration to urban conurbations, especially African-Americans from the South to dominantly European-American cities in the North, Midwest and West, began during World War II as the industrial expansion accompanying the defense build-up created a demand for labor that attracted new populations including minorities and women to roles from which they previously had been excluded. As well, the Puerto Rican migration to the East Coast and Hispanic inflows to the West increased. Immigration, which had virtually ceased during the Depression of the 1930s, was boosted by the admission of millions of European refugees in after the war, but this source of potential new citizens vanished as birthrates in Europe declined below the replacement level. In the 1960s, changes in immigration laws opened America's doors to persons from all nations and backgrounds. Supported by a philosophy of multiculturalism and a capitalistic belief that a growing population is needed for a growing economy, both in terms of demand for goods and supply of labor, legal immigrants have come in growing numbers: 4.5 million in the 1960s, 7.0 million in the 1980s, and over 9 million in the 1990s (McDonnell, 2002). Millions of illegal immigrants – just how many is unclear – supplemented this vast relocation.

The impact on U.S. cities of recent immigration from other nations is highly variable. Rapidly growing areas, particularly those on the East and West Coasts, have attracted most new residents, creating an incredible diversity of race, language, religion and talent. Slower growing areas, in contrast, often exhibit a concentration of lower income African-Americans who were part of the internal migration during and after the war. Urban schools in many parts of New York or Los Angeles may be all non-white yet, in some neighborhoods, all children are first generation Americans while in others African-American families have lived in the community for generations. In cities like Cleveland, Ohio and Rochester, New York only the latter group is found in large numbers: new immigrants have not come and Americans of European ancestry have followed the freeways to distant suburbs, gated communities, and rural solitude. Some do return, gentrifying neighborhoods and displacing low-income residents, but rarely remain to raise families or send their children to public schools (Weissmann, 2002).

The impact of demographic trends and, no doubt, the sorting of families between public and private schooling options, are evident in the ethnocultural statistics for metropolitan school systems. New York City public schools enroll approximately 1.1 million students, 37% of whom are of Latino, 35% African-American, 16% White, 12% Asian-American and less than 1% Native American. Students speak more than 170 different languages and about 15% of all students have limited English proficiency (LEP). One in eleven students is a recent immigrant. Many of these students are poor: in the 1998–99 school year, 442,000 of the 1,093,071 students came from families receiving Aid to Families with Dependent Children and 73% of the K-6 students were eligible for free lunches, compared to 5% in the remainder of the State (*Campaign for Fiscal Equity v. The State of New York*, 2001; hereafter referred to as *CFE v. NY*).

Statistics for Chicago Public Schools, which with 435,470 of students is less than half the size of the New York City system, are similar, although the concentration of African-American's is greater and fewer Whites and Asian children attend the system. Overall, 52% of Pre-school to 12th students are African-American, 35% Latino, 10% White, and 3% Asian/Pacific Islander. As in New York, most – 86% – come from low-income families and a 14% are limited in their English proficiency. The schools are staffed by both White and non-White faculty and administrators: 53% of principals are African-American, 35% White, 15% Latino, and 2% Asian or Native American; 42% of teachers are African-American, 45% White, 11% Latino, 2% Asian, and less than 1% Native American (http://www.cps.k12.il.us/CPS_at_a_Glance/cps_at_a_glance.html, 2002).

Phoenix provides a very different profile both ethnically and jurisdictionally. Unlike New York and Chicago – or even its smaller sister-city Tucson – it does not have a single major school district serving the municipalities residents. Instead, two dozen elementary, secondary, and unified districts spill across municipal lines. In a study of the rapid growth in metropolitan Phoenix, the Morrison Institute for Public Policy at Arizona State University portrayed a "deepening divide" as different populations settle in different parts of the "Valley of the Sun": in south Phoenix, the percentage of minority population increased from 47% in the 1970s to 77% in the 1990s; the percentage minority in the City of Phoenix increased from 22% to 36%; while in the more wealthy East Valley suburbs (Chandler, Glendale, Mesa, Scottsdale and Tempe) minorities increased from 13% to 22%. In central and south Phoenix, 36% of the population is in poverty vs. 10% in the five largest suburbs. In central and southwest Phoenix, students score at the 34th percentile on standardized tests vs. the 66th percentile for those in the eastern suburbs. One south Phoenix school district, the Roosevelt Elementary School District, which figured in a major court case discussed later, reports 17% Black, 4% White, 78% Hispanic, 1% Native American and one-tenth of 1% Asian (Roosevelt School District No. 66, 2001). The Phoenix Union High School District, which serves central and south Phoenix including the area served by Roosevelt, reports 69% Hispanic, 16% Anglo, 10% African-American, 3% Native American and 2% Asian (http://www.phxhs.k12.az.us/district/statistical_profile.htm, 2002).

Economically and demographically, urban America has become a different nation from suburban and rural America: it is less wealthy and more diverse. These differences are magnified in the public school systems, where students are more likely than the population as a whole to be poor and members of a minority group.

HUMAN, SOCIAL AND CULTURAL CAPITAL

Accompanying economic and demographic shifts in urban centers are changes in the non-material but nevertheless potentially valuable assets of the population. Several overlapping and variously defined concepts are useful in this regard: human, social, and cultural capital. The first, used by economist for over a half century and foretold even in the work of Adam Smith more than two centuries ago, is the notion of human capital – the knowledge and skills developed through experience, formal education or training that allow one to participate in and profit from a market economy. The concept parallels the notion of physical capital, resident in machines and structure, and financial capital that takes the form of accumulated wealth whose value can be realize through investment in physical capital. The most common method used by economists to measure human capital is years of schooling. An individual or group with more years of education than another is expected to outperform others in earning wages because they possess value-adding skills and knowledge that can be devoted to the tasks at hand. Conversely, a region with a high proportion of school dropouts would be identified as one in which the accumulation of human capital is declining. Recently, greater emphasis also has been placed on student test scores as a measure of human capital in the belief that simply completing a year of school is not sufficient evidence that learning has taken place. The validity of this newer measure, although widely endorsed and the foundation of the current emphasis on state and local testing, is nevertheless questioned: research actually linking test scores with higher earnings, all other things being equal, is scanty (Levin, 1993). Nevertheless, it is reasonable to treat all three variables – years of education, dropout rates, and test scores – as valid indices of human capital.

James Coleman and others developed a complementary notion referred to as social capital that refers to the social networks of trust, solidarity and reciprocity that exist among members of a community. At is most elemental level the strength of family and kinship ties indicate the level of social capital; more inclusively it may refer to a civic body in which there exist many cross-linked organizational ties and shared common beliefs. Measures of social capital would include the proportion of families with both parents in the home, the proportion of families with other family members in the community, and the numbers of religious and other institutions supported by community members. Typically, high levels of social capital support the acquisition of human capital because other persons are present to guide, assist, and promote individuals as they develop a life beyond the walls of the home.

Cultural capital, a term used by French sociologist Pierre Bourdieu, may refer to all forms of immaterial capital, including human and social capital, or be restricted to immaterial cultural elements acquired or available to individuals that fall outside the scope of the two preceding concepts. It is this sense that it is used here to include, especially, ethnocultural knowledge and traditions that are valued by specific groups and communities but not immediately convertible into economic advantage. Examples of such cultural capital include, in the United States, languages other than English, traditional foods, formal and informal religious practices, and the like. Typically, such cultural capital is not valued and is often ignored or even suppressed by formal public institutions, including schools. Forbidding children to speak a language other than English at school is one common example, as is celebration, say, of St. Patrick's Day in a school the is mostly Asian while Lunar New Year Celebrations are overlooked.

The human, social and cultural capital of urban school districts can be assessed by considering both student and teacher variables. Human capital accumulated by students is indicated by measures such as graduation or dropout rates and test scores; their social capital by the percentage that live in single parent homes; and their cultural capital by counts of languages spoken or the vitality of cultural and social institutions operating outside the formal structures instituted by government agencies. Development of students' human capital is very dependent upon that of their tutors; factors such as the proportion of fully certificated teachers, the proportion of secondary teachers instructing in their specialty areas, the absentee rate among teachers, and the availability of skilled substitute teachers.

In New York City, about 30% of all students who enter the 9th grade to not graduate. Although a third of these eventually obtain GEDs (i.e. passing the test of General Education Development), according to Henry Levin of Teachers College Columbia, "GED recipients are the functional equivalents of dropouts" (*CFE v. NY*, p. 34) in that the armed services do not accept individuals with GEDs and fewer than 2% of those with GEDs who attend college ever graduate. The relatively low rate of accumulating human capital was confirmed in standard tests: "21.3% of the City's fourth graders scored at level one [the lowest for four levels] . . . while only 5.8% of fourth grade student in the rest of the State scored in level one" (*CFE v. NY*, p. 37). One factor accounting for this situation may be the human capital of their teachers: approximately 10 to 14% of the City's district public school teachers lack certification and about 20% taught outside their area of certification vs. a statewide average of 9%. "BOE records show that as of October 1, 1999, 476 uncertified teachers taught high school biology, 152 taught high school chemistry, and 435 taught high school mathematics" (*CFE v. NY*, p. 15). The New York Supreme Court inferred that the last statistic means that "54,375 students were taught high school mathematics by an uncertified teacher" (Ibid.).

Chicago's public schools exhibit similar difficulties in ensuring the city's youth develop economically valued knowledge and skills. Dropout rates for the 1994–2000 cohort varied from 16% for Asian-Americans to 46% for African-Americans, with Latinos (39%) and Whites (34%) between these extremes. Consistently, male dropout rates (46%) exceeded those for females (38%). That for African-American males exceeded 50% (Allensworth and Easton, 2001). Test scores for Chicago students lag somewhat behind national norms, as measured by the Iowa Test of Basic Skills (ITBS): at age 14 (i.e. 9th grade), females scored at the grade equivalent levels of 8.21 in reading and 8.32 in math vs. 8.02 and 8.30 for males (Easton, et al., 2000). Similarly, the Phoenix Union High School District reports an 8% annual dropout rate and 55% graduation rate; the Morrison Institute study reports that students score at the 33rd percentile in central and southwest quadrants of the metropolitan Phoenix area.

In spite of high dropout rates and below-average test scores, there have been recent improvements in both New York City and Chicago. Test scores in both cities have increased. In Chicago, at age 14 males now score almost one full grade equivalent higher in reading than they did in 1992; a similar although somewhat more modest increase of 0.86 grade equivalent occurred on their math scores. Females gained 0.71 grade equivalents for both reading and math. Central Phoenix, too, has experienced improvement: the Phoenix Union High School district dropout rate, at 8%, is half what it was in the mid-1990s and its graduation rate has climbed by 8%, from 51% to 55%. As well, there is a tremendous amount of hidden cultural capital in our urban areas: students in New York City's public schools district speak almost 180 different languages. James McBride's autobiographical portrait, *The Color of Water* (McBride, 1996), a Black man's tribute to his white mother, suggests the kind of possibilities that exist underneath the often bleak statistics.

REVENUE FOR SCHOOLS

In the first half of the last century, wealth was concentrated in America's urban areas where modern educational systems developed by creating a vast array of programs, including Kindergarten, special education and adult continuing education. Today, political and economic power has shifted the ring cities and exurbs, the latter being close-in rural areas beyond suburbia (Alltucker, 2001). Consequently, urban areas find themselves unable to fund the types of educational services needed to improve the caliber of teaching staff, school programs and student performance.

Layers of federal, state and local rules often work at cross purposes as they direct and redirect funds as on their way into districts, schools and classrooms (Wong, 1999). In 1959, states on average funded 38% of educational expenditures, local districts contributed 57% and the federal government 5% (op. cit., p. 46); in 1998–1999, states provided 48.7%, local districts 41.7%, the federal government 7.1% and private parties 2.5% (National Center for Educational Statistics, 2002, Table 158). According to Wong (1999) an inverse relationship exists between the level of government providing funds and the degree to which funds are targeted at youth with higher needs. Local wealth tends to be inversely related to need: more wealthy districts tend have students with lower levels of need. State funds are somewhat more targeted, equalizing to a degree the wealth of districts; and federal funds are closely tied to student needs. Table 2 provides for each state an overview of the share of funding from each level of government and the average expenditure per pupil in attendance.

State shares vary from a high of 87.8% in Hawaii, with only a half of 1% generated locally, to New Hampshire, where 84.7% is local and just 8.9% is state. Federal funding varies from 13.8% in Alaska (omitting the District of Columbia's 16.8% and even higher percentages in "Outlying Areas" including Puerto Rico

Table 2. Revenues for Elementary and Secondary Schools, 1998–1999.

State	Percent federal	Percent state	Percent local and intermediate	Private
United States	7.1	48.7	41.7	2.5
Alabama	9.1	61.6	24.1	5.2
Alaska	13.8	61.0	22.5	2.7
Arizona	10.0	43.2	44.1	2.7
Arkansas	10.2	57.8	26.2	5.7
California	8.6	59.3	30.9	1.1
Colorado	5.1	42.5	48.0	4.4
Connecticut	4.0	39.0	54.4	2.7
Delaware	7.4	64.3	27.1	1.2
District of Columbia	16.5	na	83.1	0.4
Florida	7.9	50.3	39.3	3.5
Georgia	6.7	49.1	42.4	1.7
Hawaii	9.8	87.8	0.5	1.8
Idaho	7.1	61.5	29.7	1.7
Illinois	7.2	30.1	60.6	2.2
Indiana	5.0	52.5	39.7	2.8
Iowa	5.6	50.5	38.5	5.4
Kansas	6.1	61.6	29.6	2.7
Kentucky	9.2	61.8	26.6	2.4
Louisiana	11.5	50.4	35.8	2.3
Maine	7.5	45.9	45.5	1.1
Maryland	5.5	39.5	52.0	3.1
Massachusetts	5.0	42.1	51.6	1.4
Michigan	7.1	64.7	26.2	2.1
Minnesota	5.0	57.6	34.3	3.1
Mississippi	14.0	54.9	27.7	3.4
Missouri	6.5	39.0	50.5	4.0
Montana	11.3	44.9	39.5	4.3
Nebraska	6.9	37.1	50.8	5.2
Nevada	4.6	32.4	59.4	3.6
New Hampshire	4.0	8.9	84.7	2.4
New Jersey	3.7	41.3	52.7	2.2
New Mexico	13.4	72.5	11.9	2.1
New York	6.0	42.2	50.9	0.9
North Carolina	6.9	68.7	21.9	2.6
North Dakota	13.0	40.3	41.4	5.3
Ohio	5.8	42.1	48.4	3.8
Oklahoma	9.1	60.2	25.5	5.2
Oregon	7.0	56.8	32.7	3.5
Pennsylvania	6.0	38.2	53.9	1.9
Rhode Island	5.6	41.6	51.5	1.3
South Carolina	8.2	52.1	35.5	4.2
South Dakota	10.5	35.9	50.7	2.9
Tennessee	8.8	47.2	37.0	7.0

Table 2. Continued.

State	Percent federal	Percent state	Percent local and intermediate	Private
Texas	8.5	42.2	46.7	2.5
Utah	7.0	61.1	29.4	2.4
Vermont	5.8	74.4	18.0	1.8
Virginia	5.2	33.8	57.8	3.1
Washington	6.8	64.6	26.3	3.3
West Virginia	8.5	62.7	27.5	1.2
Wisconsin	4.6	53.4	39.8	2.2
Wyoming	7.4	52.3	38.5	1.7
Outlying Areas				
American Samoa	74.3	19.3	6.3	0.1
Northern Marianas	29.3	70.2	0.3	0.2
Puerto Rico	27.7	72.3	na	na
Virgin Islands	18.5	na	81.3	0.1

Source: National Center for Educational Statistics (NCES), 2002.

with 27.7%) to 3.7% in New Jersey. Table 3 focuses on the federal role in the U.S.'s ten largest school districts and Hawaii's statewide system. Federal percentages range from a low of 4.4% for Clark County Nevada, home to Las Vegas and a poverty rate of 14%, to a high of 13.4% for Chicago which has a 31% poverty rate for youth ages 5 to 17 years old. The average federal percentage for the ten city districts is 9.3%, almost one-third greater than the national average (NCES, 2002, Table 94).

The federal role in education is carried out under the "general welfare" clause of the *U.S. Constitution* since education was not referenced in the document and the Tenth Amendment reserved other matters "to the states respectively, or to the people." Today, state constitutions include requirements for state provision of a form of free public education. Hence, although urban school districts may appeal and lobby for federal funds, they know that the states have plenary power over education and are thus the primary agents responsible addressing the well being of urban school systems. When urban centers were the primary source of wealth (as is yet the case in Nevada), relying on local revenue was to urban schools' advantage. Today, this is no longer the case. As the tables have turned, however, state legislators have not generally rushed to their cities' aid. Increasingly, urban school systems have turned to the courts for leverage.

Two state court cases, one in New York and one in Arizona, illustrate the use of the courts as a legislature of last resort, so to speak. Wirt and Kirst (2001, p. 285) comment that, "The courts are involved in areas that scholars debate – how to measure educational adequacy and how to relate finance to

Table 3. Enrollment, Poverty and Federal Funds for 10 of the Largest School Districts, 2001–2002.

District	Enrollment fall 1999	Poverty rate for 5–17 year olds 1996–1997	Total revenue 1997–1998	Federal 1997–1998	Federal as percent of total	Federal revenue per student 1997–1998	Revenue per student: 97–98 revenue/ 1999 enrollment
New York City, NY	1,075,710	34.9	$9,155,552,000.00	$870,540,000.00	9.5	$812.00	$8,511.17
Los Angeles Unified, CA	710,007	36.0	$4,923,865,000.00	$454,297,000.00	9.2	$668.00	$6,934.95
City of Chicago, IL	431,750	30.6	$3,083,835,000.00	$412,494,000.00	13.4	$983.00	$7,142.64
Dade County, FL	360,138	26.1	$2,557,027,000.00	$202,952,000.00	7.9	$587.00	$7,100.13
Broward County, FL	241,094	15.9	$1,552,136,000.00	$99,409,000.00	6.4	$442.00	$6,437.89
Clark County, NV	217,526	14.2	$1,223,364,000.00	$54,219,000.00	4.4	$284.00	$5,623.99
Houston ISD, TX	209,716	30.6	$1,197,041,000.00	$123,456,000.00	10.3	$585.00	$5,707.91
Philadelphia City, PA	205,199	28.6	$1,554,208,000.00	$182,186,000.00	11.7	$856.00	$7,574.15
Hawaii Dept. of Ed.	185,860	14.5	$1,279,125,000.00	$107,149,000.00	8.4	$564.00	$6,882.20
Detroit City, MI	167,124	39.7	$1,420,219,000.00	$147,128,000.00	10.4	$842.00	$8,498.00
Dallas ISD, TX	160,477	30.0	$940,014,000.00	$95,848,000.00	10.2	$608.00	$5,857.62

Source: National Center for Educational Statistics (NCES) (2002). *Digest of education statistics*. http://nces.ed.gov/pubs2002/2002130b.pdf Table 94. Enrollment, poverty, and federal funds for the 100 largest school districts: 1996–97, 1997–98, 1999, and 2001–02.

pupil attainment?" They also comment on the similarities that exist "between what courts and legislatures do. Formal litigation seems different from the sweaty legislative committee rooms or boisterous chambers, but the differences are only matters of form" (Ibid., pp. 286–287).

In *Campaign for Fiscal Equity v. State of New York*, the issue became not just one of equity, but also one of adequacy: what does constitute a sound basic education in the 21st century? In his judicial opinion, State Supreme Court Justice Leland DeGrasse of Manhattan rejected the arguments that the problem with New York City schools was one of efficiency and effectiveness in the use of adequate and equitable funding, a position taken by a number of neo-conservative economists such as Eric Hanushek, who is noted for his 1981 article "Throwing Money at Schools" in which he concluded there was little or no relationship between the amount school districts spend on education and the outcomes of schooling as measured by test scores, graduation rates and the like. Instead, Justice DeGrasse attended to the differences between New York City and surrounding high-income counties in which class sizes were smaller, teachers better trained, the buildings newer, and administration more systematic. The judge endorsed the traditional notion of a production function for schooling in which the amount and quality of inputs effects the amount and quality of outputs. Specifically, the court found, "Effective teachers and school administrators can boost student performance. . . . Smaller class sizes can have a marked positive effect on student performance, particularly in early grades. . . . [B]etter school facilities can boost student achievement by providing students with the resources they need, such as up-to-date science labs, adequate climate control, and sufficient electrical capacity for computers and other instructional aids" (*CFE v. NY*, pp. 42–43). In a battle of statisticians, Robert Berne of New York University convinced the court that "minority students receive less State aid as their overall concentration increases in a particular district" (p. 61). The court found that "wealth equalization can do actual harm, where, as in the case of New York State, it is not coupled with funding mechanisms that effectively take account of differences in districts' student need" (p. 62).

In fact, in 1999–2000, New York City public schools spent less per pupil than the average district in the state. According to the Educational Priorities Panel (2002), the average expenditures of the top one-fifth of fiscally independent school districts (i.e. of all districts except Buffalo, Rochester, Syracuse, Albany and New York City) spent 60% more per pupil than did New York City – $15,984 per pupil vs. $9,921 per pupil – a difference "amplified by the fact that New York [City] is in a high cost region and has a high concentration of students with special needs." The Court concluded that the state, with its plenary powers over education, could not let the needs of the City's public school student go unmet and that the state must provide: "(1) Sufficient numbers of qualified teachers, principals and other personnel. (2) Appropriate class sizes. (3) Adequate and accessible school buildings with sufficient space to ensure appropriate class size and implementation of a sound curriculum. (4) Sufficient and up-to-date books, supplies, libraries, educational technology and laboratories. (5) Suitable curriculum, including an expanded platform of programs to help at risk student by giving them 'more time on task.' (6) Adequate resources for students with extraordinary needs. (7) A safe orderly environment." Not surprisingly, given this remedy, the court also declared that the state's "method for funding education . . . violates . . . The Education Article of the New York State Constitution" (pp. 65–66). Finally, the court ordered the state to place reforms of school financing and governance in place by September 15, 2001, a date since put aside when the state appealed the case to the Appellate Court, beyond which there is the New York State Court of Appeals, the highest court in the state (New York State Unified Court System, 2002). Regardless of its final outcome, the decision, along with that in *Abbott v. Burke* in New Jersey, stands as a hallmark of contemporary debate about educational adequacy in urban education.

The outcome of *Roosevelt v. Bishop*, in which Roosevelt School District took on the State of Arizona, is already clear. The district won its case by convincing the Arizona Supreme Court – which is the highest court in Arizona – that the state's system for funding the construction of new schools, which put virtually the whole burden on local property tax payers, violated the state constitution's education clause, Article XI, which requires a "general and uniform public school system." The legislature, after several years of debate, false starts, and a judicial threat to close all schools by forbidding the state to fund them (Jones-Sanpei, 1998), finally enacted StudentsFIRST, an initiative to ensure adequate school facilities across the state (Lawton & Schilling, 2002).

> The court relied on the state's requirements for course-work and its competency standards to conclude that the financing scheme did not enable all districts to provide the facilities and equipment necessary to give their students the opportunity to meet the state standards . . . . To meet the court's requirements for a constitutional system, the legislature and governor moved responsibility for funding school construction and other capital items away from local districts to the state and phased out those local property taxes used to support capital expenditures. The new law created a School Facilities Board to administer the system and directed the Board to include technology, transportation, and the facilities and equipment necessary and appropriate to achieve the state's academic standards in its facilities guidelines (ACCESS, 2002).

Under StudentsFIRST, the state has assumed responsibility for setting the standards for new school buildings, for maintaining school buildings, and for bringing existing buildings up to state standards. Yet, these standards leave some still feeling disadvantaged: "The Higley Unified School District had $23 million to spend on its first high school [for 1,700 students] .... Yet it lacks some of the amenities many [suburban] ... schools have taken for granted. There's no auditorium for drama performances ..., no racquetball courts, a limited number of chemistry labs and nothing special about the 'modern-industrial' look of the building." The problem, the superintendent explained, is "with the formula is that one size does not fit all" (Hopkins, 2002). While some suburban boards may still be able to convince voters to levy override taxes to build auditoriums and racket ball courts, districts in some older urban areas, remote rural communities, and rapidly growing bedroom communities may not. Nevertheless, the court made clear in its judgment that, "nothing in the constitution prohibits a school financing system that allows districts to go above and beyond state-mandated adequate facilities by individually accessing local financing sources .... Indeed, we have noted that 'local control' is a historically important value that may contribute to the overall effectiveness of the public school system .... Financial disparities caused by local control do not run afoul of the state constitution because ... the ability to go above and beyond the state system is the key to local control ....' Financial disparities caused by "[f]actors such as parental influence, family involvement, a free market economy, and housing patterns are beyond the reach of the 'uniformity' required by art. XI, [of the state constitution.]. But the general and uniform requirement will not tolerate a state funding mechanism that itself causes disparities between districts" (*Hull v. Albrecht*, 1998).

Unlike *CFE v. State of New York*, in *Roosevelt v. Bishop* the court did not try to prescribe a standard but chose to review the constitutionality of each solution proposed by the legislature. The Court finally found one it liked. It is ironic that a small urban district in Arizona, a state known for its right-to-work, free-market ideology and as home to more charter schools than any other state, managed to leverage the court system in order to create a state funded and managed uniform capital allocation system, while America's largest school district, located in a state known for a strong centralist character by virtue if its Board of Regents, is still fighting its cause in the state courts.

LINKING RESOURCES TO EFFECTIVENESS AND EQUITY

The approaches to addressing urban school needs endorsed by the courts in both *Roosevelt v. Bishop* and *CFE vs. State of New York* might be termed liberal solutions in that they endorse a more uniform allocation of resources by the state authority. Invariably, liberal solutions are delivered through organizations rather than through markets. They specify better inputs – higher quality teachers and buildings – and alternative modes of delivery – year-round schooling, preschools, tutoring, and the like. An alternative approach depends on market control rather than control by means of organizational mandates and emphasize typical initiatives such as charter schools, open enrollment, magnet schools, privatization, vouchers and tax credits. In practice, these sorts of initiatives have been more the purview of governors and legislatures rather than the courts. In *Governing America's Schools: Changing the Rules*, the Education Commission of the States foresees two types of publicly funded schools systems, one publicly operated and one independently operated (1999). This dichotomy captures the alternative paths of reform that often are portrayed not as opposites but rather as complements.

Provocatively, another school finance and governance case wending its way through the Arizona courts may test whether charter schools – and other neo-conservative, market-based approaches to reform – meet the "general and uniform" clause of the state constitution (Sowers, 2002). Also notable was the omission of charter schools from the StudentsFIRST legislative initiative that settled *Roosevelt v. Bishop*. If charter schools withstand the "general and uniform" test as independently operated public schools operating in parallel to those operated by public school boards, does it not follow that they merit the equivalent access to capital resources? In addition, at the federal level, the Cleveland voucher case (*Zelman v. Simmons-Harris*, No. 001751) was considered by the U.S. Supreme Court which decided in favor of the constitutionality of the provision of vouchers to parents, 99.4% of whom have decided to send their children to religious schools. That is, it found such vouchers do not violate the separation of church ensured by the first amendment to the U.S. Constitution which states, "Congress shall make no law respecting an establishment of religion, or prohibiting the free exercise thereof . . ." (Greenhouse, 2002).

Both organizational reforms and market reforms have similar purposes: to promote the effectiveness and, sometimes, efficiency of schooling. While ends are similar, the means and the alignment of interests that support the competing means differ. Market reforms, it should be emphasized, tap administrative, market and value-based solutions, which include the choice of religiously oriented schools, whereas organizational reform of public school districts tap administrative solutions and civic values. Detailed analyses of these strategies for change are treated in depth elsewhere in this volume.

CONCLUSION

Urban America has experience a dramatic shift in population and economic prowess in the period since World War II, a shift that has been fueled in many regions by the acceleration of immigration in the past decade. The love-hate relationship with central cities – loved as a place to work or play but despised as a place to live – does not seem about to change for family-oriented Americans who have the financial choice to live elsewhere. Nevertheless, there is evidence that the impact of financial and administrative reforms initiated by courts and legislatures have had positive effects.

One striking feature of many reforms is the extent to which outside groups have, for better or worse, come to see urban school systems as laboratories for experimentation. Legal cases and legislative initiatives focused on school finance have been transformed into administrative and systemic reforms targeting urban centers. To be sure, initiatives such as charter schools and statewide testing cover all districts, but many actions suggest that it is urban education that is most in need of reform. Whether urban parents and children are positively disposed to these actions is another question; that most teachers and administrators are opposed is evident.

Perhaps it is time for school finance reform, including relevant court cases, to return to their beginnings and to focus on equitable allocation of funds rather than mandated tinkering with administrative processes. Questions of means are too uncertain and variable in their effects to assume that there is one best solution. Also, federal resources, more than state and local funds, are targeted at high need students, suggesting that the federal government must play a greater role in achieving higher levels of equity and adequacy of funding within and among urban areas. Given that the federal government controls immigration, which is the major factor driving change in urban schools, it is incumbent upon it to bear a greater financial responsibility.

How courts will react to the notion of parallel publicly funded school structures, as envisioned by the Educational Commission of the States, is uncertain. While the convictions that built and maintained public school districts for a century and half remain deeply held, the possibility that alternative approaches and the successes they could brings might be excluded seems inappropriate for a nation composed largely of immigrants and entrepreneurs who share an optimistic commitment to "life, liberty and the pursuit of happiness."

Jane Jacobs, in *The Economy of Cities*, concludes that in the future, "cities will not be smaller, simpler or more specialized. . . . Rather they will be more intricate, comprehensive, diversified, and larger . . . and will have even more complicated jumbles of old and new things. . . . The bureaucratized, simplified cities, so dear to . . . city planners and urban designers . . . run counter to the processes of city growth and economic development. Conformity and monotony . . . are not attributes of developing and economically vigorous cities . . ." (1970, p. 251). One can surmise that the schools in such cities necessarily will be as diverse as the opportunities open to their citizens.

REFERENCES

Abbot v. Burke (153 N. J. 480). *http://lawlibrary.rutgers.edu/courts/supreme/a-155–97.opn.html*

ACCESS (Advocacy Center for Educational Success with Standards) (2002). Retrieved March 3, 2002, from http://www.accessednetwork.org/litigation/lit_az.html

Allensworth, E., & Easton, J. Q. (2001, July). *CPS dropout rates by race and gender: Addendum to calculating a cohort dropout rate for the Chicago Public Schools*. Chicago, IL: Consortium on Chicago School Research.

Alltucker, K. (2001, March 25). Welcome to the exurbs: Farther-out rural areas attract new residents. *The Cincinnati Enquirer* [On-line]. Retrieved March 3, 2002, from http://enquirer.com/editions/2001/03/25/loc_welcome_to_exhurbs.html

Education Commission of the States (1999, November). *Governing America's schools: Changing the rules*. Denver: Author.

Greenhouse, L. (2002, February 21). Cleveland's school vouchers weighed by Supreme Court. *The New York Times* (Vol. CLI, No. 52,036), A1, A21.

Jacobs, J. (1970). *The economy of cities*. New York, NY: Vintage Books.

Jones-Sanpei, Hinckley A. (1998) Roosevelt v. Bishop: Balancing local interests with state equity interests in school financing. *BYU Education and Law Journal* [On-line]. Retrieved March 4, 2002, from http://www.law2.byu.edu/jel/v1998_1/html/Jones.htm

New York State Unified Court System (2002). *Structure of the courts.* Retrieved April 2, 2002, from http://www.courts.state.ny.us/ctstrct99.pdf

Chicago Public Schools (2002). *Chicago Public Schools at a glance*. Retrieved March 17, 2002, from http://www.cps.k12.il.us/CPS_at_a_Glance/cps_at_a_glance.html

Easton, J. Q., Rosenkranz, T., Bryk, A. S., Jacob, B. A., Luppescu, S., & Roderick, M. (2000, May). *Annual CPS test trend Review, 1999. Research data brief: Academic productivity series.* Chicago, IL: Consortium on Chicago School Research.

Educational Priorities Panel (2002). *State funding equity*. Retrieved March 22, 2002, from http://www.edpriorities.org/Info/StateFunEqui/TotalExpend_Print.html

Hanushek, E. A. (1981). Throwing money at schools. *Journal of Policy Analysis and Management*, *1*, 19–42.

Hopkins, A. (2002, March 3). School funding: One size fits some. *East Valley Tribune*, pp. A1, A8.

Hull v. Albrecht (Ariz. 1998). Arizona Supreme Court No. CV-98-0238-SA http://www.supreme.state.az.us/opin/pdf98/cv980238.pdf

Jones-Sanpei, H. A. (1998, Spring). Roosevelt v. Bishop: Balancing local interests with state equity interests in school financing. *Education & Law Journal*, 223–241. http://www.law2.byu.edu/jel/v1998_1/Jones.pdf

Lawton, S. B., & Schilling, N. (2002). Shifting paradigms of equity and accountability. Paper presented at the annual conference of the American Education Finance Association, Albuquerque, NM.

Levin, H. M. (1993). Education and jobs: A proactive view. In: D. Corson & S. B. Lawton (Eds), *Education and Work* (pp. 61–69). Toronto, ON: The Ontario Institute for Studies in Education.

McDonnell, P. J. (January 10, 2002). Wave of U.S. immigration likely to survive September 11th. *Los Angeles Times* [On-line]. Retrieved March 8, 2002, from http://www.latimes.com/new/nationworld/nation/la-011002immig.story

McBride, J. (1996). *The color of water*. New York, NY: Riverhead Books.

Morrison Institute for Public Policy. (2001). *Hits and misses: Fast growth in metropolitan Phoenix.* Phoenix, AZ: Author. Retrieved March 4, 2002 from http://www.asu.edu/copp/morrison/growth.htm

National Center for Educational Statistics (NCES). (2002). *Digest of education statistics, 2002.* http://nces.ed.gov/pubs2002/2002130b.pdf

Roosevelt School District No. 66 (2001, October 1) Ethnic count. Photocopy.

Roosevelt Elementary School District No. 66 v. Bishop, 877 P.2d 806, 808 (Ariz. 1994).

Sowers, C. (January 11, 2002). Charter case hits high court. *Arizona Republic* [On-line]. Retrieved March 7, 2002, from http://www.childrenfirstamerical.org/DailyNews/02Jan/0111024.htm

Wirt, F. M., & Kirst, M. W. (2001). *The political dynamics of American education* (2nd ed.). Richmond, CA: McCutchan Publishing Company.

Weissmann, D. (2002, February). Gentrifiers slow to buy CPS [Chicago Public Schools]: Displaced students paying the price. *Catalyst* [On-line]. Retrieved March 3, 2002, from http://www.catalyst-chicago.or/02–02/0202main1.htm

Wong, K. K. (1999). *Funding public schools: Politics and policies.* Lawrence, KS: University of Kansas Press.

PART II:
ACCOUNTABILITY AND EQUITY

7. THE STRUCTURE OF INEQUALITY: TRACKING AND EDUCATIONAL OPPORTUNITY IN AMERICA'S PUBLIC SCHOOLS

Paul Green

ABSTRACT

A study of tracking literature reveals incomplete and contradictory findings. This chapter will provide a theoretical synthesis of tracking and attempts to explain the conclusions of early research by focusing on the various social, political, legal and cultural forces that influence tracking. In so doing, the chapter will develop broad-based assumptions, supported by research, which may provide the basis for new educational policy as well as a sociological assessment of this educational practice. The intention of this chapter is to determine if tracking undermines the notion of education as the "great equalizer" and ultimately, supports the existing structures of dominance.

INTRODUCTION

Schooling in America has often been identified and extolled as an avenue of upward mobility. For some Americans, education has provided a means to social, economic and political opportunity. The importance of education has

Challenges of Urban Education and Efficacy of School Reform, Volume 6, pages 123–143.

ISBN: 0-7623-0426-X

been supported by historical belief that education is valuable and desirable in and of itself but also by our commitment since the nineteenth century to education as a tool of social engineering. In short, an integral part of the American opportunity structure has been the belief in education as the surest path to economic and social equality. Clearly, the belief in education and schooling in our society has been reflected in the vast number of schools, the increasing enrollment, as well as the high level of education completed by the general population.

Researchers, on the other hand, have questioned the belief in schooling as a panacea for social inequality (Jencks, 1972; Coleman, 1966) Christopher Jencks was one of a number of researchers to question whether educational opportunities have become more equally distributed, or if social inequalities persist. His controversial study concluded that educational attainment, while related to occupation, is not necessarily indicative of financial wealth nor social mobility. Rather, the considerable variation in the income of workers with exactly the same education could only be attributed to "luck."

In addition, more recently, others have suggested that educational structures within the very schooling process often act as determinants of educational outcomes and may even serve to limit the academic and affective development of students (Oakes, 1985; Kozol, 1991; Persell, Catsambis & Cookson 1977, 1992; Riordan, 1997; Rosenbaum, 1980. Still others have viewed stratified educational structures as attempts to reproduce and legitimate the existing social, economic and political systems (Bowles & Gintis, 1976; Katz, 1968). An important educational structure often accepted by educational decision-makers as "sound" educational practice is tracking, or separation by ability and curriculum. The process of tracking or "ability grouping" usually includes sorting students into high, average and low tracks based on prior achievement and perceived intellectual ability (Oakes, 1985, 1992; Kilgore, 1991; Gamoran, 1992; Avery, 1995; Hutto, 1996). A closer examination of deleterious effects of tracking in public education is the subject of this paper.

Importantly, a closer examination of tracking research reveals incomplete and often contradictory findings. Most studies are concerned primarily with the impact on cognitive achievement. More recent studies discuss issues of affective development. This paper will provide a theoretical synthesis of tracking by assessing years of research and data. Unlike earlier summaries, this paper sheds light on some of the earliest research studies of tracking as well as recent research on its impact.

Since the issues that underlie tracking are laden with politics and history and often go beyond the practice of pedagogy, the various social and cultural forces that have shaped this educational structure will also be reviewed. The chapters' comparative approach will also enable readers to see how the social mood of the day played a role in the conclusions reached by the various studies. In so doing, it is the chapters' intention to develop some broad-based generalizations, supported by research, which might provide the basis for new educational policy as well as a sociological and pedagogical re-assessment of this educational practice.

Theoretical Contexts of Educational Opportunity in American Schools

Tracking remains a structural and organizational reality in the American educational system. In their analysis of public schools, Findley and Bryan (1970) note that 76% of elementary and secondary school administrators included in their study report some type of tracking within their schools. In her study of twenty-five American schools, Jeannie Oakes (1985) also notes that approximately one-third of all classes are tracked, additionally, most students remain within the same track year after year. Goodlad's research (1984) also concludes that organizing elementary classes into tracks for the purpose of reading and arithmetic is as necessary in American schools as the daily recess. In spite of the prevalence of tracking in our schools, not all members of the educational community favor this educational structure.

Arguments for and against tracking appear in several forms. Supporters of tracking emphasize its efficiency or capacity to enhance self-development, while critics bemoan its deleterious consequences on social and educational opportunity for poor students and students of color. Educational tracking becomes a means of increasing societal efficiency by contributing to the proper selection and channeling of national human resources.

Educational Efficiency as Opportunity

The concept of industrial efficiency informed by scientific management shaped the form schooling has taken to provide different but equitable forms of education. The idea of the factory busily engaged in a neatly standardized and controlled process of mass production scientifically determined "best" methods and practices resulting in ready made goods all designed to improve the quality of American life. The essence of the factory was efficiency. The movements of workers were controlled, coordinated and channeled into machine-like parts, with minimal waste of material or duplication of effort (Oakes, 1991). Scientific Management made possible a system of production based one top-down decision-making, a rigid division of labor, elaborate rules and regulations, and of impersonality toward the worker (Nelson, 1980).

Education, civic and business leaders throughout America courted and welcomed the incorporation of "scientific management" into schools. Managers of most school systems were formerly successful corporate businessmen with measurable outcomes as their guide posts of achievement. Compared to private industry, schools were considered in inefficient and unsuccessful. In a burgeoning industrial environment, measurable outcomes quickly became an acceptable means to manage the diversity of children's abilities (raw material) and provide different educational opportunities. This was accomplished through the infusion of division of labor, standardization, specialization and a division of labor into schools.

Schools and related educational structures focused students into different levels of social, economic and political opportunity in the labor market based upon their educational track. Vital to this approach was the use of I. Q. testing, early identification of student ability, tracking and the practice of vocational training and guidance. Proponents of this approach view tracking as an educational tool that insures the best and most efficient use of human resources. In his vision of the perfect state, Plato places considerable emphasis on the early identification and appropriate training of selected youth, "before they become tarnished by exposure to lesser sorts." He likewise stresses the role of schools and schooling in creating the efficient society and recommends the "sorting of each individual into their proper niche" (Turner, 1960, p. 23).

As exemplified in the writings of Rosenbaum (1976), and Young (1971) the school is viewed as a social sorting mechanism designed to guide, counsel and provide select curricula for students of different abilities. Viewing school resources as limited, tracking is seen as the most efficient means of increasing cognitive achievement of students whatever their abilities. In this view, the affective development of students is also enhanced when they and others do not invidiously compare their work with that more able peers. Assumptions underlying this approach include the belief that early selection is accurate, tracking is efficient and that tracking improves academic achievement.

The Self-Development Perspective

From another perspective, tracking is viewed as a pedagogical device, which improves self concept and self-development in the overall leaning experience. Through tracking, students are allowed to advance at an appropriate pace with students of similar ability. By not having to make invidious comparisons with more able peers, students develop more positive self-concept and motivation. Positive self-concept, in turn, facilitates academic achievement (Campbell, 1965; Lecky, 1945; Brookover, Thomas & Patterson, 1964). According to this perspective, the most significant contribution of tracking becomes the improved self-concept and affective development that results from this educational practice. Proponents of this approach also claim that tracking enables instructors to adapt their individual styles to the particular classroom group rather than attempt to teach the average student and miss the slow and gifted leaner. However, not everyone views the educational structure of tracking in such a favorable manner.

The Conflict Perspective

Neo-Marxist view tracking as an attempt to perpetuate the stratification system and reinforce the separation of youth along ethnic or socioeconomic lines (Bowles & Gintis, 1976; Hallinan, 1996). Schooling is viewed as an attempt to instill in workers those attitudes essential to any work force, namely: order, docility, discipline, sobriety and humility. Proponents of this perspective agree that schooling in the U.S. is associated with the extension of the wage labor system and view the repressive nature of the schooling process grading and discipline as an attempt to develop in students, traits corresponding to those required on the job.

According to the Conflict Perspective, stratification developed within the schools as a reaction to the influx of working class and immigrant children. As a result of this influx, the older ideology of the common school was replaced by a special curriculum developed for children of 94 select families while the academic curriculum was reserved for those needing it. The personality traits encouraged in students varied with their expected position in the work hierarchy. For those in the lower sector, obedience and submission were stressed, while decision making and independent thought were emphasized for those at the top. In sum, Neo-Marxist view the attempt to tailor education to the needs of all children as the desire to establish class-related curricula culminating in a highly stratified track system. Thus tracking becomes a major means of maintaining the stratification system in the American society. Still other research employing the Conflict Perspective concludes that tracking affects teacher expectations of student performance and may even impact on misconduct and demeanor (Goodlad, 1984; Reed, 1995). In sum, supporters of soft-tracking emphasize its efficiency and its capacity to enhance self-development, while critics underscore the negative consequences of stratification, separation, and misconduct.

Tracking: Educational Opportunity Versus Inequality

Tracking has enjoyed a long and controversial history in the United States. Interestingly, this educational structure has followed cycles of popularity and suspicion. Although the practice reached a peak in the 1920s, its roots can be traced to the middle of the nineteenth century when the first segregation by ability, the Harris Plan, was instituted in the public schools of St. Louis, Missouri.

Formerly, schooling in the U.S. was tutorial and most instruction was individualized. However as America became more urbanized and children abandoned the farm for the schoolhouse, a more efficient technique was required to handle the large number of students entering the schools. The Monitorial Plan offered the first such modification in the form of a master teacher aided by student assistants. This teaching technique enabled one instructor to teach large numbers of students but was soon abandoned because of its rigidity. In time, the schools adopted a form of age grading, which was also quickly abandoned because of its inflexibility.

Impacted by the new compulsory education laws, the growing trend in urbanization and immigration, as well as the increased flow of southern Blacks into northern cities, the school system was called upon to accommodate an even larger and more diverse student population. The fairly homogeneous curriculum and democratic ideology of the common school was clearly challenged by the influx of culturally diverse manual workers and newly arriving immigrants. "Dramatic was its failure to deal effectively with the seething urban masses of European immigrants of peasant origin. As large numbers of working class and particularly immigrant children began attending the schools, the older democratic ideology of the common school gave way to a new philosophical belief that education should be tailored to the needs of each child" (Bowles & Gintis, 1972).

> "Their dullness seems to be racial," wrote Lewis Terman of the new immigrants, "and while they cannot understand abstract concepts, they may be transformed into efficient workers" (Terman, 1923).

As public distrust of the schools and their inefficiency continued to mount within the general population, Americans looked to the economic sector to provide a solution to the problems within the Schools. Truly, leadership in America had fallen in love with the factory and its promise of efficiency. A variety of raw materials could be transformed into efficient and much desired products in a timely and organized manner. Standardized and controlled, it provided the most efficient means of improving the overall quality of American life.

Spurred on by the concept of Social Darwinism as well as the natives of the day, Americans searched for a comparable instrument to transform the diverse populations entering the Schools into productive and well socialized citizens. Tracking soon surfaced as the answer to this need. In time, the old uniform curriculum gave way to a new and more efficient one, a curriculum that could bridge the increasing intellectual gap between the new divergent school populations.

A curriculum that could provide scholarly knowledge to the upper class and technical know how to the poor. Academic and vocational tracks became standard features at most schools. Students were casually sorted into the various programs, too often by their race, ethnic or economic background. The procedure was considered both scientific and egalitarian in that it provided the most efficient means of socializing the human "raw" material that continued to enter the schools in ever-increasing numbers. In time, the development of the IQ examination added an air of scientific objectivity to the tracking process and provided the necessary rationalization for the sorting of students into various tracks. Tracking provided an efficient response to the common school, but somehow, the frankness by which the students were channeled into curriculum tracks on the basis of race, economics, and ethnicity raised serious concerns about the openness of the American class system (Bowls & Gintis, 1972).

The Birth of Intelligence Testing as Educational Practice

The practice of tracking seemed to reach its peak in 1920 aided by the development of a revolutionary new test designed to measure intelligence. In 1916, Lewis Termini, a leading expert in applied psychology and a proponent of intelligence testing, published the newly developed Bidet Intelligence Test at Stanford. A well-known Social Darwinist, whose views on immigrants were consonant with the natives of the time, Termini looked upon the tests as a means of identifying "abnormal" children for a differentiated curriculum. The fact that so many of the immigrants tested were found to be below acceptable levels of intelligence failed to convince Termini or his supporters that they might not necessarily provide an objective measure of intelligence.

In a 1912 study supported by the U.S. Immigration service, approximately 80% of the newly arriving Italians, Hungarians, Jews and Russians were categorized as feeble-minded based on the results of these new tests (Kandal, 1974). Rather than question the results, Termini delighted in their possible use.

> The school must take account of a student's vocational possibility at every step in his progress. Our investigations indicate that an IQ lower than 70 points should qualify an individual for nothing better than unskilled labor, a range of 70 to 80 points is qualification for semi-skilled work; while an IQ range of 80–100 can entitle one for a skilled or clerical position. This information will be of great value in planning the education of children entering our schools (Terman, 1926, p. 23).

Spurred on by the writing of John Dewey and the support of the Rockefeller Foundation, some Americans began to view the new tests as a way to provide a scientific justification for a new separatism in the schools. Testing was therefore the tool used to legitimize the emerging educational structure of tracking in schools.

The practice of tracking by ability, facilitated by IQ tests, quickly gained favor in American schools. Moreover, the academic community attempted to justify its use by assessing its effectiveness. Of 140 research projects reviewed by Billet in 1928 only four concluded that the new educational structure of tracking was detrimental to the academic development of students. Few, if any, negative results were attributed to it. Affective development was not even considered and grouping based on ability, even though it resulted in segregation by class, was not deemed to be problematic. Intelligence testing and tracking, therefore, seemed to support the philosophy of the day, which espoused separate curricula for different children.

From 1935 to 1950, as the social and cultural forces that led to its inception tapered off, tracking fell into disuse. Beginning in 1950, as a direct response to the Russian launching of Sputnick and the accompanying American concern for identifying the gifted, tracking was once again revived in the schools. Coincidentally, this period also witnessed a surge in the number of college applications made by lower socioeconomic immigrant groups who had gained admission to secondary education and now desired admission to college. In addition, the percentage of technical workers in the U.S. labor force increased by almost 10% between 1950 and 1970. New fields requiring more than a high school diploma figured significantly in this growth and college seemed the logical training ground for these specialized programs (Trow, 1966).

Tracking as a Function of Educational Outcomes

The literature has related tracking to a number of possible outcomes. First and foremost among these is academic achievement.

One of the most obvious reasons for tracking is that it promotes academic achievement on all levels. Interestingly, research failed to uncover evidence in support of this assumption. However, some earlier studies do reveal limited gains for students grouped homogeneously, especially average and superior students. In 1924, Cook observed 9th and 10th grade students ranked into two ability levels and found significant gains for upper track students (while male-English speaking) in history and for slower students in math. Few if any problems were associated with the practice of grouping by ability. Mover (1924) observed ninth grade students grouped by ability for mathematics and language.

After a period of one semester, the study also revealed gains for the upper track students in language. On the other hand, the average ability group performed better in both math and language. Jones and McCall's 1926 analysis of 67 matched pairs of grammar school students pointed to a slight advantage for ability grouped superior students. Similar results were uncovered by other studies at this time (Billet, 1928; Cook, 1924; Mover, 1924; Jones & Mecca, 1926; Worlton, 1926; Walton, 1928; Holy & Button, 1930; Barthelmess & Boyer, 1932; Wyndham, 1914).

While most early research in tracking reveals some academic gains by at least one if not all of the ability groups observed, more recent research finds that ability grouping has no clear cut positive or negative effect on the average scholastic achievement of students (Daniels, 1961; Goodlad, 1984; Goldberg, 1966; Persell, Catsambis & Cookson, 1977; Oakes, 1985; Rosenbaum, 1980). In fact, current research suggests that grouping improves only the cognitive achievement of high ability groups at the expense of average and slow groups (Borg, 1966; French, 1966; Gamoran, 1991; Oakes, 1985, 1991, 1994). In short, students in low ability groups suffer from the loss of intellectual stimulation generally associated with students possessing more social and cultural capital.

On the contrary, it does not appear that upper track students suffer when left with low ability students. Research reveals that these students perform as well when placed in heterogeneous groupings (Exposit, 1973; Nolan, 1985; Dar & Reecho, 1986). It may further be the case that the improved academic benefit to upper track students is a result of processes occurring within the tracks. Unacknowledged in academic achievement of upper tracked students are the processes of curricula differentiation, teacher expectations, friendship patterns, track composition, and affective development rather than placement in the track. An analysis of each of these processes is profoundly important in the papers' review of tracking.

Differentiated Curricula: Opportunities to Learn

In public education the assumption that a uniform body of information is taught to all students within the same grade level. However, a review of the research literature confirms the fact that grouping sets in motion a process of differentiated curricula with variations in both the content and method of instruction. In turn, this educational policy or practice of differentiated curricula impacts on the Opportunity to Learn (hereafter referred to as OTL) or the academic rigor of the curriculum content that is made available to students. For example, OTL is measured by the percentage of intended curricula, which is made available to students, and contemporary research indicates that it has a direct bearing on academic achievement.

The opportunities to learn are important if students are to achieve. In her review of tracking procedures in 25 public schools, Oakes (1985) found that educational content and rigor consistently varied by track. In one instance she reports, "while upper track students were leaning Shakespeare, lower tracks were calculating sales tax" (Oaks, 1985, p. 34). Goodlad's analysis of over three hundred schools further revealed a differentiated curricula in the classics, literary genre and critical thinking exercises cannon to the upper tracks (1984).

Similar variations in content, differential student interaction, teaching time and pace of instruction were reported in the current research. Teachers were found to interact more frequently and offer more praise and support to students in the upper tracks (Allington, 1983; Grant & Rothenberg, 1986). Bennett's (1986) comprehensive study uncovered the fact that lower track students received less instructional time from their faculty than did students in the upper tracks. Moreover, higher track students were afforded a greater opportunity to work independently and engage in higher order thinking. The study also revealed that lower tracks were more often provided with remedial books and secondary sources. Similar conclusions were reached by several other researchers (Bennett, 1986; Alexander, 1989; Riordan, 1997; Demarrais, 1999; Pallas et al., 1994; Dreeban & Bar, 1988; Gamoran, 1986; Grant & Rothenberg, 1986; Firestone & Rosenblum, 1988). Thus, differentiated curricula on occasion results in differentiated resources, (teachers, texts, facilities) and social interactions.

Importance of Friendship Patterns and Social Interactions

The term's social and cultural capital is often employed in the sociology of education to understand exactly how social class influences life chances and outcomes. Social capital refers to the capacity for family and friends to invest attention and support in others. Cultural capital is concerned with the capacity to participate in high status cultural experiences. Therefore, it is not unreasonable to suggest that track assignment influences friendship patterns, which in turn affects the development of both cultural and social capital opportunities.

Friendship patterns or social interactions and their the manner in which they impinge upon a student's school plans and academic achievement have been the subject of considerable research (Duncan, Hailer & Portes, 1968; Candle & Lesser, 1969; Williams, 1972; Heynes, 1974; Persell, Catsambis & Cookson 1992). Heyns (1974) finds that an advantage of participating in an upper track may be the opportunity to associate with economically advantaged, and academically oriented peers. Alexander and McDill (1976) assert that enrollment in an upper track appreciably increases the possibility of befriending economically advantaged students. Their research also points out that minimal, if any, academic or social interaction is encouraged between lower and upper track students.

In almost all cases, current research indicates that tracking is responsible for the development of a relatively separate and distinct informal pattern of friendships. In fact, only one study conducted in 1964 by Deidrich, reveals no appreciable difference in the selection of friends between the tracked groups. The one significant difference in this study is that all students in the upper and lower tracks are members of the middle class. Hence, tracking may not necessarily influence friendship patterns when lower and upper track students have the same or similar socioeconomic backgrounds. Considerable research is available which documents that tracking also serves to separate students along economic lines.

Social Economic Status and Educational Tracking

Some research suggests that tracking result in the separation of students along racial, socioeconomic, and ethnic lines. In light of this research, tracking is viewed as an educational structure which limits the potential range and experiences available to students, seriously impacting on their social and cultural capital. Consistently, both early and contemporary studies reveal that students from the upper classes are found disproportional in upper tracks while lower socioeconomic students are found in the lower tracks.

Maurice Each (1961) notes that ability grouping at an early age seems to favor the placement of children of high socioeconomic groups in upper tracks. The author also finds that group practices separating students on the basis of ability also reduce the possibility that students would be exposed to a broader range of ethnic and cultural differences in society. Douglas (1964) finds that upper class students are disproportionately represented in higher ability groups while students from lower classes are found primarily in the low-ability classes.

This study of English concludes that tracking by ability reinforces the process of social selection since middle class children stand are placed in upper tracks more frequently than their ability tends to justify. Heathers (1969) study also reveals that low ability groups in grammar schools have a disproportionate number of children from lower class and minority origin. He concludes that tracking serves as an agency for maintaining class and caste stratification in American society. The intractable relationship between social class and track placement is consistently noted by researchers. For instance, conflict theorists argue that public schools serve as agencies for reproducing the stratification system. By selecting and sorting students into various tracks, they reproduce the social relations of production necessary to maintain a system of stratified labor. Researchers have further suggested that lower ability groupings tend to include a disproportionate number of poor whites and children of color (Bennett, 1991; Borka & Eisenhart, 1986; Coleman, 1965; Erickson, 1976; Gamoran & Berends, 1987; Heath, 1983; Persell, Catsambis & Cookson, 1992; DelGado-Gaiton, 1988).

Early research exploring the effects of tracking on self-concept and other aspects of affective development, in general, was relatively non-existent. Many early tracking studies focused on the impact of this educational structure on academic achievement. This focus is difficult to understand, since tracking was viewed as the most efficient method of providing an education or vocation to the diverse groups entering the schools at that time.

On the other hand, research studies conducted in the early 1960s were primarily concerned with the impact of tracking on the "gifted." Clearly, space exploration (launch of Sputnik), the Cold War stimulated American interests in increasing federal funding for science and math programs in America's public schools. In response to federal involvement, educational research has directed attention to the question of affective development on all students. Research concludes, for the most part, that tracking tends to stimulate a negative self-concept on the part of students assigned to lower tracks.

While considerable research concludes that tracking tends to stimulate negative self-concept in lower track students, some studies suggest that tracking is not related to different self-concepts of students (Goldberg, 1966). The however, was conducted in a predominately white middle class school. It is possible the socioeconomic homogeneity of the school may have influenced the relationship between self-concept and grouping. Sorenson (1970) speculates that the tracking of students can have a negative or positive effect. If the separation is looked upon or in some way presented as a punishment, it is certain to have detrimental effects. However, the stigmatizing effect of the tracking can be counteracted by a change in classroom competition. Slower students may be able to raise their self-concept when interacting with other slow students. He theorizes that the stigmatizing effect will depend on the visibility of the tracking.

The majority of the tracking studies included in this analysis report negative consequences for the self-concept of average and slow students. Tracking often creates a self-fulfilling prophecy of behavior in which the student internalizes their ability or inability to achieve based upon their track position. This means that that tracks have the potential to lower self esteem and negative attitudes toward school for lower track students (Alexander & McDill, 1976; Exposito, 1973; Rosenbaum, 1980).

Additionally, low track students do not seem to suffer loss of self-esteem when placed in classes with average and brighter students. Findley and Bryan

(1970) conclude that tracking reinforces positively the self-concept of high ability groups and reduces the self-esteem of low and average groups. This research further suggests that this educational structure does not build healthy self-concepts and desirable attitudes. In another interesting analysis, Mann (1965) interviews over one hundred 5th graders in an American public school, and requests the children to identify their specific class section.

While upper track children were more aware of their level, all the children responded that they were in "the best" or "the lowest" rather than by the name of the teacher. Additionally, when asked why they were placed in that specific section, all responded by saying that they were "smarter" or "dumb" or "lazy," clearly reflecting the impact on self-concept. Persell's (1977) analysis of individual research articles indicated that tracking by ability may be detrimental to the self-concept of low and average ability students. While tracking seems to be negatively correlated with self concept for lower track students, students in upper tracks tend to develop very positive expectations for their performance and in turn seem to generate a "Rosenthal Effect" quite independent of the actual educational content of the track as well as the style of presentation (Persell, 1977; Rosenthal & Jacobsen, 1968; Oakes, 1985).

Finally, the work of Clark (1962); Sorenson (1970); and Page (1987) help us to understand how this erosion of self-confidence takes place. Revisions of self-confidence may take place in a variety of ways. Students who are unaware that they possess upper track academic ability while grouped randomly may, upon being assigned to an upper track, become more actively aware of their academic status and incorporate this into their self-concept. Students of presumed low ability may not be as acutely aware of their status until they are publicly assigned to a low track which in turn might lead to a downward revision of self-concept.

Misconduct and Ability Grouping

The subject of serious misconduct in schools is one of more recent nature. Most early studies of tracking do not focus on schooling and the part that it may play in the development of youthful misconduct. McPartland and McDill (1976) are one of the first to suggest that schools can encourage misconduct in a variety of ways. By use of self-reports, these authors reveal that students reporting greater satisfaction with participation in rule making and with existing rules also report less truancy and misconduct. Some research is also available which suggests that assignment to a lower track may contribute to hostility and resentment on the part of students toward school, eventually leading to rule violations and possible withdrawal.

Schafer and Polk (1971) suggest that while a causal link between misconduct and track position is difficult to prove, assignment to a lower track, probably does lead to frustration and rebelliousness on the part of students. In their analysis, 19% of the upper tracks compared to 70% of the lower track students admit to three or more school violations.

If lower track students redefine their self concept as a function of track position, it is possible that this may lead to general dissatisfaction with education and the entire schooling process. Additionally, teachers may reinforce this feeling of dissatisfaction by identifying and placing value on students according to track position. Students in high achieving tracks are often referred to as high achievers while those in lower tracks are considered slow learners. A number of more recent studies documents the fact that assignment to lower tracks leads to misconduct, truancy and eventual withdrawal from school (Schafer & Olexa, 1971; Goodlad, 1984; Oakes, 1985). Additionally, Goodlad's study revealed that teachers of lower track students spent more time in disciplinary measures and that lower track students were more often perceived as discipline problems.

Teacher Expectations and Ability Grouping

Current research suggests that the educational structure of tracking may influence the expectations which instructors hold for individual students. Initially, what teachers know about students very often comes from the student's track position and in general, teachers hold lower expectations for lower track students and higher expectations for those in upper tracks (Keddie, 1971). In fact, Richardson's research reveals that when school records disagree with teachers' perceptions of student performance as indicated by track placement, teachers more often disagree with the official record of the student (Richardson, 1989).

Other studies have considered the extent to which teacher expectations for student's performance influence cognitive achievement. This synthesis reveals that teachers hold more positive expectations for students in higher tracks and tend to convey these expectations to the students. In turn, this positive expectation seems to impact on the academic development of the students involved (Brophy & Good, 1970; Persell, 1977; Rist, 1970; Rosenthal & Jacobson, 1968). Of sixteen studies analyzed by Persell (1977), only three do not reflect an academic impact on the students observed.

The process by which the expectation is translated to students' academic performance is relatively simple. Since teachers hold higher expectations for upper track students, experienced teachers more often prefer teaching a higher track class and often express disappointment when assigned to a low group (Riordan, 1997). Teacher expectations can likewise influence their own behavior. This adjusted behavior for a higher or lower track can in turn translate into the quality and quantity of instruction. Teachers report spending more time and interacting more frequently with students for whom they hold higher expectations (Adams & Cohen, 1974; Riordan, 1997; Jeter, 1973, Allington, 1983; Grant & Rothenberg, 1986).

Higher track students are often provided with greater opportunity to work independently and engage in higher order thinking. They are afforded access to innovative programs, while students in lower tracks spent more time in remedial drills. Teachers were also observed to be more friendly, supportive and encouraging to students labeled as bright (Bennett, 1991; Daltoii, 1973; Persell, 1977; Delgado-Gordon, 1988, 1999). Finally, since teachers held lower expectations for students in lower tracks, they paced their instruction at a relatively slower rate (Wheelock, 1992; Cooper, 1995).

Some research also enables us to understand how the differential expectations are communicated to students. Rosenthal's research (1968) underscores the different ways in which teacher expectations are transmitted to students via a variety of affirmative gestures employed by teachers which include creating a climate of warmth and encouragement, verbalizing more praise, conducting more teaching and calling upon certain students more frequently. Ethnomethodologists have also studied the positive effects of visual cues including eye contact, forward lean when communicating with students, affirmative head nods and smiles on developing positive academic performance. Each of these cues was more frequently observed in upper track classes (Rist, 1970; Cooper, 1971; Chaikin, Sigler & Derlega, 1974; Gumpert, 1975).

In sum, this theoretical synthesis lends support to the conclusion that tracking impacts on teacher expectation and behavior, which in turn influences cognitive achievement. While material resources in schools can provide a rich atmosphere for learning, the power of positive teacher expectations – the expectancy factor – can go far in developing positive academic achievement.

CONCLUSIONS

In an era of renewed focus upon educational reform at the federal, state and local levels, more research is needed to determine the organizational and institutional value of tracking and ability grouping as educational opportunity. Tradition and educational practice have an impact on tracking and ability grouping as an educational policy decision. Tracking as a matter of educational opportunity is embedded in the culture of effective schooling rather than a function of educational achievement or effectiveness. In most instances, it represents a well-intentioned effort on the part of municipal and civic leaders, administrators, teachers and parents to provide an effective educational delivery system for students.

This paper concludes that the educational structure of tracking places children, especially those of minority groups, at a distinct disadvantage. Like many other school policies, tracking and ability grouping appear to be well-intentioned practices based not so much on pedagogy, but rather on organizational assumptions disconnected from educational opportunity.

Tracking is deeply entrenched in the contemporary American system of education. It has been part of the schooling process in the United States since the end of the Civil War and is employed today in virtually all public elementary and secondary schools. At first, it represented an efficient method of teaching American culture and vocational skills to the newly arriving immigrant groups while still providing a humanities education to the children of the affluent.

Track placement is relatively permanent within a student's career. In fact, contemporary research indicates that the academic development of lower and upper tracks becomes more sharply differentiated with each passing semester. Additionally, the pattern of sequential course taking generally locks students into a very specific sequence of opportunities, which also impacts on future career selection.

Importantly, research supported the assumption that tracking improves the academic achievement of all learners. While this research lacks the methodological rigor of current studies, it also provides support to the nativism of the time and the desire to segregate the incoming flood of poor immigrants, farm laborers and southern blacks pouring into the northern cities.

Current research does not support earlier educational assumptions except in cases where brighter youth seem to benefit from instruction with peers and in all probability this may be a function of an enriched and differentiated curriculum. Research also reveals that tracking and the unique processes, which occur within the tracks, serve to widen the academic gap between students in low and high tracks over time, thereby creating an even greater degree of inequality over time.

Early research fails to assess the impact of tracking on the affective development of students. This is probably due to the fact that affective concerns were difficult to assess. Additionally, little concern existed for the impact of schooling on the urban poor at a time in our history when Schooling was looked upon as the most efficient means of Americanizing foreigners. Most contemporary research suggests that tracking helps to foster lower self-concept among lower track students who are generally labeled as underachievers and slow learners. In turn, this label seems to act as a self-fulfilling prophecy, which serves to lower future life and career aspirations and helps perpetuate the existing structure of dominance in society.

Research also finds track placements related to class, race and gender, suggesting that the educational structure of tracking work against the concept of schooling as the Great American Equalizer. Obviously, students are not sorted into tracks on the basis of these variables and some research is available which enables us to understand exactly how this may be accomplished. A review of the literature finds that most schools track students according to one or a combination of the following: IQ, past grades and teacher recommendations.

Regretfully, IQ is still perceived as a fixed measure of ability and future predictor of academic potential rather than as a flexible indicator of student's achievement career – a composite of genetics and life experiences. While very explicit knowledge is required to answer questions on an IQ test, many social scientists agree that a student must also possess a high degree of implicit knowledge. This implicit knowledge of how to sit for an exam, or practice in problem solving and critical thinking represents skills that can be learned. These skills are also not typically stressed in lower class families or in lower tracks.

In view of this, lower class groups enter school at a natural disadvantage and are more readily sorted into lower tracks. Due to the unique processes that occur within the respective tracks, they are also more likely to remain in the lower track and experience an even greater academic deficit over time.

When test scores are used as the basis for sorting students, it is interesting to explore what knowledge and information is assessed as essential to have in order to be placed in an upper track. Information, which is deemed as essential, may be considered insignificant in the overall total universe of information. Additionally, who decides on what information is generally a function of social class and becomes critical in determining how students are sorted. The information that student's receive is also related to Opportunity to Learn and upper track students are more likely to receive more of this subject matter than students in lower tracks. While this information may not necessarily explain the reason for the initial track placement, it may help us to understand the widening gap in academic achievement over time between upper and lower tracks.

When track placements are generated by teacher recommendations it is also interesting to explore the basis upon which these recommendations are made. Some research is available, which reveals that students are often sorted on the basis of language, dress, and behavioral patterns, factors that are impacted by race and social class.

In conclusion, most studies show that more learning takes place in higher tracks, even after controlling for initial ability, gender, race and socioeconomic status. Often, the course content of higher tracks contains information of a more implicit nature that involves critical thinking skills, problem solving and decision-making. On the other hand, memory and rote skills are stressed in the lower tracks. Some studies also find an emphasis on conformity and appropriate behavior in lower tracks.

Finally, our conclusion is inescapable; the inequality caused by tracking causes many students to fail. The fault lies not with the cultural or genetic deficit of students but with the educational structures in our schools. Our task is not to repair children but to alter and transform the atmosphere and policies of the schools. Only by a radical transformation of the schools can we hope to change its product.

The educational practice of tracking and ability grouping remains a common management strategy for organizing students in many American schools. However, like so many other practices, tracking seems to be a well-intentioned practice, which tends to deter educational opportunities for both upper track and lower ability groups. Questions in the literature do not suggest that upper track students miss the invaluable experiences and learning opportunities lower ability students have to share with them. Moreover, more research needs to evaluate the tracking of teacher labor and skills as a resource and its deleterious impact on teacher effectiveness in upper and lower ability classrooms. Most importantly, though, a growing body of literature seems to cast serious doubts on it's the educational efficacy of tracking and ability grouping as an effective educational strategy.

REFERENCES

Adams, G., & Cohen, A. (1974). Children's physical and interpersonal characteristics that effect student-teacher interaction. *Journal of Experimental Education*, *43*.

Alexander, J., & McDill, E. (1976). Selection and allocation within schools: Some causes and consequences of curriculum placement. *American Sociological Review*, *41*(6), 963–980.

Allington, R. (1983). The reading provided readers of different abilities. *Elementary School Journal*, *83*.

Barko, H., & Eisenhirt, M. (1986). Students conceptions of reading and their reading experiences in school. *Elementary School Journal*, *86*.

Barthelmess. H. & Boyer, P. (1932). An evaluation of ability grouping. *Journal of Educational Research*, *26*.

Bennett, K. (1986). Study of reading ability groups. Unpublished Doctoral Dissertation, University of Cincinnati.

Billett, R. (1932). *Administration and supervision of homogeneous groupings*. Columbus, OH: Ohio State University Press.

Borg, W. (1966). *Ability grouping*. Madison, WI: Dembar Educational Research.

Bowles, S., & Gintis, H. (1976). *Schooling in capitalist America*. New York, NY: Basic Books.

Brookover, T., Thomas, S., & Paterson, A. (1964, Spring). Self-concept of ability and school achievement. *Sociology of Education*, *37*(3), 271–278.

Campbell, P. (1965). Self-concept and academic achievement in middle grade public school children. Unpublished doctoral Dissertation. Wayne State University.

Charkin, A., Sigler, E., & Derlega, V. (1974). Nonverbal mediators of teacher expecting effects. *Journal of Personality and Social Psychology*, *30*.

Coleman, J. S. et al. (1966). *Equality of educational opportunity*. U.S. Department of Health, Education and Welfare, Office of Education. Washington, D.C.: U.S. Government Printing Office.

Cook, R. (1924). A study of the results of homogeneous grouping. *National Society for Study of Education*, *23*.

Cooper, J. (1971). *Self-fulfilling prophesy in the classroom*. Educational Data, 06'453.

Dalton, W. (1973). Exploring the expectancy effect phenomenon. Doctoral Dissertation, George Peabody College for Teachers. DAI 34. 359B.

Daniels, J. C. (1961). The effects of streaming. *British Journal of Educational Psychology*, 31–45.

Dar, Y., & Resh, N. (1986). Classroom intellectual composition and achievement. *American Educational Research Journal*, *23*.

Deidrich, F. (1964). Comparisons of sociometric patterns of 6th grade students in two school systems. *Journal of Educational Research*, *57*.

Delgato-Gaitan, C. (1988). The learning of conformity. *Anthropology and Educational Quarterly*, *19*.

Delgato-Gaitan, C. (1990). *Literacy for empowerment*. New York, NY: Falmer Press.

Dreeben, R., & Barr, R. (1988, July). Classroom composition and the design of instruction. *Sociology of Education*, *61*(3), 129–142.

DeMarrais, K. (1991). *The ways schools work*. New York, NY: Longmans.

Douglas, J.W.B (1964). *The home and the school*. London, ENG: MacGibbon and Kee.

Duncan, O. D., Haller, A. O., & Portes, A. (1968, September). Peer influences on aspirations: A reinterpretation. *American Journal of Sociology*, *74*(2), 119–137.

Dunn, R., & Dunn, K. (1993). *Teaching students through their learning styles*. New York, NY: Allyn and Bacon.

Dyson, E. (1965). A study of the relationship between acceptance of self, academic self-concept and two types of grouping procedures. Doctoral Dissertation, Temple University, *Dissertation Abstracts*, *26*, 1475.

Erickson, F. (1975). Gatekeeping on the melting pot. *Harvard Educational Review*, *45*.

Esposito, D. (1973). Homogeneous and heterogeneous ability grouping. *Review of Educational Research*, *43*.

Findley, W. G., & Bryan, M. M. (19). *Ability grouping: Status, impact and alternatives*. Athens, GA: Center For Educational Improvement, University of Georgia.

Firestone, W., & Rosenblum, S. (1988). Building Commitment in High Schools. *Educational Evaluation and Policy*, *10*.

French, J. (1960). Evidence from school records on effectiveness of ability grouping. *Journal of Educational Research*, *54*.

Gamoran, A. & Berends, M. (1987). The effects of stratification in elementary schools. *Review of Educational Research*, *57*.

Gamoran, A. (1986, October). Instructional and institutional effects of ability grouping. *Sociology of Education*, *59*(4), 185–198.

Goldberg, M. (1966). *The effects of ability grouping*. New York, NY: Columbia University Press.

Goodlad, J. (1984). *A place called school.* New York, NY: McGraw Hill.

Grant, L., & Rothenberg, J. (1986). The Social Enhancement of Ability Differences. *Elementary School Journal, 87.*

Gumpert, H., & Spring, J. H. (1975). *The superschool and the superstate: American education in the 20th century.* New York, NY: Wiley Publishers.

Hallinan, M. (1996). Track mobility in secondary school. *Social Forces, 74.*

Heathers, G. (1969). Grouping. In: R. Ebels (Ed.), *Encyclopedia of educational research* (pp. 559–576). New York, NY: Macmillan.

Heath, S. B. (1983). *Ways with words.* New York, NY: Cambridge University Press.

Heyns, B. (1974, May). Social selection and stratification within schools. *American Journal of Sociology, 79*(6), 1434–1451.

Haly, A., & Sulton, R. (1930). *Ability grouping in the public schools.* Madison, WI: Educational Research Service.

Jeter, L. (1973). Teacher expectancies and teacher classroom behavior. *Educational Leadership, 30.*

Johnson, D., & Johnson, A. (1993*). Cooperative, competitive and individualistic procedures for educating adults.* Minneapolis, MN: University of Minnesota, Cooperative Learning Center.

Jones, V., & McCall, W. (1926). Application of two techniques in evaluating policies dealing with bright children. *Teachers College Record, 27.*

Kandal, D., & Lesser, G. (1969). Educational plans for adolescents. *American Educational Review, 34.*

Kozol, J. (1991). *Savage inequalities.* New York, NY: Harper Perennial.

Lecky, P. (1945). *Self-consistency: Theory of personality.* New York, NY: Island Press.

Mann, M. (1960). What does ability grouping do to self-concept. *Childhood Education, 36,* 356.

McPartland, J., & McDill, E. (1976). *The unique role of schools in causes of youth crime.* Baltimore, MD: Johns Hopkins University, Center for the Social Organization of Schools. Report 216.

Moyer, E. (1924). A study of the effects of classification by intelligence tests. *National Society for the Study of Education, 23.*

Nolan, T. (1985). *The effects of ability grouping.* Dissertation. University of Colorado, Boulder.

Oakes, J. (1985). *Keeping track.* New Haven, CT: Yale University Press.

Oakes, J, Gamoran, A., & Page, R. (1992). Curriculum differentiation: Opportunities, Outcomes and Meanings. In: P. W. Jackson (Ed.), *The Handbook of Research on Curriculum Education* (pp. 570–608). New York, NY: MacMillan Publishers.

Ogbu, J. (1986). The consequences of American caste. In: U. Neisser (Ed.), *The School Achievement of Minority Children* (pp. 58–75). Hillsdale, NJ: L. Erlbaum Associates.

Pallas, A., Entwisle, D. R., Alexander, K. L., & Stluka, M. F. (1994, January). Ability-group effects: Instructional, social or institutional? *Sociology of Education, 67*(1), 27–46.

Page, R. (1987). Lower track classes at college preparatory high schools: A caricature of educational encounters. In: G. Spindler & L. Spindler (Eds), *Interpretive Ethnography of Education at Home and Abroad* (pp. 447–474). Hillsdale, NJ: Lawrence Erlbaum Publishers.

Persell, C. H. (1977). *Education and inequality: The roots and results of stratification in America's schools.* New York, NY: Free Press.

Persell, C. H., Catsambis, S., & Cookson, P. W., Jr. (1992, July). Differential asset conversion: Class and gender pathways to selective colleges. *Sociology of Education, 65*(3), 208–225.

Reed, W. (1995). *Segregation 41 years later.* New York, NY: Beacon Publishers.

Richardson, V. (1989). *School children at risk.* New York, NY: Falmer Press.

Riordan C. (1997). *Equality and achievement.* New York, NY: Longman Press.

Rist, R. (1970). Student social class and teacher expectations. *Harvard Educational Review, 40.*

Rosenbaum, J. (1980). Social implications of educational grouping. In: ? Berliner (Ed.), *Review of research in education* (pp. 361–401). Washington, D.C., American Educational Research Association.

Rosenthol, R., & Jacoboson, L. (1968). *Pygmalion in the classroom*. New York, NY: Holt, Rinehart and Winston.

Sadker, B., & Sadker, D. (1994). *Failing at fairness: How America's schools cheat girls*. New York, NY: Scribners.

Schafer, W., & Olexa. P. (1971). *Tracking and opportunity*. Scranton, PA: Chandler Publishers.

Sorenson, A. B. (1970). Organizational differentiation of students and educational opportunity. *Sociology of Education*, *43*(4), 355–376.

Spindler, G., & Spindler, L. (1987). *Interpretive ethnography of education at home and abroad*. Hillsdale, NJ: Lawrence Erlbaum Publishers.

Terman, L. (1923). *Intelligence tests and schools*. New York, NY: World Book Company.

Turner, R. (1968) Sponsored and contest mobility in the public school system. In: R. R. Bell & H. R. Stub (Eds), *Sociology of Education: A Sourcebook* (2nd ed.). Homewood, IL: Dorsey Publishers.

Trow, M. (1966). The secondary transformation of American education. In: R. Bendix & S. M. Lipset (Eds), *Class, Status and Power: A Reader in Social Stratification*. New York, NY: Free Press.

Walton, R. (1928). *Ability grouping in the public schools*. Madison WI: Dembar Educational Research Services.

Wheelock, A. (1992). *Crossing the tracks*. New York, NY: Press.

Williams, T. (1972). Educational aspiration. *Sociology of Education*, *45*.

Worlton, J. (1926). The why of homogeneous classification. *Elementary School Journal*, *27*.

Wyndham H. S. (1934). *Ability grouping: Recent developments. City, State*: Melbourne Publishers.

8. THE DIGITAL DIVIDE IN AMERICA'S PUBLIC SCHOOLS

Philip T. K. Daniel

ABSTRACT

Through a national debate inaugurated by A Nation at Risk, a United States government-sponsored report, there has developed at least tacit accord that a digital divide exists in public schools and there are stark differences in technology training and availability of computers in communities based on race, other demographics, and disability status of students. Access to the instruments of the information and computer world are only part of the problem. Availability of broadband and other high speed Internet services and speciality servicing are also issues to be addressed. In addition, teacher training and teacher attitudes are variables that contribute to the divide, especially where students of color or students with special needs make up a large percentage of the school population. The divide increases exponentially each year, thereby widening the gap between the "haves" and "have nots" within the information enterprise. This chapter outlines these concerns, providing areas of liability that could be faced by school district personnel who fail to render an equal educational opportunity to students in the 21st century.

INTRODUCTION

The "computer revolution" in the public schools was ushered in to the U.S. in the 1980s with aggrieved and cheerless commentary from the National

Challenges of Urban Education and Efficacy of School Reform, Volume 6, pages 145–164.

ISBN: 0-7623-0426-X

Commission on Excellence in Education. The Commission, an offshoot of the U.S. Department of Education, submitted a report entitled *A Nation at Risk: The Imperative for School Educational Reform* (Nation at Risk, 1983). The report found that the education offered up to students was in a malaise, and was so mediocre as to place the American populace in a strategically vulnerable position vis a vis all other industrialized countries. One important recommendation of the commission was to get busy in the country, especially in the public schools, with training students on the use of the computer. The report, and others like it, started an avalanche of activity and helped foster an industry whose financial boundaries have yet to be determined. The process was facilitated with the marketing of the desktop and laptop computers and the ultimate infusion of billions of dollars into higher education and public school districts (Green, 1991, p. 6). Several universities, beginning in the 1980s, required students to purchase computers as a component of admission (Roszak, 1986, p. 58). One researcher estimated that in the 1980s 2.4 million computers were being used in American K-12 schools where, at the time, there were 40 million children. This translated to approximately one computer for every sixteen children (Becker, 1991). Another study found that there was one computer for every thirty-seven students in the public schools, thus reducing figures quoted in the earlier study suspected of being inflated by counting both administrative and instructional use.

Along with the marketing of computers to all of education, a level of support and rhetoric appeared to promote computer technology as an intellectual panacea. Several higher education professionals postulated, just as the *Nation at Risk* report had done, that computers would deeply transform every academic subject and exponentially increase the quality of student work, (Alexander, 1992; Morell & Fleisher, 1991; Kling, 1991). Others hailed the computer as the progenitor of a second revolution in the United States and a change agent for the world. Information processing, a term encompassing the new forms of technology including data collection, data exchange, voice conversions, multimedia presentations, and all of computer technology, was viewed as suddenly and permanently transforming the culture of education into an all-empowering institution. (Nunn, McPherson, & Rust, 1998; Sculley, 1989).

The new technology was not without skepticism and critics. Perhaps the most prominent in challenging the prospect that computers somehow promote intellectualism was the former president of Harvard University:

> Experience should . . . make us wary of dramatic claims for the impact of new technology. Thomas Edison was clearly wrong in declaring that the phonograph would revolutionize education. Radio could not make a lasting impact on the public schools even though

> foundations gave generous subsidies to bring programs into the classroom. Television met a similar fate in spite of glowing predictions heralding its powers to improve learning.
>
> In each instance, technology failed to live up to its early promise for three reasons: resistance by teachers, high cost, and the absence of demonstrable gains in student achievement. There is yet no evidence that computers and videodiscs will meet a happier fate (Bok, 1985, p. 30).

Another Harvard academic went much further and boldly criticized the report, *A Nation at Risk* (Willie, 1982). The report had claimed that computers were only so good as the support rendered for academic excellence in the schools. The report then went on to warn that such a push could interfere with the attainment of equity in the schools suggesting that the two might not be compatible. The researcher, a professor of sociology and education at Harvard, claimed that the report violated its own warning in that it championed the development and use of technology at the sacrifice of most of the students in the public schools, where there was a clear and continuing dearth of subject matter and training in the electronic media (Willie, p. 7).

Other criticism took place with the claim that the report did not relate the problems within schools to the malaise within the larger society. (Banks, 1983). *A Nation at Risk* implied that the major cause of the nation's problems were in the schools, saying nothing of societal-based discrimination against protected populations. In addition, there was nothing suggesting how the computer revolution was impacted by other social problems, thus producing a 21st century kind of reality into the haves and have nots of computer ownership and use. Moreover, the report was accused of being rather elitist inasmuch as the voices of public school teachers, administrators, and other educators were absent from the ultimate findings. (Banks, p. 3).

Strangely, these latter criticisms, produced in the early 1980s, were prophetic, giving apt descriptions of concerns about computer use in the third millennium. We are said to be in a technological period that is best described as a "digital divide" or " the differentiation or separation between those with access to the essential tools of the information society and those without access" (Spectar, 2000, p. 9). It is also, "the gap between those with access to the infrastructure of the networked society . . . (the tech-haves) and those who lack access (the tech have- nots)" (Spectar, p. 9). Access to the Internet (Sperry & Daniel, p. 610)[3] and to computer use is circumscribed by those society ills that the *Nation at Risk* failed to address. For many, such access is, as yet, an unfulfilled promise, determined by issues of race, disability, and geography. Such access is also restricted by the paucity or absence of computers in public education, teacher training, administrator training, and the attitude of such professionals in the schools.

THE DIVIDE AND ITS COMPLICATIONS

Through a national debate, there has developed at least tacit accord that a digital divide exists based on income, clearly influenced by race, geography, and disability status. The divide is both international and national, and curiously, involves the same set of variables. At the international level, little of the data being produced is disputed. The U.S. accounts for almost 40% of Internet use; this increases to 57% worldwide when the rest of North America is included. (Brennan, 2002). When combined with Europe, the World's most industrialized countries are responsible for 90% of global Internet consumption (Brennan). According to one recent report, between 98 and 99.5% of all the people in Asia, Africa, and Latin American have no connection to the Internet (Brennan). This disparity involves the expanse of information technology as described above.

The debate in the U.S. concerning the digital divide has been sharpened by various reports pointing to stark differences among classes of populations. Still other reports counter this with the claim that while there may be huge gaps, the line between certain populations is closing rapidly.

According to William Kennard, former chair of the Federal Communications Commission (FCC) during the Clinton administration, affordability plays a prominent role in computer ownership and Internet access in the United States (Kennard, 1999). The FCC commissioned a study by the Telecommunications and Information Administration which listed and pinpointed the digital divide, indicating that families with incomes of $75,000 or more were seven times more likely to own a computer than families with incomes of $25,000 or less (Kennard). The disparity is less pronounced when education level is introduced especially if households have at least one breadwinner with a college degree (Hammond, 2002, p. 141). Gender disparity is said to be "all but eliminated except when cross-referenced with income or heading a household" (Hammond) There is a severe racial divide despite income or education level. (Kennard, 1999; Hammond, 2002). The Clinton administration, under the leadership of Kennard, sponsored various programs for the purchase of computer equipment for the less advantaged so as to reduce the technological divide (Kennard, 1999). Other studies agree with the racial disparities, but claim that gains by blacks and Hispanics have changed the dynamics, even within the past few years, although people of color still lag behind whites by several percentage points. One report, for example, found that 57% of whites were on the Internet in the year 2000; this was compared with 43% of blacks and 47% of Hispanics (Hernandez, Eddy & Muchmore, 2001, p. 1964).

Disadvantaged status also plagues persons with disabilities. It could be argued that students with disabilities fall on the bottom rung of the technology access ladder. While the potential benefits of computer use are prodigious for such students, the reality is discouraging. For example, a Department of Commerce study has found that persons with disabilities have access to the Internet at a level half that of non-disabled persons and that 95% of most websites are simply not geared for use by people with visual, auditory, or ambulatory handicaps, (U.S. Department of Commerce, 2000). Accessibility for such persons becomes an issue when technology designers only have persons without disabilities in mind for target audiences. According to a government study, people with disabilities use computers one quarter the time as able-bodied individuals and 60% of disabled persons have never used a computer (Vass, 2002; Dispenza, 2002). It is estimated that the vast majority of available websites are not fully accessible to persons with visual, auditory, or ambulatory impairments (Dispenza, 2002). This pattern of active or benign discrimination against disabled persons is clearly being addressed by ongoing as well as contemporary Congressional legislation to be described in another section of this chapter.

Access to the instruments of technology and to the World Wide Web (Sperry & Daniel, p. 611) does not entirely envelope the complexities associated with participation in the Information Highway (*ACLU v. Reno*, 830). Availability of broadband connections or high speed Internet services, and specialty servicing or "Web lining" are also issues to be addressed. With wealth and education as variables, many inner city and rural communities in the U.S. do not have the available equipment or networks, or specific wiring services typically germane to other more affluent urban or suburban areas. "Availability" of such equipment and services, hence, is another cause of the digital quality divide. The disparities are often predicated on the absence of sophisticated broadband features such as Digital Subscriber Line (DSL) (search Networking.com, 2002). DSL is a technology for bringing high-bandwidth information to Internet users over telephone lines that offer such service. DSL provides data reception and retrieval that are over six times the speed of ordinary electronic media service. Internet companies have been accused of using demographic data and deliberately avoiding minority communities in laying wire for broadband access. The data is informative. The Government Accounting Office found that poverty rate plays an important role in high speed data access pointing out the communities with overall average family incomes of less than $28,000 were found to be twice as unlikely as communities with overall average incomes of $36,000 not to have such service (Hernandez, Eddy & Muchmore, 1962). The absence of high-speed access, where such access is a major and basic component of the communication medium itself, could have a chilling effect on those communities that are less privileged and further contribute to racial and wealth-based disparities that cause adults and children to fall further behind along the Information

Highway. Information and computer technology represents a form of literacy. Information-based employment positions are replacing those in industrial fields at an exponential rate. This means not only should students be exposed to formal computer training, but also that computer access must be at the advanced level.

It should be noted that the new chair of the Federal Communications Commission, Michael Powell, has all but dismissed the whole notion of a "digital divide" classifying the term as just another activist approach begun by the Clinton Administration (*New York Times*, p. C1). Nominated by current President George W. Bush, Mr. Powell has considered the term "digital divide" to be a "dangerous phrase" used to justify inappropriate government initiatives designed to provide poor people with cheap access to technology (*New York Times*). He ridiculed the idea of a divide with the statement, "I think there is a Mercedes divide; I'd like to have one, but I can't afford one" (*Washington Post*, p. C1). He claimed that the outcome that favors the rich over the poor was a satisfactory one since, in a capitalist society, "wealthy people always get these products first" (*New York Times*, p. C1).

THE DIGITAL DIVIDE IN PUBLIC EDUCATION

Those contributing to the debate about the "digital divide" have adhered to the national call to improve education as listed in the report, *A Nation at Risk*. Part of the effort is to bridge the information technology divide in all schools with the federal government taking the lead. Former Vice-President Al Gore was one of the first of the elected public officials to understand that computerized communication had much application for public schools. The Internet automates a process of gathering and communicating information for the development of knowledge and skills. The Information Highway (the term coined by Gore (as Senator) in reference to the World Wide Web [Gore, 1990]) gives students and educators at all levels, " the ability to instantly create elaborate visual models of the world around [them] and watch the way its elements interact, without the limitation of time and space" (Gore, p. B3). President William Clinton demonstrated support of technology in the public schools in his second state of the Union Address by stating that:

> Our challenge is to provide Americans with the educational opportunities we will all need for this new century. In our schools, every classroom in America must be connected to the information superhighway, with computers and good software, and well-trained teachers. We are working with the telecommunications industry, educators and parents to connect 20% of California's classrooms by this spring, and every classroom and every library in the entire United States by the year 2000. I ask Congress to support this education technology initiative so that we can make sure this national partnership succeeds (Clinton, 1996).

In response to the President's directive, the U.S. Department of Education released a plan, in 1996, to integrate technology into the nation's public schools systems. Labeled, the *Getting America's Students Ready for the 21st Century: Meeting the Technology Literacy Challenge*, the plan sought to present " a far-reaching vision for the effective use of technology in elementary and secondary education to help the next generation of school children to be better educated and be better prepared for the evolving demands of the new American economy." (U.S. Department of Education, *e-Learning*). Between 1995 and 2000 the federal government, through the Clinton-Gore administration and Congress, allocated over eight billion dollars to the states to purchase technological equipment for schools, educational programs, and libraries (Shelley et al., 2002). The U.S. Department of Education then unveiled its National Education Technology Plan, providing the nation with five educational technology goals:

(1) All students and teachers will have access to information technology in their classrooms, schools, communities, and homes;
(2) All teachers will use technology effectively to help students achieve high academic standards;
(3) All students will have technology and information literacy skills;
(4) Research and evaluation will improve the next generation of technology applications for teaching and learning;
(5) Digital content and networked applications will transform teaching and learning (Shelley).

By autumn, 2000 the Department of Education, based on an assessment of its success, was announcing that 98% of public schools had some connection to the Internet, up from only a 35% access rate in 1994 (U.S. Dept. of Ed., 2001). This was made possible through the Telecommunications Act of 1996 where Congress and the Clinton Administration provided additional funds to provide support for schools and libraries (Telecommunications Act, 2000). Specifically, through a Universal Service Fund, or Education-rate (E-rate) monies are made available to elementary and secondary schools with significant reductions in the price of technology services such as telephone hook-ups, internal and external line connections, Internet access, and advanced telecommunication services. During the Clinton years, discounts awarded were determined by demography (an urban, suburban, or rural locale), and poverty level, defined as whether schools or a school district participated in federally-based free lunch programs, and whether schools addressed the needs of students with disabilities.

These technological initiatives on the part of government, while somewhat effective and well meaning, have still not overridden the digital divide. A positive finding was that many more schools were making access to the Internet more available after school hours. This was especially true of schools with high enrollments of students of color; such school districts were likely to make computers available 61% of the time, while those with low minority enrollments permitted after school use only 46% of the time (U.S. Dept. of Ed., 2001). The availability of computers for minority students had increased substantially not only because of school participation, but also because of local libraries, who, as noted, were also recipients of E-rate funds. While the courts have supported libraries as playing a crucial role in closing the digital divide (*Ashcroft v. Free Speech Coalition*, 2002), statistics show that these places of information have yet to accept the responsibility, particularly in minority communities. A late 2000 government report announced that only 1.9% of the population had accessed the Internet from a public library (United States Department of Commerce, 2000).

The report of the Department of Education, while finding a clear increase in the number of computers and wider Internet access also discovered that technology continues to be more available in affluent communities. The ratio of instructional computers with Internet access was still greater in poverty areas at over 9 to 1 while more wealthy suburbs had a ratio of less than 6 to 1 (U.S. Dept. of Ed., 2001). This pattern was also present relative to Internet access by types of connections, especially those with broadband linkage. Students in urban areas tended to lag far behind their suburban counterparts by as many as ten percentage points in dedicated lines, dial-up connections, and access to T1 and T3 lines (U.S. Dept. of Ed.). The variable of percent of students in schools on free or reduced-priced lunches was even more telling; schools with 35% or fewer such students tended to have greater Internet access by as many as 14 or 15 percentage points then those schools with 75% or much such students (U.S. Dept. of Ed.). In fact, William Kennard, noted in his research that while 78% of schools in affluent communities have sophisticated Internet access, less then 50% of those in low-income communities have such access. Moreover, low-income children tend not to have a computer or Internet access at home or school and "as many as three-quarters of Black high school and college students [do] not have a PC (Kennard, 1999, p. 554). Mr. Kennard commented, finally, that many urban areas, where there are large concentrations of people of color, are technologically isolated. This impacted school districts with disparate wealth levels (Kennard). Students in the same school districts, but with different wealth and racial background, had the same Internet access experiences as students living in different school districts predicated upon class and race. This tends to suggest that in schools the digital divide is steady state or growing larger, mirroring experiences of the larger society. Assessing the rhetoric of the Bush administration, led by Michael Powell, current Chair of the Federal Communications Commission, this phenomenon can be justified as a "Mercedes Divide" rather than a digital divide. Mr. Powell has indicated that skewed technological access does not undermine diversity or the progress of the underclass (Powell, M., 2001).

SCHOOL DISTRICTS AND COMPUTER ACCESS LIABILITY

Race

> Computers give us a world where people are judged not by the color of their skin or their gender or their family's income but by their minds – how well they can express themselves on those screens. If we can teach our children these values, they can learn to respect themselves and each other (Clinton, 1998).

The development of computer technology has created a profound change in communication with users accessing a limitless array of information. The technology, when used effectively in education, can positively enhance teacher-based instruction, student discovery, as well as the learning of important skills. School districts have the responsibility of providing students with the necessary instruction to utilize the electronic media; such skill acquisition is important to one's education and future employment. In surveying this area of school district responsibility, few researchers have examined liability for training or access. Most have concerned themselves with looking at behavior once the requisite skills have been attained by students, surveying the legal minefields that become elevated based on student's abusive conduct over the Internet and the Constitutional and other protections of such activity (Daniel & Pauken, 2002; Daniel & Daniel, 2000); Daniel & Pauken, 1999; Daniel 1998; Daniel, 1997). For example, students have been disciplined for threatening violent acts through email or chat rooms, for accessing pornographic sites, for making defamatory remarks against teachers and other students, for violation of copyright and other intellectually property infractions, and for attempting to hack into or otherwise disrupt school-based main frames. The extant research, therefore, also focuses on the authority of school districts to control or limit student access to objectionable materials or sites and to punish those students who commit transgressions or otherwise violate school rules or acceptable use policies.

A school district may establish time, place and manner restrictions on the use of school equipment, including computers. This is also true of Internet access, and school personnel have no obligation to ensure that entry into the World Wide Web will always be available or that software installed on school computers will always perform as designed or expected. In addition, school districts are not responsible for lost data or failures that are frequent and endemic to every element of a computer. They may, however, be accountable as to whether training and accessibility are available to students between and within schools especially if differentiated access is compounded by racial, ethnic, or disability status.

While there is no case law decided to date addressing a racial digital divide, or access to computer use or Internet access in schools specifically distinguishing race, judicial decisions addressing wider perspectives may apply and, hence, suggest areas of liability for school personnel.

Since 1954, with the advent of the U.S. Supreme Court decision in *Brown v. Board of Education, Topeka*, courts and legislatures have taken an active role in redressing many of the obstacles that inhibit equal access in education. The decision, of course, could extend to and help determine whether a denial of equal access and opportunity to the use of computers exists relative to racial discrimination in the public schools or is founded upon some decision by public school personnel. As the Supreme Court stated in *Brown*:

> Today, education is perhaps the most important function of state and local governments . . . [It] is doubtful that any child may reasonably be expected to succeed in life if he is denied the opportunity of an education. Such an opportunity, where the state has undertaken to provide it, must be made available to all on equal terms (Brown, p. 493).

The history of discrimination in education involving race is not only based upon social interaction, but also, just as importantly, equipment and facilities. The direct consequence of decisions as regards access was that students of color for many years received an inferior education with substandard instructional materials (Daniel, 1980). The *Brown* Court addressed the question as to whether school districts could discriminate against students on the basis of the availability and access to school equipment and facilities, and whether such discrimination deprived students of equal educational opportunities. The Court responded by stating, "We believe it does" (Brown, 1954, p. 493).

Proving that school officials engaged in discrimination targeting race will be a formidable task for any current day student plaintiff. If a complaint is brought under an Equal Protection argument, as was the case in *Brown*, the complainant must prove that similarly situated students were treated dissimilarly relative to the distribution of benefits or burdens (U.S. Constitution). Even where a school policy appears to be neutral, it too may be challenged if it is intended to have a discriminatory effect. But, to establish unconstitutional racial imbalance within a school system, a student must demonstrate that school authorities created differentiated usage or access patterns and that their actions were motivated by discriminatory intent. This intent must, in fact, be directly linked to a segregative or discriminatory action that actually caused harm to the student. This is a high bar to vault, but not impossible.

Such was the case in *Keyes v. School District No. 1* (1973), where a school board had engaged in discrimination against students of color by making decisions pertaining to school boundaries, school placements, and the purchase and placement of equipment and facilities. School authorities had created the discriminatory practices in only certain sections of the district. The U.S. Supreme Court declared the procedure unconstitutional and indicated that school personnel could have chosen less taxing and restrictive plans to alleviate racially discrimination. The Court placed the burden on the system to show that discrimination had not occurred throughout the whole system if discriminatory actions were found in just a few schools. The *Keyes* decision has gone through several iterations resulting most recently in the lifting of the desegregation decree. A portion of the decision from the seventeenth-appealed recurrence by the same name, however, left a clear indication of school responsibility as to availability and access of school facilities:

> No student shall be discriminated against on account of race, color or ethnicity in any service, facility, activity, or program (including extracurricular activities) conducted or sponsored by the school in which he or she is enrolled. The District shall provide its resources, services and facilities in an equitable, nondiscriminatory manner (Keyes, 1987, p. 1517).

In a more recent case a federal court found school district disparities in materials and supplies and access and use of school equipment including computer and computer software (*People Who Care*, 1994).[1] The differences were organized by race and the percentages of students in schools. They were also determined by segregated policies within schools. Schools with large minority populations had for years been deprived of such equipment and materials. So as to expose majority students to the equipment, and, ipso facto, to deprive minority students of such equipment, students were "tracked." Very often a black student who had tested out as mathematically or technologically gifted found himself or herself in a lower track, thus prohibiting access to advanced instruction or computer exposure. The court described the practice as "insensitive" and "astonishing" ". . . labeling the students by color-coding them for all of the student body to see" (People Who Care, p. 913). The court held that school officials had established a rigid system of ability grouping with no intent to ameliorate disparities and which were designed to give students of color no hope of ever advancing to higher levels of achievement.

School district administrators regulating the use of school computer facilities should be instructed by this decision. Liability may be found where large percentages of students are underserved relative to equipment access while percentages of different race students are readily served. The school district in the above set of facts distributed different levels of facilities to schools that were literally down the street from each other. Moreover, as noted, students in the same schools received different treatment. This was said by the court to be the denial of an equal opportunity to an education incorporating the improper use of race.

Racial discrimination cases finding a denial of access to sophisticated facilities continue in the third millennium where students are apportioned into schools based on desegregation consent decrees. This was the case involving a magnet school featuring computer technology programs (Hampton, 2000). School personnel denied African-American students admission to the school exclusively based on racial reasons of supposed parity. Such parity was a part of the consent decree. Black parents challenged the admissions policy claiming that it was discriminatory and therefore unconstitutional. Ultimately, a federal district court gave decision to the parents ordering that within all magnet schools in the school district admission must be competitive and admission cannot be based on race. According to the court, magnet schools offer special programs such as computer technology that may not be available in regular schools. Denying such an opportunity would impose an impermissible harm and deprive such students of an equal educational opportunity (Hampton, p. 377).

School personnel may face liability as well if students are profiled based on neutral, private, discretionary acts that appear to be independent of official action. For a number of years the school district in *People Who Care* operated in a manner that permitted parent gifts and other private gifts to provide a better educational experience for white students over students of color (*People Who Care*, p. 921). The gifts were not only received from parents, but Parent Teacher Organizations and Associations. The school board argued that not only was this an exercise of private discretion, but that because the funds were raised and allocated by private groups there was no taint on the exercise of authority by school board members. The court disagreed, labeling the practice as affirmative state action and that the school officials were put on notice by virtue of the positions they occupied that the gift practice had a disparate impact on students of color (People Who Care).

Disability

Students with disabilities are protected by three federal statutes specifically designed to address participation in the educational environment. These include the Individuals with Disabilities Education Act (IDEA), Section 504 of the Rehabilitation Act of 1973 (Section 504), and the Americans with Disabilities Act (ADA). In this era of information technology the U.S. Congress also passed the Assistive Technology for Individuals with Disabilities Act, which acknowledges the issues of access to computer resources and provides financial assistance to the states so as to "maintain[] and strengthen[] a permanent comprehensive statewide program of technology-related assistance" (Assistive Technology for Individuals with Disabilities Act: § 3001(b)(1)). The practice of excluding students with special needs from public education collided with the Civil Rights movement. Each of these laws, and especially IDEA, owe their beginnings to the decision rendered in *Brown v. Board of Education*. As noted above, *Brown* established that African-American children had the right to an equal educational opportunity and that segregated schools and school facilities denied them that right. Advocates for disabled children argued that such children were also entitled to equal access to schools and facilities (Kirp, 1973).

IDEA, an affirmative action statute, provides for extensive, detailed, substantive rights for children in public schools who have at least one enumerated, federally defined, disability and who qualify for special education intervention. The fundamental premise of IDEA is that qualifying students are entitled to a free appropriate public education, which encompasses special education and related services provided in the least restrictive environment. The Act contains extensive procedural requirements centering on the development of an individualized educational program (IEP) containing long and short-term goals and objectives. It is the IEP team that selects a student's related program, including related services such as adaptive software, assistive technology, and accessibility needs. The Act specifically stipulates that school districts must provide special needs students with related services, which are consistent with their individualized programs including computer technology. Public schools may not deny such students an opportunity to participate or benefit from aids or services germane to a free appropriate public education.

The 1997 Congressional reauthorization of IDEA accentuated the necessity of computers and information technology in the education of special needs students and the importance of promoting state of the art aids and services within the public school enterprise. Much of the new legislation emphasizes assistive technology for students so as to satisfy the governmental preference for full integration as well as access to the general curriculum. The legislation not only obligates school districts to use assistive technology devices such as computers with students, but also compels school officials to train teachers with the requisite education and background in a full range of technology uses.

Notwithstanding the presence of Congressional determination under IDEA, the growth of technology may be outpacing technological accommodations for disabled students and this, together with limited school budgets, may cause such students to face a digital divide. Schools are mandated to provide effective communication for students with disabilities through accessible means. However, many school districts either cannot or do not adhere to the Congressional commands. For example, the parents of a learning disabled student complained that their school district had denied their son access to a computer class because the teacher was not able to communicate with him in his native language, and because the class was not geared to address the needs of special education students. The school district explained that the computer class was not a special education class but a mainstream elective. In addition, a teacher who at one time taught the class, no longer taught it. Although the school district attempted to accommodate the student's needs by providing him with a tutor, the parents remained dissatisfied. The parents' concerns related to their son's inability to understand what was going on during class. An impartial hearing panel found that despite the student's limited skills in English, the IEP Team did not take into account his limited English proficiency when determining appropriate services for him. The school district was ordered to test the student for language skills as well as the use of technology equipment and the addition of technology services (San Francisco, 1998).

Disabled students protected by IDEA may face a digital divide not only as regards the absence of computer technology, but also because sufficient assistance is not provided to use the equipment or technology. The parent of a student with cerebral palsy and quadriplegia who used a wheelchair alleged that the school district denied her daughter a free appropriate public education by failing to provide her with an accessible computer, and adequate aide time to allow her to participate in regular education. Although the district provided the student with a computer and software, it failed to provide the necessary equipment – a knee switch, to enable the student to use the computer without assistance. At first the switch was simply not ordered. This was followed by the fact that, although an order was placed, significant delays in delivery caused the student to miss much instruction delivered in class. A hearing panel concluded that, because the District failed to provide the student with an accessible computer, it was unable to deliver the services deemed appropriate for her in her IEP, and thus deprived her of a free appropriate public education (Colton Joint Unified Sch. District, 1995).

The Americans with Disabilities Act and Section 504 of the Rehabilitation protect students from discrimination based on disability. Section 504 addresses discrimination allegedly committed by federal fund recipients. This would include every public school district in the U.S. Congress passed the Americans with Disabilities Act because, even after the passage of Section 504, millions of disabled persons were still subject to discrimination. Therefore, in order to "provide a clear and comprehensive mandate for the elimination of discrimination against individuals with disabilities" (ADA, §12101(b)(2)), the ADA was enacted. Both statutes protect the same substantive rights. Unlike Section 504, which only addresses those receiving federal funding, the ADA extends protection against public entities, state and local governments and places of public accommodation. The preventive language of each of the laws reads as follows:

Section 504

> No otherwise qualified individual with a disability in the United States . . . shall, solely by reason of . . . disability, be excluded from the participation in, be denied the benefits of, or be subjected to discrimination under any program or activity receiving Federal financial assistance (Section 504, §794(a).

Americans with Disabilities Act

> No qualified individual with a disability shall, by reason of such disability, be excluded from participation in or be denied the benefits of the services, programs, or activities of a public entity, or be subjected to discrimination by any such entity (ADA, §12132).
>
> No individual shall be discriminated against on the basis of disability in the full and equal enjoyment of the goods, services, facilities, privileges, advantages, or accommodations of any place of public accommodation by any person who owns, leases . . . or operates a place of public accommodation (ADA, §12182(a).

The regulations implementing the ADA require "public entities" to offer reasonable aids, or equipment so as offer an equal opportunity to participate in a service, program, or activity. This means that public schools are required to provide effective communication to students with disabilities including the use of computers. This may also require Internet access if program information and information about goods and services is offered on line. Such information must also be offered to students by accessible technological means.

At least one federal appeals court has decided that websites are places of public accommodation, hence, by federal law, prohibited from excluding persons with disabilities as regards access (*Doe v. Mutual of Omaha*, 1999). The U.S. Department of Education, Office of Civil Rights has issued complaint letters under the Americans with Disabilities Act placing sanctions against universities regarding Internet access (U.S. Department of Education, Office of Civil Rights, 1997). The institutions were required to ensure that such communications were as effective as those provided to able bodied persons; this meant supplying assistive technology in its various forms depending on the disability of the person. The letters also listed the requisite caveat for such student complainants: such services may only be based on a reasonable accommodation and schools are under no obligation to make such materials available if, in doing so, it would produce an undue hardship or burden or fundamentally alter the nature of services or activities.

Section 504 of the Rehabilitation Act of 1973 is the oldest of the disability discrimination statutes and protects "otherwise qualified individuals" that are also handicapped. The guidelines of the statute indicate that federal fund recipients provide services, benefits and aids for disabled persons that are as effective as those afforded to non-disabled persons, including assistive and technological devices.

The Rehabilitation Act was amended in 1998 expanding the technological access provisions of the legislation. The revisions require federal agencies to make federal websites accessible to persons with disabilities. Under Section 508 the definitions of electronic and information technology have been augmented to include computer hardware and software, websites, Fax's, and copiers. The U.S. Department of Education has interpreted Section 508 to apply to the states and state agencies, including boards of education, because such entities receive federal funds under the Assistive Technology Act of 1998.

While students with disabilities clearly are challenged by the digital divide, they have formidable protections from the federal statutes described above. Congress has seen fit to promulgate a number of directives to educational institutions for accessibility by disabled persons to electronic and information technology. Public schools would do well to pay attention not only to equipment needs, but to proper staffing and technical training of teachers and other school personnel.

CONCLUSION: A DIVIDE BY ANY OTHER NAME

According to Moore's Law, computer technology advances exponentially every eighteen months and, as such, only the most sophisticated "tekkie" could ever hope to remain current (Brockman, 1996). Moreover, advances in technology tend to stratify according to necessity and use; business and government, hence, tend to employ computer use more than educators, and by extension, upgrade at a faster rate. This has lead educational researchers to argue that educators can contribute little to reducing the problem of the digital divide and that this should not even be an important objective. They see the divide as not so much a separation of "haves" and "have nots," but, of "those who: (1) own state-of-the-art computers and subscribe to an internet service provider, (2) have access to computers and the internet at work, libraries and know how to use them, (3) have rare or minimal access to computing technologies and little facility with them, and (4) experience their everyday lives untouched by computer and information technologies)" (Damarin, 2000). Such researchers see the job of educators not as assuring ready access to state-of-the-art technology, but, instead, certifying that students are served as much as possible in what schools have to offer.

Such an approach in addressing the problem with the divide is consistent with current educator attitudes and training in computer technology. Many of today's educators went through teacher training programs with no technology component. They do not use computers for instruction, claim that they haven't the time to do so, and those that are computer proficient claim that they either lack a computer in the classroom or, if one is present, it is not Internet connected. One study has opined that "for the average teacher the use of technology has not been an empowering experience" (Jin & Abate, 1999).

The theory of the digital divide seeks neither to address the whims or budgets of school districts nor the preferences of teachers to become a technology leader. The divide is about training, or lack of it, and it is about remaining current in a field whose growth is staggering. President William Clinton found this out in the year 2000 as he announced his desire to provide tax advantages for businesses donating computers and software to schools in low-income areas that were just a few years old. Educators responded that the only ones to benefit from such a scheme would be the private companies since the equipment would be entirely too dated for closing the digital divide among students (Mendels, 2000). Each of the states has responded similarly, creating new laws requiring up-to-date teacher training in the use of computers (Daniel & Nance, 2002). And courts of law have been quite consistent in supporting state-based "accountability" or "reconstitution" movements that permit boards of education to terminate administrators or even re-staff whole schools where high student achievement in the mathematics and technology is not demonstrated (Daniel & Nance). Courts have found portions of state constitutions to be unconstitutional when sufficient and up-to-date equipment is not equitably distributed among all schools (*DeRolph v. State of Ohio*, 1997; *Abbot v. Burke*, 1990).

No matter how the "divide" is defined, educator responsibility cannot be overlooked or avoided. This may mean that professional preparation programs, including formal degree coursework as well as in-service seminars, must be developed so that teachers and administrators are trained, brought up to speed, and maintained in their expertise of computer technology. It must mean that school districts apportion a level of the budget to such needed materials. It must also mean that multimedia instruction and the purchased equipment be equitably distributed both between schools and within schools. Only then will discrimination in this area be diminished and only then will all students, regardless of their differences, have an equal opportunity to a 21st century education.

NOTES

1. On appeal, the Court of Appeals for the Seventh circuit found the remedies ordered by the district court judge inequitable, but kept in tact the findings of discrimination against the school district.

2. The authors indicate that federal government investment in the E-rate had increased to over $10 billion dollars by 2002. The additional funds demonstrate the force of federal legislation vis-à-vis continued support of schools and libraries in the technology enterprise. It also evidences that such assistance has slowed considerably with the inauguration of the Bush Administration and the platform of the FCC chair, Michael Powell to limit federal spending in this area. Funds slated for the training of teachers in technology have been substantially reduced, thereby furthering the digital divide in the United States.

3. Sperry and Daniel define the "Internet" as a "giant network of innumerable smaller groups of linked computers." The World Wide Web serves as an on-line store of knowledge and information.

4. This portion of the Constitution has three clauses, "privileges and immunities," "due process," and "equal protection." The precise language reads, "No state shall make or enforce any law which shall abridge the privileges or immunities of citizens of the United States; nor shall any State deprive any person of life, liberty, or property, without due process of law; nor deny to any person within its jurisdiction the equal protection of its laws.

REFERENCES

Abbot v. Burke, 575 A.2d 359 (N. J. 1990).

ACLU v. Reno, 929 F.Supp. 824 (E. D.Pa. 1996).

Alexander, J. C. (1992). The promise of a cultural sociology: Technological discourse and the sacred and profane information machine. In: R. Munch & N. J. Smelser (Eds), *Theory of Culture* (pp. 293–323). Berkeley and Los Angeles: University of California Press.

Americans with Disabilities Act, 42 U.S.C. § 12101 et. seq. (2001).

Ashcroft v. Free Speech Coalition, 122 S.Ct. 1389 (2002).

Assistive Technology for Individuals with Disabilities Act, 29 U.S.C. §3001 (2001).

Banks, J. (1983). A response to a Nation at Risk, King County Library Service Association Meeting, University of Washington, on file with the author.

Becker, H. J. (1991). How computers are used in the United States: Basic data from the 1989 I. E. A. Computers in Educational Survey. *Journal of Educational Computing Research*, *17*(4), 385–406.

Bok, D. (1985, May/June). Looking into education's high-tech future. *Harvard Magazine*, 29–38.

Brennaman, N. (2002, Summer). G8's dotforce initiative: Bridging the digital divide or widening it? *Minnesota Journal of Global Trade*, *11*, 311–336.

Brockman, J. (1996). *Digerati: encounters with the cyberlite.* San Francisco: Hardwired.

Brown v. Board of Education, Topeka, 347 U.S. 483 (1954).

Clinton, W. (1996, January 23). Presidential State of the Union Address, *U.S. Capitol*, http://clinton2.nara.gov/WH/New/other/sotu.html (visited June 27, 2002).

Clinton W. President Bill Clinton, Future of the Net. *<http://www.cnet.com/Content/Features/Dlife/Future/Visionaries/Interviews/int.clinton.html>* as quoted in Gable, W. Internet Use Policies Required in School Districts That Allow Pupils On-line Access, *McGeorge Law Review*, (29), 573–582.

Colton Joint (Ca) Unified School. District (1995). *Individuals with Disabilities Education Law Reporter, 22*, 895–901.

Damarin, S. (2000). The digital divide vs. digital differences: Principles for equitable use of technology in education. To appear in *Educational Technology*.

Daniel P. T. K., & Pauken, P. (2002). The electronic media and school violence: Lessons learned and issues presented. *Education Law Reporter, 164*, 1–40.

Daniel P. T. K., & Pauken, P. (1999). The impact of the electronic media on instructor productivity and institutional ownership within copyright law. *Education Law Reporter, 132*, 1–20.

Daniel, P. T. K. (1998). Copyright law, fair use, and the internet: Information for administrators and other educational officials. *Education Law Reporter, 122*, 899–911.

Daniel, P. T. K. (1997). The electronic media and student rights to the information highway. *Education Law Reporter, 121*, 1–42.

Daniel, P. T. K., & Daniel, V. (2000). A legal portrait of the artist and art educator in free expression and cyberspace. *Education Law Reporter, 140*, 431–459.

Daniel, P. T. K., & Nance, J. (2002). The role of the administrator in instructional technology policy. Accepted for publication in the *Brigham Young Journal of Education and Law.*

Daniel, P. T. K. (1980). A history of discrimination against students in Chicago secondary schools. *History of Education Quarterly, 20,* 147–162.

DeRolph v. State of Ohio, 712 N.E.2d 125 (Ohio, 1997).

Dispenza, M. (2002). Overcoming a new digital divide: Technology accommodations and the undue hardship defense under the Americans with Disabilities Act. *Syracuse Law Review, 52,* 159–181.

Doe v. Mutual of Omaha Insurance Company, 179 F.3d 557, 559 (7th Cir. 1999).

Gore, A. (July 15, 1990), Communications: Networking the future. We need a national "Superhighway" for computer information. *Washington Post*, p. B3.

Green, K. C. (1991, Jan./Feb.). A technology agenda for the 1990s. *Change*. Green postulates that during the 1980s higher education institutions spent as much as $16 billions on computers.

Hammond, A. (2002). The digital divide in the new millennium. *Cardozo Arts and Entertainment Law Journal, 20*, 135–156.

Hampton v. Jefferson County Board of Education, 102 F.Supp.2d 358 (W. D.Ky. 2000).

Hernandez, G., Eddy, K., & Muchmore, J. (2001, Fall). Insurance web lining and unfair discrimination in cyberspace. *Southern Methodist University Law Review, 54*, 1953–1972.

Individuals with Disabilities Education Act, 20 U.S.C. §1400 et.seq (2000).

Jin, S., & Abate, R. (1999, February 28-March 4). Teachers and technology tools in the middle school, Site 99: Society for information Technology and Teacher Education International Conference (San Antonio, Texas). ERIC: ED 432285.

Kennard, W. (1999, May). Equality in the information age. *Federal Communications Law Journal, 51*, 553-556.

Keyes v. School District No. 1, 670 F.Supp. 1513 (D. Colo. 1987).

Keyes v. School District No. 1, 413 U.S. 189 (1973).

Kirp, D. (1973). Schools as sorters. *University of Pennsylvania Law Review, 121*, 705–751.

Kling, R. (1991). Computerization and social transformation. *Science, Technology, and Human Values, 16*, 342–367.

Labaton, S. (2002, Feb. 7). New F. C. C. chief would curb agency reach. *N.Y. Times*, p. C1.

Mendels, P. (2000, March). Offered old computers, some school officials decline. New York Times, <http://www.nytimes.com/library/tech/00/03/cyber/education/22education.html> (visited, June 30, 2002).

Morell, J. A., & Fleischer, M. (1991). The impact of computer systems: Revolution or incremental change. In: J. A. Morell & M. Fleischer (Eds), *Advances in the Implementation and Impact of Computer Systems* (Vol. 1, pp. xii–xxiii). Greenwich, CT: JAI Press.

National Commission on Excellence in Education (1983). *A nation at risk: The imperative for educational reform*, p. 1. Government Printing Office.

Nunn, J., McPherson, S., & Rust, W. (1998, March). Preparing teachers for school-based technology leadership. In: *Society for Information Technology and Teacher Education International Conference Proceedings.*

People Who Care v. Rockford Board of Education School District 205, 851 F. Supp. 905 (N. D.Ill. 1994). *People Who Care v. Rockford Board of Education School District* 205, 111 F.3d 528 (1997).

Powell, M. (2001). Testimony on telecommunication and the internet. *Hearing Before House Energy and Commerce*, 108th Cong. 54 (2001), 2001 WL 312498.

Roszak, T. (1986). *The cult of information: The folklore of computers and the true art of thinking*. New York: Pantheon.

San Francisco (CA) Unified Sch. District. (1998). *Individuals with Disabilities Education Law Reporter*, (29), 912–914.

Sculley, J. (1989, Sept.). the relationship between business and higher education: A perspective on the 21st Century. *Communications of the ACM, 32,* 1056–1061. searchNetworking.com. http://searchNetworking.techtarget.com/sDefinition/0,,sid7_gci213915,00.html (visited, June 24, 2002).

Section 504 of the Rehabilitation Act of 1973, 29 U.S.C. § 794 et.seq. (2001).

Shelly, G., Cashman, T., Gunter, R., & Gunter, G (2002). *Integrating technology in the classroom*. Boston: Course technology.[2]

Spectar, J. (Fall, 2000). Bridging the global digital divide: Frameworks for access and the world wireless web. *North Carolina Journal of International Law and Commercial Regulation, 26*, 57–103.

Sperry, D., Daniel, P. T. K., Huefner, D., & Gee, E. G. (1998). Education law and the public schools: A compendium.

Statement of Michael Powell, Chairman, FCC, *Testimony on Telecommunication and the Internet: Hearing Before House Energy and Commerce, 108th Cong. 54 (2001)*, available at 2001 WL 312498.

Stern, C. (2001, February 7). New FCC chairman favors a non-activist approach. *Washington Post*, p. E1.

The Telecommunications Act of 1996, 47 U.S.C. § 251 et seq. (2000).

U. S. Constitution, Amendment XIV, § 1.[4]

United States Department of Education, Office of Educational Technology. (2001). Internet access in U.S. public schools and classrooms: 1994–2000, *http://nces.ed.gov/pubs2001/* internet access. (Visited June 27, 2002).

United States Department of Education, Office of Educational Technology. (1996). e-learning: Putting a world-class education at the fingertips of all children: http://www.ed.gov/Technology/elearning;index.html (visited June 27, 2002).

United States Department of Education, Office of Civil Rights. (2001). Agreement to resolve OCR complaint between North Carolina State University and the U.S. Dept. of Education, Office of Civil Rights: <http://www.icdri.org/north_carolina_state_ university.htm> (visited, June 29, 2002).

United States Department of Commerce (2000). Falling through the net: Toward digital inclusion, http://search.ntia.doc.gov/pdf/fttn00.pdf. (visited, June 27, 2002).

Vaas, L. Web blind spots. eWeek, at http://www.eweek.com (visited June 24, 2002).

Willie, C. (1982). On excellence and equity in higher education. Paper on file with the author.

9. SUPERVISION'S PRIMARY TASK: SYNTHESIZING PROFESSIONAL DEVELOPMENT TO MEET INDIVIDUAL TEACHER NEEDS AND ATTAIN SCHOOL ORGANIZATIONAL GOALS

Stephen Earl Lucas

ABSTRACT

This chapter views the leadership function of instructional supervision through three lenses: organizational improvement, teacher development, and student growth and achievement. This chapter argues that quality supervision is a product of the principal developing and maintaining a trifocal view of (a) improving the school as an organization by (b) developing teacher capacity to (c) address the growth and achievement needs of students. Failure to adequately address any of these three areas leads to inadequate and unproductive supervisory behavior. Conversely, principals who develop this trifocal approach facilitate a synergistic system that enables the school, its faculty, and its students to grow.

Challenges of Urban Education and Efficacy of School Reform, Volume 6, pages 165–186.

ISBN: 0-7623-0426-X

INTRODUCTION

The discourse regarding American public education since the early 1980s has centered upon the issue of reform. Numerous studies, reports, and legislative initiatives have led both the public and the educational community to critically examine both the processes and outcomes of the nation's public education enterprise. Much of this activity has been concerned with determining what makes for effective schools, teaching, and teachers, and, as a corollary, what processes can be used for improving schools, teaching, and teachers.

A primary role of the school principal is that of instructional supervisor, and that role has five major tasks: direct assistance to teachers, group development, professional development, curriculum development, and action research (Glickman et al., 2001). The viewpoint of this chapter is that the professional development task of the principal is the one that has the most potential for effecting both individual teacher and school organizational change. Additionally, the chapter focuses on the task of professional development because "if one is to look for a place to improve the quality of education in a school, the sensible place to look is the continuous education of educators – that is, professional development" (Glickman et al., 2001, p. 360).

The term "professional development" is used in this chapter to encompass all activities which are undertaken by educational organizations to improve schools, teaching, and teachers. On-the-job training, renewal, human resource development, continuing education, professional growth, and staff development are terms often used as synonyms for professional development. Professional development can be defined as "the provision of activities designed to advance the knowledge, skills, and understanding of teachers in ways that lead to changes in their thinking and classroom behavior" (Fenstermacher & Berliner, 1985, p. 283).

Unfortunately, however, within the education community professional development often has a poor reputation. Professional development activities are frequently viewed as irrelevant, disjointed, and ineffective. Teacher attendance on professional development days is frequently poor, and even teachers who actually do attend these activities often leave the sessions feeling that they have gained little, if any, useful knowledge or skills. Nevertheless, the reform efforts of recent years and the increasingly diverse needs of America's schoolchildren are combining to make effective professional development even more important than it has been in past years.

This chapter first explores the literature related to the historic and recent context of professional development, professional development as the improvement of education, possible sources of dissatisfaction with professional development, the use of professional development for individual teacher development and the attainment of school organizational goals, and the possibility of professional development that synthesizes individual and organizational development. A two-dimensional framework is then employed to describe the needs assessment, planning, delivery, implementation, and evaluation of professional development activities that are either high or low in individual or organizational development emphasis. The framework illustrates the advantage of developing professional development programs that emphasize meeting both individual teacher needs and school organizational goals.

THE HISTORICAL AND RECENT CONTEXT OF PROFESSIONAL DEVELOPMENT

Professional development activities have existed in American public schools since the early years of the nation (DeLuca, 1991). The supervision of beginning teachers by more experienced teachers, state-run normal schools, Horace Mann's in-service education, four-year teacher colleges, reading circles, collaborative action research, self-directed professional growth activities, and organizational development programs have all been utilized to improve schools, teaching, and teachers. Staff development in the twentieth century consisted primarily of workshops conducted prior to opening day in larger districts, state teachers' conventions held in the fall, teacher institutes on Saturdays, and off-campus courses offered by colleges and universities (Dillon-Peterson, 1991).

Despite the wide historical variation of activities deemed to be professional development, any discussion of recent professional development history and practice must be framed in terms of the effective schools research of the 1970s, the reform movement of the 1980s, and the public demands for school accountability in the 1990s (March et al., 1993). The effective schools research of the 1970s established that student achievement is unequivocally affected by the actions of schools, principals, and teachers (Clark et al., 1984). Edmonds (1982) lists several characteristics of effective schools, including the principal's leadership, a broadly understood instructional focus, a school environment conducive to teaching and learning, teacher expectations of student achievement, and program evaluation based upon measures of student achievement.

The reform movement of the 1980s followed on the heels of the effective schools research of the 1970s. The more than 20,000 educational reform reports issued in the United States during the 1980s developed a broad consensus for increased teacher authority and accountability as the primary basis for authentic reform of the schools; this increased authority and accountability on the part of teachers necessitated a renewed emphasis on professional development programs (Futrell, 1991). Fagan (1995) points out that Goals 2000, the primary federal legislation which emerged from the reform movement, placed a renewed emphasis on professional development by adding it to the list of national goals as well as providing funds at the local school district level for improved professional development programs.

The 1990s was the decade in which American public schools began redefining education in terms which emphasized accountability (Gallegos, 1994). Rather than focusing on "processes, procedures, and inputs," schools began emphasizing "product, results, and outcomes" (p. 34). This change of emphasis was a massive transition, or paradigm shift, for educators to understand, and professional development was seen as playing an important role in helping teachers and administrators work through the changes in practice this shift necessitated.

THE IMPROVEMENT OF EDUCATION AS THE AIM OF PROFESSIONAL DEVELOPMENT

While Harris (1989) and Fenstermacher and Berliner (1985) broadly define professional development activities as those designed to bring about improvement and advancement in teaching and learning in schools, Miller and Wolf (1978) specify professional development's goal as being the "promotion of change in educators and schools that improves the conditions for learning and teaching" (p. 141). Glickman et al. (2001) note that over 85% of school budgets is devoted to employee salaries; thus, the improvement of educational quality is contingent upon the improvement of educators themselves. Richey and Sikorski (1993) contend that the education sector must follow the lead of business and industry in viewing ongoing professional development as a necessity, rather than a luxury, especially in light of the profound changes facing society.

Hansen (1980) argues that staff development in schools is necessary for the following reasons: change is a fundamental element of our world today and the schools must be a part of that change; new knowledge and new skills are being required of our citizenry; there is a professional responsibility and need that the most valid and relevant skills and subject areas be included in school programs; renewal is characteristic of a dynamic and improving profession; and inservice education is a means of assisting the professional educator to be the best he or she might become (p. 68). Asayesh (1993b) quotes Guskey and Sparks, who assert that "if improvement results from change, there must be something to initiate that change. And what's going to initiate it other than staff development?" (p. 24). Asayesh also cites Showers, who contends that "there's fairly good evidence that no one has pulled off substantial change efforts, especially with improvement in student outcomes, without a substantial staff development program" (p. 24).

SOURCES OF DISSATISFACTION WITH PROFESSIONAL DEVELOPMENT

However, teachers, schools, and school districts often doubt the effectiveness of professional development programs. Azin-Manley, Sachse, and Olson (1996) attribute this attitude to professional development efforts which are sporadic in nature, unclear in intent, and unlinked to school goals and student achievement. Gilman et al. (1988, p. 2) cite three studies when discussing the sources of teacher dissatisfaction with professional development: Westcott's claim that "administrators sometimes 'fail to recognize the considerable knowledge and expertise in their own teaching staffs' "; Smith-Westberry and Job's belief that "many inservice programs are one-day sessions which. . . are viewed by teachers as 'disorganized, dull and irrelevant to their needs' "; and Van Cleaf and Reinhartz's assertion that "the worst failure of these inservice efforts is the lack of any follow-through."

Schiffer (1978) contends that such disenchantments with staff development are fundamentally due to a disagreement between teachers, on the one hand, and schools and districts, on the other hand, as to the purpose of staff development activities:

> Some staff-development models are over committed to training teachers to fulfill organizational goals they have had little or no part in formulating. These models generally rest upon rational assumptions about the change process, and tend to ignore the diversity and stability of values held by individual staff members .... Another set of one-sided staff-development models is over committed to making personal change ... [these models] that focus almost exclusively on upgrading teachers' competencies, improving group interactions and problem-solving skills, or changing teacher behavior are insufficient (pp. 21–22).

The essentially conflicting perspectives as to the desired purpose of professional development depicted above by Schiffer is likely a fundamental source of poor attitudes about professional development. Schools and districts, on the one hand, see professional development primarily as a means of achieving organizational goals, and teachers, on the other hand, see professional development primarily as a means for addressing their individual needs as teachers. It may be that the solution to this conflict does not rest in choosing one approach over the other, but in somehow harmonizing the two. Education is both an individual and an organizational endeavor. Virtually all learning today takes places within a social context, yet it must be acknowledged that learning is most meaningful when it is fully developed and grasped by each individual within that social context. In the words of Leiter and Cooper (1978),

> If no one wants to make the investment in changing the scope, quality, and direction of in-service (and preservice) teacher education, then we will continue our *ad hoc* crisis-oriented

> relationship to teacher training and education service deliver . . . the opportunity exists for collaborative, systematic professional development that is organic, relevant, and productive of real gains to the subjects of the educational process – our students. The need is obvious, the failures of current approaches legion, and the benefits of a change in approach compelling (pp. 123–124).

PROFESSIONAL DEVELOPMENT FOCUSED ON INDIVIDUAL TEACHERS

Showers et al. (1987) highlight the individual nature of teaching by asserting that what a teacher thinks about teaching determines what the teacher does. It is important to recognize that teachers control the most important aspects of how classrooms operate, and that teachers have strong opinions and feelings about the ways in which they are asked to do their jobs (Weissglass, 1991). Hord and Boyd (1995) declare that schools will not be renewed until individual teachers themselves are renewed. Little (1993) believes that effective staff development can only take place within settings which take into explicit account the individual contexts and experiences of teachers, and even offer support for informed dissent.

Clift et al. (1990) write that staff developers must consider the context of the individual in planning staff development, including: (a) a recognition that staff development cannot be segmented as an entity wholly separate from the lives of teachers; (b) an accommodation of teacher feelings about change and a resolution of potential conflict; (c) the need of teachers and administrators to conduct and learn about current research; and (d) the necessity of providing encouragement, ideas, time, and resources to teachers in order to avoid passive or hostile attitudes toward staff development. Levine (1989) incorporates the adult phase development theories of Erik Erikson, Daniel Levinson, and Roger Gould into a call for staff development programs which carefully consider the personal and career needs of teachers as individuals who face major life tasks and conflicts.

Shroyer (1990) believes that staff development should, in fact, provide opportunities for personal self-actualization, be carried out with divergent approaches, and encourage diversity and experimentation on the part of individual teachers. Killion and Harrison (1990) call for staff developers to create organizational structures that accommodate and support the changes individuals are expected to make. Glatthorn (1987) enumerates many of the commonly used individual and peer-based approaches to staff development, including cooperative development, colleague consultation, peer coaching, and small groups engaged in self-directed professional dialogue, curriculum development, and action research. Hall and Loucks (1978, p. 37) propose a "concerns-based adoption model" as a framework for formulating staff development programs considerate of the individual. This model asserts that: change is a process, not an event; the individual teacher must be the focus of strategies designed to effect change in the classroom; change is an experience which is highly individual in nature; the change process itself is experienced in different ways by individuals; staff development is best achieved by using a teacher-centered methodology emphasizing a diagnostic-prescriptive approach; and staff developers need to work within the overall system while adapting their approaches to individual needs.

Caffarella (1993, p. 30) urges the use of "self-directed learning" models in which individual teacher needs serve as the outline for staff developers to facilitate activities and supervision which enhance individual teacher growth. Small (1990), however, cautions that the historically individualistic nature of staff development needs to be tempered by expecting individual teachers to focus energy toward change and development that is more balanced and productive. Doing so enables the organization to facilitate and support individual decision making and development. Similarly, Miller and Wolf (1978, p. 141) envision a "staff development/school change" model which cycles through: individual concerns; individual action; dialogue about action; collaborative action, and organizational change and support for change. However, Vojtek (1992) reports that recent staff development funding practices still reflect a budgetary orientation which emphasizes individual staff development practices rather than organizational practices.

PROFESSIONAL DEVELOPMENT FOCUSED ON SCHOOL ORGANIZATIONAL GOALS

The most recent literature addressing the individual-organizational aspect of staff development planning appears to lean more toward the organizational side. Sparks (1994) contends that staff development is being altered by the prevalence of systems thinking – the recognition of the complex, interdependent relationships among the various parts of organizations such as schools and school districts. As a result, reports Vojtek (1992), staff developers are becoming organizational developers to a greater extent.

Thus, the focus of staff development may be beginning to change. Little (1993) argues that staff development should place classroom practice within the larger contexts of school practice and the educational careers of children. Shroyer (1990) calls for staff development to increase organizational collegiality, self-analysis, and self-sufficiency. As a consequence, asserts Conway (1990), the development process focuses on asking, looking, and examining in order to discover organizational needs, which may or may not coincide with the perceived needs of teachers.

Duttweiler (1989) and Hinson et al. (1989) both emphasize that staff development that is more organizational in orientation tends to be more ongoing, coherent, systematic, and long-range than that which is more individual-oriented. Watson (1994) contends that organizationally-focused development should enhance teamwork and communications skills, while Showers, Joyce, and Bennett (1987) believe that organizationally-focused development increases social cohesion and increases teachers' willingness to try new ideas. Organizationally-focused development, according to Joyce et al. (1989) increases vertical-horizontal cohesiveness, reducing administrator-teacher divisions. Consequently, believes Small (1990), organizations should experience a transformation which increases productivity, cooperation, and teamwork.

Leithwood et al. (1995) report that schools with a coherent sense of direction are better able to cope with the numerous initiatives they develop or have thrust upon them; what is key, however, is that all staff members share a common understanding of the school's overall purpose. Glickman and Calhoun (1991) assert that schools which actually accomplish student learning goals because of staff development programs do so because the schools are able to tie their staff development activities to the school's overall purpose. This is possible because the staff has an underlying belief and commitment to the site-based priorities and commitment it has developed.

DuFour and Berkey (1995) urge site administrators to implement the following practices in order to ensure successful, site-based organizational development: create consensus about the school's future; identify, promote, and protect shared values; monitor the critical elements of the school improvement effort; ensure systematic collaboration throughout the school; encourage experimentation; model a personal commitment to professional growth; provide individual staff development opportunities; provide staff development programs that are purposeful and research-based; promote individual and organization self-efficacy; and stay the course in difficult times and situations.

Daniel and Stallion (1996) list as critical components of site-based organizational development: preparing an articulated mission; planning for professional development at the school and individual practitioner level; implementing the school professional development plan; providing broad support for professional development; building and maintaining the capacity to perform; and evaluating the professional development program.

By contrast, Asayesh (1993a) lists some common obstacles of long-range planning: the typically brief tenure of superintendents; the lack of quality planning time for teachers and administrators; a lack of commitment for school leadership; a lack of adequate school staff support; a lack of training and preparation in long-range planning; and the lack of ongoing attention paid to the long-range plan.

Finally, according to Wood and Thompson (1993), the school, rather than the district, should be the primary focus of improved practice and staff development. Lipman (1991) reports that school-based staff development leads to: more positive teacher response to staff development; better focus on school needs and goals; increased collaboration in thinking about and planning of instruction; more positive attitudes about professional development in general; and more teacher-planned and led staff development activities. However, contend Guskey and Sparks (1991), it is more important to remember that school organizational development must still take place within the context of the district's total improvement effort, especially in regard to organizational climate and culture in relation to innovation.

THE POSSIBILITY OF AN ORGANIZATIONAL-INDIVIDUAL SYNTHESIS

The nature of the education enterprise is both individual and organizational, and much of the recent literature on staff development has begun to address a possible harmonization between these two aspects. Duttweiler (1989) asserts that while staff development should be school-focused, it should also be teacher-driven. Wood and Thompson (1993) believe that staff development programs should support opportunities for both school improvement and individual professional growth. Organizational development, as defined by Killion and Harrison (1990), should have a broader view that requires a planned approach to change based on the needs of both the people and the organization.

Joyce and Showers (1996) propose a three-pronged synthesis of aims for staff development: serving individual teachers by enhancing their clinical skills and academic knowledge; taking collective actions through studying school improvement processes; and serving the school district by implementing districtwide initiatives in curriculum, instruction, and technology. Caldwell (1991) believes that programs which foster increases in teacher professionalization can improve not only the instructional process but also the development of teachers as leaders who actively participate in reshaping of schools and districts.

According to Richardson et al. (1990), the movement toward organizational development should be a process undertaken to define and meet changing self-improvement objectives, while making it possible for the individuals in the organization to meet their personal and professional objectives. Nebgen (1990) believes that the technique of strategic planning is effective in improving the organizational adaptability of schools in a way that is dynamic, self-renewing, creative, visionary, and has the support and commitment of both the staff and the community. McCarty (1993) calls for learning organizations to incorporate nine key concepts into staff development activities in order to facilitate this synthesis, including: safety; identity; connectedness; power; meaningfulness; risk-taking; models and mentors; counseling; and fun. Shafer (1995) believes that the identification of specific individual problems can lead to collaborative action which results in both the goal of problem solving and the goal of individual teacher professional growth.

A specific action that must take place to effect this synthesis, according to Hord and Boyd (1995), is the establishment of norms of continuous critical inquiry and improvement that govern individual and organizational behavior; this is possible only within a community of professionals. Richardson et al. (1990) call for the development of organizational climates that are respective, supportive, and positive, and which have as their aim better learning for students and continuous, responsible self-renewal for educators and schools. Leithwood et al. (1995) argue that these climates are ones which address the acknowledged concerns of teachers, and allow them to socially process, with other educators, the problems and the information they encounter in staff development activities.

In addition to these norms, Rothberg and Bozeman (1990) emphasize the necessity of: trust and conflict resolution; shared leadership; clearly articulated control procedures; effective interpersonal communications; clear problem-solving and decision-making processes, and a climate of creativity. Nowak (1994) adds the need for understanding personal factors in professional growth; the relationship of adult development to staff development; organizational and curricular needs; the importance of staff development for all staff, not just teachers; the combination of cognitive, affective, and behavioral growth characteristics; the necessity of site-based staff development; group facilitation skills; outcomes-based staff development; research-based practices; the dynamics of organizational development; the nature of the change process, and the changing role of the staff developer as a facilitator.

Katzenmayer and Reid (1991) point out the need for staff developers themselves to recognize a paradigm shift in their work, with a new focus upon their ability to facilitate change and emphasize the development of teams and organizations. Fullan et al. (1990) believe that this new kind of staff development work will emphasize: teachers, administrators, and higher education personnel in collegial partnerships; improving student experiences and learning; a renewed spirit of inquiry; schools as living laboratories for action research; curriculum and instruction as priorities; the management of change, and the systemic linkage of classroom, teacher, and school improvement.

Baskett and Dixon (1992) assert that staff developers will need to develop the following strategies to work within this new model of staff development: the adoption of continuous improvement as an organizational strategy; linking individual contributions to organizational goals; rewarding and supporting individuals who take responsibility for their own learning; developing values that support the organization's structure and purpose and are in harmony with the values of individual teachers; encouraging administrators to set examples by learning themselves; valuing differences; supporting risk-takers; developing effective communication systems that include a network of all stake holders, flexible support structures and processes, and a supportive culture; fostering collaboration in work and play, and encouraging learning by implementing rewards and processes that support creativity and innovation.

Consequently, contends Watson (1994), staff development should evolve from needs identified by the staff which facilitate the shaping of shared vision, enable the formulation of corresponding management plans, and develop leadership and technical skills. Small (1990) points out the need for both individuals and organizations to have a clear sense of purpose, while Wood and Thompson (1993) emphasize the necessity of individual and collective commitment and ownership of new practices in order for effective change to take place. Clark et al. (1984) assert that teachers are able and willing to implement change when they are provided with opportunities to plan implementation, receive appropriate training, are able to interact with each other, having breathing space for experimentation and failure, and receive continuous assistance and support.

Finally, Little (1993) calls for a governance of staff development that ensures bureaucratic restraint and a balance between the interests of individuals and the interests of institutions. Small (1990) is careful to characterize the relationship between individual and organizational development as being informal and evolving, and Shroyer (1990) advises that staff development be based on the interrelationship between individual and organizational effectiveness. Murphy (1993) suggests that all staff development efforts be conceptualized in terms of individual, site, and system components, and Munger (1995) envisions job-embedded staff development processes that balance top-down with bottom-up processes that will change, combine, and balance the seemingly contradictory factors of organizational simplicity and complexity, structural looseness and tightness, and strong leadership and participatory decision making.

A TWO-DIMENSIONAL FRAMEWORK FOR ANALYZING PROFESSIONAL DEVELOPMENT

The focus of professional development – along with the needs assessments, planning, delivery, implementation, and evaluation processes associated with it, can be envisioned and analyzed within a two dimensional framework (Fig. 1).

	Low Emphasis on Attainment of School Organizational Goals	**High Emphasis on Attainment of School Organizational Goals**
High Emphasis on Individual Development of Teachers	**Quadrant Two** Organizationally ineffective	**Quadrant Four** Synthesized
Low Emphasis on Individual Development of Teachers	**Quadrant One** Random	**Quadrant Three** Individually irrelevant

Fig. 1. A Framework for Analyzing Professional Development.

In quadrant one of the framework, professional development activity is low on both individual and organizational emphases, with a resultant lack of purpose or focus. Quadrant two describes professional development that emphasizes individual teacher development significantly more than school organizational development, while Quadrant three contains professional development activity that has just the inverse emphases. Quadrant four professional development activity is characterized by a meaningful synthesis of both individual teacher and school organizational development. This framework enables the analysis of professional development activities along their five phases, or stages: needs assessment, planning, delivery, implementation, and evaluation.

Quadrant One: Low Individual and Organizational Emphases

Needs assessment. In this quadrant, there is a lack of authentic needs assessment at both the individual teacher and the organizational levels. The school's improvement plan – if there is one – is not used to generate growth goals that can be addressed through professional development. There is little or no effort made by school leadership to help individual teachers identify their individual needs as professionals. Quite often, needs are "identified" by reading the most recent professional development marketing brochures that arrive in the school mail. Consequently, there can be no meaningful correlation between professional development activities and either individual or organizational needs.

Planning. Because there has been a failure to conduct a meaningful needs assessment, planning for professional development activities in this quadrant is typically haphazard and incoherent. Too often, the school administrator charged with professional development conducts "planning" by selecting a packaged workshop to be delivered by an outside expert or consultant and making arrangements for payment to be made. As a result, there is very little possibility that the days or weeks leading up to the activity can be used to set the stage for a meaningful development activity.

Delivery. As might be expected, delivery of professional development activities in this quadrant tends to take place in stand-alone, isolated events such as one-time workshops brought into the school (as a pseudo-organizational activity) or attended by teachers offsite (as a pseudo-individualized activity). While the workshop (or other activity) may be delivered in a highly expert manner, its isolated nature mitigates its connection with either individual teacher or school organizational needs and growth.

Implementation. Whatever knowledge, dispositions, or skills are learned in a quadrant one professional development activity are likely to go unused. The fundamental failure to connect the activity with either individual or organizational needs results in learning that lacks urgency and, hence, application in the school. While the occasional professional development activity that has been selected and delivered in this way will strike a chord with a teacher or two and be put into practice (perhaps even to positive effect), there is nothing systematic about this process that leads to long-term, meaningful improvement of teachers or the school as a whole.

Evaluation. The evaluation of the usefulness and applicability of quadrant one professional development activity is likely to be as indiscriminate as the processes that led up to its selection and delivery. If evaluation is conducted at all, it probably lacks meaning because the focus of the activity itself had little or nothing to do with what teachers or the school needed for growth. As a result, the results of any evaluation conducted are of little use for the shaping of future professional development activities.

Quadrant Two: High Individual Emphasis but Low Organizational Emphasis

Needs Assessment. In quadrant two professional development activity, needs assessment in conducted primarily, if not exclusively, at the individual teacher level. Little attention is paid to how the individual developmental needs of the teacher – however legitimate they may be – mesh with the overall improvement of the school. In schools characterized by this approach, teachers may or may not be guided by a leader or peer who can help them accurately assess their professional growth needs. In better situations, teachers can experience positive – although very individualistic – growth; however, in other situations, teachers may undergo a fairly random series of professional development activities that end up leading to very little, if any, growth.

Planning. Similar to quadrant one professional development, little if any planning is done by school administrators or teachers in quadrant two. Rather, because these activities are typically delivered by individuals or organizations external to the school, preparation is normally restricted to making arrangements to attend a workshop or activity. In better situations, however, the possibility exists that some preparation may be required to make the actual professional development activity more meaningful. However, the highly individualized nature of this quadrant's activities make it unlikely that this preparatory work will be conducted in a way that is authentically job-embedded or in collaboration with other teachers or administrators in the school.

Delivery. Delivery in quadrant two professional development is similar to that of quadrant one. Typically, it is not on the school site, is not consistently embedded in the teacher's work, and is often delivered in stand-alone, disconnected events. Too often, an individual attending such an activity is the sole participant from his or her school, limiting the possibilities for collaborative dialogue either at the session itself, on the ride home, or back in the school. As a result, such experiences tend to become somewhat formal, segmented, and unconnected with either the individual teacher's work experience or the school's communal life.

Implementation. At times, quadrant two professional development can result in high levels of implementation by individual teachers. However, this implementation is highly contingent upon the effectiveness of both the activity itself and the motivation and efficacy of a teacher learning, and acting upon the learning, in relative isolation. Because there is little, if any, systematic connection in this quadrant between the individual teacher and the school (or at least a group of teachers within the school), there is a high likelihood that whatever implementation occurs will be brief, at a surface level, and ineffectual. Only in rare instances do such activities engender more than relatively isolated improvement in individual teachers.

Evaluation. The very nature of quadrant two professional development limits the value of its evaluation. While it is certainly true than any individual teacher can assess the value of an activity in relation to his or her unique needs, there is no guarantee that his or her assessment will be accurate. Without the sort of confirmatory assessment that can be conducted in group or whole-school professional development, it is likely that the individual's evaluation of the activity's worth will be idiosyncratic and – too often – driven by prepared evaluation forms created by the developer and deliverer of the professional development activity itself. Hence, whatever evaluation does emerge is based on suspect criteria and judgment and is likely to be of little use in determining whether the activity is valuable for either future individual or organizational growth.

Quadrant Three: High Organizational Emphasis but Low Individual Emphasis

Needs Assessment. Unlike the highly individualized needs assessment of quadrant two, in quadrant three needs are assessed primarily with a view toward organizational change and growth. In more positive situations, administrators and teachers collaborate to determine what teachers need to learn and how they need to develop in order to support the overall positive growth of the school as an organization. In less positive situations, formal leaders may attempt to gauge the faculty's development needs with little or no input from the teachers. This is particularly likely when there is either no explicit school improvement plan, or the plan has been developed solely by school administrators. In these situations, of course, there is a high likelihood of mismatch between perceived organizational and individual teacher needs for professional development.

Planning. As in needs assessment, there exists the possibility in quadrant three professional development for collaborative administrator-teacher planning of professional development activities. However, in situations in which the focus of professional development is too heavily weighted toward organizational development – even to the exclusion of individual teacher development – planning can become hierarchical, top-down, and unilateral. When this happens, the opportunity to develop key teacher leadership is lost. In addition, given the numerous and pressing demands facing administrators, planning done in isolation by formal leaders is unlikely to be as deliberate and meaningful as that which is done in collaboration with teachers.

Delivery. The delivery of quadrant three professional development tends to occur more frequently at the school site than it does in quadrants one and two. Professional development in this quadrant tends to be delivered by either outside parties or the school administration itself, although it must be acknowledged that principals will often tap teachers to deliver (or help deliver) professional development activities in which they have expertise. Because quadrant three professional development emphasizes organizational over individual needs, the sessions can tend to be somewhat formal, with teachers attending but not actively engaging. This is particularly true if there has not been significant administrator-teacher collaboration in the needs assessment and delivery stages.

Implementation. Quadrant four professional development implementation is likely to be haphazard, like in quadrant two, but in a different way and for a different reason. If the needs assessment, planning, and delivery stages have led to a mismatch between the needs of the teachers and what the professional development activity delivers, there is likely to be wholesale failure to implement what has been taught or modeled. This is in contrast to the implementation pattern of quadrant two, where implementation is likely to be hit or miss with individual teachers rather than the whole faculty. While the individualized focus of quadrant two leads to a lack of mutual knowledge and support among teachers, an overly-organizational focus in quadrant three may quite likely lead to a high degree of mutual knowledge and support among teachers – unfortunately, however, that knowledge and support will be garnered to block implementation of the professional development learning.

Evaluation. Professional development activities in quadrant three will be evaluated almost exclusively by the degree to which they happen (or don't happen) to meet the individual needs of teachers. Again, particularly in schools in which there is not a living, collaboratively developed school improvement plan, professional development in this quadrant tends to be hierarchically developed and insensitive to teacher needs. As a result, teachers can arrive at these activities focused primarily on the mismatch between organizational goals and their individual needs. Consequently, the deck is stacked against meaningful evaluation of the activity, and those activities that are truly beneficial are devalued simply because of the failure to link (and make explicit that linkage) between organizational and individual development.

Quadrant Four: High Individual Emphasis and Organizational Emphases

Needs Assessment. Schools and principal that emphasize both individual needs and organizational goals in professional development make the effort to explore and articulate the connections between individual teacher development and the attainment of the school's organizational goals. Consequently, quadrant four professional develop needs assessment is characterized by an explicit linkage between what the school as an organizational needs to learn how to do to be better as a whole and what individual teachers needs to learn how to do better to contribute to that overall growth. Hence, needs assessment is conducted at two levels. First, the administrators and teachers together determine what growth opportunities are needed by the faculty as a whole to achieve the school goals that have been collaboratively developed. Second, within that overall school needs framework, individual teachers are helped by their peers and by leaders to assess where they may need more individualized support to achieve significant growth in particular areas. As a result, some professional development activities are identified that meet whole school needs, others are identified that meet individual teacher needs, and the two sets of needs and activities are coherently linked within the context of overall school improvement.

Planning. Similar to needs assessment, planning of quadrant four professional development is multi-leveled. Because professional development needs were assessed in reference to both the overall goals of the school and the individual needs of the teachers, planning is carried out collaboratively at both the whole-school and the individual teacher levels. Teams of administrators and teachers develop activities (or, where appropriate and meaningful, contract with outside parties) that connect with the school's overall plan for growth. This, of course, results not only in the development of plans, but of teachers as leaders within the school. Then, administrators or teacher-leaders help individual teachers plan for participation in other activities that are targeted for their particular needs. Because this individualized planning takes place within the context of the overall school planning, the possibility exists for school personnel to develop targeted activities within the school instead of relying exclusively on outside parties and experiences as in quadrant two.

Delivery. Delivery of professional development in quadrant four can take many forms, most of which look, on the surface, similar to delivery in the other three quadrants. However, while they may look the same, they are fundamentally different in impact because they are now being delivered within the context of a collaboratively developed improvement process that addresses both organizational and individual needs. Thus, depending on the nature of those organizational and individual needs, varying mixtures of locales, formats, groupings, and timing can be employed. Regardless of the specific nature of these delivery variables, however, the synthesis of organizational and individual needs results in activities that by their very nature tend to lead to job-embedded, meaningful activities that lead to collaborative processing and reflection by participants. Additionally, there exists much more potential for authentic teacher leadership in the delivery of the activities, as well as administrator delivery that is more meaningful than that found in quadrant three.

Implementation. Because the stages of needs assessment, planning, and delivery have been executed within the context of an individual-organizational synthesis in this quadrant, the likelihood, quality, depth, and persistence of implementation are much more likely than in the other three quadrants. Implementation is higher because the school as a whole has already bought into the rationale for the particular dispositions, knowledge, and skills delivered through the professional development activity. Mutual motivation and support is higher when the whole faculty is on the same page in terms of the school's overall goals. The inclusion of individualized professional development within the school's overall goals context enables each teacher to gain the support needed to bring them up to speed on particular aspects of the organizational plan. Teachers sense that they are important both as individuals and as organizational members, and respond by working harder to implement the strategies they have collaborated to identify and learn.

Evaluation. Evaluation of quadrant four professional development is more meaningful than in the other three quadrants for a number of reasons. First, because the activities have been collaboratively identified in relation to the school's explicit goals, there is a set of common expectations for what participation in the activities should have accomplished. Second, because a large portion of the activities have been experienced, processed, and implemented in a collective, rather than individualistic, fashion, the possibility of triangulating perceptions and experiences across the faculty is more likely. Finally, teacher judgments about the individualized activities they do participate in are more meaningful because they are executed within the context of overall school improvement. Even if a teacher is the only one who experiences a particular activity, he or she can evaluate their learning in terms of the criteria that have been either explicitly developed by the school or can be reasonably inferred from the emphases of the school's improvement plan and process.

SUMMARY

This chapter has delved into the possibility of redefining quality supervision by principals as providing leadership for professional development that synthesizes the meeting of individual teacher needs and the attainment of school organizational goals. It has done so by first exploring the literature related to the historical and recent context of professional development, professional development as the improvement of education, possible sources of dissatisfaction with professional development, and the use of professional development for individual teacher development and the attainment of school organizational goals. A four-quadrant framework, based upon high and low emphases on meeting individual teacher needs and school organizational goals, was employed to analyze what professional development needs assessment, planning, delivery, implementation, and evaluation typically look like in schools.

Because schools are organizations comprised of numerous individuals, their principals must work to identify goals for improvement that will be meaningful at both the organizational and individual levels. Merely identifying goals is not enough, however; principals must use their formal roles as instructional leaders and supervisors to facilitate professional development activities that enable both the organization and its individuals to attain those goals. Failing to link professional development to either individual teacher needs or organizational goals leads to random (quadrant one), organizationally ineffective (quadrant two), or irrelevant (quadrant three) activities and programs. Taking the time and developing the expertise to synthesize the individual and the organizational in professional development will lead to meaningful needs assessment, planning, delivery, evaluation, and – most importantly – implementation of teaching and learning strategies that improve individual teaching and schools for their students.

REFERENCES

Asayesh, G. (1993a). Long-range planning for individual and organization development. *Journal of Staff Development, 14*(2), 12–15.

Asayesh, G. (1993b). Staff development for improving student outcomes. *Journal of Staff Development, 14*(3), 24–27.

Azin-Manley, M., Sachse, T., & Olson, C. (1996). *Staff development needs assessment survey (October 1996).* Jackson, WY: Region V Board of Cooperative Services Center for School Improvement, Wyoming Department of Education.

Baskett, H. K. M., & Dixon, J. (1992, July). Conditions enhancing self-directed learning in the workplace. Paper presented to the Social Sciences and Humanities Research Council of Canada, Ottawa, ON.

Caffarella, R. S. (1993). Facilitating self-directed learning as a staff development option. *Journal of Staff Development, 14*(2), 30–34.

Caldwell, S. D. (1991). Integrating individual growth and organization development. *Journal of Staff Development, 12*(1), 7–8.

Clark, D. L., Lotto, L. S., & Astuto, T. A. (1984). Effective schools and school improvement: A comparative analysis of two lines of inquiry. *Educational Administration Quarterly, 20*(3), 41–68.

Clift, R. T., Holland, P. E., & Veal, M. L. (1990). School context dimensions that affect staff development. *Journal of Staff Development, 11*(1), 34–38.

Conway, J. A. (1990). Lessons for staff developers from an organizational development intervention. *Journal of Staff Development, 11*(1), 8–13.

Daniel, P. L., & Stallion, B. K. (1996). Implementing school-based professional development in Kentucky. *Journal of Staff Development, 17*(4), 30–32.

DeLuca, J. R. (1991). The evolution of staff development for teachers. *Journal of Staff Development, 12*(3), 42–46.

Dillon-Peterson, B. (1991). Reflection on the past, present, and future of staff development. *Journal of Staff Development, 12*(1), 48–51.

DuFour, R., & Berkey, T. (1995). The principal as staff developer. *Journal of Staff Development, 16*(4) 2–6.

Duttweiler, P. C. (1989). Components of an effective professional development program. *Journal of Staff Development, 10*(2), 2–6.

Edmonds, R. R. (1982). Programs of school improvement: An overview. *Educational Leadership, 40*(4), 4–11.

Fagan, T. W. (1995). A new approach to federal legislation and professional development. *Journal of Staff Development, 16*(2), 18–22).

Fenstermacher, G. D., & Berliner, D. C. (1985). Determining the value of staff development. *The Elementary School Journal, 85*(3), 281–314.

Fullan, M. G., Bennet, B., & Rolheiser-Bennett, C. (1990). Linking classroom and school improvement. *Educational Leadership, 48*(9), 13–19.

Futrell, M. H. (1991). Staff development and the imperative for emancipation. *Journal of Staff Development, 12*(1), 2–3.

Gallegos, J. L. (1994). Staff development strategies that facilitate a transition in educational paradigms. *Journal of Staff Development, 15*(4), 34–38.

Gilman, D. A., Emhuff, J., & Hamm, J. (1988). *Improving teacher attitude and morale through maintaining teacher effectiveness: An Indiana staff development model.* Mount Vernon, IN: Metropolitan School District.

Glatthorn, C. D. (1987). Cooperative professional development: Peer-centered options for teacher growth. *Educational Leadership, 45*(3), 31–35.

Glickman, C. D., & Calhoun, E. E. (1991). Heaven and staff development. *Journal of Staff Development, 12*(1), 6–7.

Glickman, C. D., Gordon, S., & Ross-Gordon, J. (2001). *Supervision and instructional leadership: A developmental approach.* Boston: Allyn and Bacon.

Guskey, T. R., & Sparks, D. (1991). Complexities in evaluating the effects of staff development programs. (ERIC Document Reproduction Service No. ED331795.)

Hall, G. E., & Loucks, S. (1978). Teacher concerns as a basis for facilitating and personalizing staff development. *Teachers College Record, 80*(1), 36–53.

Hansen, J. M. (1980). Why inservice? An obligation of schools to provide the best. *NASSP Bulletin, 64*(440), 67–73.

Harris, B. M. (1989). *In-service education for staff development.* Boston: Allyn and Bacon.

Hinson, S., Caldwell, M. S., & Landrum, M. (1989). Characteristics of effective staff development programs. *Journal of Staff Development, 10*(2), 48–52.

Hord, S. M., & Boyd, V. (1995). Professional development fuels a culture of continuous improvement. *Journal of Staff Development, 16*(1), 10–15.

Joyce, B., Murphy, C., Showers, B., & Murphy, J. (1989). School renewal as cultural change. *Educational Leadership, 47*(3), 70–77.

Joyce, B., & Showers, B. (1996). Staff development as a comprehensive service organization. *Journal of Staff Development, 17*(1), 2–6.

Katzenmayer, M. H., & Reid, G. A., Jr. (1991). Compelling views of staff development for the 1990s. *Journal of Staff Development, 12*(3), 30–33.

Killion, J. P., & Harrison, C. R. (1990). An organizational development approach to change. *Journal of Staff Development, 11*(1), 22–25.

Leiter. M., & Cooper. M. (1978). How teacher unionists view in-service education. *Teachers College Record, 80*(1), 107–125.

Leithwood, K., Jantzi, D., & Steinbach, R. (1995, April). An organizational learning perspective on school responses to central policy initiatives. Paper presented at the annual meeting of the American Educational Research Association, San Francisco, CA.

Levine, S. L. (1989). *Promoting adult growth in schools: The promise of professional development.* Boston: Allyn and Bacon.

Lipman, P. (1991). *Formative evaluation of school-based staff development: Focused interviews in pilot schools.* Scarborough, ON: Scarborough Board of Education Research Centre Program Department.

Little, J. W. (1993). Teachers' professional development in a climate of educational reform. *Educational Evaluation and Policy Analysis, 15*(2), 129–151.

March, J. K., Peters, K. H., Schwartz, M., & Crisci P. E. (1993, April). The long-term impact of a staff development program on student performance in an urban setting. Paper presented at the annual meeting of the American Educational Research Association, Atlanta, GA.

McCarty, H. (1993). From deadwood to greenwood: Working with burned out staff. *Journal of Staff Development, 14*(2), 42–46.

Miller, L. & Wolf, T. E. (1978). Staff development for school change: Theory and practice. *Teachers College Record, 80*(1), 140–156.

Munger, L. (1995). Job-embedded staff development in Norwalk schools. *Journal of Staff Development, 16*(3), 6–12.

Murphy, C. (1993). Long-range planning for individual and organizational development in Georgia. *Journal of Staff Development, 14*(2), 2–3.

Nebgen, M. K. (1990). Strategic planning: Achieving the goals of organization development. *Journal of Staff Development, 11*(1), 28–31.

Nowak, S. J. (1994). New roles and challenges for staff development. *Journal of Staff Development, 15*(3), 10–13.

Richardson, M. D., Flanigan, J. L., & Prickett, R. L. (1990, November). Staff development as a function of organizational development. Paper presented at the annual meeting of the National Council of States on Inservice Education, Orlando, FL.

Richey R. C., & Sikorski, J. K. (1993). Instructional design can make a difference in staff development. *Journal of Staff Development, 14*(2), 44–47.

Rothberg, R. A., & Bozeman, W. C. (1990, November). Restructuring: A school-based plan of action. Paper presented at the annual meeting of the Southern Regional Council for Educational Administration, Atlanta, GA.

Schiffer, J. (1978). A framework for staff development. *Teachers College Record, 80*(1), 4–22.

Shafer, R. A. (1995, April). Interactional processes and support structures which foster professional development: A qualitative study. Paper presented at the annual meeting of the American Educational Research Association, San Francisco, CA.

Showers, B., Joyce, B., & Bennett, B. (1987). Synthesis of research on staff development: A framework for future study and a state-of-the-art analysis. *Educational Leadership, 45*(3), 77–87.

Shroyer, M. G. (1990). Effective staff development for effective organization development. *Journal of Staff Development, 11*(1), 2–6.

Small, S. E. (1990). *Decision-making and professional development: A focus on the individual.* (ERIC Document Reproductive Service No. ED 328 534.)

Sparks, D. (1994). A paradigm shift in staff development. *Journal of Staff Development, 15*(4), 26–29.

Votjek, R. O. (1992, April). Integrating staff development and organization development: An empirical study of staff developers. Paper presented at the annual meeting of the American Educational Research Association, San Francisco, CA.

Watson, R. S. (1994). The role of professional development in restructuring schools. *Journal of Staff Development, 15*(2), 24–27.

Weissglass, J. (1991). Teachers have feelings: What can we do about it? *Journal of Staff Development, 12*(1), 28–33.

Wood, F. H., & Thompson, S. R. (1993). Assumptions about staff development based on research and best practice. *Journal of Staff Development, 14*(4), 52–57.

10. SCHOOL LEADERSHIP FOR 21st-CENTURY URBAN COMMUNITIES

Leonard A. Valverde

ABSTRACT

Because schools have historically failed to educate satisfactorily students of color, dynamic leadership is required to focus on pedagogy (teaching & learning), thoroughly knowing student population served, expanding beyond learning to serve community needs and building a support network and partnerships. In short, innovative leadership that will design and bring about new educational curricula and organization will be proposed. New paradigms from educational leaders are necessary.

INTRODUCTION

As early as the 1960 census count, the U.S. became officially an urban populated nation. That is to say, the majority of the population of the U.S. could be found living in urban settings, called cities (over 100,000 residents). This trend of urban residency has continued to the present day. In fact, urban populated America was accentuated in the following decades (1970s and 1980s) when major urban cities grew into metropolitan complexes. Joining the traditional major cities of New York, Los Angeles, Chicago, San Francisco, and Detroit were such places as Miami-Dade, Dallas, Philadelphia, Atlanta, Denver, Seattle, Houston, Phoenix, etc.

Challenges of Urban Education and Efficacy of School Reform, Volume 6, pages 187–198.

ISBN: 0-7623-0426-X

Along with the urbanization of the U.S. the population of these urban cities (since the 1960s) was predominately mixed in racial and ethnic composition. The core or inner cities were composed primarily of persons of color: African American, Hispanic, Asian, and a constantly shrinking number of whites. Many of the city's residents were recent immigrants or first-generation American-born children. While these urban centers were mixed in population, they were also segregated into racial or ethnic-specific ghettos or barrios. Furthermore, most of these families of color were economically below the average U.S. family income.

These demographic trends (or status changes) of urban growth, diverse metropolitan population make up, and low income were and have *not* been matched with commensurate changes by the educational systems. For example, the majority rank and file of the teaching force, administrative personnel pool, and state departments as well as state legislators, and to a lesser extent, local governing boards, are middle-class whites. The consequences of this mismatch between urban school students and parents with school personnel will be discussed further momentarily. Beyond and along with this intra-school, counter-group difference, there is the greater division reflected in the schools, that of society's racial discrimination practices. Since before the forming of the U.S., racist practices have been extremely detrimental toward African Americans, Latinos (Mexican Americans in the Southwest), Native Americans and Chinese. The point being that even though the *Brown v. Topeka Kansas School Board* Supreme Court ruling of 1954 supposedly ended school segregation, it only minimally decreased misunderstanding about students of color, their abilities, desire to learn, high expectation by parents of their children's school success, etc. School personnel, like society in general, still harbor stereotypes about students of color, as reflected by low teacher expectation, ignorance by educators of students of color learning styles, and so forth. As a result of this banal view toward people of color, schools have neither overcome the inequities nor systemically changed the educational programs for such students.

As rapidly and comprehensively as urban America has changed in the past four decades leading to the 21st century, projections of student enrollments indicate the trends are to continue, solidifying these identified metropolitan and school characteristics. Recent immigration growth has boosted school enrollment. Most recent arrivals (migrants) first settle in major cities (see Table 1, Projected Student Enrollments).

Related to the above projected student growth, in 1999, it was reported that 38% of public school students were students of color and since 1972, this increase was equal to 16%. The largest concentration of students of

Table 1. Projected Elementary & Secondary School Enrollment.

Year	Total
1999	46,812,000
2000	47,026,000
2001	47,176,000
2002	47,269,000
2003	47,373,000
2004	47,436,000
2005	47,475,000

Source: *The Condition of Education*, 2001, Table 2-1.

color was in the West (47%) and South (45%) (*The Condition of Education,* 2001, p. 8).

CHARACTERIZING PRESENT DAY URBAN SCHOOLS

Schools in urban areas typically can be described as follows: First, school facilities are old, most built in the early part of the 20th century. As such they are in major need of renovation to accommodate new instructional technology that could be used by teachers and students. Because the greatest growth in the United States has taken place in metropolitan areas, these schools are over-crowed. Please see Table 2. It is not uncommon to find some classes being held in rooms originally designed to be custodial supply rooms, closed-off hallways, converted offices, etc. Because urban schools are located in low-income communities, school districts are under-funded. That is, even if they tax themselves high, the property value is so low that it generates low district funds. Public elementary and secondary school expenditures show that central city schools on

Table 2. Overcrowding in Schools.

Local	Overcrowded	
	6–25% Over Capacity	More than 25% Over Capacity
Central City	15	11
Urban Fringe (Suburbs)	17	8
Rural	11	6

Source: *The Condition of Education*, 2001, Table 45-2.

the average during 1996–1997 expended $5,727 per student, while the same year non-metropolitan schools expended on the average per pupil $5,995 (*Condition of Education,* 2001). As such these schools cannot pay a competitive salary to attract enough teachers to have a reasonable teacher pupil ratio. Therefore, typically urban schools are under-staffed in teacher numbers and have a large percentage of teachers without full state certification. Even more, we find a high percentage of teachers in science and mathematics classes who are not majors in either subject field.

The student body make up is typically over 80 to 90% students of color, with one specific racial or ethnic population being dominant. High racial/ethnic make-up is due to high birth rate, larger family size, and high concentration of immigrants. In addition, because inner cities are still segregated by neighborhoods and because there has been major white flight, even if there is school bussing, school composition is typically students of color. One other major student characteristic must be mentioned. With student diversity growing, so languages other than English are increasing. It is now common for urban school districts to have more than 20 different languages spoken by students. In major metropolitan areas the number of languages increases to over 50! Languages from the Far East, Middle East, Europe, Central and South America, Indian tribes, etc., can be heard across the country, but mostly accentuated in large city schools.

Psychological Characteristics of Urban Schools

Language is more than a form of communication. It is a carrier of culture and in so doing preserves culture and reinforces personal identity and nurtures cultural roots. When schools do not account for the full importance of language, there is a culture clash and unnecessary conflict between teachers and students. The educator's attitude toward language with students of color has been different than their view toward white students. For white students, learning a second language has always been valued. However when students of color come to school speaking a language other than English, their mother tongue is seen as a deficit instead of a positive. This view of language is reflective of a larger educational perspective toward students of color. Historically, the mission of schools has been to socialize or Americanize African Americans, Latinos, Native Americans, Chinese, and other non-white populations. Not until these student populations have converted from their cultural identity to the American identify (i.e. as one example, giving up speaking their mother language for English), do schools change their mission from acculturation to education. The problem is and has been that schools do not make the transition from being assimilation agents to become instructional institutions, their true purpose!

Because this country was predicated and many of its public institutions shaped by the "peculiar institution" commonly called slavery, because American Indians were "in the way" of Westward expansion, because Mexico had to be removed from the Southwest so the U.S. could fulfill its manifest destiny, and because Chinese labor was necessary for railroad construction, these population groups came to be categorized as problematic and as such *inferior*. This unfounded view of inferiority (based partly on political intent and economic favoritism) has been reinforced, sometimes directly and other times not spoken but understood, in teacher and administrator preparation programs. This attitude has manifested itself in schools in many different ways. In the early 1960s when the federal government recognized the need to compensate for past ills and inadequate education of "minority" students, the first Elementary and Secondary Education Act (ESEA) Title I (1964) was grounded on the concept that students of color were educationally disadvantaged and to a lesser extent culturally deprived. Consequently, the education community responded by designing deficient type programs or compensatory programs. Such programs were viewed as remedial and not good for white students.

The combination of ascribing the inferiority ability to students of color and provide remedial programs continued to yield in urban schools poor education. While some progress was made up until the mid-1980s, afterwards regressive outcomes returned. Student achievement scores still continued below national averages, reading and math grade levels lagged considerably behind white students, passing rates to next grades remained low, disproportional representation of students were found in special education programs, designated with some form of learning disability. And worst of all, the drop-out rate of students in urban schools persisted to be the highest in the country.

A Change of Leadership with Modest Results

In the late 1960s, while the spotlight was on the education of minority students, urban school districts found themselves in the forefront of attention. Parents, community advocacy groups, school boards, state departments, and the federal government were looking for improvement. At the same time, even though more resources were being added, such financial resources were inadequate to the growing demand. The only added resource came from ESEA Title I and later Title VII Bilingual Education funds. But with these federal funds came restrictions and accountability. Partially due to the above conditions and because of social activism by grassroot communities, local school governing boards began to appoint superintendents of color. In turn, school principals of color were appointed. However, leaders of color attributed their appointments for other reasons. One, they posited, was they were inheriting "bankrupt" school districts. As such, management of these under-funded operations was so difficult that traditional white male superintendent candidates were no longer seeking these types of school districts. Second, minority communities were pressuring local school boards to select leaders that were representatives of the student population. The basis for this advocacy was that such persons understood the social dynamics of minority communities and therefore had a positive belief in the learning ability of students of color. They were supposed to know the importance of culture and how family and neighborhood life either helped or prevented schools to educate students of color.

Over time (from 1960s to now) the appointment of persons of color into leadership positions (district superintendents and school principals) reached a shallow plateau and recently progress has regressed! In 1985, 3% of superintendents were classified as minority compared to 30% of students classified as minority enrolled in public schools. In 1999, the percentage of superintendents of color rose by only 2%, yet students of color rose by 8% (Hodgkinson & Montenegre, 1999). Please see Tables 3 and 4.

Similarly, the composition of teachers did not change sufficiently to keep up with the high growth of students of color. Please refer to Table 5.

Table 3. Percent of Superintendents of Color in Urban Districts.

	1997			1999		
Percent	White	African American	Hispanic	White	African American	Hispanic
Superintendent By Color	37%	47%	16%	42%	42%	14%

Source: Council of Great City Schools, *1999 Study on Superintendents.*

Table 4. Principal Percentages by Race/Ethnicity Compared to Student Percentages.

	1994		
	White	African American	Hispanic
% of Students	67%	16.6%	13.5%
% of Principals	83%	10.8%	4.5%

Source: National Center of Educational Statistics, 1998.

Table 5. Teacher Percentages by Race/Ethnicity Compared to Student Percentages.

	1993			1996		
	White	African American	Hispanic	White	African American	Hispanic
% of Students	72%	14.8%	12.6%	63.2%	16.9%	14.7%
% of Teachers	87%	9%	4%	88%	7.3%	4%

Source: NEA, *Status of Public School Teacher*, 1996.

It was hoped by urban community members that these new leaders of color in the role of principal and superintendent would bring much needed change and improvement of learning for students of color in urban schools. The basic argument for such high hope of change and improvement was centered on the belief that educators who experienced similar growing-up, living, and educational experiences of urban youth and communities knew intuitively what needed to be changed and how to bring the change about. While educators of color in urban administrative posts could quickly identify the problems and could articulate the desired outcomes, there were too many barriers to overcome. There were political, economic, bureaucratic, and social barriers as well as factors of inadequate time, intensity, and entrenchment that prevent them from being successful.

Neither space nor purpose of this chapter allow for a detailed accounting of the barriers, but one example will be shared regarding each of the above barriers in order to represent the magnitude of the situation. By so doing, a foundation will be set giving justification for the proposed preparation program for future urban school leaders, described in the next section.

A good example of a political barrier is the almost automatic resistance change agents constantly encounter. Superintendents were appointed by governing boards to bring about school improvement. To do so, superintendents acted to bring about changes on a number of common fronts: (1) personnel changes; (2) re-organization of the district; and (3) installment of new programs, etc. Existing staff members did not openly accept these changes readily and on occasion refused to accommodate the proposed changes. Groups began to organize to reject changes and make formal complaints to the governing board. Governing boards, being politically elected bodies, gave into district pressures and in the end did not support sufficiently the superintendent.

Economically, suffice it to say that the incoming revenue provided by the state formula and local community taxation base were inadequate to support the needs of urban schools and the required changes. Even the infusion of federal funds (to compensate for inadequate state support) was insufficient. Federal dollars were to stimulate and seed new programs, not sustain underfunded programs. Compounding the crummy financial picture was the fact that urban school districts were growing in student enrollment faster than state dollars. Then there was the added issue that states' formulas were unequal, i.e. suburban districts were better supported than urban districts. Finally the cost of maintaining school operations was not keeping up with the annual escalating cost of doing business.

Bureaucratic change became highly frustrating and the most difficult to accomplish. Yet, such changes were fundamentally necessary. Bureaucracy is grounded tightly to rules, usually restrictive, and to following an established set of procedures, typically cumbersome, slowing action or movement. Even making administrative rule changes, within the scope of authority of superintendents, became problematic. Vested interest groups challenged such administrative rule changes, usually citing that required time periods were not honored, or that suggested advice was not adequately sought out, or a certain step was missed, etc. Such vested group reactions caused undue delays resulting in non-action or inappropriate follow-up.

Social barriers were many. School leaders of color in urban schools had to gain the support and assistance both of external and internal groups. Externally, they sought the support of business and civic leaders. While urban areas lost a considerable number of white residents, civic and business leaders were still white. Mayors, most city council members, and to a large extent business CEOs were white. America, as the Kerner Presidential Commission on Civil Disorder (1968) wrote, was still a nation divided, one white and one black, one rich and one poor, separate and unequal. There was an element of social distance between school leaders of color and the general leadership community, a distance that got in the way of school improvement. Similarly, the majority of teaching staff within the school district was composed of white middle-class persons (mostly women). District employees resided in suburbia, commuting daily to work in the city.

The lack of time factor was just as significant in contributing toward change agents being unsuccessful. Before the 1960s, urban schools did a poor job of educating their students. There was not much attention placed on this societal function prior to this time. After 1960, when education became a national priority (stimulated by the Russian launching in 1957 of the first satellite called Sputnik) a sense of urgency emerged. Then with the dawning of the Civil Rights Movement, the urgency escalated even more. Governing boards and community advocacy groups grew impatient with the slow pace of progress.

Unrealistically, they wanted quick and immediate results. Consequently, superintendents and principals, who were hired to be agents of change, were under unrealistic time expectations to produce results and thus were unable to respond in such short order. Since these well-intentioned individuals were not given sufficient time to unfold their initiatives adequately, they were rushed and pressured to produce. When the returns were not coming in quick enough, they were removed from their administrative role.

THE NEW PREPARATION PROGRAM FOR URBAN LEADERS

With the odds substantially against the leaders who tried to bring about necessary change in urban schools, it is fairly obvious why they were mostly unsuccessful. In fact, given the above obstacles, it is a tribute to those early urban leaders that they were able to make in-roads and bring about modest improvement in urban schooling. But as formidable as the above barriers are, change agents would have been more successful in overcoming them with proper formal preparation. Much more is now known about changing organizations and teaching students of color. These are the two foci that leadership training programs should concentrate on, if urban education is to change for the better.

What follows is a broad stroke treatment of urban school leadership training. Only major components will be proposed, not specific leadership competencies. The profession will be better served by the big picture approach, given that there has been heavy emphasis during the 1980s and 1990s on identifying discrete competencies and standards for inclusion into educational leadership preparation programs. These efforts were led by the University Council of Educational Administration and the National Commission on Excellence in Educational Administration. (Please see Daniel et al., 1988.)

DIFFERENTIATED PREPARATION

Historically and currently, the preparation for the role of principal or superintendent has been generic, regardless of location or setting. That is, the general assumption is that the performance of the role does not differ substantially in schools situated in rural, suburban, or urban contexts. This concept is similar to a discarded one used in teacher preparation programs. That is, teachers used to be trained under the assumption that all students were the same as far as learning ability and styles, and therefore teaching one way to the entire class was acceptable. Teacher educators abandoned the concept of homogeneity a long time ago.

The preparation of urban education leaders should be differentiated from the preparation of rural or suburban educational leaders. First, persons wanting to provide leadership in urban settings must be provided a curriculum that is embedded in the context of urban society. What this means is that traditional courses such as school finance, school law, organizational theory, and others should have a specialized focus, representing the urban experience. Clearly, when learning about school finance issues and problems, those factors associated with urban schools are not the same as rural schools. Similarly, when reviewing court cases in school law classes, coverage of legal cases that have direct bearing on urban schools will be more meaningful to future urban leaders.

Second, a good portion of core courses should revolve around learning about the culture of various students of color or about the role culture plays in the education of students of color. Certainly, there should be a course that documents how the school's culture (system) in the past has clashed with the cultures of African American, Latino, Native American, and other immigrant groups. This course could be used to teach future urban leaders what not to do. That is, such a course could point out how this culture clash has produced unfavorable situations contributing to high drop-out rates and low achievement.

Third, there should be a series of courses that specifically help future urban educational leaders to be agents of change. As a part of this change agent strand, a course aimed at bringing about innovation is a must. A course on best practices could be another part of this strand. Furthermore, the knowledge base has progressed to examine systemic change. Clearly, urban school districts need to be not just changed, but transformed. Thus this third strand is the counter to the previous strand of what not to do.

Fourth, a strand of learning should be dedicated to designing and organizing urban schools that are to be "full service" schools. Full service urban schools are the goal of systemic change and school transformation. Schools that will go beyond just providing instruction to students, schools open longer than student hours, schools open to adults and their needs. For example, schools can be used as places where adults can come to learn about house improvements. Or open non-school staff can provide information about legal aid on immigration matters. Schools can be places to host neighborhood association meetings to discuss community-wide issues of concern. Full service schools can provide space where other community services can be accessed, such as providing free transportation late at night for grocery shopping, emergency baby-sitting for a single parent household, when the parent has to work late.

Fifth, there should be a strand of learning on how to start, maintain, and grow more formal partnerships with other entities in the city. Partnerships could be with businesses, corporations, city and county government agencies, community groups, higher education institutions, etc. Each of these various units can provide some sort of assistance to the schools. As has been pointed out, urban schools fall short of monetary and human resources commensurate to their level of need. Urban school leaders can no longer work with the normal funding streams in the hope of catching up to their level of needs.

Sixth, the learning method should be eclective. While we have suggested new strands of learning with new foci, we further suggest that these new learning foci not be just through the conventional way of formal course offerings. Courses should not be the only means. Courses should be offered off campus and in urban school settings, so that future leaders experience early the conditions of urban education. On-site formal observations should be a way of learning. Practicums, internships, and on-site mentoring should be used as learning vehicles. Field practitioners should be used to team-teach as well as to be clinical instructors. Instruction should be packaged into shorter, but intense time periods, such as four weekends, eight-hour days, or two-three concentrated weeks.

Seventh, the remaining recommendation to improve preparation programs is really targeted to improving urban education. It is centered on student recruitment and admission and faculty training and hiring. For many reasons, it is imperative that educational leadership programs assertively recruit students of color and women into degree and certification programs in much larger numbers than in the past to fill urban education administrative roles. Since the 1980s, there has been a growing desire by governing boards and community advocacy groups for a larger pool of candidates of color for leadership roles. They desire a pool of candidates trained in school effectiveness and to bring about much needed systemic change for improvement. Parents of color and community leaders of color are looking to get school leaders of color who come to the job ready to recognize the problems besetting urban schools. These leaders must be knowledgeable about problem solving and eager to attack the problems that have for too long of a time plagued students of color and urban schools. They may not be just persons of color, but also any person who appreciates and understands basically the culture of the student populations served, a person who accepts the proposition that culture does play a major role in the learning of urban students.

In the same vein of recruiting more aspiring administrators sympathetic to urban culture, it is just as critical to have such persons in the ranks of faculty in educational administration and supervision departments. Persons of color are vital, if new curriculum is to be developed, if assertive student recruitment is to take place perennially, and if continual and closer relationships are to be nurtured between educational leadership departments and urban school districts. And to be sure, inclusion of persons of color and women into the faculties must be more than one representative. Departments of educational leadership must go beyond the symbolic or token representation of today and the past. They must authentically be committed equally to diversity and cultural pluralism as they are to urban education improvement. Without true commitment to the former, there will not be significant and meaningful improvement of the latter.

REFERENCES

Council of the Greater City Schools (1999). *A study of school superintendents.* Washington, D.C.: Council of the Greater City Schools.

Griffths, D. Stout, R., & Forsyth, P. (Eds) (1988). *Leaders for America's Schools: The report and papers of the National Commission on Excellence in Educational Administration.* Berkeley, CA: McCutchan Publishing Company.

Hodgkinson, H., & Montenegro, X. (1999). *The U.S. school superintendent: The invisible CEO.* Washington, D.C.: Institute for Educational Leadership.

National Center of Education Statistics (1998). *Digest of educational statistics.*

National Education Association (1998). *Status of the American public school teacher, 1995–1996.* Washington, D.C.: National Education Association.

Report of the National Advisory Commission on Civil Disorders (1968). Washington, D.C.: Government Printing Office. Mr. Kerner, Commission Chair.

U. S. Department of Education, National Center for Educational Statistics (2001). *The condition of education, 2001.* Washington, D.C.: Government Printing Office. Retrieved March 19, 2002, from www.nces.ed.gov/programs/coe/ (please see Tables 2-1, page 107; 45-2, page 171, and 56-1, page 177).

11. ADEQUACY ISSUES IN FINANCING URBAN SCHOOLS

James G. Ward

ABSTRACT

This chapter will survey events in financing urban school districts in the United States from the period of major urban stress in the late 1970s to the present. It will consider the political, economic, and social environment surrounding urban schools and will consider whether we are making progress in both urban school finance equity and urban school finance adequacy. Major public policy initiatives will be considered.

INTRODUCTION

Seymour Sacks (1972) opens the introduction to his classic work *City Schools/Suburban Schools: A History of Fiscal Conflict* by citing a British commentator who in 1904 observed that in the U.S. we spend a large amount of money on public schools, but that we do not spend enough, especially on teacher salaries (p. 1). Some issues do not change substantially over time. This chapter explores the changing concepts of adequacy, considers some policy issues of adequacy in urban schools, discusses the political dimensions of adequacy in urban schools, and then provides some discussion of future prospects for adequate funding of urban schools.

The issue of adequately funding urban school districts is not a simple matter of how to treat a particular school district type. It actually taps at the root of

Challenges of Urban Education and Efficacy of School Reform, Volume 6, pages 199–205.

ISBN: 0-7623-0426-X

an ideological conflict that is old as the Republic itself. Simon (2002) analyzes the struggles of the early years of our Constitutional government between states' rights and a strong federal government. Embedded in this struggle was an agrarian vs. urban point of view that permeated American politics. In the first Washington Administration there was an intense disagreement over a Hamiltonian view of the new nation, which envisioned a strong federal government, with cities and commerce at its core, and a Jeffersonian view of a decentralized, agrarian society with strong rights for individual states. This clash of ideologies was not settled by the Civil War, with the clear victory of a strong federal government bolstered by manufacturing, commercial, and financial interests, but continued through the political battles over Populism, Progressivism, the New Deal, the Great Society, and beyond. This essay will make reference to the manifestation of this struggle in a number of issues relating to adequate financing of urban schools.

ADEQUACY OF SCHOOL FUNDING

Everybody seems to be in favor of adequate school funding, but there the consensus ends. The rhetoric is plentiful. The "father of American school finance," Ellwood P. Cubberley (1919) in *Public Education in the United States* defined adequacy as "a generous system of free public schools" (p. 495). What constitutes generous? That question has prompted as much political debate in American legislatures, courts, and school board meetings than almost any other question imaginable. One problem with defining adequacy is that there are widely conflicting views on the goals of American education. Without going into the intricacies of the debate, we still have major disagreements about the relationship of sometimes competing goals of preparing students for citizenship and maximizing student academic performance. Moran (1999) writes that even the U.S. Supreme Court has raised the issues that a major difficulty in dealing with school finance cases is that "educators themselves were divided on the issue of what constitutes educational adequacy" (p. 65).

The classical view of educational adequacy has been to consider it in terms of financial inputs to the educational system, as measured by either revenues per pupil or expenditures per pupil. Sacks (1972), for example conducted an extensive study of the relationship between educational financial inputs and a wide variety of other social and economic factors in comparing urban schools with their surrounding suburban counterparts. We are accustomed to see studies, which compare school districts, or states, by per pupil expenditures or per pupil revenues. Sometimes in the public finance literature, we see this is the form of per capita revenues and expenditures. While such measures are indicators of the amount of resources available, they provide little guidance as to how those resources are used and what the results are of the uses of those resources. These measures also present no absolute standard and assume adequacy to be a relative concept. If district A spends $9000 per pupil and district B spends $7000 per pupil do we conclude: (1) both are adequate, (2) both are inadequate, or (3) A is more adequate than B? This approach provides very little information for public policy purposes.

Adequacy is a political concept. Constitutional provisions regarding education are in state constitutions where terms like "high quality education," "thorough and efficient education," and "educational opportunity" appear. Generally, it is up to state legislatures to define what these terms mean within the political, economic, social, and cultural context of the state and then state education authorities, school district, and schools implement these standards of adequacy. All along the process, political decisions are made as to what is adequate and what is not. In the late 1970s, the National Institute of Education compiled state legal standards relating to educational adequacy and identified eighteen categories of those standards. More recently the trend has been to define educational adequacy in terms of student performance measures on state-set curriculum standards. In the various definitions of adequacy over time, adequacy is addressed in terms of school inputs (resources, standards), school outputs (test scores, graduation rates), and school outcomes (economic returns to education and good citizenship).

ADEQUACY ISSUES IN FUNDING URBAN SCHOOLS

Revenue Generation

A classic issue in the school finance issue has been how to raise sufficient (adequate) resources for public schools and how to distribute those resources in a reasonable manner. There is a vast literature on state grant-in-aid system for local school districts and how to best serve urban schools (Sacks, 1972; Alexander & Salmon, 1995). There is a parallel literature on urban school district fiscal stress and what factors contribute to the ability or inability of urban school districts to provide adequate resources for education (Ward, 1985). Urban school districts are generally the captive of state political systems and the relatively generosity of the state toward funding urban school districts is not only a function of the state economy, but the state political culture as well. City school districts have not fared well in state funding as the locus of political power has moved to the suburbs in many states. Former Secretary of Education William Bennett's oft-quoted observation that the Chicago schools were the worst public school system in the nation may have been interpreted by some as a call for reform, greater performance, and more accountability, but others saw it as a message to the Republican leadership in the Illinois legislature that they need not be overly concerned about Chicago school funding issues. Some politicians and others at that time referred to increased funding for Chicago schools as "throwing money down a black hole," with its obvious racial overtones. Nonetheless, there was still a recognition that funding and performance can be connected.

The New Public Management

A concern about performance at all levels of government led to the emergence of a new set of emphases in governmental management that has become known as The New Public Management (NPM), which is not only a major trend in the U.S., but in places like New Zealand, Australia, and the United Kingdom as well. There are various definitions of NPM, but commonly recognized characteristics are:

(1) Slowing down the growth of government or shrinking government.
(2) Use of privatization in the production of government services.
(3) Greater use of information technology in governmental management.
(4) The development of a more international perspective with sharing among nations of management issues and developments (adapted from Hood, 1991).

A major controversy over NPM is whether administration in the public sector should start with an emphasis on "public" or an emphasis on "management."

While it has never achieved the status of a recognized movement with a distinct name, NPM is a major issue in public education and I would simply term it New Public Management in Education (NPME). NPME, especially in urban school districts, seemed to be characterized by:

(1) A decline or stagnation of state funds for education.
(2) Greater use of privatization or semi-privatization, such as vouchers, charter schools, and use of outside education management firms.
(3) Increase power of public schools by mayors and the employment of non-educator school CEOs.
(4) An emphasis on technology in both management and instruction.
(5) A high concern for international student performance comparisons.

The rationale for NPME is twofold: (1) more competition in education will result in increased student performance, and (2) the overall performance of schools will be enhanced by adopting more "business-like" management approaches.

The results of NPME have been very mixed at best. Both vouchers and charter schools have become far more complex issues than their advocates every anticipated and there is no evidence that either one consistently improves student performance over time. The major outside education management firms have become controversial in their approaches, have failed to improve student performance, and a number are in serious financial trouble. The one consistent lesson of privatization and semi-privatization is that schools, and particularly urban schools, are much more difficult to manage well than many outside of education have thought. Competition is not a replacement for expertise.

The criticism of NPM in the public sector is that is fails to sufficiently account for issues of diversities within our society and that it further separates the provision of services from the centers of power. The criticism of NPME is its potential treat to society equity. Some educators may welcome the separation of service provision from political power, but the danger of that separation is that power and wealth are related and any such separation diminishes the power of service providers to increase funding.

Teacher Quality Issues and Urban Schools

The one clear and consistent message of educational research and examination of educational practice is that the key to providing an adequate education for children is the existence of a high quality teaching staff in all schools to serve all children. As a nation, we have an insufficient supply for high quality teachers, and the problem is more acute in urban school districts and most acute in high poverty urban schools. Good teachers have always been in short supply, especially in urban districts. Recent research has demonstrated that a good teacher has a strong set of skills, knowledge, and attitudes in both a content area of teaching and in pedagogy. Numerous studies have shown the high numbers of teachers in the classroom that are not well prepared in their content area. In urban schools, and in urban schools in poor areas, the number of poorly prepared teachers is higher than in other districts. The age profile of existing teaching staffs strongly suggests a high number of teacher retirements over the next few years. The shortage of high quality teachers will increase.

How can urban school districts address the issue of adequacy through high quality teachers? Approaches like "signing bonuses" for new teachers and placing teachers in shortage areas on a higher level in the salary schedule seem only marginally effective. Urban school districts will not be able to move toward adequacy without addressing issues of teacher salaries and teacher working conditions on a level well above what most districts are now operating. A substantial increase in teacher salary levels and restructing schools to improve teacher working conditions will produce larger numbers of high quality teachers over time, but will be expensive. The issue of staffing urban schools with high quality teachers may be the most critical finance issue now facing urban policy makers.

THE POLITICAL DIMENSIONS OF FINANCIAL ADEQUACY IN URBAN SCHOOLS

Once upon a time, urban school districts were the wealthy schools districts in the American public system. Wealth was concentrated in urban areas through much of the nineteenth century. The influx of a large number of immigrants in the 1880–1920 period place a heavy strain on urban schools, especially since many of the immigrant children were from southern and Eastern Europe and had no English skills, or very low levels of English ability. But, while this demand was increasing on urban schools, the suburbs were emerging and much of the wealth left the cities for the suburbs and this placed a strain on the ability of urban schools to provide adequate financing. The Great Depression further depressed the ability of urban schools to support high quality education and the large movement of African-American families from the South into cities in the 1930s through the 1960s increased the demands on urban schools, without increasing their fiscal capacity. Phillips (2002), among others, documents to close relationship between wealth and power. The widespread fiscal crisis of urban school districts in the 1970s and 1980s (Ward, 1985) was partially the result of the greatest need for school funding existing in urban school districts and the wealth and the power being outside the cities in many cases.

Phillips (2002) debates whether the current conservative domination of American politics began with the election of Nixon in 1968 or the election of Reagan in 1980. Nonetheless, the shift to the right in American political culture in the 1980s and 1990s has been pronounced and it has not improved the fiscal condition of most urban schools, nor made increases in state education aid for city school districts any easier to obtain. The latest development is that we have seen a new influx of Asian and Hispanic immigration into urban districts, creating a new strain on financial adequacy. The educational need says new funds for urban schools; the current political environment says no. Major corporations with production facilities in urban areas demand better educated workers, but the corporate leaders in their lush suburban corporate headquarters oppose higher taxes for schools. In summary, this is the current dilemma for adequacy in financial in urban school districts.

PROSPECTS FOR ADEQUATE FUNDING FOR URBAN SCHOOLS

The prospects are not good for the future of adequate funding of urban schools. State political support for urban schools is not strong and governors and legislatures seem very willing to leave urban school matters with mayors. The general political climate in the nation is not in favor of higher taxes and more government spending and the prospects of greater intergovernmental funding of urban schools is not encouraging. Of course, at the time of this writing, the general economic climate of the country is not encouraging either and any growth in the economy is likely to be modest and slow and benefit other parts of the country before it does urban centers. The NPME diffuses political support for public schools and diverts attention away from improvement of the public school system. Finally, the large question of how and where urban schools will find a sufficient number of high quality teachers in order to offer an adequate education and how they could pay for them if they found them is a major problem.

REFERENCES

Alexander, K., & Salmon, R. G. (1995). Public school finance. Boston: Allyn and Bacon.

Cubberly, E. P. (1919). Public education in the United States. Boston: Houghton Miflin.

Hood, C. (1991). A public management for all seasons? *Public Administration Review*, *69*, 3–19.

Moran, M. (1999). Standards and assessment: The new measure of adequacy in school finance litigation. *Journal of Education Finance*, *25*, 33–80.

Phillips, K. (2002). *Wealth and democracy*. New York, NY: Broadway Books.

Sacks, S. (1972). *City schools/suburban schools: A history of fiscal conflict*. Syracuse, NY: Syracuse University Press.

Simon, J. F. (2002). *What kind of nation: Thomas Jefferson, John Marshall, and the epic struggle to create a United States*. New York, NY: Simon and Schuster.

Ward, J. G. (1985). Predicting fiscal stress in large city school districts. *Journal of Education Finance*, *11*, 89–104.

12. STANDARDIZED TESTING AND ASSESSMENT POLICY: IMPACT ON RACIAL MINORITIES AND IMPLICATIONS FOR EDUCATIONAL LEADERSHIP

Dawn G. Williams and Laurence Parker

ABSTRACT

Despite years of education reform, America's public schools continue to provide an unequal education to many low-income and minority students. Although urban schools receive millions of dollars to correct disparities, the standardized test scores for African-American and Latino students remain much lower than those of white students. This chapter discusses the influence race and discrimination have on the achievement gap in public education. It includes a description of the gap's emergence during the 1970s, the social and political changes the caused it to widen during the 1980s and strategies for closing the gap.

INTRODUCTION

Education reform seems to be an immortal constant in the American public school system. Apple[1] (1994) recognizes the history of the multiple uses that the language of reform has. He further distinguishes its uses within a political

Challenges of Urban Education and Efficacy of School Reform, Volume 6, pages 207–220.

ISBN: 0-7623-0426-X

context. Reform can be used to help create a movement toward more democratic institutions that better meet the needs of students, teachers and communities. Secondly the language of reform can also be used as a part of a larger strategy that supports tightening control mechanisms within schools to create a closer alignment to further meet the needs of the groups in dominance.

Reform in American education can be viewed as a swinging pendulum. New ideas in school reform have come and gone – and come back again. These new ideas rest upon old reform structures. The value of equity has been a desired goal in many national reform initiatives and efforts. America has often overlooked and recently struggled with this value within the educational system as it pertains to racial/ethnic groups. The value of equity centers on the fairness of distribution of resources. Burlingame et al. (1999) argue that equity often suffers at the hand of excellence. Noguera (2001) asserts that it is a popular perception to believe that advances in educational equity for minority students would come at the expense of the educational interests of affluent White students. While some may believe resources should be distributed equally on the base of merit, others feel that need should be the determining factor of distribution to ensure equity. This battle exists not only in the classrooms but also in the boardrooms where educational policies are made.

Many civil rights battles were first won in the democratic institutions that our schools represent. The latest battle and rhetoric of national school reform is the narrowing and/or closing of the achievement gap between African-American and White students. President George W. Bush's educational plan, No Child Left Behind Act, defines the gap as "the difference between how well low-income and minority children (African-American, Hispanic and Native American) perform on standardized tests as compared with their peers (White children). For many years, low-income and minority children have been falling behind White peers in terms of academic achievement."[2] More specifically, the Black-White test score gap focuses on the academic achievement disparities noted by standardized tests in reading, math and tests that claim to measure scholastic aptitude and intelligence between Black and White students in the elementary and secondary levels (Jencks & Phillips, 1998). Sometimes the terms achievement gap and Black-White test score gap are used interchangeably. Additionally noting that researchers speaking within the context of the Black-White test score gap tend to also use the identifying terms of Black and African-American interchangeably. The same can be said for the interchangeable uses of Hispanic and Latino/a in the literature.

In the literature, it seems that the obvious and repetitive acts of racism are being overlooked as the nucleus factor affecting the achievement gap and how it influences pedagogical practice in the classroom. Noguera (2001) would agree with this accusation. He also points out that genetic and cultural theories generally locate the cause of the problems associated with the achievement gap within students (low motivation, devaluing academic pursuits, etc.), while effectively divorcing educational institutions of responsibility. This is problematic because schools, which is our most public institution, currently is serving the role of reproducing the inequality in society. While it may seem like the issues surrounding the achievement gap is the latest craze in the educational policy arena, it is by no means a new concept for debate. These issues of equity, or a lack thereof, have existed since the inception of public education for all. However, federal attention and support wasn't launched until the 1960s. It continued in the 1970s, and resurfaced in the 1990s. There was a hiatus on federal support and attention as it relates to equity during the Reagan era of the 1980s. This was evidenced in the growth of the Black-White test score gap during the latter part of the 1980s that continued to widen in the 1990s (Miller, 1995; Lee, 2002).

This chapter will give an overview of the research generated on the achievement gap, but more specifically the Black-White test score gap. It will first outline and acknowledge the current trends of the Black-White test score gap and trace its emergence since the 1970s to the present. The political and sociological factors that caused a sudden widening of the gap towards the late 1980s and early 1990s will be identified. Changes within the gap between early childhood through adolescence will be addressed. This chapter will also review the literature that identifies social and genetic factors that have been assumed as contributing factors to the widening of the gap. In its conclusion, this chapter will offer multiple strategies in successfully closing the achievement gap between African-American and White students and identify what implications can be made for educational leaders. This review of salient literature findings on the achievement gap plus some understated ideas will cause further debate and hopefully promising solutions to benefit all children and uphold the promise of equal opportunity for racial/ethnic minority students.

THE CURRENT TRENDS OF THE BLACK-WHITE TEST SCORE GAP

The National Assessment of Educational Progress (NAEP) is currently the only assessment that provides information on the knowledge and skills of a diverse representative sample of the nation's students. Currently, there are no stakes attached to NAEP scores. Therefore student motivation or performance may differ on NAEP and state standardized tests that may be characterized as high stakes. The following description of NAEP can be found on the National Center for Education Statistics web site (http://nces.ed.gov/nationsreportcard/ about/). NAEP, also known as "the Nation's Report Card," is the only nationally representative and continuing assessment of what America's students know and can do in various subject areas. Since 1969, assessments have been conducted periodically in reading, mathematics, science, writing, U.S. history, civics, geography, and the arts. NAEP does not provide scores for individual students or schools; instead, it offers results regarding subject-matter achievement, instructional experiences, and school environment for populations of students (e.g. fourth-graders) and subgroups of those populations (e.g. female students, Hispanic students). NAEP results are based on a sample of student populations of interest. National NAEP reports information for the nation and specific geographic regions of the country. It includes students drawn from both public and nonpublic schools and reports results for student achievement at grades 4, 8, and 12.

Reading and math have always been the subject matter of great national concern. Therefore, much data is available to track the progress of students in these areas at various grade levels. Recently, Lee (2002) found that the long-term trend in NAEP data results indicate that student achievement improved moderately between 1971–1999 in reading and 1973–1999 in math (p. 3). The 1970s and early to mid-1980s also showed the most substantial academic gains for African-American students when compared to Whites, as for example, the Black-White test score gaps in the NAEP reading and math fell by 20% to 40% over the 1971–1999 period (p. 3). However, Lee (2002) also pointed out in his review of the NAEP data that the largest jump in the Black-White test score gain happened between 1971 and 1986–1988; afterward the achievement level for African-Americans flattened while those for White students significantly improved. For Latino students, their comparison NAEP test score rates with Whites showed an inconsistent pattern of gains and losses during the 1973–1975 to 1999 period. In math for example, the most significant gains were made between 1975 and 1982 and remained stagnant afterward. Lee (2002) speculated that the most significant measured growth on the NAEP test scores in the late 1970s and early 1980s period corresponded with the minimum competency standards movement that was emphasized during the 1970s and early 1980s. This is consistent with earlier test data reviews conducted by Miller (1995; p. 49) in which he found that the average NAEP readings scores of African-Americans (age 9) went from 181 in 1975 to 189 in 1980 and virtually stayed at that level till 1988 but then dropped to 182 in 1990. The reading scores for Latinos of the same age group also showed regression in growth as Miller (1995) pointed out how in 1975 they had average NAEP reading scores of 183; 190 in 1980; 194 in 1988, but then dropped to 189 in 1990.

More recent NAEP data results show that in the year of 2000, 40% of White fourth graders scored at or above the proficient level, compared to only 12% of African-Americans and 16% of Hispanics. Math shows an even greater disparity. 34% of White fourth graders scored at or above the proficient level, while just 5% of African-Americans and 10% of Hispanics reached that level. Disappointing disparities in academic achievement between African-American and White students appear even earlier than the fourth grade. According to Jencks and Phillips (1998) and NCES (2001), by kindergarten African-American students already lag behind their White classmates in early reading and math skills. These disparities appear as early as kindergarten, which gives clear indication that African-American students are starting off at a disadvantage. The gap widens in elementary school and remains fixed throughout high school. The NCES study compared mathematics and reading levels of Black and White children at various points between grades 1 and 12. It concluded that Black-White gaps in mathematics and reading achievement appeared at every grade studied. Even for children with similar levels of prior achievement one or two grades earlier, mathematics and reading scores of Blacks were generally lower than the corresponding scores of Whites. This information speaks to the current gap between Black and White students in reading and math. While there has always been a gap, the growing trend of the gap has not been consistent within the past quarter-century.

HISTORY OF THE ACHIEVEMENT GAP

Although the assessment/achievement score gap has always been present, it has not remained consistent within the past 30 years. Grissmer et al. (1998)[3] reports that the NAEP shows a significant narrowing of the gap between Blacks and Whites on reading and mathematics tests between 1971 and 1996. These authors put primary focus on the reasons they felt that the Black-White test score gap narrowed in the 1970s and 1980s. However, little attention is paid to the acknowledgement and causes of the significant widening of the gap between 1988 and 1992.

The authors primarily suggested that the following factors led to the narrowing of the Black-White gap from the 1970s to the 1990s: ". . . increased parental education, smaller families, smaller classes, and rising enrollment in academically demanding courses" (p. 25). The authors also make careful note that during this time the narrowing of the gap constituted higher test scores for Blacks with very little improvement for Whites. For this scenario they assume that improvements in schooling were more valuable to Blacks than to Whites. They also recognize the support that flowed in from the federal government by way of the civil rights movement, school desegregation, affirmative action, and the War on Poverty. Federal programs such as Head Start and other expanded social welfare programs for poor families were contributing factors to the increased achievement for Black students, but had very little effect on White students.

We argue that the significant widening of the Black-White gap beginning in the late 1980s to the early 1990s has less to do with changes in testing procedures, the birth of the hip hop culture, or the increase in violence among Black teenagers. We posit that a stronger correlation can be made to the disappearance of the federal support aimed at increasing academic achievement for minorities and low-income students during this era.

With Lyndon B. Johnson's presidency of the 1960s, the role of the federal government in education was expanded. In 1981, America witnessed a new type of executive leadership. President Ronald Reagan called for a decreased role of the federal government in education. Even more drastic, Reagan sought to eliminate the U.S. Department of Education. Immediately, he began to propose federal budget cuts in education. Specifically, funds would be decreased from various programs initiated under the Elementary and Secondary Education Act (ESEA). During Reagan's first year of administration, he was characterized as not having a formal policy regarding education. The perception was that he was unconcerned about education at any level. The pressure was thick and Reagan would have to act soon to appease the public and critics.

Boyd[4] (1990) describes how strategy is sometimes better than strength as it relates to the political tactics of the Reagan administration. Initially the Reagan administration began by denying that there was an important federal role to be played in education. The administration then began to realize that education is crucial to the ability of the U.S. to compete successfully in the new global economy. Now caught between its ideological commitment to decreasing the federal role in education and the pragmatic reality of the increasing economic importance of education, the Reagan administration established the bully pulpit as its primary tool for resolving this contradiction. Boyd calls this course "efforts to reform the government without half trying." Through the use of reports, commissions, and strategic rhetoric, the administration began to place pressure on the states to assume responsibility for this new reform. Cleverly, the administration did nothing. The states took on the responsibility and the Reagan administration took credit, therefore achieving his goal to decentralize education.

A major proponent of this strategy was the use of the classic 1983 report of the National Commission on Excellence in Education, *A Nation at Risk: The Imperative for Educational Reform.* It called on improving schools for excellence in order to get our schools better prepared to compete against international economic competitors as future workers. *A Nation at Risk* brought forth a federal challenge to state governments to conduct reforms on a grand scale. Although studies have released claims on the inaccuracy of this report, it however sparked a nationwide interest in school reform. Emphasis was placed on teaching traditional academic subjects, increasing the quality and number of science and mathematics courses, and changing the career structure of teachers with the primary goal of promoting excellence for greater democratic equality.

During the 1980s, there was an obvious an overt shift from educational equity to educational excellence. All students (including poor and ethnic minority students) were expected to reach and obtain a higher level of standards, particularly in math and science. However, funding was decreased in the attempts to level the playing field. Even though many educational equity programs began in 1965 with the establishment of ESEA, not all states were in compliance at the beginning. Some states and local districts resisted and did not comply with the *Brown v. The Board of Education* of 1954 ruling until the early 1970s. Reagan's consolidation program came into effect during his first year in 1981. Therefore, many students may not have had adequate time to take advantage of these programs that were first offered during Johnson's administration. With Reagan's ideology of less government, many mandates that came with the federal money had been removed. Localities were no longer obligated to provide programs that would meet the needs of ethnic minority students in order to get the federal money. A decade of progress had come to a halt.

After the release of *A Nation at Risk*, researchers and educators alike began to consider the organization and governance of schools. One result of this re-examination was a shift toward decentralization and site-based management. Local educators and administrators were to be given more control over managing their schools, but they also were to be held accountable for the results. (Vinovskis, 1999, p. 173) In this era, educational equality comes in the tune of the term standards. When schools use standards they are asking that every child meet a certain level of proficiency. Students are expected to be taught and learn the same thing (sometimes in the same manner) to achieve this goal of excellence. However, if some schools are lacking qualified teachers, necessary resources, and adequate physical learning conditions they would not be able to fairly compete with those schools that have an abundance of the latter.

A Nation at Risk called for no new federal dollars. Instead the federal share for elementary and secondary education declined by under 6%. Autonomy was left up to state and local governments to raise student achievement to these new levels of standards. In addition to the less federal involvement or mandate in the Reagan era, monies that were formerly used for providing equal opportunities was decreased and consolidated. In the Johnson era the federal money that was given to states was targeted for specific equity programs. Reagan's administration consolidated all monies and left the power of distribution up to each individual state. They were called block grants. These block grants were a real threat to the tightly targeted categorical programs. Although federal aid was first filtered through state policy, local agencies still diffused and redirected the aims of state and federal governments, that in turn have power to the local districts to use the money where and how they see fit. This weakened the impact and the federal intentions because local districts often structure programs so as to divert funds from those children most in need. (Bennett & LeCompte, 1990) Schmitz (1990) states, "regardless of their racial background . . . urban disadvantaged children become part of the decaying landscape of the inner-city. Most tragic is that the state denies them the only leverage which could lift them from the impoverished underclass – an adequate, equal education" (pp. 1644–1645).

Irvine (1990) comments that the nation is indeed at risk, but because the fastest growing segments of the school population, Blacks and other minorities, is being systematically and effectively excluded from the benefits of educational opportunities. These educational benefits lead to individual economic independence, which this country will ultimately depend upon for its strength and survival.

The changing political climate in the Reagan era moved the nation's focus from equity to excellence in education. During this era, equity did suffer at the hand of excellence. Black students felt the wrath of new federal policies that did little to consider their academic needs.

The other chapters in this volume speak to the multiple ways in which racism and discrimination play crucial roles in creating the achievement gap between African-American and white students. This racism takes the form of: tracking and ability grouping; stereotype threats that African-American students, particularly males, experience in school systems, low teacher perceptions and expectations, lack of resources given to highly populated minority schools, blame placed on African-American families for lack of involvement in education, and poverty in African-American communities. All of these factors need to be considered by educators in terms of explaining the current social context related to racism and discrimination and its important impact on the achievement gap. We argue that some schools and school districts have chosen to use these factors as a pretext for not aggressively dealing with this problem. For example, in the Champaign and Urbana, IL school districts, on average, African-American students are between two and three years behind their White student counterparts in the 5th, 6th, and 7th grade achievement test scores in reading and math assessment tests (Hagg, 2002, pp. A1, A6). The various aforementioned reasons have been given in both communities for this persistent achievement test score gap between African-American and White students, including poor African-American student attitudes about schooling. However, some schools and school districts have aggressively attacked this problem head-on with a different set of organizational/school cultural characteristics based on social justice and service to minority communities which has resulted in dramatic gains in minority student test score achievement.

STRATEGIES TO CLOSE THE ACHIEVEMENT GAP

The research by Scheurich (1998) and Skrla, Scheurich, and Johnson, Jr. (2001), point to ways in which school districts in Texas, with majority African-American and Mexican American populations (and recent immigrants from Mexico and other countries), have been successful in raising student achievement scores. The districts and schools covered in their research represent all the ills typically associated with minority schooling in urban and rural areas (e.g. poverty, local racism). They were also some of the poorest performing districts and schools in the state. To be sure, the increased emphasis on achieving passing rates on the Texas Assessment of Academic Skills (TAAS) tests put pressure on many schools and districts in the state to seek higher comparative performances from teachers and students. However, Scheurich and others found that there were some schools and school districts that used the test mandates as an opportunity to think differently about how to change schools to meet the needs of minority students and communities. Scheurich and his group found a set of "high-pass" schools in which principals and superintendents have concentrated on working hard with teachers, parents, community members and children to create a set of core beliefs and organizational culture characteristics that have significantly raised TAAS score rates and have also resulted in greater teacher, parent, and student satisfaction about education. The test score changes resulted from a passionate commitment and loving attitude toward children with core beliefs that all children can succeed, no exceptions allowed. Creating learner-centered schools with all children being treated with love and respect, no exceptions allowed. The race, and culture of the child is always highly valued with no exceptions allowed, and the school exists for the community. The schools profiled in the research by Scheurich (1998) and Skrla, Scheurich and Johnson, Jr. (2001) also share basic organizational culture characteristics that are different from the typical organizational theory tenets; they are: a strong shared vision, loving caring environments for children and adults, strong collaborative relationships, innovative experimental openness where teachers are not afraid to fail and collective learning from past mistakes to improve, hard working but not burning out on teaching and administrative work, appropriate conduct built into the organizational culture, and the school staff holds themselves accountable for success of all children. The research highlighted here is just one example of a "living reality" from which all educational leaders can learn from in terms of seeing the increased testing as a way to fundamentally change schools for the betterment of African-American and Latino students and service to their communities.

There are other strategies that should be encouraged by the federal government for implementation on the local level in closing the achievement gap. These strategies are suggested by the North Carolina Justice and Community Development Center and the task force created that comprises the Council of Great City Schools:

- Increase the number of minority teachers. Research suggests that students respond more positively when their teachers share likenesses to themselves – even if the likeness is a racial one. Additionally, the retention of diverse teaching staff to reflect the diversity of the student population is important.
- Implement diversity training for pre-service and in-service teachers and other educational staff. Regardless of their race, they must understand the powerful role which ethnic and cultural differences play in influencing learning.
- Using multiple assessments to determine student achievement.
- Adopt a culturally relevant curriculum and pedagogy. The curriculum is far too often geared to the experiences of students who come from White, middle class households. As a result, what African-American students are taught doesn't always reflect the realities of their world and they become disengaged and made to feel less important than their White peers.
- Creating smaller schools and/or reducing class size to facilitate more individualized instruction.
- Increase community partnerships and minority mentoring programs. Provide opportunities for all students to see many examples of successful African-American adults.
- Extend learning time by providing tutoring and other individualized attention opportunities in weekend or after-school activities to supplement student instruction.

Many of these strategies will require extra funding targeted towards minority and at-risk students if the ultimate goal is to successfully close the achievement gap. Lessons can be learned from the 1960s and 1970s where federal money was loosely given and left in the hands of states assuming that they had good intentions to assure equity. Money alone will not close the achievement gap. How the money is spent will be of equal importance. History also tells us that obtaining this type of federal support will be nearly impossible. Distrust of federal education funding and programs by states and local districts has always been present. The current administration is attempting to move in this direction.

CURRENT FEDERAL INITIATIVES TO CLOSE THE ACHIEVEMENT GAP

In the *No Child Left Behind Act* (2001)[5] President George W. Bush states that closing the achievement gap between African-American and White students will be a challenge. He admits that even though schools are now desegregated, public education has failed to deliver the promise of quality education to African-Americans. His stated solution is to attack the soft bigotry of low expectations and demand that schools close the achievement gap among African-American and White students. However, this Act speaks more to identifying the gap than narrowing or closing it.

The intense focus on testing that the president advocated as governor in Texas has become the model for Title I, the federal program for education of poor children. In his education policy statement, "No Child Left Behind," President Bush concludes that testing will do much to "close the achievement gap between the disadvantaged students and their peers":

> Schools must have clear, measurable goals .... Requiring annual state assessments in math and reading in grades 3–8 will ensure that the goal are being met for every child, every year. Annual testing in every grade gives teachers, parents, and policymakers the information they need to ensure that children will reach academic success.

To expose failure and success, test data will be reported by economic background, race and ethnicity, English proficiency, and disability. This is in an effort to hold schools accountable for the academic achievement of all subgroups. Schools that meet or exceed adequate yearly progress objectives or close the achievement gap between minority and White students will be eligible for State Academic Achievement Awards. Those who fail to do so, will over time (after three consecutive years), be subject to improvement, corrective action and restructuring measures aimed at getting them back on course to meet State standards.

The president, like many other testing advocates, thinks that the combination of information, accountability, and sanctions will enable students to reach high standards. He feels certain enough about this to justify the imposition of annual testing requirements on the states, even in an administration committed to increasing state autonomy in other areas.

Research done by the National Research Council has documented that certain assumptions used to justify a heavy reliance on high-stakes tests are flawed.

They largely find that the evidence is inadequate to demonstrate that test policies will motivate the unmotivated; solve problems created by inadequately trained teachers or weak administrators; close gaps in achievement among students from different racial, ethnic, and economic backgrounds; lead to

better job candidate selection; or alter the national economy. Some of these researchers claim that the misuse of test scores to impose drastic sanctions without equalizing opportunity to learn actually can make bad situations worse and can harm the educational attainment of the most vulnerable students. Some studies document that an overemphasis on testing leads to drastically narrowed curricula and to increases in dropout rates (McNeil, 2000).

This mandate of student assessment with the *No Child Left Behind Act* has the potential to do one of two things: (1) It will force families to choose other schools to educate their children by using their Title I funds. Therefore, the policy sends across a message that symbolizes the abandonment of improving public education, particularly the education of youth attending schools in the inner cities. Furthermore, parents in minority communities will begin to lose faith in the ability of the government to educate their children seeking other enticing avenues that are looking to privatize public education. (2) This Act may create a standardized 'dumbing down' of the curriculum and similar teaching methods in order to specifically prepare students for the test in fear of sanction and in search of rewards. This segment of the plan will have the most profound negative effects in the inner cities. "Schools and educators will be asked to do the impossible, still without the resources to do even what is possible, and then blamed for their inevitable inability to do the impossible" (Fair Test, 2001).

CONCLUSION

Standardized tests can be considered a form of institutionalized racism because they lend credibility to policies that have denied, and are continuing to deny, persons of color equal access to educational and job opportunities (Weisglass, 2001). An educational accountability system based on standardized testing, which can be seen heavily throughout the *No Child Left Behind Act*, which prides itself on using standardized measurements which are reportedly neutral, objective, and color-blind only perpetuates and strengthens institutionalized racism in our schools. In order for it to be successful, closing the achievement gap has to be a goal that society endorses. It is not just a school issue. However, fairly or unfairly, what schools do or do not do will have a significant impact on the future of our global society. Schools can use the opportunities presented by the increased testing mandates to change in a fundamental way like the ones profiled in the research on High Pass schools in Texas, and move toward greater equity and social justice for African-American and Latino students. Or they can continue to fail these students, rely on reasons for minority student failure, and then find themselves behind the curve of effective new strategies and ways that address African-American and Latino student achievement.

NOTES

1. Michael Apple is a contributing author in the edited book *Changing American Education: Recapturing the Past or Inventing the Future.*
2. This definition can be found in the glossary section of www.nochildleftbehind.gov
3. David Grissmer, Ann Flanagan, and Stephanie Williamson are contributing authors in the edited book *The Black White Test Score Gap.*
4. William Boyd is a contributing author in the edited book: *Education Reform: Making Sense of it All.*
5. The No Child Left Behind Act of 2001 can be found in its entirety at www.nochildleftbehind.gov

REFERENCES

Bacharach, S. (Ed.) (1990). *Education reform: Making sense of it all.* Boston: Allyn and Bacon.

Bennett, K., & LeCompte (1990). *The way schools work: A sociological analysis of education.* New York: Longman.

Borman, K., & Greenman, N. (1994). *Changing American education: Recapturing the past or reinventing the future?* Albany: State University of New York Press.

Burlingame, M., Coombs, F., Sergiovani, T., & Thurston, P. (1999). *Educational governance and administration* (4th ed.). Boston: Allyn and Bacon.

Fair Test. (2001). Issues and arguments on Bush testing plan. Retrieved June 8, 2002 from the World Wide Web: www.fairtest.org/nattest/Bush3.html

Hagg, D. (2002, May, 5). Test score disparities challenge C-U schools. *The Champaign Urbana News Gazette,* pp. A1, A6.

Hauser, R., & Heubert, J. (Eds) (1999). National Research Council, Committee on Appropriate Test Use, *High stakes: Testing for tracking promotion, and graduation.* Washington, D.C.: National Academy Press.

Irvine, J. (1990). *Black students and school failure: Policies, practices and prescriptions.* New York: Greenwood Press.

Jencks, C., & Phillips, M. (Eds) (1998). *The Black-White test score gap.* Washington, D.C.: Brookings Institution Press.

Lee, J. (2002). Racial and ethnic achievement gap trends: Reversing the progress toward equity. *Educational Researcher, 31,* 3–12.

McNeil, L. (2000). *Contradictions of school reform: Educational costs of standardized testing.* New York: Routledge.

Miller, L. S. (1995). An American imperative: Accelerating minority educational advancement. New Haven, CN: Yale University Press.

National Center for Education Statistics (2001). *Educational achievement and Black-White inequality.* Washington, D.C.: U.S. Department of Education, Office of Educational Research and Improvement.

National Commission on Excellence (1983). *A Nation at risk.* Washington, D.C.

Noguera, P. (2001). Racial politics and the elusive quest for excellence and equity in education. *Education and Urban Society, 34*(1), 18–41.

North Carolina Justice and Community Development Center. Exposing the gap: Why minority students are left behind in North Carolina's educational system. Retrieved from the World Wide Web on May 2, 2002. Available at: http://www.ncjustice.org

Scheurich, J. J. (1998). Highly successful and loving public elementary schools populated mainly by low-SES children of color: Core beliefs and cultural characteristics. *Urban Education, 33*, 451–491.

Schmitz, A. (1994). Providing an escape for inner-city children: Creating a federal remedy for educational ills of poor urban schools. *Minnesota Law Review, 78*(6), 1639–1671.

Skrla, L., Scheurich, J., & Johnson, J. F., Jr. (Eds) (2001). Accountability and achievement in high-poverty settings. *Education and Urban Society, 33*, 227–333.

Vinovskis, M. (1999). *History and educational policymaking.* New Haven: Yale University Press.

Weisglass, J. (2001). Racism and the achievement gap. *Education Week, 20*(43), 49, 72.

13. INSTRUCTIONAL EFFICIENCY VERSUS SOCIAL REFORM: FUNDAMENTALS OF THE TRACKING DEBATE

Arthur E. Lehr

ABSTRACT

The controversy over tracking in American public schools has been more often marked by ostensibly emotional expressions than by clearly presented conclusions. This chapter examines the fundamental issues surrounding the debate over detracking. While tracking supporters contend that it provides an efficient way of organizing students for instruction, opponents contend that it perpetuates educational inequality by denying low-income and minority students access to quality schooling. This chapter considers both perspectives and their underlying assumptions and scrutinizes the reasoning and commentary drawn from both sides in an effort to broaden understanding of the controversy.

INTRODUCTION

The grouping and scheduling of students according to their perceived level of academic ability has long been a feature of American public schools, particularly at the secondary level. In the past several decades, the basic question of whether ability grouping or assignment of students to academic tracks is a

Challenges of Urban Education and Efficacy of School Reform, Volume 6, pages 221–235.

ISBN: 0-7623-0426-X

benefit or detriment has sponsored a recurring clash of logic, emotion, and research (Hopkins, 1997). Extensive research efforts to discover the actual impact of tracking on student progress have not helped to resolve the dispute.

Reviewers of studies comparing ability-grouped and non-grouped classes have generally agreed that there are few, if any, positive effects of ability grouping on student achievement (Kulik & Kulik, 1984; Gamoran, 1986; Slavin, 1990). When ability grouped classes are compared with heterogeneous classes, however, some researchers have noted a small increase in high-level student achievement from ability grouping (Loveless, 1998; Betts & Sckolnik, 2000). As this difference is negligible, some studies report it as positive, while others view it as irrelevant or inconclusive (Jaeger & Hattie, 1995).

For the past 20 years, contending sides in the debate over ability grouping or tracking have disputed research findings that did not reflect their point of view and have become more rigid in their perspectives. Some have become increasingly strident in the tone of their arguments. The following presentation is not an attempt to resolve the controversy. It is an effort to understand it more fully.

Tracking Support and Opposition

The supporters of tracking have described it as a valuable tool for organizing students and facilitating instruction. They have noted that by narrowing the range of student academic achievement in the classroom, the number of students requiring extra help is minimized and the number of students who can understand and work with difficult concepts is maximized. As a result, they have claimed that instructional efficiency and academic progress are increased (Loveless, 1999). On that basis, they have advocated the continuation of tracking for the good of students. This point of view is consistent with the rationale typically offered to explain secondary school scheduling of students and classes according to perceived levels of academic ability.

The foes of tracking have often voiced fierce opposition to its application. They have condemned it as a form of "educational apartheid" (Darling-Hammond, 1997, p. 267) and "educational child abuse" (Broussard & Joseph, 1998). They have characterized it as an "evil" practice that promotes "dumbed-down, skill-drill, ditto-driven, and application-deficient curricula" (Pool & Page, 1995, p. 1). Among the negative outcomes of tracking, they have cited the disempowering and disabling of students assigned to low-ability tracks (Cummins, 1983), inhibiting their opportunities for postsecondary education, reducing their self-esteem, and stunting their academic growth (Furr, 1993; McLaren, 1988; Oakes, 1985, 1992).

The basic concerns for the academic progress of students voiced in arguments for and against tracking are interestingly similar. Both sides of the issue make their case on the basis of essential fairness in providing students with opportunities for an adequate and appropriate education. Both sides assert that the educational needs of students must be met through appropriately structured teaching and learning situations. And, both sides claim the academic progress of all students as their primary objective. Although their concerns are comparable, their perspectives on the outcomes of tracking are poles apart.

The arguments for and against tracking appear to be shaped by rather different sets of interests. Pro-tracking is mainly concerned with classroom efficiency and instructional effectiveness; whereas, anti-tracking is primarily concerned with social equity and democratic values (Braddock & Slavin, 1995). Behind both of these positions are an array of supporting arguments and assumptions that extend to issues of race, class, economics, politics, and the fundamental role of public schooling in society. A closer examination of the rhetoric on both sides of the issue is instructive for educators, particular those in administrative positions who must make or implement policy decisions on the organization of teaching and learning and the placement of students at the secondary level.

THE RATIONALE FOR TRACKING

Whatever views may be held for or against tracking, it is a practice in widespread use, especially at the high school level. Grouping students by presumed stages of ability and assigning them to classes that reflect various levels of difficulty may typically be found in high school core curriculums, including English, social studies, math and science. Approximately 80% of math and science classes are tracked at the high school level, and many schools also track for language classes (Hallinan, 1994; Oakes, 1990). Many of the schools that use tracking, however, also typically offer a variety of untracked courses of study and extracurricular activities.

Tracking for Structure

Historically, tracking has been closely associated with the use of a differentiated curriculum at the secondary level. Nevi (1987) claims that tracking was born "the first time an enterprising young teacher in a one-room schoolhouse in the 1880 divided his students into those who knew how to read and those who didn't" (p. 24). Some form of tracking has been employed in the public schools for much of the last century, although the specific applications with which tracking or ability grouping is identified have changed over time.

Although the terms are now used interchangeably, 30 or more years ago, tracking and ability grouping were used to identify very different approaches to student placement. Ability grouping generally referred to the formation of small, homogeneous groups within elementary classrooms for reading or mathematics instruction. Tracking was the term applied to the practice of placing high school students in separate curricular tracks on the basis of achievement and IQ test scores.

According to Hallinan (1994), students in secondary schools were originally assigned to academic, general, or vocational tracks. Courses within the high (college preparatory) track were designed to prepare students for postsecondary education. Courses within the low track (vocational) were designed to prepare students for the work force. The general (middle-level) track served as a "catch-all for the huge group of students in the middle, those neither gifted nor deficient or unsure of what they would do after high school" (Loveless, 1998, p. 7). Although many schools have shifted to course-by-course placement of students according to prerequisites and perceived student abilities (Lucas, 1999), the advanced, regular, and basic course designations found in many secondary schools today have evolved from this earlier pattern.

Tracking for Fairness

Those who support tracking argue that heterogeneously grouped or mixed-ability classes are difficult to teach due to the wide range of student abilities and needs, that they slow the progress of academically talented students, and that they leave students with learning problems to struggle while others move ahead (Brewer et al., 1995). In their view, heterogeneous grouping treats students unfairly by not meeting their needs or supporting their aspirations (Loveless, 1999). In mixed-ability classrooms, as they see it, faster students are not appropriately challenged and slower students are not adequately supported because instruction must be too broadly aimed at a wide spectrum of academic abilities and intellectual interests.

Some tracking advocates reason that if children demonstrate distinct and measurable differences in their ability, motivation, and speed of learning, educators are obliged to respond appropriately to these differences and that it is unfair to students to pretend that such differences do not exist (George, 1995). By identifying the differences that characterize students, "organizing students according to these differences, and matching curriculum and instruction to the differences," schools are fulfilling their responsibility for providing optimum opportunities to all students (p. 45). This argument in behalf of tracking assumes that students will learn more effectively, gain more confidence in themselves, and have a greater motivation to learn when grouped with others who resemble their levels of academic skills and development. It also assumes that instruction may be delivered more efficiently.

Tracking for Efficiency

Proponents of tracking have claimed that ability grouping is necessary to maximize the effective delivery of instructional programs, especially those in which the curriculum is broadly differentiated and designed to serve a broad cross-section of student interests and needs. To accommodate the spectrum of student need and to individualize instruction, tracking supporters argue that school organization, class scheduling, and course content must make the best possible match between students and the instructional setting (Braddock & Slavin, 1995). Tracking students according to their abilities and needs has been described as a logical and reasonable response to the increasing diversity of the student population in America's public schools.

According to tracking advocates, the theory behind ability grouping is based on the idea that teaching efficiency is improved by allowing teachers to focus their instruction more narrowly and subsequently to provide greater depth of content for students who have the capacity for quick and viable comprehension. Teaching a group of "like-ability students allows teachers to adjust the pace of instruction to students' needs" (Slavin, 1987). Broussard and Joseph (1998) identify four basic rationales in support of tracking at the secondary level:

(1) Students learn better when they are grouped with academically similar students.
(2) "Slower" students develop more positive attitudes toward themselves and the school if they are not placed with more "capable" students.
(3) Placing students in various tracks is basically fair because it reflects their past achievement and "innate abilities."
(4) Teaching is much easier in homogeneous classrooms, as students are easier to teach and to manage (p. 112).

The placement of students on their record of past achievement assumes an accurate and reliable means for measuring that achievement, a premise that has been strongly challenged by tracking opponents.

Track assignment at the secondary level is typically based on prerequisite courses, teacher and counselor recommendations, and grade point averages, in addition to standardized test scores. Loveless (1998) notes while that academic performance measured by grades and teachers' recommendations dictate most student placements, parent and student requests are also factors in determining where students are assigned.

Although most attention is focused on tracking at the secondary level, claims for increased instructional efficiency and student achievement as a result of ability grouping are made at the elementary level as well. Slavin (1987) notes that instruction can be improved by grouping students for one or two subjects (e.g. reading instruction), by grouping students according to ability rather than age and allowing them to progress at their own rates, and by in-class grouping that breaks out two or three ability-based groups within a classroom. Slavin cautions, however, that any grouping plan must allow for frequent reevaluation of student skills and provide an easy means for reassignment of students who show progress.

Tracking for Bureaucracy

The connections between tracking practices and the bureaucratic structure of schools has been acknowledged by tracking supporters and vilified by tracking opponents. Most organizations have some bureaucratic elements within their structure, but many of the characteristics attributed to well-developed bureaucracies are easily identified in schools. Like most bureaucratic organizations, schools typically have a top-down hierarchy, differentiated work roles, formalized goals and expectations, and an extraordinary number of rules and regulations governing most aspects of their operation (Byrk & Driscoll, 1988; Rowan, 1990). In secondary schools, the organization of instruction into departments and tracks is consistent with the bureaucratic model of specialization.

Supporters of tracking argue that a school's bureaucratic focus on efficiency and product quality is entirely appropriate. They point out that instruction may be regarded as a technical activity and that curriculum is composed of discrete and fixed subject matter to be imparted through a standardized and sequenced pattern of instruction within defined subject areas (Lee & Smith, 1995). In the school setting, learning is typically assessed by measuring subject matter mastery. Students are sorted into "specialized instructional units aimed at matching their ability and interests to the subject matter" (Byrk & Driscoll, 1988, p. 243). Except in small schools where there are too few students to justify a division of classes at any grade level, students at the same grade level in most schools must be divided into separate classes. Schools are, therefore, in a good position to create specialized courses tailored to student needs (Monk & Haller, 1993).

As a technique for organizing and scheduling students, tracking offers a structured approach that evidently has strong appeal among secondary school administrators who must manage large numbers of students and a broad range of curriculum offerings. Today's high-ability tracks are focused on preparing the most capable students for postsecondary education, sometimes to the neglect of students considered less capable and assigned to middle or lower-tracks. Tracking supporters see this outcome, not as an indictment of tracking, but as a deficiency caused by insufficient support and inadequate resources. The opponents of tracking focus most strongly on the effect tracking has on students who are not selected for the high ability classes.

THE CASE AGAINST TRACKING

The opponents of tracking claim that grouping students by ability is and always has been about "race, class, and inequality – that when everything else is stripped away, maintaining special privileges for some students and denying them to others is the dominant theme of all tracking decisions" (Loveless, 1999, p. 3). They are also concerned that students are treated unfairly because their needs are not met and they become stereotyped for limited progress or outright failure. The opponents of tracking see the unfairness primarily associated with those students who are assigned to classes specifically designed for slow learners. They also claim that tracking supporters are only genuinely concerned with serving fast learners. The opponents of tracking also draw a larger picture of unfairness that they base on deeply held American social views about racial, ethnic, and class inferiority and in the ways these views affect the disposition of students in the public schools.

During the final decade of the 20th Century, the move toward detracking gained considerable momentum. Educators who had grown disillusioned with the consequences of ability grouping began advocating the replacement of tracked course programs and ability-grouped classes with heterogeneous or mixed-ability classrooms (Wheelock, 1992; Yonezawa et al., 2002). Detracking proved to be a difficult undertaking, however, as school leaders, researchers, and scholars found that they, as well as parents and students, had to rethink many traditional understandings of intelligence and academic merit that were ubiquitous to the culture (Oakes et al., 1997). Indeed, public opinion research by the Public Agenda Foundation revealed broad support for tracking among parents, students, and teachers (Loveless, 1998). Their 1996 poll indicated that only "34% of the public and 40% of teachers believe that heterogeneous grouping (as an alternative to tracking) will improve education" (Farkas & Johnson, 1996). Even so, tracking has generated fierce conflict in many school communities that has divided parents, educators, and the general public into increasingly vociferous opinion groups.

Tracking as Detrimental to Learning

Those who advocate wiping out ability grouping as a means of organizing students within the public school setting offer justifications that are grounded in goals that are both educational and social. Opponents of ability grouping see detracking as the obvious means to achieve the ultimate goal of improved learning for all students. They view public schools as obliged to recognize the principle that all children have the capacity for high-level learning and that the schools are "society's responsible institutions for developing this learning" (Wheelock, 1995).

The supporters of detracking regard it as a means for removing the social stigmas that tracking imposes on students assigned to low-ability classes and as a means for raising the levels of intellectual stimulation and inquiry for all students. Detracking is also expected to elevate the "moral and ethical consciousness of students who previously may not have been considered bright enough to discuss such weighty concerns" (Blackwell, 1995). The notion that some students, because of their family background, are not intellectually capable of higher-level learning seems to be the match that ignites the strongest protests against assigning students to different learning tracks.

Tracking as Social Discrimination

The view that tracking is a means of discriminating against some students, while favoring others, is predicated on the idea that the assignment of a student to a lower track constitutes assignment of that student to lower social as well as academic status. This connection appears to dominate the thinking of those who most bitterly oppose tracking. According to Wheelock (1992), there are four good reasons why tracking should be banned:

(1) Criteria used to group kids are based on subjective perceptions and fairly narrow views of intelligence.
(2) Tracking leads students to take on labels – both in their own minds, as well as in the minds of their teachers, that are usually associated with the pace of learning (slow or fast), thus confusing pace of learning with capacity to learn.
(3) We associate students' placement with the type of learners they are and therefore create different expectations for different groups of students.
(4) Once students are grouped, they generally stay at that level for their school careers, and the gap between achievement and levels becomes exaggerated over time (p. 2).

Advocates of detracking see a strong connection between student placement and the expectations and classroom practices of teachers.

Opponents of tracking argue that the instructional approaches and pedagogical methods applied by teachers of low-track students may be regarded as discriminatory because teachers assigned to low-ability classes are predisposed to assume that low-track students necessarily have limited academic abilities and can not be expected to perform well. Tracking opponents claim that teachers who are assigned to teach low-track classes are likely to allocate less time to instruction and to use that instructional time most often for seatwork that involves worksheets and other forms of controlled drill and practice.

As student-teacher interactions become less academically oriented, teachers are also considered to be more likely to expect students to misbehave and to focus on criticisms of student behavior than on meeting student academic needs (Eckstrom & Villegas, 1991; Oakes, 1985). More class time, therefore, is devoted to management and discipline concerns, as teacher of low-track students place greater emphasis on students' conformity to rules than to helping them to become autonomous, competent thinkers and learners (Oakes, 1995). Because they believe that students assigned to low-ability classes are held in low-esteem by teachers, the opponents of tracking conclude that students must come to regard themselves in the same way.

Tracking as the Cause of Lost Motivation

In an ideal world, students will develop through their school experiences the ability, confidence, and motivation to succeed academically. They will participate constructively in instruction because they have a respectable and respected social identity. But, the opponents of tracking assert that when students are not positioned to experience this development because of ability grouping, not only their academic growth but also their social well being is negatively affected (Cummins, 2001).

Students may come to see low-track assignment as evidence that they cannot succeed in school and that it is pointless to try. According to Neito (2000), students to placed in low-ability classes begin to believe that "their placement in these groups is natural and a true reflection of whether they are dumb or smart" (p. 90). In addition, they become alienated by the school where they are identified as losers. And, as school becomes more senseless and less rewarding, they become discouraged and drop out. Loss of self-confidence is seen as a direct route to loss of motivation to stay in school.

Research reports that, compared to students with similar abilities in mixed-ability classes, students who are placed in low tracks achieve less (Gamoran &

Mare, 1989; Oakes, 1990; Gamoran, 1990), are more likely to engage in delinquent behavior, and are more likely to drop out of school before high school graduation (Children's Defense Fund, 1988; Maddox & Wheelock, 1995; Rosenbaum, 1976; Cummins, 2001; Wiatrowski et al., 1982). Many researchers also note that the ability grouping of students has a negative effect not only on students but also on the community, as the sorting process all too frequently groups students by race or socioeconomic standing, rather than by a valid assessment of student ability and potential. Oakes (1985) asks, "Could it be that we are teaching our kids at the bottom of the educational hierarchy – who are more likely to be from poor and minority groups – behaviors that will prepare them to fit in at the lowest levels of the social and economic hierarchy?" (p. 91). The question is relevant when considering racism as a factor in tracking.

Tracking as Racism

In schools that have a tracked curriculum, students most often found in low-ability classes are African Americans, Hispanics, and the children of low-income families. The opponents of ability grouping argue that the practice of school tracking is rooted in the belief that upper income, white populations are possessed of higher levels of intelligence and ability and that African Americans, Hispanics and poor people possess lesser abilities and intellects (Oakes, 1985). They charge that tracking is a practice founded on racist intentions that continues to produce racist results (Loveless, 1999). Pollock (2001) observes that "Americans routinely think about school achievement in racial terms" (p. 1). And, although many members of local school communities and the general public typically attempt to avoid references to race in public discussions of student achievement, most are likely to be concerned about the possible association of race with student achievement patterns (Lipman, 1998). It should not come as a surprise, therefore, that individuals and groups who defend or advocate student placement on the basis of academic ability within a tracked school system may be accused of racist motives.

Opponents of tracking specifically argue that ability grouping in public schools continues to exist in order to guarantee the unfair distribution of privilege, preserving access to high-status knowledge for white students from affluent families and denying it to low-income students and students of color. A broader basis for this charge is the assertion that social stratification of intelligence and ability by race and class has been widely accepted in America and that standardized tests used to justify student tracking placements represent a misleading, but "conventional view" of intelligence and ability as "stable, unidimensional, easy to measure, and difficult to change" (Oakes et al., 1996). If this assertion is accurate, it would mean that a substantial proportion of students are being unfairly "written off" as unworthy of anything more than a token schooling effort because of their family background or the color of their skin.

Tracking as Classism

Another facet of the concept that tracking is aimed at preserving the privileges of the elite is the contention that tracking persists because good teaching is a scarce resource that is typically allocated to the students whose middle and upper income families have the highest social standing in the community and, consequently, the most political clout. The emphasis placed on competition in American society may lead parents who want the advantage of having their children enrolled in only the "best classes" to pressure the schools to give them that edge (Oakes, 1995). Considering that schools are essentially competitive systems that offer places in the high-ability track to relatively small percentages of their enrollments, it is not unexpected to have influential parents push to have their children better educated.

This situation may be further compounded by racially biased fears that "minority student enrollment in a class will lead to lower educational standards" (p. 67). Such qualms may also prompt white and wealthy parents to lobby for assignment of their children to the racially and socio-economically homogeneous classes and programs that they see as most advantageous.

Close attention by influential parents to the placement of students and the scheduling of classes may also explain why the most highly qualified teachers are usually assigned to teach the most enriched curricula to the most advantaged students (Darling-Hammond, 1997; Oakes, 1990). This often leaves the low-track classes to by staffed by less qualified, less experienced teachers. Although some schools may rotate the teaching of low and high track classes, it is likely that teachers with the most seniority or influence will be assigned to the high track, or that administrators may attempt to use class assignments as rewards or punishments. As tracking opponents see it, the least prepared and least resourceful teachers are too often assigned to the low-track classes with the greatest needs (Oakes, 1995), and the students in these low-track classes are the most likely to be from minority and low income families.

Tracking as Supporting Social Stratification

More radical explanations by anti-tracking activists of the underlying assumptions that support ability grouping include references to Social Darwinism and Neo-Marxism.

The more outspoken opponents of tracking relate it to Social Darwinism, the belief that socially advanced classes are biologically superior to others. They find that the sorting and classifying of children in schools according to their inherited intellectual abilities is a predictable response by Social Darwinism (Crosby & Owens, 1993). They charge that misguided educators who accept the notion that biologically inferior children are simply not equipped for higher-level learning will perpetuate the inequities of tracking that will result in low expectations and eventual failure for students who do not fit a socially advanced profile. The outcome for schools is the funneling of white, middleclass children into college preparatory classes, while students of color and students from poor families are placed disproportionately in lower tracks leading eventually to low skilled or unskilled slots as low-paid workers (Broussard & Joseph, 1998).

Neo-Marxists apparently suspect that the American public school system serves as no more than a sorting mechanism intended to guarantee that children of the privileged classes maintain their position. Neo-Marxists view tracking as a conspiracy to perpetuate the nation's system of social stratification through reinforcing the segregation of students along socioeconomic, as well as racial lines (Hallinan, 1996). From their position of denouncing the American public schools as an extension of the wage labor system designed to generate a low-paid labor pool (Ansalone, 2000), it is a short step for Neo-Marxists to join the opponents of tracking in citing the school system as repressive device to maintain a repressive social system for the advantage of a ruling elite.

CONCLUSION

Reformers who believe that the single most effective means of improving public schools is the complete obliteration of tracking are faced with a major struggle to gain general acceptance of their idea and to find ways to make it work. Tracking systems are extraordinarily resistant to change, as tracking is usually interconnected with and supported by other practices in the organization of instruction and the scheduling of students into classes. Detracking, therefore, must involve much more than simply moving students into mixed-ability classes.

Advocates of detracking affirm that it must be combined with changes in instructional strategies and formats; less dependence on textbooks; and the use of innovations such as cooperative learning, peer tutoring, and multilevel teaching (Neito, 2000). For detracking to work, curriculum will need to be altered and instructional materials modified to accommodate various ability levels in the classroom. Teaching will need to focus on drawing struggling students into class activities and in giving them the support they need to succeed (Watkins et al., 2001). These, and many other changes in the organizational structure and culture of schools will be necessary to bring about the move from tracking to the mixed-ability classroom.

Because tracking is so firmly entrenched, its opponents see themselves as facing an uphill battle. They feel that detracking must begin with a major change in the belief that only some students have the intellectual capacity to benefit from schooling. Educators and the public at large will need to accept that all students can profit from a curriculum that teaches children to think (Darling-Hammond, 1997). As O'Neil put it, "Once teachers realize that all students can really be smart, then they will realize the importance of detracking" (1992, p. 21). That realization may be slow in coming.

REFERENCES

Betts, J. R., & Sckolnik, J. L. (2000). The effects of ability grouping on student achievement and resource allocation in secondary schools. *Economics of Education Review, 19*(1), 17–20.

Blackwell, B. G. (1995). In the meantime: Using a dialectical approach to raise levels of intellectual stimulation and inquiry in low-track classes. In: H. Pool & J. A. Page (Eds), *Beyond Tracking: Finding Success in Inclusive Schools* (pp. 155–164), Bloomington, IN: Phi Delta Kappa Foundation.

Braddock, J. H., & Slavin, R. (1995). Why ability grouping must end: Achieving excellence and equity in American education. In: H. Pool & J. A. Page (Eds), *Beyond Tracking: Finding Success in Inclusive Schools* (pp. 7–20), Bloomington, IN: Phi Delta Kappa Foundation.

Brewer, D. J., Rees, D. I., & Argys, L. M. (1995). Detracking America's schools: The reform without cost? *Phi Delta Kappan, 77*(3), 210–215.

Broussard, C. A., & Joseph, A. L. (1998). Tracking: A form of educational neglect? *Social Work in Education, 20*(2), 110–120.

Byrk, A. S., & Driscoll, M. E. (1988). *The school as community: Theoretical foundations, contextual influences, and consequences for students and teachers.* Madison, WI: University of Wisconsin.

Children's Defense Fund (1988). *Making middle grades work.* Washington, D.C.: Adolescent Pregnancy Prevention Clearinghouse.

Crosby, M., & Owens, E. (1993). The disadvantages of tracking and ability grouping: A look at cooperative learning. ERIC/EDRS Doc. Ed358184. Clemson, SC: National Dropout Prevention Center.

Cummins, J. (1983). Functional language proficiency in context: Classroom participation as an interactive process. In: W. J. Tikunoff (Ed.), *Compatibility of the SBIS Features with Other Research on Instruction for LEP Students* (pp. 109–131). San Francisco: Far West Laboratory.

Cummins, J. (2001). Empowering minority students: A framework for intervention. *Harvard Educational Review, 71*(4), 656–675.

Darling-Hammond, L. (1997). *The right to learn: A blueprint for creating schools that work.* San Francisco: Jossey-Bass.

Eckstrom, R., & Villegas, A. (1991). Ability grouping in middle grade mathematics: Process and consequences. *Research in Middle Level Education, 15*(1), 1–20.

Farkas, S., & Johnson, J. (1996). *Given the circumstances: Teachers talk about public education today*. New York: Public Agenda Foundation.

Furr, L. A. (1993). Curriculum tracking: A new arena for school social work. *Social Work in Education, 15*, 35–44.

Gamoran, A. (1986). Instructional and institutional effects of ability grouping. *Sociology of Education, 59*(4), 185–189.

Gameron, A. (1990, April). *The consequences of track-related instructional differences for student achievement*. Paper presented at the annual meeting of the American Educational Research Association, Boston.

Gamoran, A., & Mare, R. (1989). Secondary school tracking and educational inequality: Compensation, reinforcement or neutrality? *American Journal of Sociology, 94*, 1146–1183.

George, P. S. (1995). Is it possible to live with tracking and ability grouping? In: H. Pool & J. A. Page (Eds), *Beyond Tracking: Finding Success in Inclusive Schools* (pp. 141–154). Bloomington, IN: Phi Delta Kappa Foundation.

Hallinanh, M. T. (1994). Tracking: From theory to practice. *Sociology of Education, 67*(2), 79–84.

Hallinan, M. T. (1996). Track mobility in secondary schools. *Social Forces, 74*, 983–1002.

Hopkins, G. (1997). *Is ability grouping the way to go – or should it go away*. Retrieved June 17, 2002, from http/www.education-world.com/a_admin/admin-009.shtml

Jaeger, R. M., & Hattie, J. A. (1995). Detracking America's schools: Should we really care? *Phi Delta Kappan, 77*(3), 218–219.

Kulik, C.-L. C., & Kulik, J. A. (1984). Effects of ability grouping on elementary school pupils: A meta-analysis of evaluation findings. Paper presented at the annual meeting of the American Psychological Association, Toronto, Canada.

Lee, V. E., & Smith, J. B. (1995). Effects of high school restructuring and size on early gains in achievement and engagement. *Sociology of Education, 68*(4), 287–300.

Lipman, P. (19998). *Race, class, and power in school restructuring*. Albany, NY: SUNY Press.

Loveless, T. (1998). *The tracking and ability grouping debate*. Retrieved June 17, 2002, from http://www.edexcellence.net/library/track.html#anchor996453

Loveless, T. (1999). *The tracking wars: State reform meets school policy*. Washington, D.C.: Brookings Institution Press.

Lucas, S. (1999). *Tracking inequality*. New York: Teachers College Press.

Maddox, R., & Wheelock, A. (1995, November). Untracking and students' futures: Choosing between aspirations and expectations. *Phi Delta Kappan, 7*, 222–228.

McLaren, P. (1988). Broken dreams, false promises, and the decline of public schooling. *Journal of Education, 170*, 41–45.

Monk, D. H., & Haller, E. J. (1993). Predictors of high school academic course offerings: The role of school size. *American Research Journal, 30*(1), 3–21.

Neito, S. (2000). *Affirming diversity: The sociopolitical context of multicultural education* (3rd ed.). New York: Longman.

Nevi, C. (1987). In defense of tracking. *Educational Leadership, 44*(6), 24–26.

Oakes, J. (1985). *Keeping track: How schools structure inequality*. New Haven, CT: Yale University Press.

Oakes, J. (1990). *Multiplying inequalities: The effects of race, social class, and tracking on opportunities to learn math and science*. New York: Rand Corp.

Oakes, J. (1992). Can tracking research inform practice? Technical, normative, and political considerations. *Educational Researcher, 21*(4), 12–21.

Oakes, J. (1995). More than meets the eye: Links between tracking and the culture of schools. In: H. Pool & J. A. Page (Eds), *Beyond Tracking: Finding Success in Inclusive Schools* (pp. 59–70), Bloomington, IN: Phi Delta Kappa Foundation.

Oakes, J., Wells, A. S., & Associates. (1996, September). *Beyond the technicalities of school reform.* Los Angeles: UCLA Graduate School of Education and Information Studies.

Oakes, J., Wells, A. S., Datnow, A., & Jones, M. (1997). Detracking: The social construction of ability, cultural politics, and resistance to reform. *Teachers College Record, 98*(3), 482–510.

Rosenbaum, J. E. (1976). *Making inequality: The hidden curriculum of high school tracking*. New York: John Wiley & Sons.

Rowan, B. (1990). Applying conceptions of teaching to organizational reforms. In: R. E. Elmore (Ed.), *Restructuring Schools: The Next Generation of Educational Reform* (pp. 313–58). San Francisco: Jossey-Bass.

Slavin, R. (1987). Ability grouping and student achievement in elementary schools: A best evidence synthesis. *Review of Educational Research, 57*(3), 293–336.

Slavin, R. (1990). Achievement effects of ability grouping in secondary schools: A best-evidence synthesis. *Review of Educational Research, 60*(3), 471–499.

Smith-Maddox, R., & Wheelock, A. (1995). Untracking and students' futures: Closing the gap between aspirations and expectations. *Phi Delta Kappan, 77*(3), 222–228.

Watkins, W. J., Lewis, J. H., & Chou, V. (2001). *Race education: The roles of history and society in educating African American students*. Boston: Allyn & Bacon.

Wheelock, A. (1992). *Crossing the tracks: How "untracking" can save America's schools*. New York: New Press.

Wheelock, A. (1995). Reintegrating schools for success: Untracking across the United States. In: H. Pool & J. A. Page (Eds), *Beyond Tracking: Finding Success in Inclusive Schools* (pp. 213–224). Bloomington, IN: Phi Delta Kappa Foundation.

Wiatrowski, M., Hansel, S., Massey, C. R., & Wilson, D. L. (1982). Curriculum tracking and delinquency. *American Sociological Review, 47*(1), 151–160.

Yonezawa, S., Wells, A. S., & Serna, I. (2002). Choosing tracks: "Freedom of choice" in detracking schools. *American Educational Research Journal, 39*(1), 37–67.

PART III:
SCHOOL REFORM STRATEGIES

14. INITIATING WORK TEAMS TO REFORM THE AMERICAN HIGH SCHOOL

Terri H. Mozingo

ABSTRACT

The high school reform literature shows that high school teachers work best in a structural context that promotes teamwork, values collegiality, and increases interaction. Yet, the large high school structure constrains collegiality, de-emphasizes teamwork, and is embedded with routines that increase isolation among administrators, teachers, and students. Research studies of work teams in business show an increase in employee morale and in productivity and a reduction in isolation between and among workers. The inward look at a business successfully initiating work teams provide insights into redefining the classical paradigm that supports working in isolation in high schools.

THE PROBLEM: THE LINGERING BUREAUCRACY

The idea to organize people in a hierarchical and departmentalized organizational structure whether in business or schools dates back to the late 19th century. Taylor (1911) described his management ideas in *The Principles of Scientific Management.* Taylor was a laborer, machinist, and a chief engineer who developed a mechanistic view of workers. He believed that people could be programmed as efficient machines that would accomplish production-related

Challenges of Urban Education and Efficacy of School Reform, Volume 6, pages 239–253.

ISBN: 0-7623-0426-X

tasks. According to Taylor, the tendency for man to take it easy when working resulted from a uniform standard rate of pay by the day. Hence, the better man slowed down their production gait to that of the poorest and least efficient. In pre-industrial management systems, each worker was left with the final responsibility for doing his job practically as he thought best and with little help and advice from management. But Taylor felt this isolation of workmen made it impossible for the men to perform their work in accordance with the rules and laws of science or art. Furthermore, Taylor argued that, because the science underlying each act of each workman was so extensive, the workman best suited to performing the work was incapable of truly understanding this science. Many believed during this time that the workman could only perform his task with the help of those working with him or over him because of the workman's lack or education or insufficient skills. The scientific management principles clearly favored the system over the people. In other words, Taylor consistently argued that man is incapable of being self-directed and that without systematic management, or a hierarchy, man would continue to be ill-directed, inefficient, and incapable of consistently producing his best.

Taylor's ideas were implemented in different organizations, and other writers expanded upon his ideas. For example, Hoy and Miskel (1996) described how Max Weber, a German sociologist, further enhanced Taylor's work by articulating a management system called bureaucracy. Weber's bureaucratic model contained five elements that are still prevalent in many organizations today:

(1) Clearly defined hierarchy of authority.
(2) Davison of labor and specialization.
(3) Rules and regulations.
(4) Impersonal orientation.
(5) Career orientation.

These five elements set forth a set of assumptions about how people should be organized and how work should be done in accordance with scientific principles. First, offices within a bureaucratic organization are arranged vertically, with power and authority flowing from the top to the bottom through the organization's chain of command. Second, workers are responsible for a specialized task based upon technical qualifications. Third, rules and regulations are established to provide stability and uniformity of employee actions and continuity of operations during personnel turnover. Fourth, the interaction between and among individuals and departments is formal. Decisions are based on judgment and facts vs. passion and emotion. Fifth, those who are efficient and effective are guaranteed a job and are protected from arbitrary dismissal. Hoy and Miskel (1996) contend that these five elements are present in organizations today.

In *Organizational Architecture: Designs for Changing Organizations,* Nadler, Gerstein, and Shaw (1992) describe the presence of Taylor's work in many organizations. They wrote that the fusion of Taylor's and Weber's approaches to organizing has resulted in "machine bureaucracy" (p. 112). Nadler et al. described yet another lasting effect of bureaucracy: "This approach [machine bureaucracy] has become so pervasive that we unconsciously equate the machine bureaucracy with the process of organizing; it is hard for us to think of any other way of structuring work enterprises. (p. 113).

Taylor's model, however, ignored the psychological and sociological elements of workers and the workplace. Yet, more than 20 years ago in *American Bureaucracy* Bennis (1970) stated that, although these bureaucratic principles were formulated to enhance rationality and efficiency in the Industrial Era, they have outlived their usefulness. According to Bennis, "Organizations of the future will be adaptive, rapidly changing temporary systems, organized around problems-to-be-solved by groups of relative strangers with diverse professional skills" (p. 166). He painted an image of organizations wherein people will be evaluated, not in a rigid vertical hierarchy according to rank and status, but according to competence. He predicted that the end of bureaucracy as we know it and the rise of a new social system within 25 to 50 years. If Bennis was accurate, between 1995 and 2020, organizations will begin to reflect values toward more humanistic, democratic, and teaming practices.

An inward look at a business successfully initiating work teams provide insights into redefining the classical paradigm that supports working in isolation in high schools.

The next section of this chapter presents a case example of how a company successfully started more than 100 work teams. Finally, the chapter concludes with lessons learned and implications for reforming the American high school using work teams.

We are in this for the long haul. The message sent to us indicated that the management was committed to this type of philosophy. We recognize that nothing works 100%. This is a business strategy and not necessarily a social program. We socialized the idea since 1989 by looking at management, research articles and talking to employees. We believe teaming will help us be successful. Our philosophy is less direction and this is a people-oriented initiative (Plant Manager).

THE DATA TRADEMARK STORY: INITIATING A CULTURE OF WORK TEAMS

This is the story of how Data Trademark initiated more than 100 work teams over a period of 10 years through an organizational change process. The case describes the culture of Data Trademark and the deliberate use of work teams to change the culture. Data Trademark's vision was to deliver market leadership through customer satisfaction, people, teaming, product excellence, commitment, and integrity.

Methodological Overview and Objective of Case Study

The data in this initiation case study were collected through interviews with a cross sample of more than 22 Data Trademark employees. The participants included vice presidents, plant directors, managers, supervisors, associates, and technicians. The sample was purposefully selected to provide diverse representation on jobs, roles, responsibilities, perceptions, and experiences about how and why work teams were initiated. Numerous internal and external documents between 1981 and 1995 were reviewed. The objective of the initiation case study was to identify the factors that contributed to the original initiation of Data Trademark's manufacturing work teams.

Company Profile and History

Data Trademark, a major supplier of technical products with more than 50 manufacturing facilities worldwide, conducted business in more than 75 foreign territories and countries. Its research and development activities were conducted at more than 26 centers. Revenues at the time of this research exceeded $8.5 billion and the company employed more than 57,000 people worldwide. Like other manufacturing facilities in the late 1970s, Data Trademark was a traditional hierarchical organization. Yet, they were committed to core beliefs aimed at creating excellent products with minimal errors when inspected.

Plant Operations

The plant described in this case study opened its doors in the early 1980s. More than 100 work teams were started in this facility 13 years after the plan opened. Before relocating products to other plants in the early 1990s, more than 2,000 manufacturing employees were employed at this site. At the time of the study, the site had more than 1,400 employees.

The plant's organization included a president, an assistant vice-president, a plant director, managers, supervisors, associates, and technicians. Data Trademark operated three 8-hour shifts during the week, Friday through Sunday, and they operated a 12-hour weekend shift.

Initiation and Work Teams Defined

According to Fullan (1991), "Initiation is the process leading up to and including the decision to proceed with implementation" (p. 50). For the purpose of this case study, initiation is defined as the point at which Data Trademark leaders began to contemplate starting and planning to implement work teams. Data Trademark's work teams are defined as a highly trained group of employees who worked together to complete a segment of work. As an essential step in the innovative change process, initiation represents the greatest opportunity for getting organizations to try something new. The following comment illustrated how the leadership supported innovation and experimentation.

> President Tom Smith was aware of the need to alter the original design as a group with the double-digit growth. The leadership realized that something had to change. Tom Smith, CEO sanctioned experimentation and encouraged trying something new. Tom Smith also had a growing respect for the worker. The accounting philosophy at that time was to change, trim, and move from an efficiency-based accounting [individual] to activity-based [group] outcomes (Manager).

Areas of Participation

In Data Trademark work teams, the plant director, managers, supervisors, associates, and technicians shared decision-making. This cross sample of roles represented areas such as management, engineering, quality, training, and human resources.

Areas of Non-Participation

Management handled issues that pertained to the number of products to manufacture during a given week, performance appraisal, availability, and salary.

Work Teams

While Data Trademark maintained a traditional and bureaucratic organizational structure for more than 13 years, they successfully organized 17 manufacturing process areas in this facility into more than 100 work teams. The manufacturing teams were responsible for a particular sub-assembly of an end product from the moment the raw materials entered the plant's receiving area until the finished assembly was configured for the customers. Teams ranged in size from 15–50 members. Many of the teams formed sub-teams within the larger team.

Three support teams were organized apart from the manufacturing teams: (a) management council; (b) training; and (c) human resources.

HISTORICAL AND CULTURAL DEVELOPMENT OF WORK TEAMS

The culture of Data Trademark emerged into work teams over a period of 10 years. Like other manufacturing facilities during the early 1980s, this plant tested all of its highly technical products in a linear assembly line. This linear production assembly and test operation were segmented into resource centers, which were considered separate departments. Transactions were required to transfer materials from one department to another, and different supervisors managed these departments. Prior to 1988, the workers performed job functions in a linear assembly line, punched in at a time clock, took breaks and lunch scheduled by the supervisor or his or her leader, received work schedules assigned by management, remained in the same job functions without cross-training or job rotation opportunities, and were evaluated only by management. Managers at Data Trademark made a majority of the day-to-day operational decisions, provided customer and visitor tours, performed all evaluations, and set policies and made decisions without input from the production workers.

Productivity Circles

The manufacturing unit in this case study is unique in that it has had a long history of encouraging employee participation from the grass roots level. In July 1981, Data Trademark formed productivity circles. These circles included groups of employees from the same work area, who for one hour each week under the leadership of their immediate supervisor, discussed their work area problems, investigated causes of problems, and used statistical methods to formulate solutions. The productivity circles were made up of seven to fifteen members who voluntarily met together to discuss technical problems that were familiar to all of them. The productivity circle members were trained to use the following techniques to solve problems: brainstorming, data gathering, check sheets, Pareto analysis, cause and effect problem analysis, and presentation techniques. In the early stages, the productivity circles focused on quality and technical issues, not on developing people skills. While some of the productivity circles were quite successful in developing participatory styles between leaders and workers, many of the circles failed to support the idea of increased employee involvement. One respondent described why the productivity circles were not successfully initiated:

> The productivity circles started from the middle and they lacked commitment from all of management. For example, the circles would be moving along and management would say: "Is this what I hired you for?" The fight was in the middle and there was a turf battle. The fight was because the people were being taken off the production floor. Management couldn't see the benefit of taking the people off the production floor. Remember, the people volunteered to replace them on the production floor while they were meeting. Now, teaming is no longer volunteer because the entire team is expected to participate. Teaming is in more depth, mandatory, and there is a commitment from management (Supervisor Human Relations Training Initiatives).

In 1985 three individuals from this site participated in what would eventually be remembered as a significant historical event in moving decisions to the manufacturing teams and upgrading the first line supervisors' people skills. By participating in an interpersonal training session held at another local facility that was also considering work teams, three workers discovered an interpersonal training program for employees. The program included some of the most common language principles needed within a work team. The skill-based training program aimed to help the non-supervisory employees work smarter with their peers and supervisors. The common philosophy of the training program is respecting others, and it teaches people to think of themselves as a "company within a company" that serves customers both inside and outside the organization. The four principles of the training program perfectly aligned with Data Trademark's mission and values. Themes include listening, giving feedback, taking new assignments, requesting help, presenting, informing the boss, resolving issues, responding positively to negative situations, working smarter, experiencing change, and being a team player. When asking a worker about the various training opportunities for developing work teams, she replied:

> Courses taught in the training program were fun and enjoyable. These courses made you believe that teaming could work. The courses were mostly interpersonal and this is where everyone was lacking. Our challenge was learning how to communicate. The course taught us to separate the personal from the job (Associate).

Additionally, the training program for managers was a major catalyst for beginning to getting the people more involved in the business, with each other, and between other teams. First, the culture began to shift from focusing on the person, but on the issue or the situation. Second, the self-esteem of the employees was maintained. Third, the relationships between the employees improved. Fourth, the people began to take the initiative to make things better. Finally, the leaders felt they had found a training program that provided basic human interaction skills everyone needed to succeed in the business.

Pilot Work Team

Committed to involving employees in the business and intrigued by working in teams, management at this site began to inform employees of their intention to shift toward teaming. The idea of teaming was discussed at the management, employee advisory council, and roundtable meetings. The larger question during this time was: "In a teaming environment, can we achieve our business objectives and make the quality of work life better for our employees?"

From several years, there was much talk about becoming a less directed plant and giving the workers more say in running the business. Yet, the company wanted to move in a manner that would produce long-lasting results for both the company and their workers. In the 1980s, Data Trademark trained and certified their first pilot work team. Twenty-five participants spent more than ten weeks learning more about developing better interpersonal skills to achieve results. The team was expected to appreciate and understand the external customer, and they were being asked to view each other as internal customers.

Changing the Production Processes

Data Trademark leaders knew they had to rethink the way in which their production processes were organized if they were to remain competitive and successful. They started by reorganizing the production floor to a U-shaped layout instead of a straight line manufacturing process, because in the straight line manufacturing process the worker could not see what happened at the end of the process. By eliminating the traditional, impersonal assembly line concept for work teams, the workers became more knowledgeable of subsequent operations that impacted their area because they were physically closer together. In the traditional assembly line arrangement it was difficult for the workers to increase quality in the manufacturing process because they did not have ownership from start to finish. In the new arrangement, workers in the same product area were closer together and could interact with each other within minutes about a particular concern.

Inherent within this work team arrangement were two assumptions. First, with the initiation of work teams and the further flattening of the organization, there would be significant reduction in overhead. Second, management felt that quality would be increased through a team-based workforce because teams would become more involved in production decisions and would be key to improving the manufacturing process. Results from the new physical layout reported in 1990 included more than $2M in annual cost savings from the reduction of overhead and inventory as well as improvement in quality and composite yield. According to many of the manufacturing respondents, the straight assembly line would have inhibited the successful initiation of teaming if the cellular change had not occurred.

A Teaming Champion

In the late 1980s the entire manufacturing plant, not partial, was organized into more than 100 work teams. A plant manager described by many as a teaming champion, deliberately spearheaded, supported, and pushed this innovation beyond the pilot work team of twenty-five. Some respondents also said this plant manager understood the plight of the factory worker and had a passion for employee participation. Also, this champion was described as being a risk-taker who was in a powerful position that allowed him to empower others to move forward. This comment below described how the plant manager viewed changed:

> The irony of this change was that my people said management would never listen and I said, "We are management, so let's give this a shot." I was championing something that I would back up. If champions push the ideas of ownership, then the product will be better. For example, champions are directly responsible for the budget and then they have the opportunity to walk the talk (Plant Manager).

Many of the grass root managers and supervisors working with this plant manager believed that work teams could be used to empower the workforce to share the responsibility of managing and improving the business. For example, the next respondent comment illustrated why the people viewed the plant manager as a teaming champion:

> Teaming was a plant manager and staff initiative at Data Trademark. The plant manager pushed for teaming. Teaming would never have gone without the plant manager's pushing and believing in the teaming process. It has been easy for us to take lessons from him on this and to explain our success (Supervisor).

Others described work teams as a way to improve the quality of work life for the worker, thus making the worker feel more valued. In order to help the people move from a traditional workforce to a teaming environment, this plant manager sought financial support for training from the corporate vice president. He was given full support to charge ahead with teaming from the corporate vice-president.

Getting the Teams Started

In the late 1980s each manufacturing cell started working as a team using their quality, technical, and interpersonal skills to improve the business. The plant manager did not want any detailed guidelines given to the teams, because he believed that the workers were tired of being told what to do by management. Therefore, he instructed his management team not to give the workers any guidelines to implement teams. Despite the teams' efforts to develop guidelines for how their particular area was going to operate as a team, many of them had difficulty articulating this new role.

In trying to become a team, there were team non-believers and skeptics. While the work team believers supported the transition to work teams, the skeptics supported the change with reservation, and the non-believers did not support the change and communicated their dissatisfaction. The following two respondent quotes illustrated the fears and reservations on part of the skeptics and non-believers:

> When I first heard about work teams, I was skeptical. Teaming sounded nice, but I did not think it would work. I didn't think the people would work. I was selling teaming short (Manger).

> In the beginning I did not like teaming because I felt that I would eventually lose my job. If the teams worked and became self-sustaining, I felt like I would not be needed. If these teams were up and running, I knew I would lose my job, and we [supervisors] would not be needed.I wanted things to run the way they had. Most people were apprehensive and were very concerned about their jobs. We feared losing power and control. The only concerns I have had dealt with resistance and change. We did everything for the people to managing paperwork, training, scheduling, rotating schedules, and writing reviews. This change is rather hard. We [supervisors] feel as if we have lost power and control after losing power and control, we felt expendable. We also felt that the quality of the product would drop because we were allowing the people to develop and hold their own meetings. To me, it looked as though we were losing the product due to the loss of time from the floor (Supervisor).

Developing Some Guidelines

Most of the line employees were pleased with the idea of becoming a team, but they were uncertain about translating the idea into practice. Therefore, when the workers began to ask for some teaming guidelines, management realized that this new approach had created many different emotions and feelings, and that not having an initial set of guidelines or baseline boundaries had caused most of the work team participants to feel uncomfortable in developing a work team proposal. While some of the teams charged ahead with the challenge, a majority of the teams stumbled until management developed a set of guidelines and expectations. Very few of the workers could take the lack of structure and go forward. Many respondents described their initial fears in terms of these questions:

- What does it mean to be a team?
- Where do we want to go as a company with teaming?
- What are we supposed to do as a team?
- How do we do what we are supposed to do?
- What is the supervisor's role in this framework?
- What are the boundaries?
- How do we change attitudes without proper interpersonal training?

To resolve this problem with teams, the plant manager assigned one person to work full time leading the cultural change to work teams. The training manager and members of the Team Advisory Council developed and disseminated a set of guidelines that outlined expectations, roles, tasks, and responsibilities expected of managers, supervisors, team leaders, boundaries, and team roles. The booklet also included a mission statement, objectives, core values and the employees' and management's roles in a team-based environment.

Supervisor's New Role

The supervisor's role under work teams was described as having them most crucial role in facilitating the teams' work. First, the supervisor role required two functions: supervise and facilitate. This dual role required the supervisor to participate with the team in implementing and communicating diverse objectives, goals, and expected outcomes. Of all the roles redesigned in the teaming arrangement, the supervisor's was described as having to give up the most as illustrated in this comment:

> The supervisors gave up the most in the teaming process because they had to facilitate and delegate their responsibilities (Supervisor).

Unfortunately, the supervisors experienced some fear, resentment, and anxiety about losing their control over their daily operations. For the teams, areas of participation included planning and developing a flexible work schedule, helping with business problem solving, improving customer/vendor satisfaction, and giving feedback to peers. Teams could also decide when to take their breaks and lunch, discuss training needs, manage overtime and vacation, manage rotation schedules, and discuss issues of quality, productivity, and cross-training.

For the first time, the supervisor not only directed but also solicited and interpreted information. The company expected tremendous change in skills from the supervisors. The following roles were identified for the supervisor: coach/counselor, teacher/trainer, role model, team builder, and policy administrator. Other roles incorporated within most of the teams include team leader, team coordinator, planner, champion, mentor, and meeting chairperson.

Data Trademark further developed a policy that enhanced the development of work teams. The policy provided for the provision of many options for the employees: make-up time, flex-time, no time clocks, part-time work options, flexible spending accounts, personal leave of absence, and financial reimbursement for employees who adopt children. Employee assistance programs were available to provide private, confidential counseling services for personal, family, and professional concerns.

LIFE INSIDE A WORK TEAM

Each work team included groups of employees from the same area that began their work with a ten-to-fifteen minute communication/information meeting on the production floor near the work area. It was not uncommon to see persons other than the supervisor presenting information to the team at the daily meetings. The line employees seem very comfortable in facilitating the communication meetings. During these meetings, the day's work schedule was presented, the training schedule was reviewed, and the work schedule was adjusted given any absences. Issues were handled as quickly as possible and questions were answered.

The teams met for one hour each week, in a classroom located off the production floor, under the leadership of their immediate supervisor. Issues discussed included: quality, defects, audits, cross training, overtime, production, training opportunities, and the everyday operation of the team. Rewards were also presented where production was made and other areas appropriate.

While observing teams on the production floor, there was much laughter and conversation between the workers and management. The team members moved around and talked freely about issues pertinent to their work area. Instances where there were errors on the line were immediately addressed by stopping the line. Workers were very concerned about identifying the problem and quickly resolving. The teams were committed to meeting the production schedule with a quality product. The teams have learned how to talk objectively to one another, learned how to listen to each other, and have become more involved in the business within their area. Additionally, the people have moved away from "I" to "we" as stated repeatedly by many of those interviewed. In fact, many refer to themselves as "our team."

When asking a worker about the difference between productivity circles and work teams, she replied:

> Oh yes, oh yes, there is a difference. The productivity circles were volunteer and it was hard trying to keep the production going with those remaining while the others were meeting. Also, some people will never get involved. In the work team structure, the current management

> supports the idea and it is not an option for the teams. Whereas teaming was volunteer in the past, it is now a mandate and it is tied in with a person's performance evaluation (Associate).

Teaming became a way of life inside Data Trademark, and many respondents indicated that the workers' quality of work life had improved for the better. Data analysis revealed that the people obtained basic satisfaction of their social needs by working with others. Also, embedded in the data was the idea that work teams were initiated to improve the workers' organizational life by involving them in making critical decisions that were formerly decided by management. The following respondent comment illustrated the lingering ideas of the scientific movement that promoted hierarchical relationships within Data Trademark:

> Teaming led to a better quality of work life for the people. Yeah, you work harder but, I have seen success stories. Prior to teaming, I had a traditional, hierarchical and very tall organization thinking: "I'm supervisor and you're a factory worker." Actually, the leadership style that made many people successful became the same way people failed. Teaming has gone well beyond what we expected. We learned that if you expect too little, you get too little. Maybe we had been expecting the worker to act like a robot or wallflower, but what we learned in a population of 2,000 employees was that initially the introduction of teams lead to rampant fear and a sense of helplessness. This might be due to the fact that we hold onto the odd-man-out idea and feel a sense of losing protection (Supervisor).

Data Trademark's manufacturing culture changed and it became a different kind of organizational arrangement as illustrated within this chapter. If the company was going to survive the fierce competition, its leaders assumed that initiating work teams would be the best route for making a leap in its competitive strength in the 21st century. The traditional way of organizing people in business through a top-down hierarchy was no longer a viable competitive business strategy in isolation. Data Trademark realized that through teaming, the full and competitive resources of all employees could be utilized. Achieving quality and higher productivity and remaining competitive depended on how to best use human resources. The evidence was clear that involving others in decision-making would enable Data Trademark to remain ahead in the years to come.

LESSONS LEARNED AND IMPLICATIONS FOR HIGH SCHOOL WORK TEAMS

Finally, this chapter concludes with three key lessons learned and implications for reforming the American high school using work teams. The conversion at Data Trademark from a conventional organizational system to a more innovative one did not occur overnight. The process occurred over a period of more than ten years. As in business, the initiation of work teams in high school would entail a long journey that would evolve over time. This process takes so long because the traditional ways of structuring and organizing people are hard to change, as this innovation is very difficult to get started. Do we have this kind of time in our high schools? Probably not. However, the first lesson learned is that Data Trademark found that their people felt more valued because through participation they gained increased ownership, autonomy, and independence. The first lesson implies that organizing teaching and learning in work teams will yield greater results than is being yielded in the current system. As in Data Trademark, schools must address the same question: "In a teaming environment, can we achieve our business objectives and make the quality of work life better for our employees?" It is clear that even with reform aimed at improving the high school over the past years, the review of the literature unfortunately illustrated that the high school has changed very little substantively.

Similar to business, school systems must be committed to involving employees in the business and intrigued by working in teams. It is beyond the scope of this chapter to present the intricate details of a high school organized around work teams, given that bureaucracy has been the fundamental organizational structure for high schools for more than 80 years. However, commitment as a second lesson requires that the school leaders must share the same belief and thereby support the organizing around work teams. Whereas bureaucracy places the system's need above those of the people in the system, the core of teaming is a focus on people. Changing high schools would require the examination of institutionalized norms that legitimate the traditional organizational structure. Norms such as rigid allocation of time, physical layout of the school facility, large classes, larger teaching loads, and non-teaching duties, make the interaction and exchange of information between principals and teachers almost impossible. For schools, a commitment to work teams offer hope for decreasing isolation among administrators, teachers, and students and for improving student achievement in grades 9–12. Also, a long-term commitment must be made to ongoing interpersonal and other forms of team process training.

Finally, the third lesson is the most exciting part of this chapter. By definition, work teams offer an alternative to the isolated way in which high school teachers work and go about the business of teaching and learning. Implied in this chapter is a plea to policymakers and educational leaders to recognize that high schools are places where people desire working in collegial arrangements that foster increased interaction, teamwork, and collaboration. For students, work teams offer a way to ensure engaging and minimal lecture-type instruction. For the central office, work teams serve as a way to better coordinate work, meet goals, and establish priorities.

CONCLUSION

One might argue that there is a difference in the motivation between these two organizations for considering work teams. Although the processes between these two organizations are uniquely different, in many ways the organizations are similar in that they are organized around people. This chapter does not suggest that a high school should have either departments or work teams. Instead, this chapter proposed that both departments and work teams could successfully be initiated within high schools. Together, both work teams and departments could increase collegiality and improve student achievement. However, the traditional norms institutionalized in high schools must be examined or the past will continue. Work teams would improve not only the system, but also the lives of those who teach, learn, and work in school.

REFERENCES

Bennis, W. G. (1970). *American bureaucracy.* New Brunswick, NJ: Transaction.

Fullan, M., & Stiegelbauer, S. (1991). *The new meaning of educational change.* New York, NY: Teachers College Press.

Hoy, W. K., & Miskel, C. G. (1991). *Educational administration: Theory, research, and practice.* New York, NY: McGraw-Hill.

Mozingo, T. (2001). Semi-autonomous work teams in industry: High school possibilities. Unpublished doctoral dissertation, University of North Carolina, Chapel Hill.

Nadler, D. A., Gerstein, M. S., & Shaw, R. B. (1992). *Organizational architecture: Designs for changing organizations.* San Francisco, CA: Jossey-Bass.

Taylor, F. (1911). Principles of scientific management: Theory, research, and practice. In: *Classics of Organization Theory* (pp. 9–23). Oak Park, IL: Moore Publishing.

15. CHOICE, VOUCHERS AND PRIVATIZATION AS EDUCATION REFORM OR THE FULFILLMENT OF RICHARD NIXON'S SOUTHERN STRATEGY?

Frank Brown

ABSTRACT

Formal public education of African Americans became a reality after the Civil War in the 1870s. Although some integrated schools did exist, many schools were racially segregated and remained that way until after the Brown decision in 1954. The white backlash to equal, integrated schooling for African Americans yielded a brief period of modest equality in the 1970s followed by greater inequality during the past two decades. This article addresses some of the schemes used to educate African Americans focusing on the future of education in neighborhood schools.

INTRODUCTION

The U.S. constitution leaves the role of public education to the individual states and so you have 50 state educational systems with varying degrees of educational services for their citizen. The federal government gets involvement in public education by passing and enforcing legislation to protect the legal rights of school

Challenges of Urban Education and Efficacy of School Reform, Volume 6, pages 255–282.

ISBN: 0-7623-0426-X

children under the U.S. Constitution under the general welfare clause of the Constitution. These measures protect parents and students against discrimination based upon race, gender, disability, religion, or national origin. But the degree to which these rights are enforced depends upon the philosophy of the political party in power and/or the ideological composition of the U.S. Supreme Court appointed by the political party in power over time. Currently, the U.S. Supreme Court has stopped enforcing the 1954 *Brown* Court decision requiring the racial desegregation of public schools (*Belk*, 2001). Likewise, the use of public funds to support educational services in religious schools at this level has been a violation of the federal constitution but a recent U.S. Supreme Court decisions have weaken that standard by allowing public funds to be used to pay for books, transportation, related services in K-12 religious schools and the use of publicly funded vouchers in religious schools (*Zelman v. Simmons-Harris,* 2002).

This paper addresses issues central to school choice issues in public education after the U.S. Supreme Court's 1954 decision in *Brown* making de jure racial segregation of public education unconstitutional. However, a more in depth discussion of school desegregation will be detailed in other chapters of this book. School choice experiments include: free of choice enrollment options, vouchers, magnet schools, charter schools and the privatization of educational services. I will review the impact of race on efforts to implement school choice options in K-12 public education and efforts to the use of public funds to educate children in private not-for profit schools. Currently, there are no for-profit schools operating in American which should not confused with the private management of public schools by for-profit companies.

There are also other labels related to school choice/privatization issues such as family choice, charter schools, vouchers, opportunity scholarships, magnet or public school academies, "break-the-mold" schools, "new schools," "reconstituted schools," deregulation, private money for public schools and tuition tax credits. However, I will discuss implementation, deregulation, and other school choice experiments.

Educational reform is often a metaphor for other agendas and not educational reform as stated in public announcements by educators and politicians, which often represent a combination of: political, economical, racial and educational ideas. Other common metaphors for school choice are family values, family choice, deregulation, and democratic values. But, one thing is certain, low academic productivity in public education is associated with poorly funded schools in poor communities; and most poor performing schools are located in urban communities where most students come from racial and ethnic minority households. These residents possess less economical and political capital than those who live outside of these communities. Many reformers proposing radical solutions to the problems of urban schools affecting poor minority children are political enemies of residents in these communities. Yet, privatization has its own set of problems, academic and accountability (Archer, 2000a, b; Bowman, 2000a, b).

The major supporters of vouchers are the pro-market libertarians, business and the Catholic Church and the major opponents are the educational establishment, civil libertarians and church/state separatists and African American organizations (Kennedy, 2001, p. 451). For example, recently U.S. Senator Hillary Rodham Clinton, Democratic of New York speaking for the democrats against school vouchers stated that "experiments have demonstrated absolutely no evidence that vouchers help improve student achievement; secondly, we know that vouchers do not help the students who need the help the most and they do nothing to help improve public schools. Vouchers only further segregate and stratify our public schools" (Alvarez, 2001, p. 6). Senator Judd Gregg, Republican of New Hampshire speaking for the Republicans see vouchers as helping "real people who are locked in inner-city schools who didn't have the option for a better education like folks with more money, who are seeing their children left behind; and we should give parents an option so they can compete for the American dream" (Alvarez, 2001, p. 6). However, absence credible evidence that vouchers improve educational opportunities for at-risk students support for vouchers should fade as a viable reform measure to improve education (Kennedy, 2001, p. 456).

This is a political struggle between the hegemonic European American group and marginalized minority groups, even though their continues to exist a large number of poor European Americans in society who are also seeking a better education for their children. Poor whites and poor minorities have not been able to join forces to improve education for their children. The relationship between poor people across racial groups is hindered by the willingness of poor whites to give up the struggle for equity for their privileged position as a white person (Reich, 1994, p. 472). Poor whites recognize that however inferior their schools, minority schools are worse and most of their teachers and administrators will be white who are in a position to provide a measure of protection. Racial and ethnic minority students are more likely to attend worse schools, with mostly white teachers and administrators with less understanding of their culture (Reich, 1994, p. 472). This position by poor whites reduces their desire to fight for better schools; and schools for poor minority students are more likely to be located near poor white schools than rich white schools.

I will review the implementation of privatization, deregulation and other school choice experiments affecting the education of minority children who now live mainly in large urban school districts in segregated neighborhoods. In all major U.S. cities during the last decade, from 1990 to 2000, segregation levels of Black and white children grew sharply as a result of white flight (Schmitt, 2001). In Milwaukee where the voucher experiment began, Black children now make up 61% of the public school population in 2000, up from 46% in 1990 (Schmitt, 2001). "White flight," the exit from or avoidance of racially mixed urban public schools was as strong in the 1990s as it was in the 1970s (Clotfelter, 2001). In 238 metropolitan areas from 1987 to 1996 white losses in urban public school enrollment resulted from white families moving from one district to another, enrolling their children in private schools and avoidance of moving into districts with high minority concentrations (Clotfelter, 2001). This pattern existed across small and large urban communities; and is consistent in both southern and northern urban communities.

RACE AND CHOICE

It is important to note that race plays a critical role in determining who gets to choose the type and kind of education they wish to receive from the public schools. The school choice movement, began in America with the consideration of race and social class of students. Generally, white Americans desire for their children to attend school with other white students but will accept a minimum level of minority involvement. Coons and Sugarman (1974, p. 28), two University of California at Berkeley Law School Professors and developers of California's voucher initiatives inform us that white Americans nationwide are so opposed to school desegregation that they will find multiply ways to avoid racial integrated schools almost at any costs and vouchers are the best option left for African Americans to improve their educational opportunities in this society. On the other hand, the *Wall Street Journal* (2002, p. A26) editorial board in their support of the Cleveland Voucher Program concludes that racism also affects the teaching of minority children. The editorial board (2002, p. A26) supports the use of public funded vouchers in Cleveland, Ohio, which allows parents to use public funds to send their children to religious schools. According to this newspaper the "legal question is straightforward: The state isn't choosing religious schools, parents are. In Brown, Linda Brown was forced to attend an all Black Monroe Elementary School but at least Linda Brown could learn to read and write at the Monroe School." The journal also concludes that education is a social process and while the Black teachers at the all Black Monroe Elementary School were committed to teaching Linda Brown, the plaintiff in *Brown v. Board of Education* to read and write but the white teachers at her new integrated mainly white elementary school would not teach her how to read and write regardless of their academic qualifications and additional resources compared to those at Monroe Elementary. The Journal provides a lengthy and detail editorial about how the voucher program benefited a 11-year-old Black girl who's mother is a college graduate but is confined to a low income section of the Cleveland where the school are not doing a good job of educating Black children. But the Journal failed to tell its readers that most of children receiving vouchers are white children already enrolled in religious schools. The editorial board ignored factual information reported in another section of the paper on the same day (WSJ, 2002, p. A28).

School choice and privatization (maintenance of racially segregated public schools via de facto means) began with the 1954 *Brown* decision, which declare racially segregated schools unconstitutional. First, after the *Brown* decision many white parents in the Southern states removed their children from the public schools and enrolled them in racially segregated schools citing parental choice as their rationale. The used "school choice" as a rationale for maintaining racially segregated schools, white parents sought public vouchers and tuition tax credits to fund their segregated schools commonly called "Christian Academies" to escape sending their children to integrated school (Levin, 1999).

The 1954 Court in *Brown v. Board of Education,* gave birth to the modern voucher movement under the "Southern Strategy" initiated by President Richard M. Nixon which sought to gain votes of southern whites who opposed school integration and northern whites who did not wish for their children to attend school with urban minorities but did not have the resources to move to white isolated suburban communities. The school choice movement began in the State of Virginia in 1956 to derail school desegregation and later adopted by the late President Richard M. Nixon as a part of his Southern Strategy is still in full operation and is currently being promoted by President George W. Bush (Carter, 2000, p. 820).

Politicians seeking support from this white constituency promised public funded vouchers to send their children to racially segregated schools; supported racially segregated neighborhood schools, "magnet" schools within the public schools that enhanced racial separation of students, and eliminated the use of public funds to transport children for the purpose of racially desegregating public schools. The U.S. Congress made it illegal to use federal funds for the purpose of racially desegregating public schools unless the school district was under court orders to desegregate its schools. These same anti-school desegregation forces support "market" forces and the private management of public schools as an alternative to the racial integration of public schools and shifted the focus to educational excellence away from equity.

The first federal support for school choice programs began with support for magnet schools. In October 1977, the New York State Department of Education convened a four day meeting involving officials from the U.S. Office of Education to set guidelines for Congressional approval of $7.5 million allocation to use magnet schools within public schools as part of a plan to achieve quality integrated public education. Representatives from school districts across the county with experience with magnet schools participated in the conference.

Morton J. Sobel, a New York State Education Department official, concluded that (Ambach, 1979, p. 129–140) if there are to be magnet schools with Federal Government support, the government should provide funds to make these schools the best schools possible. Magnet schools have been around for many years but they typically have not been racially desegregated. There is a strong feeling that magnet schools are designed to pacify whites by using a de facto method of voluntarism and not "forced busing" to get whites into black schools which will not work. A major element of concerning school desegregation is and this is true of magnet schools, is the victim of segregation must take the initiative. It is the victim who is being analyzed, researched, and it is up to the victim to fit the problem: make a selection to get a better education and force the power structure to make our democratic ideals work. There is little evidence that magnet schools will promote desegregated schools, but they can produce excellent schools that are more likely to develop a desegregated school situation (Ambach, 1979, p. 140).

Privatization of public education will keep racial and economic groups in their respective neighborhood schools. But supporters recommend changes by altering the leadership, from public school administrators to privately hire administrators; and second, it's believed that this change in leadership alone will improve services for students. The first goal is more important to the supporters of privatization than the second goal. Privatization of public education is designed to satisfy political motives since there is no evidence that the scheme works.

The 2000 U.S. Census reports that most white and black children live in segregated neighborhoods and attend racially segregated schools (Schmitt, 2001, pp. 5–6). This is a significant increase over the 1990 Census (Schemo, 2001, p. 12). Several big cities where most racial minorities reside are pushing to increase the percentage of white middle class residents, referred to as gentrification (Wilgoren, 2001, p. 20). Racially segregated, neighborhood public schools are often promoted (indirectly) as an incentive to attract these gentrified residents. Changing demographics among white suburbanites are also fueling this movement back to the inner cities. These gentrified residents consist of families with fewer or no children and their long commutes to work the inner cities make relocating more attractive if schooling opportunities for their children are changed (Scott, 2001, p. 18). Lipsitz (2000, p. 669) calls this "possessive investment in whiteness," where whiteness has value that includes the unequal education allocation to children of different races.

EXPERIMENTS WITH PRIVATIZATION AND VOUCHERS

The use of private for-profit companies to manage public schools is active in America but is at a stand still (Mosle, 1997, p. 32). In 1992, the Edison Project, a for profit company, raised $100 million to establish and operate 25 schools, but still has not been able to make a profit. Edison, the nation's largest for-profit venture into public education has yet to establish a for-profit school; and now has shifted its focus to managing public schools for a fee or profit. The Edison Company was the first company in America to enter this business and operates 113 schools across the country; but many of these schools are charter schools with small enrollments of approximately 160 students per school compared to a regular public school with 400 to 700 for the elementary grades and 500 to 900 for the middle grades (Mosle, 1997, p. 32). There are approximately 85,000 public elementary and secondary schools in America.

There are more than 75,000 children in the Cleveland City Schools and more than 80% are from low income and minority families. The Cleveland voucher/tuition aid is distributed to parents according to financial need (Zelman, 2002). Families with incomes below 200% of poverty are given priority and eligible to receive 90% of private school tuition up to $2,250. These lowest income families, participating private schools may not charge a co-payment greater than $250 per child. But for all other families, the program pays 75% of tuition costs, up to $1,875, with no co-payment cap. These higher income families receive tuition vouchers only if the number of available scholarships/vouchers exceeds the number of low-income children who participate. Where voucher scholarships/tuition depends upon where parents choose to enroll their child. If parents choose a private school, checks are made payable to the parents who then endorse the checks over to the private school. For parents who choose to keep their child in public school district and seek tutorial assistance through grants must arrange for registered tutors to provide assistance to their child and submit bills for those services to the State for payment. Students from low-income families receive 90% of the amount charged for such services up to $360; and all other children receive 75% of $360. The number of tutorial grants offered in a covered district must equal the number of vouchers provided to students enrolled in participating private or adjacent public school districts. In the 1999–2000 school year, 56 private schools participated in the voucher program, 46 or 82% were religiously affiliated. No adjacent schools districted participated. Approximately 3,700 students participated in the program and 96% were enrolled in private religious schools; 60% were from families with incomes below the poverty line; and about 1,400 students received tutorial assistance.

The use of public vouchers to attend private schools is legal in two school districts, Cleveland and Milwaukee and the entire State of Florida. The Cleveland and Milwaukee voucher programs are designed for low-income students and the Florida program applies to students in all academically failing public schools. In Milwaukee, where the state established a voucher system initially for poor inner city children, where most were African Americans, accommodates 1.5% of the district's student population; and Cleveland, Ohio has a similar public voucher program for a small number of inner city students are in operation. In 28 states, school districts are allowed to experiment with charter schools, autonomously operated public. Since Minnesota passed the first charter schools law in 1991 several states and the District of Columbia has statutes authorizing charter schools. About 700 charter schools out of 85,000 public schools are in operation nationwide and most are small and aimed at disadvantaged elementary and middle school students. Federal support rose from $51 million in 1995 to $85 million in 2000. In New York and several other large cities, public schools are being reconstituted or restructured to bring about increased academic improvement. But, creating a few good schools have never been difficult with enough energy and motivation, but scaling up to improve all public schools in a district have proven difficult or impossible.

The Cleveland Voucher Program is one of several such programs operating across the country. In Florida, the state allows the use of state funds to educate children from failing public schools to private schools; and allows corporations to give money to state approved scholarships for low-income students and get their state taxes reduced dollar-for-dollar based upon the total amount of their contributions to the program (Kronholz, 2002, p. A28). The Cleveland Voucher Program began in 1995 to low-income students attend private or suburban schools with the state paying $2,250 in tuition for each student. This year, 2001–2002 about 4,300 students receives vouchers to attend private or religious schools. Suburban schools refused to participate and almost all of the students are enrolled in religious schools. The Florida voucher program that will allow parents of children from low performing schools to enroll their children in a private with a $4,500 per year voucher. However, the state will only cover the cost of educating a child in a private school for that cost and the parents must pay any additional costs for a private education. However, this policy allows parents of special education children with the money to enroll their children in selective private schools and poor parents cannot afford such costs; and private schools are not required as with public schools to monitor the progress of special education students.

In 2000, the Cleveland program enrolled approximately 3,000 students for a total cost of about $12 million of which $7.5 million go directly for vouchers and remainder for related costs of transportation. Most assistance went to students attending private schools or kindergarteners; only about 200 students from public schools received vouchers. The two independent for-profit schools enroll most of the students from the public schools. Most parents used the vouchers to enroll their children in religious schools. White suburban schools refuse to participate in the voucher program.

The U.S. Federal Government is getting into the school choice movement with its financial support of charter schools, magnets schools, and ability of school districts to use federally funded Title I money to allow students to transfer out of low performing schools to higher performing schools. The federal government will now require a local educational agencies (LEA) to provide choice options for Title I students enrolled in low performing schools for two consecutive years, unless forbidden by a court ordered school desegregation plan or by state statute (Paige, 2002). This requirement seems like a self-fulfilling prophecy because by definition, Title I programs are located in low performing schools and low-income communities.

Six states provide programs that allow parents or corporations tax incentives to fund private education (Kronholz, 2002, p. A28). To date, in Florida two corporations have given $5 million to the Florida scholarship program (Kronholz, 2002, p. A28). The Tri-Tech Preparatory School in Miami open with 140 students funded on scholarships paid by corporations. The Florida program is capped at $50 million total and limited to $3,500 per student.

In Pennsylvania, a business can give up to $100,000 yearly to a scholarship fund or to projects that finance that improve public schools and take as much as a $90,000 tax credit (Kronholz, 2002, p. A28). The state has capped the program at $30 million per year. Arizona, Minnesota, Illinois and Iowa also offer similar, but different program designed for individuals to help fund public or private schools: Arizona taxpayers can take up to $650 credit of contributions to a "school-tuition organization" providing scholarships to children other than their own; Illinois parents get a credit for up to $500 in costs of tuition, books and laboratory fees at private or public schools; Iowa parents get a credit of up to $250 for private school tuition, public school fees or home schooling costs; and Minnesota give households with income $33,500 get up to $2,000 credits against tuition, tutoring, and other school expenses and higher income households can reduce taxable income by expenses of up to $1,625 per child (Kronholz, 2002, p. A28).

In 1997, the Milwaukee voucher program paid up to $5,100 per student in 2000, $38 million for 4,200 students enrolled in religious schools and for 2,300 enrolled in private non-religious schools (Nelson, Muir & Drown, 2001). In 2000 approximately 96% of the students receiving public vouchers in Cleveland attend religious schools. In 1999 the U.S. Supreme Court granted a stay in a 5 to 4 decision, permitting the Cleveland voucher program to continue after a Federal District Court had issued a preliminary injunction to halt the use of voucher to attend religious schools and before the U.S. Court of Appeals for the Sixth Circuit had a chance to hear the case. In 2001, the Bush administration asked the U.S. Supreme Court to rule on the case (Greenhouse, 2001, p. 7–8). In September 2001, the U.S. Supreme Court agreed to hear arguments for and against the Cleveland voucher program; and in 2002 the Court (*Zelman,* 2002). This request occurred after President Bush lost his fight in Congress for an educational voucher program (Rothstein, Richard, 2001, p. 14). This action by the Bush administration also came after recent statewide voucher initiatives failed in California and Michigan.

Voucher supporters argue that they provide: competition for students, innovation and diversity, competition for teachers and a more flexible employment relationship, avoiding the dead hand of public school bureaucracies. Financial access is not an issue with public education, they argue, because public schooling is available to everyone. Therefore, privatization merely provides greater choice of school settings and hopefully quality. Opponents of vouchers argue that: competition for students is not fair where all parents are not equally informed or interested, innovation and diversity is best served by the public schools, it will weaken the teaching profession, destroy the public schools, and return religion to the public schools.

To understand the impact of vouchers on students and school districts we need to know: the size of the voucher in dollar terms, who qualifies for a voucher, the financing of the voucher, the rules governing private schools that accept vouchers, and how individuals and private schools react to specific voucher policies (Goldhaber, 2001, p. 48). We do know that given a choice in selecting schools for their children, most parents give the most weight to the demographics of the school's population their child attends, which generally results in greater segregation of students by race and social class (Goldhaber, 2001, p. 51).

There have been few controlled experiments examining voucher programs, except for a few privately funded voucher programs in New York, Washington, D.C. and Dayton, Ohio. These programs are small and targeted for low-income children in grades 2 through 8 (Goldhaber, 2001, p. 63). The New York program offered 1,300 scholarships up to $1,400 per year for up to three years.

The Dayton voucher program provided 515 scholarships to children attending public schools and 250 scholarships to children already attending private schools up to $1,200 for at least four years. The Washington, D.C. program provides 1,000 scholarships per year worth 60% of the tuition or $1,700, whichever is less in the elementary grades and up to $2,200 for the high school grade. In each city researchers compared the treatment group and a control groups for two years on the Iowa Test of Basic Skills and found that: voucher participants in New York and Washington were more satisfied with their schooling and only African American students showed higher academic achievement on the tests with their controlled group of African American students (Goldhaber, 2001, pp. 63–64). However, these studies did not control for important students' demographics and ability levels of the treatment and controlled groups.

There are also several private voucher programs for public schools. Virginia Gilder decided to improve education at Albany, New York Giffen Memorial Elementary school, the lowest performing school in the district by providing $1 million to offer up to $2,000 to any Giffen student who wishes to attend a private school. About 105 students applied for the offer, but only 83 accepted to attend local Catholic schools. In San Antonio (Texas) Independent School District, a system of 61,000 students, of whom 81% are Hispanic and 7% are white, the Children's Educational Opportunity Foundation provided scholarships that covered half of the tuition cost for low-income children to enroll in private schools, with a maximum of $750. This program was in operation from 1992 and evaluated for the first four years. A study of the program revealed that choosing parents were more educated and wealthier; the children applying for the program had higher standardized test scores; the students were more likely to be white; and the dropout rate was 50% due mainly to get transportation to the private school of choice.

What are the limits to the use of vouchers to educate children from low-income families? The two states statutes with vouchers allow these vouchers to be used in private schools or in another public school district. The cost of attending many private schools are beyond what a public voucher can purchase. But what about using these vouchers to attend schools in another public school district? Vouchers have strong support from wealthy individuals and business leaders, but at the same time wealthy school districts where these wealthy individuals live are opposed to children from poor school districts attending school in their wealthy districts (Finn, 1997, p. 17). School districts outside of Milwaukee and Cleveland are not required to participate in the voucher programs in these cities designed for mostly African American children from poor families by accepting students from these two cities. Wealthy public school districts do not participating voucher programs and typically place a "bounty" on non-residents who fraudulently enroll children in their schools. This situation poses a problem for voucher programs trying to enroll low achieving students into high achieving public schools. A Cleveland, Ohio mother went to jail for enrolling her son in a wealthy suburban school (Lewin, 1997, p. 1). Illinois makes illegal school registration in another school district a misdemeanor punishable by up to 30 days in jail, a $500 fine and tuition reimbursement.

Privatization implies that: under capitalism, maximum output and efficiency by an organization can best be accomplished if there is an opportunity to make a profit; and we should encourage private vendors to enter public education with the profit motive in mind to increase productivity. The profit motive should be an advantage whether a school is operated with private funds or with state funds via a state voucher or a performance contract with a local public school system because it increases competition; and competition in education is good. But the history of "markets" in education has not been positive (Richards, Rima, and Sawicky, 1996).

America began schooling children privately administered not-for-profit schools and a few for-profit schools. As late as the 1920s three models co-existed: public schools, private non-profit religious and private independent schools, and a few for-profit independent schools.

The supply-side of voucher programs cannot be estimated due the lack of enough private schools to accommodate a large shift of public schools students to private schools and we do not know what type of private schools will be established to meet such a demand. Second, will these private schools be more effective in attracting more high quality teachers into the profession. School choice using public vouchers has the opposite effect on the teaching profession. Teachers are concerned about good working conditions: adequate salaries, fringe benefits, and a quality work environment; and deregulation via voucher programs may not improve working conditions enough to attract top quality teachers.

END GAME

Wisconsin State Democratic Representative Polly Williams of Milwaukee, an African American, and the early national spokesperson for vouchers recently admitted that she "knew that once they (conservative white Republicans and the right wing foundations) figured they didn't need me as a Black cover, they would take control of vouchers and use them for their own selfish interest" (Peterson & Miner, 2000, p. 819). Representative Williams felt that the conservatives would remove the separation of church and state; remove the income cap set at $23,000 per year level for a family of four; and the white city administration would use the voucher program to attract white people back into the city by promising that "you don't have to go to Milwaukee schools with Black children because we have opened a way for you" to send your children to school with other white children (Peterson & Miner, 2000, p. 821).

The conservative Bradley Foundation of Milwaukee funded much of that city's voucher efforts. The foundation also contributed $1 million to support Charles Murray's research in *The Bell Curve* (Herrnstein & Murray, 1994), a book that claims to document the inferior intellectual abilities of African Americans and pushed for school choice as the best strategy to help African Americans. The conservative right continues to attract individuals from a few Black groups to support voucher initiatives using the promise the African American communities will be given money and control over the education of Black children (Wilgoren, 2000). But as Representative Polly Williams of Milwaukee discovered, her goal of pursuing a better education for poor Black children was less important in the bigger scheme: a return to racially segregated schools.

School choice options promoted to improve education for African American children lack evidence that these options are superior to those offered by public schools. The promoters of school choice give the impression to Black parents that simply having the option to choose the school their children will attend, give these parents control over education of their children. The history of such programs is that there a limited number of options because of geographical distance to some schools and the attract ness of these schools for middle class families with more political influence. Also once parents leave their children at a private schoolhouse, there is no evidence they will have control over what happens inside the school. These parents may have less of a voice or influence with private schools than with public schools; and multiple private school options may not be available. It is true parents can exercise influence by with drawing their child from a private school but what are the options if they take this action, return to the public schools or enroll their child in a private school of less quality (assuming that their first choice was of superior quality). In the absence of more politically powerful consumers, vouchers may not purchase superior schooling for poor minority children; and an expansion of vouchers to all income groups may further segment schools by race, ethnicity, income and ability (Sawhill & Smith, 2000, p. 278).

CHARTER SCHOOLS AND PRIVATIZATION

Many states have authorized local school districts to grant parents or teachers the right to operate semi-autonomous public schools known as "charter" schools.

In these states parents may organize a charter school, if they can recruit enough students to enroll, with public funds on the same per pupil expenditure basis as other schools in the district. The parents may operate the school themselves or contract with a private company to manage the school for a fee. These private companies generally try to make a profit by reducing administrative cost. A private management company may contract directly with a local school district to manage their schools or contract to manage a charter school within the district controlled by parents.

A charter school allows a public school to operate outside of traditional local and state regulations. California charter schools may employ non-certified teachers and handle their own finances. In theory, charter schools foster competition since they may accept students from within or outside a single school district. To date, most charter schools are located in urban areas and operate in poor minority neighborhoods. But getting parents in the "better" economic parts of the district to enroll their children in a charter school in a poor neighborhood is not proving to be successful. It will take several years to systematically evaluate the academic success of charter schools. However, several state accountability systems that mandate annual testing of students in charter schools should provide better data on their effectiveness. In general, students in charter schools score below students in traditional public schools on standardized achievement tests, except for the few charter schools organized and operated by middle class parents (Zermike, 2001). Recently, 86 charter schools have closed and some granted charters failed to open because of a lack of enough students, staff or adequate facilities.

PRIVATE MANAGEMENT COMPANIES

Private management companies seek to manage traditional public schools and charter schools. However, parents in New York City and San Francisco oppose their school district's proposal to allow the private companies to manage schools in their communities (Wyatt, 2001a, b). Charter schools are likely candidates for management by private for-profit companies. In 28 states, school districts are allowed to establish charter schools. Since Minnesota passed the first charter schools law in 1991 several states and the District of Columbia have statutes authorizing charter schools. About 2,150 charter schools out of 85,000 public schools nationwide are in operation. Most are small and aimed at disadvantaged elementary and middle school students. Federal support to aid with start-up costs of charter schools rose from \$5 million in 1995 to \$51 million in 1997. Charter schools are public schools with administrative flexibility and may also opt to be managed by a private for-profit company.

Today, private companies manage more than 200 public schools that enroll approximately 100,000 students (Addonizio, 2001, p. 165). This is a small portion of the 53 million public school enrollment and financial success for these private management companies is rare. The Tesseract Group, Inc. that evolved from Education Alternatives, Inc. failed to get its school management contracts renewed in Dade County, Florida, Baltimore, and Hartford; and recently sold two Arizona charter schools and business college due to mounting financial losses (Addonizio, 2001, p. 166). However, Nobel Learning Communities, Inc. of Media, Pennsylvania bought the schools and now operates 151 small private and public charter schools in 16 states (Addonizio, 2001, p. 166).

Edison, the largest private company of public schools is in a battle with a Detroit area school district that may force it to withdraw from a school that was one of the first schools to sign with the company. The company president and founder, H. Christopher Whittle, stated that the company intends to reduce its growth figures and terminate contracts with several school districts. Edison manages 133 public schools enrolling approximately 74,000 students but has never made a profit. What can Philadelphia expect now that the Edison Corporation is set to take over their public school system? Based upon what the company is doing in Flint, Michigan's low income neighbors with at-risk students at Garfield Edison Partnership School Philadelphia can expect 90 minutes of reading lessons each morning in which teachers follow a set curriculum called *Success for All*; standardized tests taken on computers each week; quick disciplinary hearing for students who misbehave in class; and soon a computer in each home (Jacques, 2002, p. 17). Today, Edison manages for-profit 134 schools in 22 states, including schools in Las Vegas, Boston, Detroit; and they have lost schools in New York City and Wichita, Kansas. However, Edison results are mixed, and Wall Street has grown bearish on its stocks, which lost two-thirds of its value in the last year (Jacques, 2002, p. 17).

Some parents and teachers oppose the private management of charter schools. In Wilkinsbury, PA a suburb of Pittsburgh allows the for-profit company Alternative Public Schools of Nashville, Tennessee to manage an elementary school. The teachers went to court to oppose this private management arrangement. A local judge ruled that the state charter school law gave local school districts the option of turning over failing public schools to private not-for-profit companies only and they are not authorized contract with for-profit companies to manage charter schools (Walsh, 1999, p. 15). In Detroit, Michigan city officials lost a lawsuit to oppose the private management of a Detroit charter school by another public school district, located west of Detroit (Johnston, 1999, p. 3). The charter school enrolls about 250 students. State lawmakers are debating whether another public school district can open a school inside another public school district. Michigan's Governor John Engler backed the move by another state school district system into Detroit to promote competition. In anger, the Detroit School Board voted against joining a partnership with the mayor and governor in reforming the city schools.

In general, charter schools have not shown academic advantages over traditional public schools, but are just an advanced model of magnet schools that surfaced in the early 1970s. A study of charter schools in the State of Michigan (Miron & Nelson, 2002, pp. 195–214) suggest that charter schools in that state, charter schools are not "public" in the sense of control over what and how the students are taught and how the schools are administered. Charter schools in Michigan received more funds that public schools for the same number of students for producing less for more; and there appears to be less of an incentive on the part of state officials to provide meaningful oversight or to close failing charter schools (Miron & Nelson, 2002, pp. 204–208).

The private for-profit Sylvan Learning Systems Inc. is the largest provider of contract services for instructional programs to public schools. This New Jersey based company provides supplemental instruction only: remedial and special education services funded by federal and state sources; and tutorial services to students in wealthy public school districts. It has contracts in several states and is listed on the Stock Market (Kann, 1997, p. A14).

POLITICS OF PRIVATIZATION

On the federal level, the Republican Party has shifted its school choice campaign to the tax code (Hoff, 1997, p. 30). They seek tax-free savings accounts that could be spent on tuition at private and parochial schools. These accounts would allow parents, grandparents, and scholarship sponsors to deposit up to $2,000 free of federal income tax into an A+ account. Withdrawals could go to independent private or parochial school tuition, or out of district public school tuition. The Republicans also want a voucher program for students in the Washington, D.C. Public School District where Congress has control. Their proposed voucher program is similar to those in Milwaukee and Cleveland for children from poor families. Former President Clinton threatened to veto the voucher proposal and it was withdrawn (Janofsky, 1997, p. A12); and recently President George W. Bush withdrew his voucher proposal for the Washington, D.C. Public Schools due to a lack of support in Congress (Alverez, 2001). The President was aware of the fact that in 2,000 voters in two large states, California and Michigan defeated voucher initiatives in their states by large margins. Also there are no private schools in the District of Columbia area that will enroll students for the $2,000 included in the 1997 Voucher Bill (Loose & Strauss,

1997, p. A01) or the slightly larger amount in the 2001 U.S. Department of Education Budget (Alverez, 2001).

Private companies have been employed to manage an entire school district. The Minneapolis School District hired a private company to serve as superintendent under a performance contract for four years. At the end of the 1997 school year, the Minneapolis School Board ended it contract with the Public Strategies Group Inc., a private company hired to manage their public schools after four years (Hutchinson, 1997). The company made a claim of improving the school system according to its pay-for-performance contracts, but there is no confirmation of this claim. This private management company found that it takes a tremendous amount of energy to change schools and too much of what passes for change in education is nothing more than moving things around in hope that things will get better for children.

A for profit school management company first responsible is to its shareholders and not the its customers, the students; and society cannot afford the cost of inferior education at the cost of rewarding corporate shareholders (Conn, 2002, pp. 142, 148). The only way for these management companies to make a profit is to produce the same or a better quality of education for its students than the traditional public schools for less cost; and this seems to be illogical since most schools operated by for profit management companies are schools where students tend to need more services to keep paste educationally with their peers in the traditional public schools.

Privatization implies that: under capitalism, maximum output and efficiency by an organization can best be accomplished if there is an opportunity to make a profit; and we should encourage private vendors to enter public education with the profit motive in mind to increase productivity. The profit motive should be an advantage whether a school is operated with private funds or with state funds via a state voucher or a performance contract with a local public school system because it increases competition; and competition in education is good. But the history of "markets" in education has not always been positive (Richards, Rima & Sawicky, 1996).

Contracting with a private vendor to manage a public school, in which school system administrators, not parents, generally make the choice. Parents, generally, enroll their children in the same school, with the same teachers and schoolmates, regardless of who administers the school. Also, because of distance, money, peer pressure and parental knowledge, school choice for the urban poor is more limited than for those who have the means to leave the district, enroll their children in private schools or secure special treatment for their children in public schools (Wilgoren, 2001). This inability of inner-city parents to choose to quality schools for their children is central to a discussion of privatization because they involve children from poor urban communities with a high concentration of racial minorities (Molnar, 1996; Brown, 1991; Brown & Contreras, 1991; Carnoy, 1995; Henry, 1996).

PRIVATIZATION AS POLITICAL SYMBOLISM

The genesis of the modern privatization movement was put in motion by the 1954 U.S. Supreme Court decision, *Brown vs. Board of Education*, that declared state-supported school segregation, by race to be unconstitutional (Levin, 1999). *Brown* motivated school systems, first in the Southern schools and later in Northern schools, who were opposed to school desegregation experiments with school choice as opposition to the racial integration of public schools. The backlash against school integration increased after the passage of the 1964 Civil Rights Law, which gave the U.S. Justice Department the authority and resources to process through the federal courts compliance with *Brown* by offending school systems. School desegregation in the South and race riots in urban centers in the North combined to give the Republican Party a powerful weapon to attract conservative voters using the rhetoric of school "choice." In 1968, Republican presidential candidate Richard Nixon proposed his Southern strategy to win office. The Southern or racial strategy worked North and South. Republican presidential candidate Ronald Reagan repeated this strategy later and it worked, even though the Democratic Party enjoyed a two-to-one edge among registered voters. Reagan began his presidential campaign in the deep Southern state of Mississippi to reinforce his support for those offended by the racial integration of public schools. Reagan by this action indicated symbolically that he related voters supported a federal tax-exempt credits for tuition to help families off-set the cost of enrolling their children in segregated Christian academies; and recommend federal vouchers to support attendance at these private academies. In the North, tuition tax credits appealed to working class families with children in religious schools. Most of these voters were Democrats who were now voting for Republican candidates. Democratic candidates refused to use such overt "symbolism" of racism lost many national, state and local elections. In 1994, conservative Republicans took control of Congress, most state legislatures and governorships; and with these victories Republicans in Congress attempted to get their 30 year quest for government vouchers enacted in the District of Columbia, where the federal government has control of public education (Johnson, 1996). This proposal was defeated; and last June 2001 a similar proposal to experiment with voucher programs in three states by President George W. Bush was defeated in Congress (Alverez, 2001).

SUMMARY

The privatization of public education, a school choice program, involves the use of "market" incentives to improve education without additional financial resources. There are no for-profit schools in America but public are managed by private companies. This sounds confusing because the general public calls the private management of public schools, "privatization" of public schools. It merely means that private for-profit companies are allowed to manage public schools for a profit.

I expect the school choice movement in public schools to decline within a decade due to:

(1) The realization that without additional resources, will not improve failing schools.
(2) The preference for neighborhood schools after *Brown* will sap the energy and motivation for alternatives to public schools.
(3) Public school vouchers cannot constitute a viable option to replace public education for poor minority children.
(4) The profits that can be made from managing schools are not enough to entice more private companies into the field; or sustain the current for profit education management companies.
(5) Schools that are successful will continue to use public school administrators to manage their schools, thus limiting the market of available schools for private companies.
(6) Parents of children in failing schools will increase in their opposition to the private management of their children's schools.
(7) Elected public schools officials will continue to be guarded in their acceptance of the "privatization" of public schools, less they are voted out of office.
(8) Teachers' unions will continue to oppose this process.
(9) Wealthy school districts have not found a need to use private companies to manage their schools or get involved with voucher programs.
(10) The major incentive behind the school choice movement was the opposition of white parents to court ordered school desegregation factor in school assignment, which has ended, and no longer a major factor in drafting school district boundaries.

The desire for school choice, vouchers or privatization should not be based solely upon benefits to students. Politicians support what people want, not always what they need. Anything that has value is political and the politics of education precedes the art and science of education. Using vouchers or the private management of school to education to educate the urban poor in any form is a risky enterprise, and it is often a metaphor for other goals. When the Southern strategy is complete, a majority of the U.S. Supreme Court Justices will be individuals with racially and socially conservative views. The U.S. Supreme Court has ended court ordered desegregated public education program (Belk, 2001). This action should decrease the demand for vouchers and privatization of public education.

A few Black Americans have bought into the use of vouchers to "fix the system" with parental choice in where their children are educated are simply no match with the resources compared with the resources available to the white conservatives to push their agenda (Wilgoren, 2000). Howard Fuller, an African-American and former Superintendent of the Milwaukee public schools admits, "people with money in America today have choices" (Wilgoren, 2000, p. 10). Yet, Fuller, fails to recognize that most inner city Black parents do not have the money and will not have viable choices beyond the public school system. The *Frank Brown* (author) rule in power politics is that you never play another man's game, because you can only lose; and the use of vouchers to support education is the game of wealth and politically powerful white conservatives with the intent of implementing Richard Nixon's Southern Strategy to promote neighborhood schools and gain votes in elections.

President George W. Bush keeps searching for practical alternatives to public schools with vouchers and tax credits to individuals and corporations but cannot find viable ones (Rothstein, 2001). Few unfilled private-school seats exist in urban areas except for Catholic schools. But, Milton Friedman, the 1976 recipient of the Nobel Prize in economics and now a senior research fellow at the ultra conservative Stanford University Hoover Institution, who first recommended educational vouchers in the 1970s, feels that with approval of the Cleveland voucher program by the U.S. Supreme Court the program can now be expanded to serve children beyond the poverty level to include all children across the state of Ohio (Friedman, 2002). He notes that the Milwaukee voucher program has expanded in this direction over the past 10 years by increasing the income level of parents who may participate in their voucher program.

There are not likely to be major changes in improving the education for poor minority children with voucher programs because of the U.S. Supreme Court's approval of the Cleveland, Ohio voucher program. This voucher program provides private education to mainly poor white Catholic students; and not poor Black students enrolled in the largely Black Cleveland Public School System (Zernike, 2002, p. 3). Further, there are not enough places in the private schools to accommodate all the low performing students and suburban schools have shown no desire to participate in voucher programs, charter schools or magnet schools advanced to improve education for poor children and to increase school desegregation. It should be remembered that the Court's decision in 1954 *Brown v. Board of Education* did little to desegregate the public schools because of such strong political opposition to it and most poor Black children continue to attended segregated substandard schools (Zernike, 2002, p. 3).

The theme put forth by the major vocal force behind vouchers, such as the Black Alliance for Educational Options chaired by Howard Fuller a former schools superintendent in Milwaukee and site of the first voucher program states that his organization did not get into the voucher movement to give public money to educate middle class white children. However, 90% of the children in the Cleveland voucher program approved by the U.S. Supreme Court are white and attend Catholic schools; and only 10% of the Black children in the mainly Black Cleveland School System continue to attend the public schools. Suburban schools refuse to participate in the voucher program for the same reason they opposed busing to integrate publics, they did want to open their schools up to children from the inner cities (Zernike, 2002, p. 3).

Howard Fuller, a former civil rights activist, now turned conservative must have known the *end game* for public education vouchers sponsored by the Republican Party, to provide poor white families the opportunity to escape school desegregation like their middle class white counterparts who could not afford to live in largely racially isolated communities. At best it appears naïve or these were people out to make personal financial gains for African Americans to believe that the Republican Party who historically opposed all but voluntary efforts to de-segregation the public schools, including the use of "busing" would have such a great interest in promoting special programs to improve the education for children of parents who routinely support the Democratic Party. In addition to providing opportunities for poor white inner city children to escape school desegregation, the original voucher program was also aimed at rural southern communities where many white parents removed their children from the public schools and enrolled them in private segregated white academies. The Republican Party, for their support of alternatives (opposition) to "force busing" via vouchers and magnet gained the party the votes of urban whites and rural southerners. On the other hand, for African American inner city children the Democratic Party countered with school choice within the public schools with magnet schools and later with charter schools. The Republican Party was rewarded with what became known as the "Reagan Democrats," democratic who voted for republican political candidates. However, now that poor inner city white have the opportunity to escape school desegregation with state funded voucher programs, bread and butter issue may return to the top of their agenda and many of the poor inner city whites may return to the democratic party in national elections.

If we assess privatization from an educational perspective, the experiment is just beginning and we need more data over time before we can judge its success or failure. However, if we assess its impact on improving education for inner-city children, the experiment is a failure; most continue to be poorly educated. But, if we view school choice issues from a perspective, it is enjoying temporary success. Political candidates who use this symbolism as a political strategy are always favored to win elections. Big business and suburban voters who feel that their taxes are paying for wasteful government programs for the poor favor vouchers and the privatization of urban schools. The major opponents of privatization are the two major teachers' unions. The unions receive lukewarm support for their position from Democratic President Clinton and Democratic governors who must respect the politically successful Southern strategy. This is weak opposition compared to strong support for privatization by big business, several major private foundations, and the leadership of the Republican Party, the Christian Coalition and scholars associated with well-funded conservative think tanks.

Even if Americas were not divided along racial and social class lines, politics would still play a significant role in the allocation of school resources for the simple reason education is the largest component of local and state budgets. Second, educational resources are not evenly distributed throughout the population. Inner-city schools are generally under-funded when compared to suburban schools. It is interesting why there are so many conservative politicians from wealthy neighborhoods fighting to help inner-city children with state funded vouchers? May be because it is easier to get a program started for the poor and expanded later to help the rich.

Again, we will have to await the education success of the several choice options discussed for more long-term evaluations before conclusions may be drawn. A confluence of other social and economic issues may help determine the success or failure of privatization. On the political side, politicians who support these efforts won more votes than their opponents. Most choice programs are aimed at inner-city children. Wealthy communities have been content to watch the privatization movement with neutrality; and with the rich on the sidelines it is difficult to predict the long-term future of the movement. Polls reveal that most Americans oppose government tuition vouchers for parents to send their children to independent private or religious schools (Rose, Gallup & Elam, 1997, pp. 41–58). On vouchers, the public is evenly divided. This is not a new finding and politics do not always follow public opinion. Experiments with experiments will have to produce dramatic results for inner-city children to change the direction of public opinion about vouchers, charter schools and the private management of public schools. School district who are contracting out for instructional services must provide administrators with the training necessary to enter into agreement that will benefit children and meet the public's demand for fiscal accountability (Richards, Rima & Sawicky, 1996; Flam & Keane, 1997).

I see school choice plans and privatization of public schools coming to halt within a decade and the country will refocus on accountability measures which will lead to greater equality of funding for children enrolled in educationally disadvantaged schools. Choice and privatization plans separate school children by race and social class. But in the near future the minority population will become the majority and should bring changes in the education system. Given the winner take all format of national presidential elections in the U.S., it will be difficult for a candidate to win with a Southern strategy within a few years and continue to promote choice plans that separate children by race and social classes.

By 1986, only 3% of white children were enrolled in 25 largest city school systems in the country; and most were enrolled mainly with other white children in gifted and talented within-school programs (Levin, 1999, p. 268). In American, vouchers and privatization have more to do with racial politics than education. In short, many white parents want choice as a means of schooling their children with other white children; and African Americans want choice because they feel that the federal courts and U.S. Congress has no intention of implementing a school integration plan. Therefore, as a practical matter they should take the money (vouchers) and educate their own children. Schools also serve as a source of employment for communities and blacks remember losing public school jobs in the after attempts at school integration; and the schools remained segregated and under funded (Levin, 1999, p. 285). In America parents select schools based more upon the racial and social economic composition of the student body and schools are rated good or poor by parents based upon these characteristics. White parents want their children in schools with white students and minority parents want their children in schools with a few minority students. Parents and their children are not the only constituents of public schools; teachers are also major plays in the school choice movement (Buss, 1999); and in general, teachers are oppose school choice options unless it's within the public school system.

Experience with school choice reveals that after the first year most students get their first choice because they select the same school as their first choice. Thus, market conditions only operate in making the first choice; and the mechanism of withdrawal and competition does not work as promoted by market advocates (House, 1998, p. 103). Educational suppliers are limited to the number of children living in a specific community due to the fact that public funds are finite and limited based upon enrollment; and once parents with more information and resources make their choices, it limits the choices of other house holds. This is not the market model that comes to mind when we shop for food and other household goods; and these markets conditions are not available to the urban poor where suppliers are few.

In America, many markets do not seek consumers from among the poor and education markets follow this trend. High quality education suppliers have not fought to take advantage of public education vouchers that serve poor minority children. Public education does not respond to true market conditions. Education as a market lows its quality based upon state funding levels, not consumer demands (assuming all parents want the best for their children) by: employing less qualified teachers, a higher student/teacher ratio, and fewer support services. The motive for vouchers and privatizing public education in America is declining and will probably soon disappear as evident by minimum participation in the voucher program by poor African American children in Milwaukee and Cleveland. The voucher program sponsored by President George W. Bush was rejected by the U.S. Senate (Alvarez, 2001).

There will be other issues to review after these changes. Will the public schools lose their capacity to make the "melting pot" idea a reality with more racially segregated neighborhoods and schools? How will the teacher supply market respond to working in these new African American de facto segregated schools with greater input or control? We will have to wait for the answers. Another point that will require future analysis but is not a part of this article, the push for the principle of "neutrality" of the laws regarding race; a legal principle that gives the advantage to the majority group with the power to make most important public policy and employment decisions.

A young well-educated Black male feels that young Blacks support vouchers because they do not feel that Black political or economic power is sufficient enough to influence public education policies in ways that would benefit black children (Owens, 2002). Therefore, vouchers are the only hope for young blacks seeking quality education. He cites the failure of the black administrated school system to raise the test scores of black children, but he fails to recognize that schools offer more than education, they also offer jobs and other intangible benefits. An older black male and former school superintendent disagrees with a strong case against vouchers as implemented in Cleveland, OH, vouchers will improve conditions for most black students for the same reason that Owens cited, the failure of the hegemonic white power structure to implement an educational system that will benefit black students (Canada, 2002). The educational survival of marginalized minority students will depend upon how they manage the politics of education including school choice plans supported by the hegemonic majority.

The backlash against *Brown* and court ordered school desegregation which became known as the "Southern Strategy" that spawned the school choice movement, vouchers, magnet schools and later charter schools, and the privatization of public school management is likely to be reversed in the near future with the end *Brown* and the approval of public school vouchers by the U.S. Supreme Court. The ending of *Brown* and with the approval of public vouchers may take away the motivation of poor European Americans who now being educated in neighborhood schools with mainly other European Americans to continue to support this school choice mechanisms. This movement never had the active support of middle class European Americans who reside in largely racially isolated neighborhoods, nor did this movement have the support of most minority citizens or communities. Finally, with *Brown* gone forever and there is little possibility that the Court's voucher decision will be reverse, politically those who sought protection from *Brown* will no longer have a need for this protection by elected officials and the courts. U.S. Congress will feel less pressure to continue to fund public school choice programs such as magnet schools and charter schools; and without federal support its difficulty to envision how these programs can exist well into the future.

REFERENCES

Addonizio, M. F. (2001). New revenues for public schools: Blurring the line between public and private finance. In: S. Chaikind & W. J. Fowler, Jr. (Eds), *Education Finance in the New Millennium* (pp. 159–171). Larchmont, NY: Eye on Education.

Alvarez, L. (2001, June 13). Senate rejects tuition aid, a key to Bush education plan. *New York Times* [On-line]. Retrieved June 22, 2002, from: http://www.nytimes.com/2001/06/13/politics/13EDUC.html

Ambach, G. M. (1979). *Magnet schools for desegregation*. Albany, NY: The University of the State of New York, The State Education Department, Division of Intercultural Relations.

Belk v. Charlotte-Mecklenburg Bd. of Educ., 269 F.3d 305 (2001).

Bowman, D. H. (2000a, May 3). Charters, vouchers earning mixed report card. *Education Week, 19*(34), 1, 19–21.

Bowman, D. H. (2000b, March 1). States giving choice bills a closer look. *Education Week, 19*(25), 1, 24.

Bradford, D. F. (2000). The economics of vouchers. In: C. E. Steuerle, V. D. Ooms, G. Peterson & R. D. Reischauer (Eds), *Vouchers and the Provision of Public Services* (pp. 40–91). Washington, D.C.: Brookings Institution.

Brown v. Board of Education, 347 U.S. 483 (1954).

Buss, W. G. (1999). Race and school choice. In: S. D. Sugarman & F. R. Kemerer (Eds), *School Choice and Social Controversy: Politics, Policy, and Law* (pp. 300–331). Washington, D.C.: Brookings Institution Press.

Canada, B. O. (2002, June). Black leadership and vouchers. *The School Administrator, 59*(6), 39.

Carter, D. T. (2000). The southern strategy. In: J. Birnbaum & C. Taylor (Eds), *Civil Rights Since 1787: A Reader on the Black Struggle* (pp. 151–152). New York, NY: New York University Press.

Clotfelter, C. T. (2001, Spring). Are whites still fleeing? Racial patterns and enrollment shifts in urban public schools, 1987–1996. *Journal of Policy Analysis and Management, 20*(2), 199–221.

Coons, J. E., & Sugarman, S. D. (1978). *Education by choice: The case for family control*. Berkeley, CA: University of California Press.

Conn, K. (2002, April). For-profit school management corporations: Serving the wrong master. *Journal of Law and Education, 31*(2), 129–148.

Editorial: A chance, not a choice (2002, February 19). *The Wall Street Journal*, p. A26.

Editorial: Our *Brown v. Board* (2002, February 19). *The Wall Street Journal*, p. A26.

Finn, C. E., Jr. (1997, May 17). Cheating the child to save the 'system'. *The New York Times*, p. 17.

Friedman, M. (2002, July 2). The market can transform our schools. *The New York Times*, p. A19.

Gintis, H. (1995). The political economy of school choice. *Teachers College Record, 96*(3), 492–511.

Goldhaber, D. (2001). The interface between public and private schooling: Market pressure and the impact on performance. In: D. H. Monk, H. J. Walberg & M. C. Wang (Eds), *Improving Educational Productivity* (pp. 47–76). Greenwick, CT: Information Age Publishing.

Greenhouse, L. (2001, July 8). White house asks justice for a ruling on vouchers. *The New York Times*, pp. 7–8.

Harvey, W. B. (2000, April). Vouchers and school choice in Milwaukee: Changing like the weather. *School Business Affairs, 16*(4), 16–21.

Herrnstein, R. J., & Murray, C. (1994). *The bell curve: Intelligence and class structure in American life*. New York, NY: Free Press.

Hoff, D. J. (1997, September 3). GOP plans push on private school tax relief. *Education Week, 17*(1), 30.

House, E. R. (1998). *Schools for sale: Why free market policies won't improve America's schools, and what will*. New York, NY: Teachers College.

Hutchinson, P. (1997, September 17). The five Cs. *Education Week* [On-line]. Retrieved July 1, 2002, from http://www.edweek.org/ew/cirremt/03hutch.h17

Janofsky, M. (1997, September 17). Republicans urge voucher system for D.C. schools. *The New York Times*, p. A12.

Kennedy, S. S. (2001, February). Privatizing education: The politics of vouchers. *Phi Delta Kappan, 82*(6), 450–456.

Kronholz, J. (2002, February 19). High court's ruling will fuel fight over school vouchers: Judgment on Cleveland's taxpayer plan will subject Florida's program to more scrutiny. *The Wall Street Journal*, p. A28.

Levin, B. (1999). Race and school choice. In: S. D. Sugarman & F. R. Kemerer (Eds), *School Choice and Social Controversy: Politics, Policy, and Law* (pp. 266–299). Washington, D.C.: Brookings Institution Press.

Lewin, T. (1997, April 20). Schools get tough on illegal students from other places. *The New York Times*, p. 1.

Lipsitz, G. (2000). The possessive investment in whiteness. In: J. Birnbaum & C. Taylor (Eds), *Civil Rights Since 1787: A Reader on the Black Struggle* (pp. 669–678). New York, NY: New York University Press.

Loose, C., & Strauss, V. (1997, September 30). Few doors open to school vouchers. *Washington Post*, p. A1.

Miron, G., & Nelson, C. (2002). *What's public about charter schools? Lessons learned about choice and accountability* (pp. 195–214). Thousand Oaks, CA: Corwin Press.

Mosle, S. (1997, August 31). The stealth chancellor. *The New York Times Magazine*, pp. 30–37, 48–50, 55–56, 60–61.

Nelson, F. H., Drown, R., Muir, E., & Van Meter, N. (2001). Public money and privatization in K-12 education. In: S. Chaikind & W. J. Fowler, Jr. (Eds), *Education Finance in the New Millennium* (pp. 173–192). Larchmont, NY: Eye on Education.

Nelson, F. H., Muir, E., & Drown, R. (2001). *Venturesome capital: State charter school finance systems. national charter school finance study*. Washington, D.C.: Office of Educational Research and Improvement, U.S. Department of Education (ERIC Document Reproduction Service No. ED448514).

Olson, L. (2000, May 24). Gauging the impact of competition. *Education Week, 19*(37), 1, 18–20.

Olson, L. (2000, April 26). Redefining "public" schools. *Education Week, 19*(33), 1.

Owens, M. L. (2002, June). Why Blacks support vouchers. *The School Administrator, 59*(6), 38.

Paige, R. (2002, June 14). Dear colleague letter to education officials regarding implementation of No Child Left Behind and guidance on public school choice. Washington, D.C.: U.S. Secretary of Education, U.S. Department of Education.

Peterson, B., & Miner, B. (2000). Vouchers, the right and the race card. In: J. Birnbaum & C. Taylor (Eds), *Civil Rights Since 1787: A Reader on the Black Struggle* (pp. 819–822). New York, NY: New York University Press.

Richards, C. E., Rima, S., & Sawicky, M. B. (1996). *Risky business: Private management of public schools*. Washington, D.C.: Economic Policy Institute.

Reich, M. (1994). The economics of racism. In: D. B. Grusky (Ed.), *Social Stratification: Class, Race, and Gender in Sociological Perspective* (pp. 469–474). Boulder, CO: Westview Press.

Rothstein, R. (2001a, June 20). Lessons: Vouchers dead, alternatives weak. *The New York Times*, pp. A6, A20.

Rothstein, R. (2001b, June 20). Yes, vouchers are dead, and alternatives flawed. *The New York Times*, p. 14.

Sawhill, I. V., & Smith, S. L. (2000). Vouchers for elementary and secondary education. In: C. E. Steuerle, V. D. Ooms, G. Peterson & R. D. Reischauer (Eds), *Vouchers and the Provision of Public Services* (pp. 251–291). Washington, D.C.: Brookings Institution.

Schemo, D. J. (2001, July 20). U.S. schools turn more segregated, a study finds. *The New York Times*, p. A12.

Schmitt, E. (2001, May 6). Segregation growing among U.S. children. *The New York Times*, p. 6.

Scott, J. (2001, February 25). White flight, this time toward Harlem: Despite economic boost, wariness about newcomers and gentrification. *The New York Times*, p. 18.

Walsh, M. (2000, June 7). Losing money, Tesseract sells charters, college. *Education Week, 19*(39), 5.

Walsh, M. (1996, August 7). Proponents of private management weigh their long-range prospects. *Education Week*, [On-line]. Retrieved June 8, 2002, from http://www.edweek.com/ew/ewstory.cfm?slug=41priv.h15&keywords=private%20management

Walsh, M. (1999, December 15). Report card on for-profit industry still incomplete. *Education Week, 19*(16), 1, 14–16.

Walsh, M. (2000, January 12). Supreme court declines to hear Vt. 'tuitioning' case. *Education Week, 19*(17), 24.

Walsh, N. J. (1995). Public school, inc.: Baltimore's risky enterprise. *Education and Urban Society, 27*(2), 195–205.

Wilgoren, J. (2001, June 15). Chicago uses preschool to lure middle class. *New York Times*, pp. A1, A20.

Wilgoren, J. (2000, October 9). Young Blacks turn to school vouchers as civil rights issue. *The New York Times*, p. 9.

Wyatt, E. (2001a, March 17). 9 Council members assail school privatization. *New York Times*, p. A12.

Wyatt, E. (2001b, March 13). Higher scores aren't cure-all, a for-profit school discovers. *New York Times*, p. 1, A22.

Zelman v. Simmons-Harris (2002). 122 S. Ct. 2460.

Zermike, K. (2001, March 25). Charting the charter schools. *New York Times*, p. 3.

Zernike, K. (2002, June 30). Vouchers: A shift, but just how big? *The New York Times*, p. 3.

16. FILING FOR ACADEMIC BANKRUPTCY: THE IMPACT AND ECONOMICS OF STATE TAKEOVERS

Richard C. Hunter and Saran Donahoo

ABSTRACT

Under increasing pressure to reform low performing schools and improve the test scores of all students, many states have turned to school takeovers as way of bringing about radical reform. Although it has been more than a decade since the first state sponsored school takeover occurred, this reform strategy has yet to be proven effective. This article begins with a brief description of school takeovers. This is followed by a critical analysis of how school takeovers were constructed by, carried out in and the lasting impact on school districts in Logan County, West Virginia; Newark, New Jersey and Compton, California.

BACKGROUND AND FOUNDATION

Among other things, the accountability movement has placed even more pressure on urban schools to improve. Desperate to identify both the cause of their problems and the best way to solve them, many state boards of education are looking to school takeovers as a panacea for low performing schools. Approximately 24 states have laws authorizing school takeovers for schools or districts deemed to be "academically bankrupt." Urban areas that are utilizing

Challenges of Urban Education and Efficacy of School Reform, Volume 6, pages 283–293.

ISBN: 0-7623-0426-X

or have experimented with school takeovers include Baltimore, Cleveland, Detroit, Newark, Philadelphia and Washington, D.C.

As a reform strategy, school takeovers date back to the early days of school desegregation. Federal judges who found it difficult to get school districts to carry out desegregation orders sometimes went so far as to relieve administrations of their duties (Hunter & Donahoo, 2001; Hunter & Swann, 1999). In addition, state boards of education in California, New Jersey and Ohio have also used school takeovers to rescue school districts encountering fiscal crisis. Although these situations often resulted in leadership changes, states instituted these takeovers to provide consistent and accurate fiscal management, not academic reforms (Hunter & Donahoo, 2001; Reinhard, 1998).

Throughout the past fifteen years, the applicability of school takeovers has been expanded to include school districts that are experiencing academic difficulties. For schools in Compton and Newark, school takeovers for poor academic performance have resulted in power over the district reverting back to the state. In cities like Chicago, Detroit and Harrisburg, Pennsylvania, control over the local school district has actually been shifted to the mayor (Green & Carl, 2000; Kirst & Bulkley, 2000; Sandham, 2001; Sikkenga, 2000). Although encouraged by different motives, the result is generally the same in both cases – the end of local control by professional educators.

Despite the existence of local school boards, states are ultimately responsible for maintaining public education (Wirt & Kirst, 1989). Indeed, the U.S. Constitution provides legal justification for state sponsored school takeovers (Hunter & Donahoo, 2001).

Even so, these drastic leadership changes rarely take place without opposition in spite of the fact that states have legal justification for taking over schools. In many cases, conflict erupts as dismissed school boards and local administrators react to political scapegoating holding them responsible for problems that have been with the school district longer than they have.

THE STRUCTURE OF STATE TAKEOVERS

Whether attempting to address financial or academic problems, most school takeovers tend to have similar characteristics. First, a district must be experiencing a major or long-term crisis that the state believes cannot be solved by the existing administration. Once this is determined, the state assumes control of the district. At this point, the state removes the locally appointed superintendent and reduces or eliminates the locally elected school board's authority. A new district superintendent is also assigned, and a state-appointed school board may be established.

In many cases, states are electing to appoint non-educators to run their most troubled districts. Business and industry often criticize schools while characterizing them as inefficient for not strictly adhering to a more business-like style of management. Consequently, changes in school board composition suggest that takeovers are more an effort to satisfy business concerns than to improve failing schools (Birnbaum, 2000; Chubb & Moe, 1990; Hunter & Donahoo, 2001; Lieberman, 1989). This particular change suggests that states electing to take over schools are acting on behalf of outside business interests as well as their own.

Many states also find they must increase the amount of aid allocated to those school districts that are taken over. Facility repairs, management improvements and other previously ignored issues are primary targets for this aid. As many states now realize, hiring a new superintendent simply is not enough. These districts should be regularly addressing most of these problems to prevent accumulated wear and costly restructuring. However, most states have adopted the view that giving more funds to the most troubled districts is basically throwing away good money after bad, making it difficult for already impoverished school districts to get the financing needed to fix and prevent these problems.

CASE STUDIES

Although school takeovers have similar beginnings, states do not conduct them in the same manner. The following provides a more in-depth look at how West Virginia, New Jersey and California have used school takeovers.

Logan County, West Virginia

West Virginia took over the Logan County School District in August 1992. The takeover resulted from an audit in which the district was found to have a series of personnel and management problems dating back to 1986 (Gifford, 1992). These problems included failing to obtain proper state certification for teachers, insufficient and inaccurate record-keeping, overuse of substitute teachers, low attendance rates, high dropout rates, poor student performance, and receiving over $600,000 in federal funds for which the district was not qualified. When the state assumed control, more than one-third of the teachers working in Logan County did not have state approved certification (Gifford, 1992; Seder, 2000).

One of the first state changes made in the Logan County School District was removal of Superintendent Cosma Krites who had previously served as district director of personnel (Gifford, 1992). The state also fired the existing personnel director. Rather than disband the local school board, the state restricted its authority to maintenance and transportation matters. The state board appointed a superintendent who reported directly to them for handling all other aspects of the district's operations (Hoff, 1996; Seder, 2000). The state retained control over the district until August, 1996, when it restored full authorization and powers to the local school board (Hoff, 1996).

Some regard West Virginia's control of the Logan County School District as an example of a successful school takeover (Hoff, 1996; Seder, 2000). One fact supporting this conclusion is that, compared to takeovers in other locales, little controversy surrounded the Logan County takeover. The state minimized resistance and opposition by permitting the local school board to continue to operate. Although its powers were limited, the local Logan County school board did retain its ability to make some decisions. Some view this as an interesting compromise and method for resolving one of the issues associated with school takeovers. Specifically, the removal of a duly elected board of education may violate the Voting Rights Act of 1965 which restricts states from disenfranchising racial and ethnic minorities. Opponents of takeovers argue that dismissing duly elected school boards and establishing state-appointed boards denies their voting rights. In some areas, litigation with the intent to test the constitutionality of takeovers and related legislation (Hunter & Donahoo, 2001) has resulted. West Virginia avoided this type of lawsuit by allowing the local school board to continue operations.

In addition, West Virginia never viewed its takeover of the Logan County School District as permanent. Indeed, the state approached that takeover as an emergency intervention, not a long-term reform measure. As such, the West Virginia State Board of Education used its first year of control to assess district conditions and to establish specified goals for restoring local control to Logan County's schools. While under state control, test scores rose, attendance improved, dropout rates decreased, and many budget and personnel issues were resolved. Once conditions improved, control over the Logan County School District was returned to the local school board (Hoff, 1996). Having clearly defined goals to determine when a district takeover will end is very important and appeared to work very well in the Logan County case.

Despite gains made during its takeover years, the Logan County School District continues with the struggle to meet state standards. Based on its 2000 performance audit, only two of the district's twenty-two schools qualified for full accreditation by the state. The other twenty schools, as well as the district itself, received conditional approval. To receive full approval and accreditation, the Logan County School District and its individual schools must resolve a variety of noncompliance issues. These issues include developing effective discipline policies, addressing multicultural education and concerns, abiding by required curriculum development structure, improving parent involvement and monitoring procedures, and increasing student test scores (Office of Education Performance Audits, 2000). It is unclear whether West Virginia will institute another takeover if Logan County fails to resolve these issues. The state instituted takeover of the Lincoln County Schools in 2000 for failing its performance audit indicates this option remains viable and may be repeated in the Logan County School District.

New Jersey

In many ways, New Jersey is a trailblazer in the state takeover movement. In 1988, New Jersey became the first state to pass a law authorizing and establishing procedures for the state board of education to take over "academically bankrupt" school districts (Jennings, 1989). In the following year, New Jersey again made history by becoming the first state to assume full control of a low-performing school district. To date, New Jersey continues to be among the most willing to exercise this takeover power. The New Jersey State Board of Education has used its takeover law to seize control of three school districts. The state took control of Jersey City and Paterson school districts in 1989 and 1991, respectively, and the Newark Public Schools in 1995. In doing so, New Jersey became the first state with a tradition of local control to both financially and academically take over one of the nation's 100 largest school districts (Diegmueller & Lindsay, 1994; Walsh, 1995; Ziebarth, 1998/2002).

New Jersey took over the school districts of Jersey City, Paterson and Newark for very similar reasons. The Jersey City Public Schools were placed under state control after the state accused district administrators of committing a variety of offenses including using patronage in hiring practices, violating state bidding and contract laws, and mismanagement. Two years later, Paterson Public Schools were taken over because of continuous poor performance on state assessments and academic performance reviews (Ziebarth, 1998/2002). Likewise, the state seized control of Newark's schools after accusing the district of mismanagement and years of providing a miserable education to area students (Walsh, 1995; Ziebarth, 1998/2002).

In addition, the state approached each of these three takeovers in a similar manner. Like West Virginia, New Jersey removed the superintendents and many other top administrators in each district, holding them responsible for the poor conditions of the schools (Diegmueller & Lindsay, 1994; Walsh, 1995). However, unlike West Virginia, New Jersey dismantled the local school boards in each of these districts. State-appointed superintendents replaced local school boards (Diegmueller & Lindsay, 1994).

Although New Jersey has been most willing to assume control of school districts with academic problems, this action has not been as successful as many hoped. In some ways, however, the districts under state control have improved. For example, student performance on the New Jersey High School Proficiency Test (HSPT) has increased in all three districts (New Jersey Department of Education, 1999; Seder, 2000). During the 1998–1999 school year, HSPT math scores increased by 6.1% in Jersey City, 7% in Newark and 9.4% in Paterson from the previous year. In that same year, the Jersey City Public Schools were also honored with five awards for "Best Practices" (DeSando, 1999). Moreover, the number of students attending school in Newark increased by 1.4% throughout the district and 2% at the high school level (Johnston, 2000a).

Despite these gains, some argue that New Jersey's takeovers have not been very effective (Green & Carl, 2000; Johnston, 2000a; Seder, 2000; "Takeovers Don't Bring Turnaround," 1999). Although student performance has generally improved, scores in Jersey City are still lower than the state average ("Takeovers Don't Bring Turnaround," 1999). Even as math scores rose between 1997–1998 and 1998–1999, reading scores actually decreased in Jersey City, Newark and Paterson by 5.1%, 9.8%, and 12.2% respectively (DeSando, 1999).

In addition to having minimal influence on student performance, Newark's school district actually experienced new financial problems while under state control (Johnston, 2000b; Keller, 2000; Reid, 2001). During the 1999–2000 school year, Newark's schools had a budget deficit of more than $70 million (Johnston, 2000b; Reid, 2001). Although the state argues that takeovers have led to improvements in district budgeting and management procedures, the deficit cited above developed while Newark's schools were being managed by the state, suggesting that changes in these areas may not have a lasting impact. Indeed, frequent leadership changes at both the state and district levels appear to have made it difficult for significant reforms to take root in Newark (Keller, 2000). Rather than revamp and restore failing school districts, New Jersey's approach to school takeovers appears to have increased their deterioration.

Although each of these districts continues to have some of the same problems in place before the state took control, New Jersey may be getting out of the school takeover business (David Hespe, personal communication, October 26, 2000). New Jersey began the process of reestablishing local control in Jersey City in 1999 and formally returned power to the local school board in 2000 (A History of Intervention, 2002; Peretzman, 1999). Paterson and Newark are likely to follow the same path in the near future. Perhaps New Jersey may be giving up on school takeovers because modest gains experienced in those districts are not strong enough to justify the political and economic costs of takeover efforts.

Compton, California

Although the Compton Unified School District is not the first district in California subjected to state intervention, it was the state's first district to be placed under direct control due to poor student performance (Diegmueller, 1992; Ziebarth, 1998/2002). In 1993, California took over the financial operations of Compton's schools by contending that the district had mismanaged its funds. Around the same time, the California Assembly passed legislation authorizing the state to take over school districts that exhibited poor academic performance, thus enabling the state to assume control over educational operations as well (Hendrie, 1997; Ziebarth, 1998/2002). When the state took over Compton's school district for financial difficulties, it had the lowest standardized test scores in the state (Diegmueller, 1992).

The structure of Compton's takeover combines elements of approaches used by both West Virginia and New Jersey. Similar to takeovers in West Virginia and New Jersey, California dismissed many top administrators when it took control of Compton's schools. Like West Virginia, the state did not completely disband Compton's local school board. Although the power to administer various aspects of the district's operations was lost in the takeover, the local board was allowed to continue in an advisory capacity (Hendrie, 1997).

In spite of personnel changes and a $20 million loan from the state, the takeover has not really improved the Compton's situation. Many of the same problems persist, including poor facilities, high teacher turnover rates, and continued reliance on emergency credentials to fill positions requiring state certification. Similar to New Jersey's state controlled districts, test scores in Compton have experienced only slight improvements. Further, Compton has found it difficult to maintain consistent leadership. Between 1993 and 1997, Compton was led by five different state-appointed superintendents. In fact, the district went through four superintendents in 1996 alone (Hendrie, 1997).

After eight years of state control, Compton Unified School District was restored to local control in January 2002 (A History of Intervention, 2002). Like New Jersey, California seems to have reached a conclusion that changes in leadership are simply not enough. Rather than return the district to local control as a reward for making required improvements, the state seems to have given up on Compton fearing that even they are not equipped to improve the district.

THE COSTS OF STATE TAKEOVERS

In addition to producing questionable academic results, state takeovers are also financially risky. Whether successful or not, takeovers generally require revenue increases in addition to leadership changes. Indeed, the willingness of states to financially support takeovers may be one key to ensuring some measure of success. For example, the state took control of Newark's schools during the 1995–1996 school year, at which time the district received $392,502,219 in state aid (B. Rarick, personal communication, July 24, 2001). During the 2000–2001 school year, this amount rose to $406,314,144, a modest 3.5% increase from the district allocation when it was initially taken over (2001–2002 State Aid Summary, 2001). Although this amount rose to $446,583,090 for the 2002–2003 school year (an increase of 13.8%) since direct state control began, it may not be enough to help the state save either the Newark district or its plan to take over failing school districts (2002–2003 State Aid Summary, 2002).

Conversely, West Virginia was much more supportive during its takeover of Logan County's schools. During the 1991–1992 school year when the state determined that local control was not functioning adequately in Logan County, the district received $24,021,290 in state aid. The Logan County School District regained local control during the 1996–1997 school year. During that same year, the school district received $28,630,691 in state aid (W. Watson, personal communication, January 11, 2002), an increase of 19.2%. Despite the fact that many schools in Logan County are not yet eligible for full state accreditation, this district fared much better during its takeover than Newark. Although state aid is not the only difference between these two districts, it is difficult to expect an "academically bankrupt" school system to repair itself without adequate financial support.

California's financial response to problems in the Compton Unified School District was very different from the approach used by either West Virginia or New Jersey. In spite of a $20 million district loan provided by the state, Table 1 suggests that California was never quite sure about how to fund a district with the academic and financial problems it found in Compton.

Table 1. Compton State Aid, from 1992–1993 to 1999–2000.

Fiscal/School Year	State Aid	Change in $/year	% Change/year
1992–1993	$74,624,216	N/A	N/A
1993–1994	$65,938,701	–($8,685,515)	–(11.6%)
1994–1995	$58,314,980	–($7,623,721)	–(11.6%)
1995–1996	$60,858,577	$2,543,597	4.4%
1996–1997	$72,108,075	$11,249,498	18.5%
1997–1998	$74,533,154	$2,425,079	3.4%
1998–1999	$83,415,999	$8,882,845	11.9%
1999–2000	$86,411,618	$2,995,619	3.6%

Source: "District Profiles and Reports," Education Data Partnership.

Although state aid to the district increased by 15.8% overall during the years of state control, Compton actually suffered significant reductions in state aid during the first two years of its takeover ("District Profiles and Reports," 2002). Moreover, the dubious results from California's takeover of Compton's schools indicates that even financial support increases do not produce the immediate results states feel pressured to make in struggling districts.

CONCLUSION

As indicated by the outcomes in Logan County, Compton and Newark, school takeovers do not repair failing school districts. Despite leadership changes and increases in state aid, each of these districts continues to experience academic problems. These districts did have some problems that were resolved by state funding increases, suggesting that these increases were long overdue. Although increased state financial allocations proved insufficient to guarantee the success of a takeover, they did help to improve the overall condition of the failing districts.

Many takeover supporters point to Logan County as the best example of a successful school takeover. Even so, school takeovers have failed as a reform measure since they have not had a significant and lasting impact on student performance. Moreover, the fact that takeovers failed in Compton and Newark does not bode well for other urban school districts. Although Chicago, Detroit and other big-city school districts tend to favor mayoral control vs. state sponsored takeovers, there is little reason to believe these districts will fare better than others under that option. Although it seems politically advantageous for mayors to take over urban schools, New Jersey's abandonment of this reform strategy implies that states are beginning to move away from school takeovers.

REFERENCES

A history of intervention (2002, January 9). *Education Week*, *21*(16), 14.

Birnbaum, R. (2000). *Management fads in higher education: Where they come from, what they do, why they fail.* San Francisco, CA: Jossey-Bass Inc., Publishers.

Chubb, J. E., & Moe, T. M. (1990). *Politics, markets, and America's schools.* Washington, D.C.: Brookings Institution.

DeSando, B. (1999, July 7). *Jersey City test scores show impressive gains – progress noted in Newark and Paterson* [Press release]. Trenton, NJ: New Jersey Department of Education. Retrieved January 9, 2002, from http://www.state.nj.us/njded/news/1999/0707jc.htm

Diegmueller, K. (1992, September 16). Academic deficiencies force takeover of Calif. District. *Education Week on the Web*, *12*(2). Retrieved March 9, 2002, from: http://www.edweek.org/ew/vol-12/02–2comp.h12

Diegmueller, K., & Lindsay, D. (1994, August 3). N. J. moves toward takeover of Newark schools. *Education Week, 13*(40). Retrieved from: http://www.edweek.com/ew/ew_printstory.cfm?slug=40new.h13

District profiles and reports-District financial statement: Los Angeles County, Compton Unified School District [Data file]. (2002, February 4). Sacramento, CA: Education Data Partnership. Retrieved March 9, 2002, from: http://www.ed-data.k12.ca.us/dev/District.asp

Gifford, S. K. (1992, September 9). W. Va. Board assumes control of district for 1st time. *Education Week, 12*(1). Retrieved from: http://www.edweek.com/ew/ewstory.cfm?slug=01–1wva.h12&keywords=west%20virginia

Green, R. L., & Carl, B. R. (2000, May). A reform for troubled times: Takeovers of urban schools. *The Annals of the American Academy of Political and Social Science, 569*, 56–70.

Hendrie, C. (1997, June 11). Calif. district takeover faces political threat. *Education Week, 16*(37). Retrieved March 9, 2002, from: http://www.edweek.org/ew/ew_printstory.cfm?slug=37comp.h16

Hoff, D. J. (1996, September 18). W. Va. Leaves district better than it found it. *Education Week, 16*(3). Retrieved from: http://www.edweek.com/ew/ewstory.cfm?slug=03wva.h16&keywords=west%20virginia

Hunter, R. C., & Donahoo, S. (2001, September). Sanctioning school failure: School takeovers and big-city politics. *School Business Affairs, 67*(9), 20–23.

Hunter, R. C., & Swann, J. (1999, February). School takeovers and enhanced answerability. *Education and Urban Society, 31*(2), 238–254.

Jennings, L. (1989, October 11). Board in New Jersey completes takeover of troubled district. *Education Week, 9*(29). Retrieved March 10, 2002, from http://www.edweek.org/ew/ew_printstory.cfm?slug=09090029.h09

Johnston, R. C. (2000a, May 31). N. J. takeover of Newark found to yield gains, but lack clear goals. *Education Week, 19*(38), 17.

Johnston, R. C. (2000b, April 26). State audits find new budget shortfalls in Newark. *Education Week, 19*(33), 3.

Keller, B. (2000, February 2). Red ink in Newark mars state takeover. *Education Week, 19*(21), 1, 24–25.

Kirst, M., & Bulkley, K. (2000, March). 'New, Improved' Mayors take over city schools. *Phi Delta Kappan, 81*(7), 538–546.

Lieberman, M. (1989). *Privatization and educational choice*. New York, NY: St. Martin's Press.

Office of Education Performance Audits (2000, September). *Final education performance audit report for Logan County Schools*. Charleston, WV: West Virginia Board of Education, Author.

Peretzman, P. (1999, June 2). *State board considers the establishment of a process to return Jersey City School District to local control* [Press release]. Trenton, NJ: New Jersey Department of Education. Retrieved January 9, 2002, from: http://www.state.nj.us/njded/news/1999/0602jc.htm

Reid, K. S. (2001, February 14). Newark sues state, district over losses. *Education Week, 20*(22), 1, 18.

Reinhard, B. (1998, January 14). Racial issues cloud state takeovers: Interventions often face legal challenge. *Education Week, 17*(18), 1, 18.

Sandham, J. L. (2001, January 10). Mayoral takeover of schools off to tumultuous start in Pa. Capital. *Education Week, 20*(16), 5.

Seder, R. C. (2000, March). *Balancing accountability and local control: State intervention for financial and academic stability* [Policy Study No. 268]. Los Angeles, CA: Reason Public Policy Institute. Author, pp. 1–32. Retrieved March 9, 2002, from: http://www.rppi.org/educ.html

Sikkenga, A. M. (2000, Winter). Detroit school reform: A necessary means to improve the schools and end the cycle of mismanagement. *University of Detroit Mercy Law Review*, *77*, 321.

Takeovers don't bring turnaround in student achievement. (1999, May). *School Reform News*. Retrieved March 9, 2002, from: http://www.heartland.org/education/may99/turn.htm

2001–2002 state aid summary cash basis (2001). Trenton, NJ: New Jersey Department of Education. Retrieved July 24, 2001, from: http://www.state.nj.us/njded/stateaid/0102/cash_aidsearch.htm

2002–03 state aid summary cash basis (2002). Trenton, NJ: New Jersey Department of Education, Finance. Retrieved March 10, 2002, from: http://www.state.nj.us/njded/stateaid/0203/cash_aidsearch.shtml

Walsh, M. (1995, August 2). State-appointed Newark chief vows to improve condition of buildings. *Education Week, 14*(41). Retrieved from: http://www.edweek.org/ew/ew_printstory.cfm?slug=41newark.h14

Wirt, F. M., & Kirst, M. W. (1989). *The politics of education: Schools in conflict*. Berkeley, CA: McCutchan.

Ziebarth, T. (1998/2002). *State takeovers and reconstitutions* [Policy Brief]. Denver, CO: Education Commission of the States. pp. 1–18. Retrieved March 10, 2002, from: http://www.ecs.org/clearinghouse/13/59/1359.htm

17. AFRICAN AMERICAN PARENTAL INVOLVEMENT IN URBAN SCHOOL REFORM: IMPLICATIONS FOR LEADERSHIP

Linda C. Tillman

ABSTRACT

Much has been written about the importance of parental involvement and its relationship to the social, emotional, and academic achievement of students. Research on parental involvement indicates that parental involvement enhances school climate and is a necessary component of effective schooling. This chapter will explore the role of the school site administrator in facilitating parental involvement of African American parents in the context of urban school reform.

INTRODUCTION

Much has been written about the importance of parental involvement in K-12 schooling and its relationship to the social, emotional, and academic achievement of students. Researchers, as well as school personnel at the district and school site levels have suggested that there is a direct link between the active involvement of parents and the educational success of students, and particularly in large urban school districts. Early research on parental involvement (Epstein, 1987;

Challenges of Urban Education and Efficacy of School Reform, Volume 6, pages 295–312.

ISBN: 0-7623-0426-X

Haynes, Comer & Hamilton-Lee, 1989) as well as more recent research (Beck & Murphy, 1999; Brown & Hunter, 1998; Casanova, 1996; Davies, 1991) indicates that parental involvement can significantly enhance the school climate and is a necessary component of effective schooling.

Many of the current discussions as well as current research on parental involvement is situated within the context of school reform. Broadly conceptualized, school reform efforts are typically designed to improve urban public schools, and have been implemented in cities such as Chicago, Detroit, Atlanta, and Baltimore. One of the more widely used reform approaches is site-based management – a collaborative governance model that can include teachers, administrators, parents, community leaders, and students as members of the school site governing body. While the particular features of site-based management vary according to the specific school district, the primary goal is improved student performance. Although site-based management remains a popular choice in school reform efforts in many urban school districts, researchers have found that there is limited evidence to suggest that such initiatives actually contribute to increased student achievement (Beck & Murphy, 1999; Brown & Hunter, 1998; Fine, 1993) According to Beck and Murphy, concrete measurable indicators of student performance in schools using site based management models are limited and results are inconclusive with regard to improved student achievement.

But while there may be limited empirical evidence to suggest that a more collaborative decision-making model that includes and empowers parents actually contributes to improved student performance, parental involvement is still considered to be a critical element in the successful schooling of students in large urban districts. Over the past decade, school districts as well as state and national education committees, have called for models, legislation, and other mandates intended to provide opportunities for active parental involvement. Two initiatives that are prominent in the literature on schools, communities, and families are Epstein's (1995) model for community/school/parental involvement and the National Education Goals (Goals 2000), a national policy initiative on education. Epstein is the Director of the Center on School, Family, and Community Partnerships at Johns Hopkins University. In Epstein's model, parental involvement can occur along a continuum that ranges from low to high levels of involvement, with the level of involvement being dependent on the perceptions of parents and school personnel regarding the importance of involvement. According to Epstein's model, "the highest level of parental involvement occurs when the resources of the community and parents are integrated with those of the school in a total effort centered on the child" (Casanova, 1996, p. 30). The eighth goal of Goals 2000 specifically targets parents and states, "By the year 2000, every school will promote partnerships that will increase parental involvement and participation promoting the social, emotional, and academic growth of children" (Patrikakou & Weissberg, 1999, p. 1). This increased attention to the importance of parental involvement has implications for institutionalizing both micro (district and school level) and macro (state and national level) programs and policies.

Although the literature is instructive with regard to the importance of parental involvement, there has been less emphasis placed on the role of the school site administrator (the principal) in facilitating structures and incentives that lead to effective parental involvement within the context of urban school reform. In addition, while reform models such as Accelerated Schools (Levin, 1987), the Comer Model (1988), and Schools Reaching Out (Davies, 1988) do provide opportunities for parental involvement, these models do not explicitly define the role of the school site administrator in promoting effective, long-term models of parental involvement. The absence of such discussions indicates a need to broaden our conceptualizations of parental involvement to include the principal's role in planning and implementing models of parental involvement that support improved student achievement.

While the importance of parental involvement is not unique to any one type of school district or any particular race/ethnicity, much of the focus on parental involvement has been on urban schools that serve large numbers of African American and other minority and low income children (Brown & Hunter, 1998; Hampton, Mumford & Bond, 1998; Henig, Hula, Orr & Pedescleaux, 1999; Norwood, Atkinson, Tellez & Carr Saldaña, 1997). Given the persistently moderate to low performance of African American students on state mandated standardized tests, the active participation of parents has become a key issue in the reform movement. In this chapter I will explore the role of the school site administrator in facilitating the involvement of African American parents in the context of urban school reform. A brief review of the literature on parental involvement in urban school reform will provide a framework for this discussion, followed by a discussion of micro level parental involvement programs, and a discussion of macro level parental involvement in urban school reform in four major cities. I will conclude this chapter with recommendations that emphasize the role of the principal in planning and implementing effective models of parental involvement for African American parents.

Background

My discussion of African American parental involvement in urban schools is based on several assumptions. First, research indicates that parental involvement is a fundamental ingredient in the social, emotional, and academic success of urban school children (see for example Davies, 1991; Epstein, 1995; Hampton, Mumford & Bond, 1998; Hoover-Dempsey & Sandler, 1997). A second assumption posits that parents are and should be considered legitimate partners in their children's education (see for example Brown & Hunter, 1998; Epstein, 1995; Nardine, 1991). Third, parents want a "voice" in their children's education and desire to actively participate in the decisions that may affect their opportunities for a quality education (see for example Beck & Murphy, 1999; Epstein, 1995; Hoover-Dempsey & Sandler, 1997; Siddle Walker, 2000). A final assumption is directly linked to the first three assumptions – parents cannot be separated from their children in the educational process (Epstein, 1995). According to Epstein, "The way schools care about children is reflected in the way schools care about the children's families" (p. 701). Epstein has argued that schools *cannot* (emphasis added) view parents as separate from their children; rather, school personnel must view parents as partners and key stakeholders in the educational process. Thus, schools (and especially principals) must conceptualize parental involvement as an on-going relationship that positions parents as active participants rather than members of an audience (Smock & McCormick, 1995) or guest observers (Brown & Hunter, 1998).

These assumptions are particularly important for African American parents whose children are enrolled in large urban school districts-school districts that are struggling to implement effective school reform initiatives that will lead to improved student performance. While such reform initiatives are also designed to empower parents and to include them in the governance and decision making processes at the school site level, historically African American parents have felt excluded and isolated from the important decisions that affect their children's education (Brown & Hunter, 1998). School reform models may not always be structured to provide meaningful opportunities for parent empowerment and collaborative decision-making that will directly benefit African American students. As Brown and Hunter (1998) have reported, African American and other minority parents have rarely been given the opportunity for equal participation with school personnel; rather, decisions about their children's education are often made absent the consideration of parents' wishes for their children's education.

These assumptions suggest that researchers and school site administrators may need to engage in a re-conceptualization and re-definition of the concept of parental involvement. Davies (1991) reports that traditional definitions of parental involvement may be insufficient to make any significant impact on policies and practices in urban schools that serve large numbers of poor and minority students. Additionally, several researchers report that social and economic changes have left parents of poor and minority children with less access to schools than middle class and affluent parents (Davies, 1991; Henig et al., 1999; Lipman, 2002). Davies reports that Schools Reaching Out, a national project of the Institute for Responsive Education has adopted definitions of parental involvement that: (1) broaden the term *parent* to recognize that families may include grandparents, sisters, brothers, aunts, uncles, and legal guardians who are charged with caring for the child and may act as parents; (2) include community and social service agencies that provide services for children, and particularly those that service urban children and their families; (3) move beyond using the school site as the only meeting place for parent conferences/interaction; (4) consider more innovative methods for communicating with "hard to reach parents" (parents who may be apprehensive about communicating with school personnel for various reasons); (5) include agendas and priorities families; and (6) replace deficit theorizing about urban parents and their children with definitions that emphasize family values, cultural differences as strengths, and parents' desires to become active participants in their children's education. Two of these points are particularly important with regard to re-defining parental involvement for African Americans: replacing the agendas of school personnel with the agendas parents, and replacing the pervasiveness of deficit theorizing about African American parents and their children with theorizing that considers the academic potential as well as the positive social and cultural aspects of this group. While cultural, social, and economic differences may position African American parents as outsiders in schools as they are presently structured, it is not necessarily the case that these parents are uninterested in the emotional, social, and academic success of their children. Like parents of other racial and ethnic backgrounds, African American parents want their children to have educational opportunities that significantly increase their life chances for professional and personal growth and development. Thus, it is imperative that teachers and principals view African American students as members of the school family rather than "other peoples children" (Delpit, 1995). The literature suggests that teachers who engage in deficit theorizing are not likely to adopt this view on their own (Brown & Hunter, 1998; Lipman, 1997). Thus, school site administrators must implement structures and incentives that are designed to position African American parents as co-constructors of their children's educational experience. This view also positions the school principal in a leadership role that requires a vision for and commitment to progressive parental involvement. Such a vision and commitment would emphasize the many ways African American parents can help their children, rather than what racial, ethnic, and socio-economic groups they fall into (Davies, 1991).

There is an extensive amount of literature that focuses on parental involvement models and programs. A common theme in these micro level models is the attempt to link parental involvement to school reform. Davies (1991) reports that models such as the Comer Model, the Accelerated Schools Model, Epstein's model for school and family connections, and Rich's Home and School Institute are similar and have three common themes: (1) providing success for children (all children can achieve academic success regardless of cultural, social and economic differences); (2) serving the whole child (the emotional, physical, and academic growth of children are linked and are a primary focus at home and at the school site); and (3) sharing responsibility (the responsibility for the social, emotional, physical, and academic development of children is shared among the family, school, and social and community organizations) (p. 377). Davies, in his work with the Schools Reaching Out project proposes enhancing micro level parental involvement by implementing parent centers, home visitations, and action research teams. The use of action research teams may be beneficial in facilitating parental involvement in urban school districts. Action research teams combine the knowledge, experiences, and skills of teachers in "studying home/school/community relations and in devising actions to improve their own practices" (p. 380). Davies reports that some schools have considered including parents in action research teams – a strategy that would enhance both the teachers' and parents' knowledge about home/school relations and that would also promote shared responsibility among all members of the school community.

The participation of African American parents in their children's education can be traced back to the early 1900s. Siddle Walker (2000), in her discussion of segregated schools in the south reports that African American parents in these schools had a history of active participation in their children's education. According to Siddle Walker, African American parents played supportive roles that included providing finances and other resources, acting as advocates for their children, and attending school meetings and other school functions. But while it appears that African American parents were visible and were active participants, Siddle Walker indicates that there is little evidence that African American parents were decision-makers in school policies and practices. This finding is consistent with other research that suggests that African American parents are severely under-represented in the decision making process at the school site level (Brown & Hunter, 1998; Henig et al., 1999).

African American parents have participated in micro level parent involvement programs in some urban school districts. Hampton, Mumford, and Bond (1998) conducted a study of the Project FAST (Families Are Students and Teachers), a collaborative parental involvement project between the predominantly African American East Cleveland, Ohio school district and Cleveland State University. Project FAST was designed to serve students who were primarily from single parent families living at or below the poverty line. The major goal of the project, which was piloted in five kindergarten classrooms, was improved student achievement through enhanced school/family relationships. The project was guided by the concept of an extended family and long-term relationships between the school and the home. A three year plan was developed to create "an educational environment that offered students and parents a sense of structure and consistency" (p. 415). In the FAST model, students remain with the same teacher for three years, parents have the opportunity to collaborate with teachers, parents are invited to attend monthly meetings and workshops, and an extended family concept is developed. Hampton et al. found that Project FAST benefited students and their families in several ways that included: (1) teachers began the school year with important information about students' home life, and their social, cultural, and emotional needs; (2) students and parents began the year with a knowledge of teacher expectations for acceptable work and behavior; (3) the concept of parental involvement as a process over time, rather than as isolated events was promoted; (4) monthly parent workshops provided parents with knowledge and skills needed to assist their children at home and in school; and (5) basic parenting assistance was provided for low income parents in an economically depressed urban area. While the researchers reported that student outcomes could not be directly linked to Project FAST, it was possible to compare the performance of Project FAST students on two standardized tests to other students of the same grade in the same school, as well as to students across the district. Students were tested at the end of each of the three years. Results indicate that the achievement levels of Project FAST students on standardized tests in reading, language arts, and math "was significantly above that of other students in the same school and of students in the district at large" (p. 423). The authors indicate that when "time and commitment are devoted to strengthening relationships between home and school, positive results occur" (p. 426).

Norwood, Atkinson, Tellez, and Carr Saldaña (1997) describe the results of a collaboration between a university school of education, school of social work, and a community school to develop a culturally responsive parent education/involvement program. A parent involvement model that validated the cultural standpoints, values, and frames of reference of the participants was designed and implemented over a two year period. The second year of the program was focused on developing a parental involvement model for African American parents. Organizers worked to remove artificial barriers (i.e. language differences, unequal power relations), establish a sense of community through supportive sharing of all participants, and respect the cultural backgrounds of the parents. One researcher acted as a "cultural broker" or mediator by helping other members of the research team to examine and consider the consequences of using workshop materials that might suggest biases or deficit theorizing. One of the major goals of the program was to "provide a supportive environment whereby the participating parents might acquire new child-rearing knowledge and skills" (p. 419). Norwood et al. report that since the majority of the participants were African American, the "focus of all instructional practices was sensitive to this specific cultural group" (p. 421). Thus, while the workshop topics were similar to topics covered in other parent-education programs, "they were always presented in the context of the culture and the immediate community" (p. 421). Findings from survey and interview data indicate that parents were pleased with the format and content of the weekly sessions, and many parents modeled session activities in their homes. A particularly important finding was that parents felt empowered and more confident about their interactions with teachers and administrators in schools. Findings also indicate that children of program participants scored better in math and reading on standardized tests than did students whose parents received no services. This finding supports other research mentioned in this chapter that suggests a positive relationship between parental involvement and student achievement. These findings also support research that suggests that it is what parents do rather than their social, cultural, and economic background that is most important, and the imperative to recognize issues of race and class in the design and implementation of parental involvement initiatives (Beck & Murphy, 1999; Davies, 1991; Patrikakou & Weissberg, 1999),

Each of these micro models of parental involvement focuses on helping parents to support student achievement. Additionally, the models are intended to promote positive relations between parents and school personnel. The use of a culturally responsive approach to parental involvement as described by Norwood et al. (1997) appeared to have a positive effect on student achievement as well as parents' sense of self efficacy. This suggests that concerted efforts, the use of appropriate models, and committed participants can positively affect the educational environment. Although these findings are encouraging, a key question remains unanswered: What is the role of the principal in providing leadership in such programs? It seems doubtful that these programs were successful absent the direct involvement of the principal. It is important to make explicit the leadership strategies that were used to promote parental involvement in these settings.

Parental Involvement and Urban School Reform: Four Case Studies

The Color of School Reform: Race, Politics, and the Challenge of Urban Education (Henig, Hula, Orr & Pedescleaux (1999) provides an insightful analysis of school reform and urban education in four major cities-Baltimore, Washington, D.C., Atlanta, and Detroit. Each of these cities have majority African American populations and corresponding majority African American public school systems. Thus, the education of African Americans in the context of school reform efforts is a primary focus of the book. Although the book is written from a political science perspective, it is instructive with regard to macro level parental involvement in large urban school districts. In their chapter titled *Parental and Community Participation in Education Reform,* the authors discuss the activities of informal grass roots parent coalitions as well as formally structured parent groups in each city, and efforts to institutionalize parental involvement. Unlike the micro level programs that I discussed earlier in this chapter, parental involvement initiatives in these four cities were primarily in the form of large scale district/community wide efforts. According to the authors, parents represent one group whose participation (as well as the lack of) can be a crucial factor in the success or failure or urban school reform. In addition, the authors assert that as a group, parents can build coalitions with schools and other community organizations to "accomplish goals that could not be accomplished either separately or competitively" (p. 161).

Atlanta

Henig et al. (1999) found that before the 1970s Atlanta public schools consistently experienced low levels of parental involvement. In an effort to improve parental involvement and participation, particularly among African Americans, several Atlanta school superintendents implemented various initiatives such as forming school-business/community partnerships to increase a sense of ownership among parents. Former superintendent Alonzo Crim created a cabinet level position to act as liaison between the school system and the community. In addition, PTA membership campaigns, volunteer campaigns, minimum requirements for system wide parental participation, and the Atlanta Partnership for Business and Education were all implemented in an effort to increase parental participation in the Atlanta Public Schools. Henig et al. report that these actions suggest that the Atlanta Public School System placed a high priority on parent participation, and these initiatives dramatically increased parental participation from the 1970s through much of the 1980s. However, with the turnover of superintendents, the Atlanta school district again began to experience a decline in parental participation. For example, Henig et al. report that while every school in the Atlanta district had a parent center, these centers were under-used and under-staffed. In the 1990s parental participation was usually initiated by local community groups whose efforts were primarily aimed at addressing issues affecting the district as a whole (i.e. school closings, budgets, school board elections,) rather than school site issues such as school climate and student achievement. The authors do not discuss in detail the roles and responsibilities of the school site principals, and it appears that principals played only a minor role in facilitating parental participation. For example, in most cases principals were only required to submit quarterly reports that documented the number of parent and business volunteers, the number of school site activities, and the status of the PTA.

Baltimore

In Baltimore parents were mobilized for participation primarily through Baltimoreans United in Leadership Development (BUILD), a community wide organization whose membership consisted of a large number of Black churches and three labor unions. This group recruited parents for the specific purpose of implementing a site-based management model that would benefit low income and minority students. While respondents in this study indicated that "a key indicator of a successful school is the amount of parent involvement" and were concerned "that many parents do not realize the power that they have" (p. 174), parental involvement declined dramatically when BUILD began to redirect its efforts to other community issues. Unlike Atlanta, no district wide initiatives designed to involve parents in PTAs and other parental activities were implemented until the late 1980s. In 1987, the Baltimore school system began a collaboration with Johns Hopkins University, and implemented the Baltimore School and Family Connections Project. The focus of this program is *teachers*– helping them to improve and increase parental involvement in the Baltimore schools. Under a recent school reform effort, parents were encouraged to participate in site-based management teams. Thus, parents could participate in developing school improvement plans for improved student achievement and the specific means to measure student performance. Interestingly, while parents were invited to become members of the school site teams, there was no evidence to suggest that the decision making processes were collaborative; that is, it is not clear that parents were actually involved in making decisions that would affect their children. Similar to Atlanta, there is also little evidence to suggest that principals played a major role in facilitating parental involvement at the school site level. Neither is there evidence to suggest that principals played key roles in district initiatives. While the authors note that the Baltimore school system experienced difficulty in mobilizing parents to participate in a recent Educational Alternatives, Inc. (EAI) reform effort, it is not clear whether school site principals were actively involved in the planning and implementation of this effort.

Detroit

In Detroit, only 17% of survey respondents named parents as key players in educational policy making in the public school system. One respondent indicated that "parental involvement is probably the largest single weakness of the system" (p. 176) referring to the absence of parents at school site and district meetings and their failure to ask questions about district wide issues that would affect their children. The lack of parental involvement was considered to be a major challenge in the Detroit Public Schools. Yet, the authors note that Detroit is "distinguished by having been the focus of the earliest efforts to institutionalize community control" and groups such as Citizens for Community Control "endorsed community control as the salvation of Detroit public schools" (p. 176). Since the late 1980s, much of the focus of system wide parental participation in Detroit has been on "Empowerment Schools" and school choice. Coalition groups such as the Parental Task Force and the Citizens Education Committee included parents who worked to promote school choice and to de-centralize the Detroit school system. One of the recommendations of the CEC regarding empowered schools was that schools would be expected to involve parents and be held accountable for student achievement. Empowerment schools were specifically designed to provide opportunities for family participation, and to increase a sense of ownership, commitment, and accountability among parents, principals, teachers, and students. Each empowerment school operated on a shared decision making model. However, the authors report that in the Detroit reform efforts parents were rarely involved in the decision making process because parents were generally viewed as threats by principals. It appears that similar to Atlanta and Baltimore, principals in the Detroit system did little at the school site level to encourage and facilitate parental involvement. Although the system adopted an "empowered schools" philosophy, it is unclear how principals promoted this philosophy with regard to parental involvement. In addition, if principals viewed parents as threats (suggesting both race and class conflicts), it is unlikely that the majority of these principals were engaged in significant efforts to promote parental involvement.

Washington, D.C.

Unlike Atlanta, Baltimore, and Detroit, macro level parental involvement initiatives in the Washington, D.C. school system were primarily implemented to affect specific changes at the school site level. Community organizations such as the D.C. Congress of Parents and Teachers, and Parents United worked to produce significant changes in the D.C. public schools in the areas of school funding, school choice, and through legal cases. For example, Parents United had two specific goals: (1) to identify issues that required legal action, (the group often filed lawsuits on behalf of schools); and (2) to collect, analyze, and disseminate data concerning individual schools and their student performance. Thus, while Parents United represented all parents in the D.C. system, its efforts were focused on issues in individual or groups of schools. The authors note that Parents United was responsible for implementing reforms that included smaller class sizes, a full day pre-kindergarten, and availability of texts and supplies. The Washington, D.C. example presents both a micro and a macro approach to parental involvement in school reform.

Several issues are common in the four cities. First, each city choose to use formally structured and broad based, grass-roots approaches to parental participation and involvement. Thus, efforts to involve parents in education reform were more often initiated at a macro level with control resting with elite groups such as Parents United and BUILD, while low income and minority parents usually participated as the audience or guest observers. Second, race and class conflicts appeared to be a key factor in the level of parental participation. The authors note that one of the major problems affecting parental involvement in these cities was "Black educators vs. Black parents"; that is, some principals felt threatened by low income African American parents and/or did not fully involve parents in the decision making processes, particularly in site based management models. Third, there is very little evidence to suggest that principals played leadership roles by encouraging parental involvement and by providing opportunities for their involvement. While this study did not specifically seek to explore the roles of school site principals, it could be argued that many of the failed initiatives could have been enhanced by the active participation of the school site principal. Additionally, while it cannot be determined from the results that are presented, it is possible that the failure of the school districts to consider principals as "key players" in efforts to mobilize parents may have contributed to the inconsistent patterns of parental involvement at the school site level. There may be a variety of reasons for the lack of principal leadership-reasons that are specific to the social, cultural, and political norms of each of the cities. Whatever the reasons, it seems clear that a more direct approach was needed to address the inconsistent levels of parental involvement in these cities. Although the imperative for school site leadership is implied in the research literature and in the examples presented here, the findings suggest that the role of the school site leader was a secondary issue.

School Leadership and Parental Involvement: A Necessary Combination

There is sufficient evidence to indicate that there have been and continue to be low levels of parental involvement in most urban school districts. This may be particularly applicable to African American parents whose children attend urban schools (Brown & Hunter, 1998; Henig et al., 1999). Research on minority parental involvement indicates that there are a variety of reasons why African American parents in urban school districts generally do not have high levels of parental participation. As indicated in this discussion, these reasons include but are not limited to, race and class differences/conflicts, adversarial relationships between the school and the home, unequal power relationships between parents and school personnel, deficit theorizing on the part of school personnel about certain racial and ethnic groups, and role perception by parents and school personnel. Other reasons such as lack of transportation, conflicts in meeting times and parents' work schedules, and mis-communication between the school and the home may also contribute to the lack of African American parental involvement. While the reasons for lack of parental involvement given here are by no means absolute and should not be construed as applicable to only African American parents, it is this group of parents whose involvement and participation is most needed if we are to improve the social, emotional, and academic life chances for African American students in urban schools.

As a former educator in an urban school district, I was often puzzled by the lack of parental participation by African American parents. Despite the fact that many of their children were scoring poorly on standardized tests, and often had poor attendance and discipline problems, many African American parents in the district appeared to take little interest in attending school site meetings or other activities relating to their children's social, emotional, and academic growth. I remember well the frustration of my colleagues and I, as well as the principal, when discussing the low numbers of parents who attended parent-teacher conferences or who responded to communications from the school. Again, while this dilemma was not always specific to African American parents in the schools in which I worked, there appeared to be a direct link between African American student achievement and the lack involvement by their parents. In addition, as a university professor, I have taught school-parent-community relations courses and I have heard first hand accounts from graduate students concerning their own frustrations about the low levels of parental involvement in their schools. It is interesting that the majority of the students in these classes who expressed frustration about the lack of parental involvement either taught or were administrators in predominantly African American school districts. Only rarely have I heard these same concerns expressed by students who were teachers or administrators in the school districts that served primarily White and middle class students. This fact should cause African American parents and school site leaders to re-examine their commitment to educating children, and the means by which we must go about this. The lack of African American parental involvement is a dilemma in school systems across the country-a dilemma that requires our serious attention.

Based on my experiences as a public school educator and as a university professor, I believe that the key to structured, effective parental involvement and participation is the *school site principal*. The principal of any school provides the vision, the structures, and the incentives for any initiative that is intended to improve the social, emotional, and academic growth of *all* students. As the instructional leader, it is the principal who must model the type of attitudes, behaviors, and purposeful actions that lead to collaborative and successful partnerships with parents. The principal must do more than send home monthly newsletters and communicate with parents only when there is a problem with their children. Principals must take responsibility for parental involvement in their schools by re-examining their own assumptions about parental involvement. As Brown and Hunter (1998) have noted, principals often "blame minority parents who cannot meet their definition of adequate involvement as measured against parent participation by middle class White parents" (p. 117). Thus, principals must re-think their own definitions and motives for parental involvement in their schools. Principals must also do more than appoint a committee to work with parents. Principals must begin to view parental involvement as relationship building and as a process that occurs over time (Hampton et al., 1998) rather than as a series of isolated events such as PTA meetings, parent-teacher conferences, and discipline hearings. Norwood et al. (1997) report that many parental involvement initiatives in urban school reform lack systematic interventions that are designed to assist parents of inner-city children to become empowered advocates for their children, assist them in transcending barriers to involvement, and assist them in understanding and choosing from the various ways that they can participate in their children's education. This suggests that principals must design and implement systematic, long-term approaches to parental involvement that include knowledge of the parent population, a needs assessment, a multi-year plan, and an evaluation component.

Systematic, long-range planning for effective parental involvement must necessarily include a core team of teachers and other school personnel who are committed to working with parents in order to enhance the social, emotional, and academic achievement of every student in the school. While many urban school districts have adopted site based-management models, these initiatives have either failed or experienced only moderate success because of a lack of *commitment* on the part of school personnel to working with low income and minority parents. The result has been the continued dismal performance of many minority students, and particularly African American students. In addition, I agree with Norwood et al. that "parents in the urban school reform milieu require a model for a parent involvement program that serves to validate their cultural frames of reference, values, and heritage" (p. 414).

Given this discussion, it is imperative that principals assume a more active leadership role in facilitating parental involvement. In short, it is the principal who must assume a leadership role by taking charge of the planning and implementation of systematic, long-term parental involvement efforts that focus on students and their parents. It is the principal who must move parents from a position of passive interest to active involvement in their children's education. It is the principal who must view parents as partners rather than as threats to the status quo (Davies, 1991).

Based on a careful reading of the literature and my own experiences in public schools, the following recommendations are offered for facilitating African American parental involvement. First, both aspiring and practicing principals should enroll in a school-parent relations course at the local university. University leadership preparation programs offer courses that provide opportunities for both aspiring and practicing principals to become familiar with the literature on parental involvement, and to apply theory to practice through discussions and projects. School site leaders must be willing to engage in the theoretical and practical acquisition of knowledge and skills that will enable them to successfully address the needs of diverse populations of parents and to work toward the success of all students. Elsewhere (Tillman, 2001) I have argued that leadership preparation programs must include course work that prepares principals for the challenges and promises of working with an increasingly diverse population. Similarly, principals must recognize that there is no "ideal" type of school and no "one size fits all" plan for parental involvement. The exposure to various theories on parental involvement as well as interactions with other principals from various school districts can provide a knowledge base from which to choose appropriate models of parental involvement.

Second, using the knowledge and information gained from school-community relations courses, principals should form a core team of teachers, counselors, parents, other school personnel, and community and social service leaders/ volunteers. The specific purpose of the team should be to develop a parental involvement program that will allow African American parents to engage in meaningful participation. Principals must be actively involved in the planning and should be actively engaged in deciding on the specific goals of the initiative given the social, cultural, and academic realities and needs of students and their parents. As Norwood et al. (1997) have suggested, the implementation of a culturally responsive model of parental involvement should be given serious consideration. The use of action research teams (Davies, 1991) is one way to approach the development of a culturally responsive model of parental involvement. Action research teams composed of teachers and parents can help to make explicit the perceptions and expectations of all key stakeholders in the educational environment. The importance of encouraging parents to become members of the action research team cannot be overemphasized. Principals must be aware of and understand what it is that parents believe is important for their children's educational growth and development. Principals must also understand that their own perceptions of and expectations for acceptable procedures, attitudes, and behaviors may be different from some of their parents. This will require flexibility on the part of principals, teachers, and parents. Thus, principals must educate themselves and their staffs about the parents that they serve (i.e. parents level of education, socio-economic status, cultural norms, etc.) Principals and teachers cannot work in isolation from the parents they serve; that is, effective parental involvement must be a collaboration between key stakeholders. Involving parents should be considered a priority rather than an option.

Third, the principal should investigate opportunities for the school to become a member of a parental involvement network. Such networks provide models, materials, newsletters, opportunities to attend conferences, and access to current research on parental involvement and student achievement. Much of the information is specific to schools that serve large numbers of low income and minority students and students who are placed at-risk for various reasons such as poverty and crime. For example, Epstein's Center on School, Family, and Community Partnerships is open to any school and offers a wealth of material at minimal cost to the schools. Membership in a national organization can help to bring focus and structure to parental involvement efforts at the school site. Because information is periodically updated and is accessible on-line, principals, teachers, and parents can access current research about parental involvement initiatives in other school districts across the country. In Henig et al.'s (1999) discussion of parental involvement in Atlanta, Detroit, Baltimore, and Washington, D.C., the Baltimore school district was the only district that entered into a partnership with a national network focused on students and their families. Principals must investigate all avenues of support for parental involvement.

These suggestions do not represent the complete range of possibilities for increasing the levels of African American parental involvement in urban schools. However, these suggestions do represent a starting point for re-conceptualizing parental involvement that supports student achievement. Principal preparation through university course work, the use of a core team of committed individuals, and membership in a national parental involvement organization can assist principals in promoting African American parental involvement that supports an improved school climate as well as student achievement.

CONCLUSION

I have used the phrase "the principal must" in my discussion of the importance of Afican-American parental involvement. This was an intentional effort on my part to emphasize the importance of the principal's role in facilitating African American parental involvement. We are all aware of the dismal performance of many African American children on standardized tests, poor graduation rates in many large urban cities, and the decreasing numbers of African American students who pursue post-secondary education. After more than a decade of school reform, African American students continue to be under-served and under-educated in urban schools. As educators we must be committed to the success of every African American child. We must do more through our research and our writing to encourage school site leaders and parents to become active participants in the continuing struggle to educate African American children. The life chances of African American children can be significantly enhanced by effective leadership, principals who care and are committed to their success, and parents who are given every opportunity to exercise their right to full participation in their children's education.

REFERENCES

Beck, L., & Murphy, J. (1999). Parental involvement in site-based management: lessons from one site. *International Journal of Leadership in Education*, *2*(2), 81–102.

Brown, F., & Hunter, R. (1998). School-based management: Involving parents in shared decision making. *Urban Education*, *33*(1), 95–122.

Casanova, U. (1996). Parent involvement: A call for prudence. *Educational Researcher*, *25*(8), 30–32, 46.

Comer, J. (1988). *A brief history and summary of the School Development Program*. New Haven, CT: Yale Child Study Center.

Davies, D. (January, 1991). Schools reaching out: Family, school, and community partnerships for student success. *Phi Delta Kappan*, 376–382.

Delpit, L. (1995). *Other people's children: Cultural conflict in the classroom*. New York: The New York Press.

Dryfoos, J. (1996). Adolescents at risk: Shaping programs to fit the need. *Journal of Negro Education*, *65*(1), 5–18.

Epstein, J. (1995, May). School/family/community partnerships: Caring for the children we share. *Phi Delta Kappan, 701–712.*

Epstein, J. (1988). How do we improve programs for parent involvement? *Educational Horizons*, *66*(2), 58–59.

Fine, M. (1993, Summer). [Ap]parent involvement: Reflections on parents, power, and urban public schools. *Teachers College Record*, *94*(4).

Hampton, F., Mumford, D., & Bond, L. (1998). Parent involvement in inner-city schools: The Project FAST extended family approach to success. *Urban Education*, *33*(3), 410–427.

Haynes, N., Comer, J., & Hamilton-Lee, M. (1989). School climate enhancement through parental involvement. *Journal of School Psychology*, *27*, 87–90.

Henig, J., Hula, R., Orr, M., & Pedescleaux, D. (1999). *The color of school reform: Race, politics, and the challenge of urban education*. Princeton, NJ: Princeton University Press.

Hoover-Dempsey, K., & Sandler, H. (1997). Why do parents become involved in their children's education? *Review of Educational Research*, *67*(1), 3–42.

Lipman, P. (2002). Chicago school policy and the politics of race: Toward a discourse of equity and justice. Paper presented at the Annual Meeting of the American Educational Research Association, New Orleans, LA.

Lipman, P. (1997). Restructuring in context: A case study of teacher participation and the dynamics of ideology, race, and power. *American Educational Research Journal*, *34*(1), 3–37.

Norwood, P., Atkinson, S., Tellez, K., & Carr Saldaña, D. (1997). Contextualizing parent education in urban schools: The impact on minority parents and students. *Urban Education*, *32*(3), 411–432.

Smock, S., & McCormick, S. (1995). Assessing parents' involvement in their children's schooling. *Journal of Urban Affairs*, *17*(4), 395–411.

Patrikakou, E., & Weissberg, R (February, 1999). The seven P's of school-family partnerships. *Education Week, 18.*

Tillman, L. (2001). Success for all children: Implications for leadership preparation programs. *University Council for Educational Administration Review*, *62*(1), 10–15.

Siddle Walker, V. (2000). Value segregated schools for African American children in the South, 1935–1969: A review of common themes and characteristics. *Review of Educational Research*, *70*(3), 253–285.

18. RECONSTITUTION, SMALL SCHOOLS, SCHOOL-BASED MANAGEMENT, ETC.

James E. Lyons

ABSTRACT

This chapter addresses three reform strategies that have been employed in American schools to effect improved teaching and learning, particularly better student performance on standardized tests. These three reform initiatives are school-based management, small school initiatives, and reconstitution of failing schools. All of these strategies seek to change the way schools are structured, governed and operated. This chapter provides an overview of these reform initiatives and discusses how each of these has been implemented in America's public schools. Some examples of states or school districts where these initiatives have been broadly implemented are presented and discussed.

EVOLUTION OF RECENT REFORM MOVEMENT

Most scholars contend that the federal government's publication of the 1983 report, *A Nation at Risk: The Imperative for Educational Reform* (National Commission on Excellence in Education, 1983), served as the clarion call that spurred the national effort to reform and improve America's schools. This report was produced by the National Commission on Excellence in Education, which had been appointed in 1981 by then Secretary of Education, Terrell Bell, to examine the

Challenges of Urban Education and Efficacy of School Reform, Volume 6, pages 313–337.

ISBN: 0-7623-0426-X

quality of education in the U.S. The commission concluded that a "rising tide of mediocrity" was sweeping across the educational system, which would eventually cause America to lose its competitive edge in competing with other industrialized nations. In addition to calling for a more rigorous, demanding curriculum, it recommended that a nationwide system of state and local achievement tests be administered at major transitions points from one level of schooling to another. Although there are scholars such as Berliner and Biddle (1995), among others, who contend that erroneous conclusions were reached in the report, it ushered in the reform era in public education that has continued to the present and will likely affect education for the foreseeable future. Nevertheless, the fact that some indicators of educational quality had been steadily declining during the seventies served to corroborate the suspected decline in public education and boosted the arguments for school reforms. Many critics came to view public education as an ineffective, sluggish monopoly with little incentive to reform. Concerns about the quality of schooling in American's public schools, coupled with the demands for a better, highly trained workforce, fueled the flames of reform.

The overall effort to improve public schools in the U.S. came to be commonly known as restructuring. Although the various reforms done under the rubric of restructuring have taken a variety of forms, fundamentally they have addressed the issues of how schools are governed, organized, and operated for the purpose of improving teaching and learning. Specific intervention strategies have addressed one or more of the important elements of schooling, including governance, decision-making, instruction, curriculum, teaching practices, professional development, parental and community involvement, and school support services. While the early efforts to reform schools began at the local and state level, a national framework to reform schools was soon organized. It eventually culminated in a 1989 Education Summit when President George H. Bush convened the states' 50 governors in Virginia and established national education goals for America's schools.

The initial reforms made, generally categorized as first wave reforms, dealt primarily with top-down mandates from the state legislatures. Ornstein (1991) notes that nationwide, more than 1,000 state statutes affecting some aspect of school reform were enacted within the seven year period between 1983 and 1990. The approach most frequently taken was the passing of an omnibus education bill by the state legislature that contained a combination of regulations and incentives. Since these state legislators assumed the schools within their respective states were more alike than different, reform statutes tended to be across the board, one size fits all (Metz, 1988). The vast majority of these first wave reform proposals assumed a "top-down" strategy wherein decisions made at the state level, usually by the legislature or state board of education, were handed down to local school districts to be implemented at the classroom level.

These mandates primarily called for tougher graduation standards, more testing of students and teachers, longer school days and years, more emphasis on student mastery of the basic skills, more courses in mathematics, science, foreign language, more remedial programs, etc. (Ornstein, 1991). Based upon the speed at which states across the country attempted to reform education by statutes and mandates, it may be concluded that lawmakers sincerely believed that they could legislate educational quality, if not excellence. However, in spite of these reforms, significant and pervasive improvement in student achievement was not realized. Some school reformers have noted that these first wave reforms were based upon a false premise. Undergirding most of them was the belief that many administrators and teachers were either not competent and/or were simply not working hard enough. It viewed professional educators as a major part of the problem, not as part of the solution. Thus, these initiatives were geared to make the old system work more efficiently and effectively. Owens (1998, p. 96) notes that by the 1990s, however, many thoughtful observers were expressing alarm that these regulatory approaches were, in fact, counterproductive for two reasons. First, these bureaucratic approaches, which often reflected mindless rigidity, failed to account for individual needs of students, specific circumstances in schools, etc., and hampered teachers in making professional judgments about the curriculum and teaching strategies needed in schools. Second, a growing body of research had begun to show that many highly qualified and motivated teachers were increasingly frustrated by their inability to exercise their professional judgments in a school environment that was becoming steadily bureaucratized. Moreover, these first wave bureaucratic initiatives failed to recognize the important role that school culture, school norms, human relationships, and organizational dynamics play in schools. Sarason (1990) aptly addresses this phenomenon in his book, *The Predictable Failure of School Reform.* When it had begun to appear that first wave reforms were not particularly effective in effective in improving student achievement, second wave initiatives were introduced.

Second wave educational reformers advocated giving professional educators, including teachers, sufficient professional autonomy and leeway to identify and solve educational problems at the school level and then to be held accountable for the results of their decisions and acts (Owens, 1998). Research studies conducted during this second wave of school reform underscored the importance of managing schools so that teachers are respected, treated as professionals, and allowed to exercise autonomy commensurate with their professional status. Moreover, these reformists advocated shared decision making among school constituencies – including teachers, administrators, parents and students – each of whom had a vested interest in improved schools and student achievement. They also called for new approaches that would restructure the roles and relationships among school staff and parents under the leadership of school principals who would serve as strong instructional leaders.

Owens (1998) contends that second wave reforms were based upon an entirely different view. They were based upon the premise that the "front line" of schooling lies in the individual school rather than in a distant bureaucracy and that educational problems can best be identified, addressed, and solved by those closest to them through exercising their own professional judgment. Moreover, this approach recognized and called for a collaborative school environment with fully engaged and highly motivated teachers taking ownership for the work needed to effect success with their students. In exchange for this autonomy and the accompanying right to exercise greater professional responsibility at the school level, principals and teachers would be held more responsible for their decisions and, most important, for the academic achievement of students in their schools.

The third and most recent wave of reform might appropriately be called the standards and accountability movement. To determine if consistent progress was being achieved, however, it soon become apparent to policy makers that statewide standards would be necessary to make meaningful comparisons between student achievement in schools and school districts. Although the National Assessment of Educational Progress (NAEP), known as the Nation's Report Card, has been administered since 1969, it only tests samples of students in grades 4, 8, and 12 from specific geographic regions across the country in reading, mathematics, science, writing, U.S. History, civics, geography, and the arts. It does not provide scores for individual students or schools. It is governed by the National Assessment Governing Board and administered by the National Center for Education Statistics in the U.S. Department of Education.

Some state legislatures have passed what is literally known as Excellent School Acts or other acts closely akin in name. To effect high educational quality and pursue excellence, most policy makers concluded that it was necessary to set high standards that specified what students should know and be able to do as they matriculated through the educational system. Also, they perceived that it was necessary to use standardized tests to measure whether educational goals were being met and to reward success and sanction failure. All of the 50 states have now adopted educational reform initiatives that encompass some combination of high standards, challenging content, or school district or school accountability (Goertz & Duffy, 2001). Most frequently, these reforms establish a statewide accountability system and set goals for school districts or individuals schools within districts. Additionally, many of the states have identified performance standards and determined how they will measure annual progress toward their achievement. There is wide variation in performance goals and standards among the states; however, there are many common elements of these accountability systems which usually include assessments, standards, performance reporting, and, in most cases, consequences of performance (Goertz & Duffy, 2001). Every state except Iowa has established standards in some subjects, and 44 states have standards in the core academic discipline (English, math, history, and science). Forty-eight of the states have statewide testing programs, and most have aligned the tests to the standards in at least one subject (Thernstrom, 2000).

Among the states that have comprehensive accountability systems, a few stand at the forefront. These include North Carolina, Texas, Florida, Kentucky, Colorado, Arkansas, Louisiana, Ohio, and Virginia. For example, North Carolina has its Accountability, Basics, and local Control (ABCs) Program; Texas has it Texas Assessment of Academic Skills (TAAS) Program; and Virginia has its Standards of Learning (SOLs) Program. Most of these standardized accountability programs are designed to measure if students learn a predetermined body of knowledge to a particular level of accomplishment. To hold school districts and schools accountable, most of the states have developed a high stakes testing program to measure student academic achievement. In the majority of cases, there are consequences for school districts, schools, administrators, teachers, and students when significant numbers of students do not reach expected levels of achievement on these tests.

THREE REFORM INITIATIVES

School Based Management

The "second wave" of school reform discussed earlier had promulgated the notion that administrators and teachers in the schools were better positioned to discern the most appropriate manner to structure the curriculum and determine teaching strategies. Moreover, since the top down approach had been minimally successful in effecting broad school improvement, policy makers were willing to allow professional educators the opportunity to use their expertise to improve their schools generally and student achievement in particular. Coincidentally, at approximately the same time, Deming's total quality management (TQM), which advocated allowing those closest to the problem to have input in the solution and shared decision making, was being widely adopted in the corporate/business sector. This approach to organizational management and leadership advocated broad staff participation in decisions affecting their work, staff empowerment, and staff ownership of issues, challenges, and opportunities at their level of the organization. Given that many representatives from the business community directly or indirectly influence and shape educational policies, they saw the possibilities that might ensue from transferring these principles and practices to the business of education. The practice of delegating responsibility and decision making to the school level led to the restructuring initiative known as school based management.

School based management (SBM), often used synonymously with site-based management, is a form of decentralization that identifies the individual school as the primary unit of improvement and relies on the redistribution of decision-making authority as the primary means through which improvements might be stimulated and sustained (Malen, Ogawa & Kranz, 1990). Although various hybrids of school based management have been attempted in American schools during the last thirty years, it has been implemented to its greatest degree since the early 1990s. It should be noted, however, that during this approximate time period some form of school based management had also been implemented in schools in many other countries, including Canada, England and Wales, New Zealand, Sweden, Austria, Denmark, Finland, Portugal, Belgium, France, Germany, Norway Spain, and Switzerland (Meuret & Scheerens, 1995). Although the procedures and practices of school based management may differ in schools where it has been implemented, Herman and Herman (1991, p. 261) note that the following are some common elements:

(1) a shift occurs in decision making, relocating some, or a substantial part of it, to individual buildings with some degree of central office collaboration;
(2) at the building level, control over such critical decision areas as budgeting, personnel, and instruction is exercised;
(3) district, and even state policies and regulations are often waived to facilitate greater building-level autonomy;
(4) the local building creates its own policies and regulations; and
(5) at the building level, a number of "stakeholders" – administrators, teachers, paraprofessional, parents, students, members of the community, and local businesspeople – make decisions affecting that individual school.

At its core, school based management requires that fundamental changes be made in the roles and relationships at both the school district and school levels. It is a process of decentralization and deregulation in which the individual school becomes the focal point of school leadership, planning, and decision making. First, central office administrator roles must change and be redefined as more decisions and responsibility for making them are shifted to the school building level. Thus, the traditional, authoritative role previously carried out by central office administrators must change to accommodate school-based management. If they are unwilling or unable to do this, then friction and power struggles are likely to occur as principals, teachers, parents, and students seek to exercise more control over decision making at the building level.

Second, the role of principals, teachers, and school stakeholders will change as school based management is implemented. The principal's role is the one that normally must change most dramatically in the process. Meriwether (1996) notes that the principal must function more as a leader rather than a manager/administrator as he/she facilitates decision making without (unilaterally) making decisions and participates in leadership by relinquishing authority to the adopted management structure in the school. Likewise, the role of teachers must change as school based management is implemented, as they normally assume a greater role and more responsibility for making decisions. Although many teachers often feel overwhelmed by the demands of their job, they are expected to play a key role in school based management by more actively participating in the decision making process at the building level. Similarly, parents, or at least parent representatives, must assume a greater role in helping to participate in the school planning and decision making.

Normally, in school based decision making, a school site council is established at the building level that includes the principal, and teacher and parent representatives. In secondary schools, students are sometimes included, also. Ideally, the council seeks concerns and issues from all school stakeholders, i.e. teachers, parents, paraprofessionals, students, etc., and brings them to the council meeting for discussion and, if deemed warranted, action. To function effectively, most school site councils usually need some training in group process skills, consensus decision-making, and conflict resolution. Moreover, the principal or another administrator needs to keep the council informed in a timely manner about pertinent school issues that are likely to come before the council. Since school based management is a process rather than a product, significant time and experience is needed to implement, refine, and assess its effectiveness. Hoyle (1992) has noted that the process requires 5 10 years to fully implement in schools.

If school based management is to be successful over the long haul, areas of decision making must be clearly identified that will be transferred from the central office to the school level. Most frequently, the areas of decision making transferred to schools include budget, personnel, and curriculum, although the amount of flexibility for decision making in these areas various from district to district. When implementing school based management, Lewis (1989) notes that the most common order of areas of implementation includes the budget first, personnel and staffing second, and curriculum third. Within these broad areas, individual schools often are allowed some flexibility in terms of policies, rules and regulations, staffing, and school governance (Herman & Herman, 1992).

Two places where school based management has been implemented on a very broad scale to effect school improvement is Chicago and the state of Kentucky. As a result of the Chicago School Reform Act of 1988 (Illinois P.A. 85-1418), all schools were required to implement school based management and, through this process, establish local school goals and a system for redistribution of resources. The Chicago reforms were enacted to respond to low student academic achievement in the district with a goal of increasing the percentages of students performing at or above national norms on standardized tests. Hess (1991) provides a detailed description of the Chicago School Reform Act and the events that led the Illinois Legislature to pass it. Also, in a journal article in Educational Policy, he provides a comprehensive description of the school based management reforms instituted in Chicago and the changes added to those reforms in 1995 to enhance accountability (Hess, September, 1999). Wong (1999, p. 313) notes that the act was guided by the belief that that parent and citizen empowerment through local school councils would improve educational performance and restore public confidence by granting parents substantial ownership over the schools. Fundamentally, the goal of the Chicago reformers was to free individual schools from the control of the central office bureaucracy and provide them with sufficient resources and the flexibility to use them so that they might best use them to address the needs of students served at each school site.

A key element of the Chicago School Reform Act is the requirement that Local School Councils (LSCs) be created comprised of six parents, two community representatives, two teachers, the principal, and, in the high schools, a student. The Local School Council, which is elected by a school's constituents and must be chaired by a parent, has three primary responsibilities: to enact a school improvement plan, to adopt a school budget to support the plan, and to hire and/or fire the principal (Hess, 1999). Principals, who lost tenure as a result of the 1988 act, were made accountable to these councils rather than to the central district administration. Since there was more than an 80% turnover of principals between 1989 and 1995, it might be concluded that the councils were willing to exercise their authority to remove principals when they deemed it necessary (Hess, 1999).

The results of mandated school based management in Chicago have been deemed mixed at best in terms of its effectiveness for a number of reasons (Wong, 1999). First, voter turnout to elect LSCs steadily declined by 68% over a 5-year period (1999) and, as a result, fewer candidates ran for office to serve on the councils. Wong notes that by 1993, one out of every three schools lacked a full slate of candidates. Therefore, it might be concluded that there was a lack of interest by eligible members to serve on the LSCs. More important, on those factors that represent school success such as attendance, graduation rates, and academic achievement, Polsby cited in (Walberg & Niemiec, 1996) did not find any systematic indicators of school improvement. He also found that high schools were even further behind the elementary schools on national standards. Hess (1999) notes that by 1993 only a third of Chicago's elementary schools were engaged in systematic reform efforts, another third were adding programs in a haphazard way, and the other third had made little effort at improvement, either due to resistance or reduced capacity to envision or implement reform.

To address the problem of low academic achievement, in spite of a major reform to introduce school based management through LSCs, the Chicago School Reform Act of 1988 underwent some major changes through amendments made in 1995 to strengthen local school accountability. These amendments, known as the Chicago School Reform Amendatory Act, took effect in July 1995. It reversed a seven year effort to effect local decentralization of authority and redesigned the system to reflect an integrated governance model wherein fewer policy actors would compete for decision-making authority (Wong, 1999). Among other things, the amendments led to the establishment of standards based on the percentage of students being tested in each school who were at or above norms on the Iowa Test of Basic Skills (ITBS) or its high school counterpart, the Test of Achievement and Proficiency (TAP) (Hess, 1999). Specifically, the 1995 amendments substantially changed how the school system managed its finances; gave the mayor new authority to directly appoint a new, smaller Reform Board of Trustees and the top five managers of the school system; and provided the central administration with the authority to hold low-performing schools accountable by directly intervening to put schools on probation and to reconstitute the staffs of the worst of these (Hess, 1999). Hess notes that a year and a half after taking office following when the 1995 amendments were enacted, the Reform Board of Trustees placed about a quarter of the system's schools on probation because fewer than 15% of their students were performing at national norms. When schools were placed on probation, they received more scrutiny from the central office; their expenditures were subject to the approval of probation managers assigned to each school; their principals were more closely monitored; and the central office was on alert to intervene when schools were considered to be in crisis (Hess, 1999).

In 1990, the Kentucky General Assembly passed the Kentucky Education Reform Act of 1990 (KERA). This followed a Kentucky Supreme Court ruling that declared the state's public school system to be unconstitutional and invalidated the entire body of school law. In ruling on a lawsuit brought by sixty-six of the state's poorest districts, the court charged the legislature with developing a whole new educational system that would meet the needs of all students (Starr, 2001). Starr notes that KERA has often been referred to as the most sweeping educational reform in history because it took on all aspects of education at once: funding, governance, curriculum, instruction, and assessment (2001). Similarly, Guskey and Oldham (1997) observed that KERA addressed nearly every aspect of public education in the commonwealth, including administration, governance and finance, school organization, accountability, professional development, support for at-risk students, curriculum, and assessment. However, by attempting to address multiple aspects of the public educational system in a relative short time frame, they contend that inconsistencies and unintended consequences were created when too many initiatives were introduced simultaneously. An example of this, cited by Guskey and Oldham, was the mandate that schools create School-Based Decision Making Councils with the authority to govern individual schools. However, at the same time, the mandated primary school program dictated how students should be grouped for instruction, class structures, and instructional formats to be employed. As a result, they note that these inconsistencies made certain reform components highly controversial and confounded implementation efforts. Major school reforms mandated by the act included extended school services, family resource/youth services centers, financial equity among school districts, expanded preschool programs, flexible grouping in primary grades, professional development, and educational technology investments (Education, 2000).

Under KERA, individual schools became self-governing under the leadership of School-Based Decision Making (SBDM) councils made up of one administrator, three teachers, and two parents. By mandating SBDM in the state statute, legislators attempted to treat local school staffs as professionals and empower them, in concert with parents, to make decisions that were in the best interests of students. Moreover, policy makers were attempting to convey the idea that the most sound decisions would emanate from those who were closest to the students and understood the local school context, special circumstances, etc. Guskey and Oldham (1997) note, however, that perhaps the greatest inconsistency of all in KERA was that the legislature employed mandated, top down decision making to require that decisions be made from the bottom up.

The most crucial component of the KERA comprehensive testing program was that it mandated and set two-year improvement goals for schools and allowed the state to directly intervene with those that did not do well and gave cash bonuses to those that met their goals (Kirchoff, 1998). The testing program, known as the Kentucky Instructional Results Information System (KIRIS), serves as the state's high-stakes testing program. Jones and Whitford (1997) note that student performance on the test is converted to a "school score" that the "state uses to determine rewards or sanctions for teachers and administrators. (The school score is technically called the accountability index). If the score exceeds the state's expectation for a school, the teachers and administrators receive substantial bonuses. If the score is not high enough or does not continue to improve over time, the teachers and administrators can be placed on probation, and the school can be taken over by the state" (1997, p. 276). Jones and Whitford argue that Kentucky's accountability system has served to undermine decision making at the school level, an effect diametrically opposite to the intention of the KERA-mandated school councils. They note further that, instead of giving teachers a greater say in curriculum, the accountability system has led to the creation of a state curriculum as local educators have continued to pressure the state to become more and more precise about what will be tested (1997, p. 279). The conclusion reached by Jones and Whitford is that Kentucky's high-stakes accountability program (KIRIS) has now become the engine that drives school reform in the state and that it has now undermined the very changes in teaching and learning that it was intended to promote. They conclude that it is not yet possible to claim that KIRIS has improved student learning due to the many other variables that come into play; however, they observed that the political environment will unlikely allow policy makers to back away from it. Moreover, they note that, in an ironic twist, the state has begun employing more, not less, bureaucratic controls to effect school improvement. This, they argue, is diametrically the opposite of what was envisioned by the reform goal of providing administrators and teachers more decision making autonomy at the individual school level. In their view, the next stage of educational reform in the United States needs to be one in which those who hold power over the schools are able to give up their controlling role in favor of a collaborative one (1997, p. 281).

School based management often fails for a number of reasons. Most frequently, the reasons for failure arise from problems with the school site councils and how they function. These include limited participation, strong views suppressing dissent, high status individuals (usually the principal) exercising undue influence, group think, excessive time spent with too few decisions being reached, difficulty managing the meeting and sticking to the agenda, low quality decisions, different agendas of participants, and inadequate training (Ethridge, Horgan, Valesky, Hall & Terrell, 1994). Also, because of the time commitment involved in studying complex educational issues, practices, and innovations, school site councils frequently resort to addressing more easily understood school issues such as discipline and extra-curricular activities.

The Small School Initiative

For more than a half-century schools in America have been growing in size primarily as a result of the consolidation of schools and schools districts. This phenomenon has been particularly pervasive in the case of high schools and, to a lesser extent, middle and elementary schools. Often characterized as one of America's most widespread education reform movements between 1940 and 1990, the number of schools in the U.S. dropped nearly 70%, and average enrollment in schools rose fivefold (Foundation, 2001). This reform movement was greatly energized when James Bryant Conant, former president of Harvard University, conducted a study of high schools in the late 1950s that culminated in the book, *The American High School Today*, published in 1959 (Conant, 1959). The major recommendation from Conant's study was that the number of small high schools must be drastically reduced through district reorganization (Bracy, 2001). Since the Russians had launched Sputnik in late 1957, Bracy notes that Americans were already in a "tizzy about their schools" and were inappropriately blaming them for letting the Russians get into space first (2001, p. 413). Therefore, Conant's call for consolidating and increasing the size of high schools was dutifully followed. It has been noted, however, that the large comprehensive high school that Conant called for would have no fewer than 400 students (Viadero, 2001). By today's standards, this would be deemed a very small high school. Ostensibly, an essential reason for creating larger high schools was to offer a broader, more advanced curriculum, including more courses in foreign language, science, mathematics, etc. In fact, Conant recommended that high schools be sufficiently large to offer rigorous academic courses such as calculus, physics, and advanced foreign language. As school continued to grow in size, coupled with their burgeoning course offering, concern developed that the curriculum had expanded to include too much. The book, *The Shopping Mall High School*, by Powell, Farrar, and Cohen (Powell, Farrar, Cohen, National Association of Secondary School Principals (U.S.), and National Association of Independent Schools, Commission on Educational Issues, 1985), quite aptly addressed this issue. Its thesis is that these large high schools often give students too much latitude to choose what they want rather than what would be challenging for them or useful for them in their postsecondary careers (Bracy, 2001, p. 2).

As this movement to larger high schools developed, many of them were built or expanded to accommodate over two thousand students. In some large urban areas, some even enrolled over three thousand students. Some of the envisioned advantages were realized: an expanded and more advanced curriculum was offered; better athletic teams, bands, orchestras, and theatrical groups were featured; more clubs and activities were offered to develop student academic and avocational interests; economies of scale were realized which lowered costs per student; and a more diverse student body was usually brought together. In some cases, the latter goal was accomplished as school districts sought to comply with desegregation orders. As this movement grew, educational policy makers, including local school boards, realized there were economies of scale ensuing from large schools, so this trend for building large schools at the elementary and secondary level grew in popularity, particularly in urban and suburban areas. Rural areas followed the trend by consolidating smaller schools into larger ones to which students were bussed. Currently, the U.S. Department of Education figures indicate that nearly 44% of all public elementary and secondary students attend schools of 750 students or more (Viadero, 2001).

Although these larger schools had some advantages, there were many trade-offs in creating them. Researchers have cited some of the major disadvantages of large schools. Frequently, there are problems with student attendance, student alienation, disorder and discipline problems, violence, theft, substance abuse, gang participation, and low percentage of student participating in extra-curricular activities. Perhaps the greatest problem presented, particularly in high schools, is student anonymity which goes hand in hand with student alienation. In a Kappan article, title "Musings in the Wake of Columbine," Raywid and Oshiyama (2000) present a very illuminating view of the causes of violence in schools in the United States in light of the shooting at Columbine High School. They contend that in large schools many students often remain virtually anonymous during their entire stay there, and that it is very difficult to have community in a school of several thousand or more students. Also, they note that, since teachers tend to focus more on their content than on getting to personally know students, they tend to not establish very close relationships with students. As a result, students often affiliate with sub-communities and cliques that invariably develop. Students who are not accepted by or affiliated with a clique often become loners and/or outcasts. Feeling rejected and unwelcome in their schools, Raywid and Oshiyama (2000) note that these students may become alienated and filled with rage that sometimes leads to tragedies such as the one that occurred at Columbine. Consequently, they advocate that schools be organized around a small school concept reflecting a sense of community wherein all students are personally known by one or more adults. From their perspective, school violence is far less likely to occur in small schools or schools-within-a school where students are known by and have positive relationships with adults in the school and are made to feel welcomed and accepted.

Also, it should be noted that, due to their size, large schools require an enormous amount of administrative time, effort, and energy to simply manage the logistical functions necessary to keep them functioning on a day-to-day basis. In addition to the required administrative functions like attendance, discipline, building supervision, security, transportation, etc., much attention must be devoted to such issues as planning, scheduling, recordkeeping, and dealing with staff and student personnel issues. By their very nature, these large schools often create impersonal, institutional environments that do not foster close, caring relationships between students, staff, and parents.

In contrast, many advantages of small schools have been cited based upon large-scale quantitative studies of the late 1980s and early 1990s that firmly established small schools as more productive and effective than large ones (Raywid, 1999). Lee and Smith (1995), in summarizing the findings of these studies, note that they confirmed that students learn more and better in small schools. They also found that disadvantaged students perform better academically in small schools. Similarly, Howley and Bickel (1999) conducted a comprehensive study of four states (Georgia, Ohio, Texas and Montana) to examine the relationship between poverty, school size, and achievement. In this study, titled *The Matthew Project: National Report,* they found that smaller schools reduce the damaging effects of poverty on student achievement and help students from poorer communities narrow the achievement gap between them and students from wealthier communities. Pittman and Haughwout (1987) found that students are generally more satisfied in small schools and are less likely to drop out. In addition, Stockard and Mayberry (1992) found that students behave better in small schools, which results in fewer minor and major discipline problems and rule infractions. Michael D. Klonsky, the Director of the Small Schools Workshop in Chicago that supports efforts to create small schools, has noted that the research consistently shows that both teachers and students report feeling safer in small schools. In his own research, cited in Viadero (2001), Klonsky observes that federal statistics show that violent incidents are eight times more likely to occur in schools with 750 or more students than they are in schools of fewer than 350 students. Katheleen Cotton (1996a), a researcher at the Northwest Regional Laboratory in Portland, Oregon, who has done extensive research on small schools, has noted that students are much more likely to take part in extra-curricular activities in schools of fewer than 400 or 500 students. She also notes that, for both elementary and secondary students, research has repeatedly found small schools superior to larger ones on most measures and equal to them on the rest (Cotton, 1996b). In addition to creating a greater sense of belonging, small schools are able to accommodate flexible scheduling of students for learning activities. Small schools also benefit parents, as they tend to become more involved in the school community and their children's learning (Foundation, 2001). It has also been noted that small schools foster more staff collaborative planning, cooperation, and better staff development.

Two comprehensive empirical studies done in Chicago identified clear advantages of smaller schools. One is the study in which Lee and Loeb (2000) examined data from nearly 5,000 teachers and 23,000 students in grades six and eight to identify relationships among school size, teacher attitudes, and student achievement. They found that small size (fewer than 400 students) has a beneficial effect on both: (1) teacher attitudes about collective responsibility for learning; and (2) student learning itself. Also, they found that positive teacher attitudes about collective responsibility was positively related to student achievement. The other one is the Bank Street College of Education study by Wasley and colleagues (2000) in which they examined an enormous range of data on achievement, social relations, satisfaction, morale, and other variables in elementary schools. They found that small schools increased student attendance rates and significantly increased student persistence and student performance. Also, they found that more students completed courses, got higher grades, and graduated. Further, they found that parents, teachers, students, and community members were all more satisfied with their schools, believed in them, and wanted to see them continue to grow. However, they found that smallness did not assure school success, as they found a range of quality and effectiveness in the small schools studied.

During the last 10–15 years, the small school movement has been evolving as a reform strategy for school improvement in America. There is an ever-growing body of research that supports the benefits of small schools for students. Raywid, one of the most prominent researchers in this area, has noted that the findings confirming the benefits of smaller schools over larger schools has been "confirmed with a clarity and at a level of confidence rare in the annals of education research" (Raywid, 1999; Raywid & Oshiyama, 2000). Some researchers argue that a major factor in the movement to establish charter schools and other smaller schools is the belief that they can be more effective than large schools. To support the small schools movement, the Seattle-based Bill and Melinda Gates Foundation has awarded $277 million toward efforts to create smaller schools or smaller learning communities within large schools (Viadero, 2001). Also, to help facilitate efforts to make large high schools smaller, Congress earmarked $45 million in the 2000 Appropriations Act for the Department of Education to fund Section 10105 of the Elementary and Secondary Education Act. Entitled the Smaller Learning Communities Program, this section of the act was planned to help local education agencies (LEAs) plan, development, implement, or expand smaller, more personalized learning communities in large high schools. In FY 2001, the Department planned to award up to $125 million to LEAs under this program.

Increasingly, organizations are being created to foster and support the development of small schools. Prominent among these are The Small Schools Workshop and the Cross City Campaign for Urban School Reform, both in Chicago. The Small Schools Workshop, affiliated with the College of Education at The University of Illinois at Chicago, consists of a group of educators, organizers, and researchers that work with teachers, administrators, and parents to create new, small learning communities in public schools. Others include the Rural School and Community Trust (a Washington based non-profit education and advocacy group), the Small Schools Project in the Center on Reinventing Public Education at the University of Washington, and the Small Schools Coaches Collaborative, which provides sustained support for schools that receive grants from the Bill and Melinda Gates Foundation. The Maryland-based Annie E. Casey Foundation has also provided support for the development of small school initiatives.

Recognizing the benefits of small schools, this small school reform effort has been an increasingly popular solution to the problems of failures and low student achievement in cities such as Chicago, Denver, Los Angeles, New York, Philadelphia, Oakland, and Seattle. Since it has not been possible to build new, smaller schools in some areas, the solution to creating smaller schools has been to create smaller autonomous learning communities, often called schools-within-schools. Other terms used for this practice include all of the following: houses, clusters, pods, mini-schools, theme/focus schools (traditional, arts, math & science, etc.), academies, etc. Under this arrangement, one or more small schools are established within a larger school. However, the degree to which schools-within-schools establish separate identities varies. They may function as a sub-unit of the "host" school or they might function quite autonomously with each school having its own teachers, administrators, climate, and culture. Ordinarily, however, they still share common spaces such as the library, cafeteria, gym, art and drama facilities, etc. Other variations of the school-within-a school model include freshman transition academies and multi-year groups in which a groups of teachers stay with the same group of students for two or more years to foster closer relationships, trust, and teacher-student advising.

Although there is not a consensus among researchers regarding what are ideal size schools, most of the recommendations coming from the research suggests the following: elementary schools (300–400 students); middle schools, 400–600 students; and high schools, 600–1,000. Most of the authorities suggest that, ideally, schools should have enrollments at or below the mid-ranges in these categories. Several researchers believe strongly that schools that exceed 1,500 students are simply too large for students and staff to realize the advantages that ensue from smaller schools. Given the current average size of schools in the United States, some economies of scale would be lost in terms of cost per students if schools were downsized to reflect the above recommendations. However, there are some researchers who argue that the average cost per graduate would be about the same, if not less, in terms of the increased number of students that would remain in school until they finished (Stiefel, Iatarola, Frucher & Berne, 1998).

School Reconstitution

As mentioned earlier in this chapter, publication of the report, A Nation at Risk, ushered in a plethora of school reforms. Pipho (1997), among others, has listed the evolutionary path of these reform initiatives: minimum competency testing, a move toward criterion-reference testing, international test comparisons, the national education goals, the creation of strong academic standards to be met by students, and high stakes testing with an enforcement arm to measure the effectiveness of school districts and individual schools. He argues that the accountability movement has given over to academic bankruptcy provisions, state takeovers of school districts, and state and/or district reconstitution of individual schools. Of all the school reform strategies employed during the last two decades, the most radical and controversial one is school reconstitution. According to Pipho (1997), putting the focus on low performance has now become the "name of the game." Increasingly, political leaders, particularly at the national and state level, are taking the position that students cannot and should not be allowed to languish in failing schools, making little academic progress and not being adequately prepared for the world they will enter after leaving school. Twenty-three states now have policies for intervening and mandating major changes in low-performing schools, and 17 states grant this authority at the district level (Doherty & Albernathy, 1998).

Although researchers do not seem to have a universally agreed upon definition of school reconstitution, it has been defined as those "intervention strategies that range from the restructuring of school leadership, mandated redesign of a school's program and instructional practices, to state takeover of school governance. In its most extreme form, reconstitution involves disbanding the existing faculty and replacing nearly all the school staff. Most frequently, under a new principal, displaced staff members may apply to return to the reconstituted school. This latter approach to reconstitution has garnered the most attention and engendered the greatest controversy" (Doherty & Albernathy,

1998). Doherty and Abernathy (1998) note that reconstitution usually involves several components: (1) identifying schools that are significantly underperforming on a measure defined by the state or district; (2) vacating (or granting the authority to vacate) staff and administrative positions; (3) sometimes appointing a new principal; and (4) hiring back a proportion of incumbent teachers and filling the other positions with new staff.

Reconstitution is most frequently the reform of last resort when it has been determined that other intervention strategies have not been successful in schools where large proportions of students are scoring significantly below specified standards. Several researchers have noted that, in many cases, these schools have developed dysfunctional or toxic cultures which makes it very difficult to turn these schools around and make them effective (Deal & Peterson, 1998). Although individual teachers in many of these schools might have been effective, school officials generally perceive that these schools as a whole have developed a school culture that is nearly impossible to change. These schools often suffer what has been described as a "legacy of failure." For whatever reasons, the staff in these schools is usually perceived by school officials to be unable or unwilling to work together cooperatively to successfully develop and implement a comprehensive school improvement plan that leads to sustained student achievement. Given the dynamic nature of schools in terms of their context, climate, culture, instructional practices, mix of staff and students, use of resources, and varying schedules, it is often difficult to identify the most effective strategies for turning them around. Deal and Peterson (1998) contend that schools in this condition may need to be "recultured." Reconstitution serves as the vehicle for accomplishing this task.

Reconstitution was first employed in a substantial manner in the San Francisco public schools. Ironically, it was desegregation rather than student achievement that precipitated the series of events that led to reconstitution. In 1982, as a result of a lawsuit filed by African-American parents and the National Association for the Advancement of Colored People against the San Francisco public schools, the district agreed in a court degree to integrate its schools (Ruenzel, 1997). However, school officials deemed that integration alone would not remedy the problems in schools characterized by decrepit facilities, poor student performance, low parent involvement, and teacher apathy which they believed contributed to low performance of black and Hispanic students, who lagged farthest behind (1997). Therefore, in 1984, the staffs in three elementary schools and two middle schools were notified that they would be dismissed. New principals were appointed and new teachers were hired who agreed to 11 school district "philosophical tenets" believed necessary to turn these schools around. In 1992 an evaluation panel assigned by the court found that African

Americans students in reconstituted schools were performing better than those from similar backgrounds in other parts of the city (Program, 2002). Having been institutionalized, during the next five years sixteen other San Francisco schools were subsequently reconstituted. With the arrival in 1992 of a new superintendent (Bill Rojas) from New York, who had already had some experience there with school reconstitution, this practice was continued with eight additional schools being reconstituted between 1994 and 1996 (Ruenzel, 1997). Other cities that have been substantially involved in reconstituting schools include Chicago, Cleveland, Houston, Denver, Baltimore, and Prince George's County Maryland.

Opponents of reconstitution argue that the process is often used to make scape-goats of staff in low-performing schools who have not been successful in raising the academic achievement of students who are usually poor, disadvantaged, and transient. They contend that it serves to embarrass and further demoralize teachers who are already frustrated at their students' poor performance. Although they are usually reassigned within the district, displaced administrators and teachers from failing schools often perceive that they have been stigmatized, making it difficult for them to obtain other desirable school assignments. Since these schools often have developed reputations as failing schools within the districts as well as in the community, few experienced teachers are willing to transfer into them. Thus, frequently, when they are re-staffed, new principals find that the vast majority of teachers willing to come to them are new, inexperienced teachers who find themselves lacking veteran colleagues to help them confront the challenges new teachers normally face. In some cases it should be noted, however, newly assigned principals prefer to employ new teachers who are likely to be more innovative, enthusiastic, and open to new ideas. Thus, there is sometimes a tradeoff between enthusiasm and expertise. In most cases, teacher unions have resisted and fought the practice of reconstitution, particularly the manner in which it has been carried out in most urban districts. The Chicago Teachers Union and the Philadelphia Teachers union are cases in point. In New York, administrators and teachers worked out an acceptable plan for redesigning failing schools. However, the American Federation of Teachers (AFT), the dominant union in urban districts, has suggested that school officials collaborate with teachers to identify low-performing schools, identify the causes of failure, and set high standards for student achievement and behavior.

On the other hand, proponents of reconstitution view it as a very legitimate response to schools with a history of chronically low student achievement. Many argue that just the threat of reconstitution, where it is an available option, can motivate a school's staff to find solutions to improve student achievement. They further note that, in most instances, a new, student focused culture is needed in these schools to effect improved student achievement. Moreover, given the current accountability systems in place in many states, districts have little choice but to intervene in cases were schools are continually failing to show any appreciable gain in student achievement. Fearing the sanctions that now exist in nearly half of the states to address chronic low school performance, local school officials are more likely to move quickly and decisively to reconstitute schools in this category.

Given the number of school districts, particularly in urban areas, that have reconstituted schools, one might conclude that clear evidence exists to show the efficacy of this reform. However, this would be a false assumption. In terms of increased student academic achievement as measured by standardized tests, there is very little concrete evidence to support this reform strategy, although some districts have achieved improved student achievement in some schools. According to officials with the Education Commission of the states, evidence is still lacking on the effects of reconstitution and results from standardized tests are uneven in reconstituted schools (Association, 1999). Also, Doherty (2001) notes that there is little evidence that reconstitution alone leads to dramatic turnaround in academic performance. Notwithstanding, when compared with their status prior to reconstitution, some school officials report that staff, student, and parental relationships are more positive in reconstituted schools and the climate and culture is usually more positive in them. Some scholars, however, note that it is too early to tell whether reconstitution ultimately will yield positive results over time. At this junction, however, they do concur that reconstitution is no magic bullet for improving for failing schools.

Based upon efforts to date in reconstituting schools, some lessons have been learned to guide those faced with this task. The following are some of them.

(1) Displaced staff must be treated in a humane and professional manner consistent with local policies and union contracts;
(2) Teacher organizations, including unions, must be included in the process and kept properly informed in a timely manner;
(3) Strong and capable leadership in the reconstituted school, particularly from the principal, is a must;
(4) Recruiting and selecting the new staff is crucial;
(5) Inadequate time for recruitment and preparation of the new staff can jeopardize reconstitution efforts;
(6) New and/or returning staff members must share a similar philosophy and a commitment to work as a team for school improvement;
(7) A vision and coherent strategy for school improvement is a must;

(8) Rebuilding a low performing school requires a clear break with the past;
(9) Some additional resources may be needed (i.e. to lower class size);
(10) Expect some unanticipated consequences (i.e. too much staff displacement may have a destabilizing, negative effect on the staff as a whole;
(11) District support and assistance will be needed after reconstitution;
(12) Reconstitution is enormously complex and does not guarantee improved student learning; and
(13) The impact of reconstitution may not be immediately seen, as it often takes several or more years for significant results to show (Doherty & Albernathy, 1988; Peterson, 1998).

SUMMARY

During the last two decades, pervasive efforts to reform and improve the public schools have swept across the American educational landscape. Most scholars credit publication of the report, *A Nation at Risk*, by the National Commission of Educational Excellence as the triggering event that fostered the school reform movement. By likening the public education's performance to a "rising tide of mediocrity," the commission contended that systemic school improvement efforts were needed to reverse the downward turn in student academic achievement in America's schools. Eventually, with prodding from the executive and legislative branches of the federal government, comprehensive efforts were undertaken in virtually all of the states to improve their public schools. Initially, in what is known as first wave reforms, most states enacted top down regulatory reforms that primarily required tougher standards, more student and teacher testing, more emphasis on mastery of basic skills, longer school days, etc. After recognizing the disadvantages of mandating top down reform initiatives, including the failure to adequately involve school based professional educators, second wave reforms were adopted which recognized the expertise of school personnel, and provided them more autonomy in fashioning school improvements since they were closest to the problems and challenges. In return for more autonomy, school personnel, particularly teachers and principals, were held more accountable for student academic achievement. By the late 1990s, the third wave of reforms had evolved, which has become known as the standards and accountability movement.

This chapter has addressed three of the major reform strategies that evolved out of the national effort to improve the public schools. The first of these, school based management, was an initiative to respond to second wave reforms. Fundamentally, it moves more responsibility for school governance and decision making from the district level to school stakeholders (i.e. principals, teachers, parents, etc.) at local school sites. Principally, through shared decision making, these stakeholders are empowered to make many of the crucial decisions regarding local school budgeting, staffing, curriculum, and instructional practices. In return, principals and teachers are held more accountable for school results, particularly student academic achievement.

The Small Schools Initiative, which began in earnest during the second wave reform movement, is a restructuring effort to create free standing smaller schools or smaller schools-within-a school to foster more intimate learning environments, better teacher-student relationships, and more effective student advising. Smaller schools are also intended to negate student anonymity, isolation, discipline problems and to prevent students from falling between the cracks. Data from an increasing number of empirical research studies have shown smaller schools to be inherently more effective, particularly with poor and disadvantaged students. These studies have also shown that small schools usually have better student attendance, and less student alienation, less violence and theft, less disorder, and fewer drug and discipline problems. Better staff collaboration and coordination have also been found in smaller schools in contrast to larger ones.

When the standards and accountability movement became widely adopted in the various states, state-wide specific standards with rigorous student assessments were put in place. As noted by Airasian and Abrams (2002), the stakes and consequences associated with performance on state-wide standards significantly surpassed those of other previous school reforms. Annual assessment of students, often referred to as "high stakes testing," drives the process. In many states, there are rewards for school based personnel (usually pay bonuses) when students do well, and consequences when they do poorly. In many states, when schools develop a pattern of chronic poor performance, school reconstitution is an option. It is the process wherein the school's current staff is vacated, and a new staff is appointed to the school, usually under the leadership of a new principal.

Taken as a whole, each of these reform initiatives has proponents who perceive them to be effective strategies for effecting school improvement. There are places where student achievement has improved when each of these reforms has been implemented. However, in terms of empirical research, cause-effect relationships are nearly impossible to find, as is the case with most educational research. This is particularly true with school based management and with school reconstitution reforms. Although it is more in the realm of correlational research, there is more evidence to support the efficacy of small schools in terms of student achievement. To date, there is scant evidence to definitively conclude that school based management and school reconstitution leads to appreciable improved student achievement. However, given the degree to which all of these reforms have now been institutionalized in public school districts in the U.S., they will likely continue for the foreseeable future.

REFERENCES

Airasian, P. W., & Abrams, L. M. (2002). What role will assessment play in school in the future? In: R. W. Lissitz & W. D. Schafer (Eds), *Assessment in Educational Reform: Both Means and Ends* (pp. 50–65). Boston, MA: Allyn & Bacon.

Berliner, D. C., & Biddle, B. (1995). *The manufactured crisis: Myths, fraud, and the attack on America's public schools*. New York, NY: Addison-Wesley.

Bracy, G. (2001). Small schools, great strides. *Phi Delta Kappan, 82*(5), 413–415.

Conant, J. B. (1959). *The American high school today*. New York, NY: McGraw-Hill.

Cotton, K. (1996a). *Affective and social benefits of small-scale schooling* [ERIC Digest]. Charleston, WV: ERIC Clearinghouse on Rural Education and Small Schools. (ERIC Document Reproduction Service No. ED401088).

Cotton, K. (1996b). *School size, school climate, and student performance* [Closeup #20]. Portland, OR, Northwest Regional Educational Laboratory.

Deal, T. E., & Peterson, K. D. (1998). *Shaping school culture: The heart of leadership*. San Francisco, CA: Jossey-Bass.

Doherty, K., & Albernathy, S. (1998). *Turning around low-performing schools: A guide for state and location leaders*. Washington, D.C.: U.S. Department of Education.

Doherty, K. M. (2001, December 12). Reconstitution. *Education Week*.

Education, K. S. D. o. (2000, January 1). *Results matter: A decade of difference in Kentucky's public schools*. Frankfort, KY: Kentucky Department of Education.

Ethridge, C., Horgan, D. et al. (1994). *The challenge to change: The Memphis experience with school-based decision making*. Washington, D.C.: National Education Association.

Goertz, M. E., & Duffy, M. C. (2001, April 18). All over the map. *Education Week, 20*(31), 44–45, 60.

Guskey, T. R., & Oldham, B. R. (1997). Despite the best intentions: Inconsistencies among components in Kentucky's systemic reform. *Educational Policy, 11*(4), 426–443.

Herman, J. J., & Herman, J. L. (1992, May/June). Educational administration: School-based management. *Clearing House 65*(5).

Hess, G. A. J. (1991). *School restructuring, Chicago style*. Newbury Park, CA: Corwin Press.

Hess, G. A. J. (1999, September). Expectations, opportunity, capacity, and will: The four essential components of Chicago school reform. *Educational Policy, 13*(4).

Howley, C. B., & Bickel, R. (1999). *The Matthew project: National report*. Charleston, WV: ERIC Clearinghouse on Rural Education and Small Schools (ERIC Document Reproduction Service No. ED433174).

Hoyle, J. R. (1992, November). Ten commandments for successful site-based management. *NASSP Bulletin, 76*(547), 81–87.

Jones, K., & Whitford, B. L. (1997). Kentucky's conflicting reform principles. *Phi Delta Kappan, 79*(4), 276–281.

Kirchoff, S. (1998). Congress looks to Kentucky for lesson on education. *Congressional Quarterly Weekly Report, 56*(9), 491–496.

Lee, V. E., & Loeb, S. (2000). School size in Chicago elementary schools: Effects on teachers' attitudes and students' achievement. *American Educational Research Journal, 37*(1), 3–31.

Lee, V. E., & Smith, J. B. (1995). Effects of high school restructuring and size on early gains in achievement and engagement. *Sociology of Education, 68*(4), 241–270.

Lewis, A. (1989). *Restructuring America's schools*. Arlington, VA: American Association of School Administrators.

Malen, B., Ogawa, R. T. et al. (1990). What don't we know about school-based management? A case study of the literature – A call for research. In: W. H. Clune & J. F. Witte (Eds), *Choice and Control in American Education: The Practice of Choice, Decentralization, and School Restructuring* (Vol. 2, pp. 289–342). London, ENG: Falmer.

Meriwether, C. O. (1996). Site-based management in secondary schools. *NASSP Practitioner, 22*(3).

Metz, M. H. (1988). Some missing elements in the educational reform movement. *Educational Administration Quarterly, 24*, 446–460.

Meuret, D., & Scheerens, J. (1995). An international comparison of functional and territorial decentralization of public educational systems. Paper presented at the annual meeting of the American Educational Research Association, San Francisco, CA.

National Commission on Excellence in Education (1983). *A nation at risk*. Washington, D.C.: Government Printing Office.

NEA (1999). Can reconstitution fix failing schools? *NEA Today, 17*(4).

Ornstein, A. C. (1991). Reforming American schools: The role of the states. *NASSP Bulletin, 75*(537), 46–55.

Owens, R. G. (1998). *Organizational behavior in education*. Boston, MA: Allyn and Bacon.

Peterson, K. D. (1998). *Reconstitution and school improvement: Early lessons*. Final Report to the Joyce Foundation and the Spencer Foundation. Madison, WI: University of Wisconsin.

Pipho, C. (1997, November). How good is good? How bad is bad. *Phi Delta Kappan, 79*(3).

Pittman, R. B., & Haughwout, P. (1987). Influence of high school size on dropout rate. *Educational Evaluation and Policy Analysis, 9*(4), 337–343.

Powell, A. G., Farrar, E. et al. (1985). *The shopping mall high school : Winners and losers in the educational marketplace*. Boston, MA: Houghton Mifflin.

West Ed's Policy Program (2002). *Does "reconstitution" work?* Retrieved February 7, 2002, from: http://www.wested.org/pub/docs/266

Raywid, M. A. (1999, January). *Current literature on small schools* [ERIC Digest]. Charleston, WV: ERIC Clearinghouse on Rural Education and Small Schools. (ERIC Document Reproduction Service No. ED425049).

Raywid, M. A., & Oshiyama, L. (2000). Musing in the wake of Columbine. *Phi Delta Kappan, 81*(6), 444–448.

Ruenzel, D. (1997). Do or die. *Teacher Magazine, 8*(6), 23–30.

Sarason, S. B. (1990). *The predictable failure of educational reform*. San Francisco, CA: Jossey-Bass.

Starr, L. (2001). Ten years of puzzling about audience awareness. *Clearing House, 74*(4), 191–197.

Stiefel, L., Iatarola, P. et al. (1998). *The effects of size of study body on school costs and performance in New York city high schools*. New York, NY: New York University, Institute for Education and Social Policy.

Stockard, J., & Mayberry, M. (1992). *Effective educational environments*. Newbury Park, CA: Corwin (ERIC Document Reproduction Service No. ED350674).

The Annie E. Casey Foundation (2001). *Success in school: Education ideas that count*. Baltimore, MD: The Annie E. Casey Foundation.

Thernstrom, A. (2000). Testing and its enemies. *National Review, 52*(17).

Viadero, D. (2001, November 28). Research: Smaller is better. *Education Week*, *21*(13), 28–30.

Walberg, H., & Niemiec, R. P. (1996, May 22). Can the Chicago reforms work? *Education Week*, *15*(35).

Wasley, P. (2000). *Small schools: Great strides*. New York, NY: Bank Street College of Education.

Wong, K. K. (1999). Political institutions and educational policy. In: G. J. Cizek (Ed.), *Handbook of Educational Policy* (pp. 297–324). San Diego, CA: Academic Press.